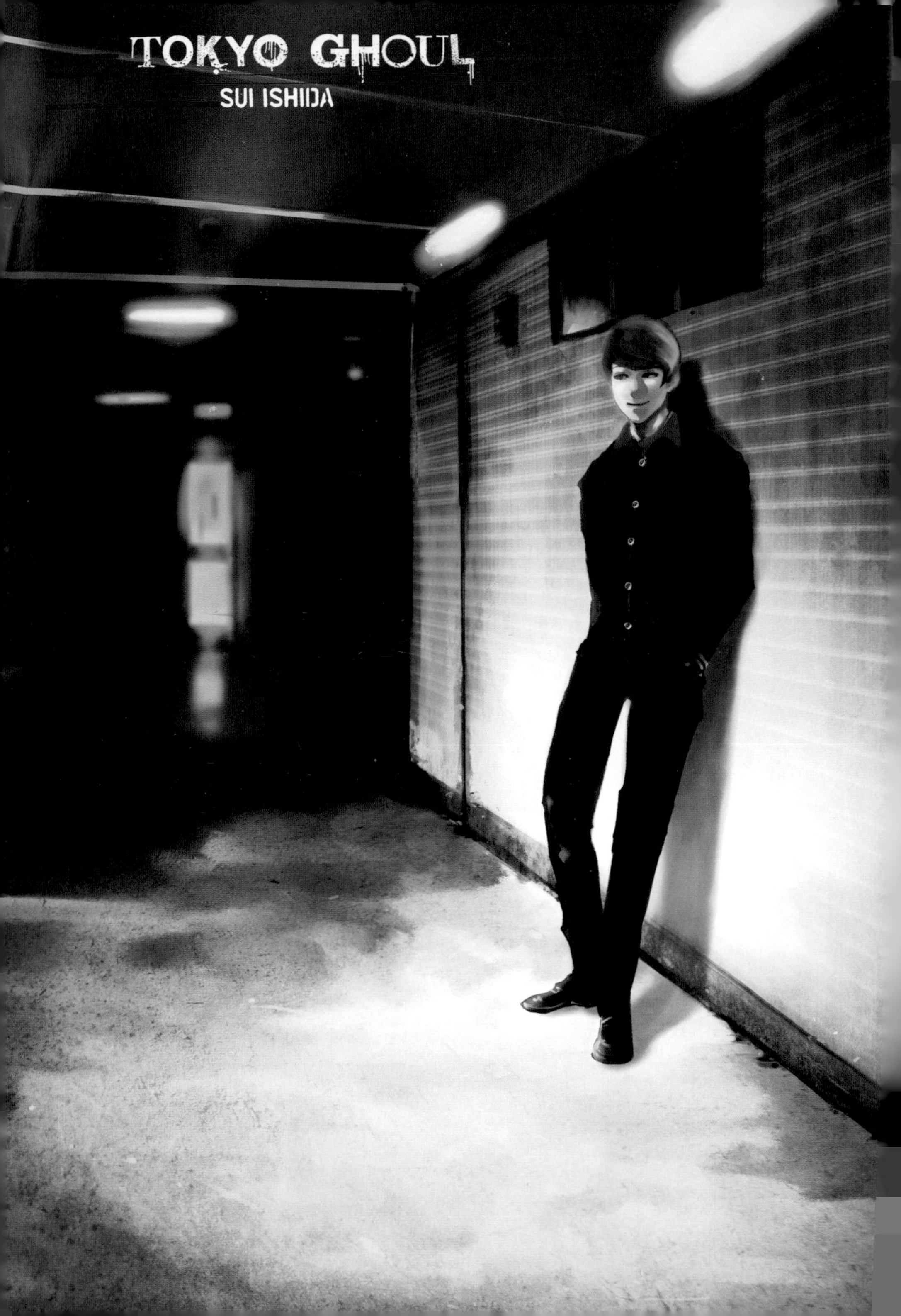
TOKYO GHOUL
SUI ISHIDA

T O K Y O G H O U L

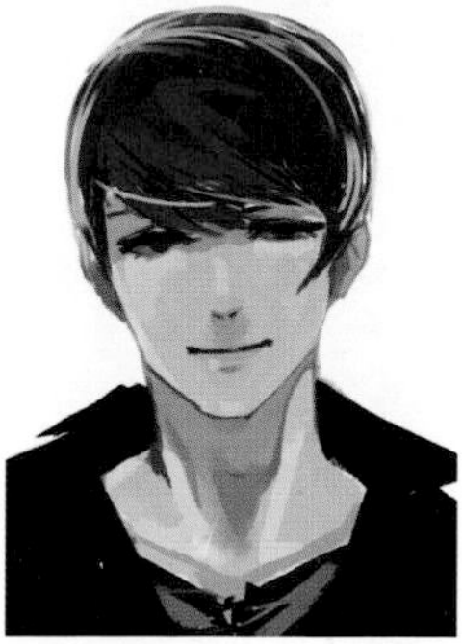

S H U
TSUKIYAMA

月山 習（ツキヤマシュウ）

BORN March 3rd Pisces

Seinan Gakuin University Human Sciences
Department of Social Services 4th Year

BLOOD-TYPE: A

Size: 180 cm 71 kg FEET 27.5 cm

Likes: Self-discipline, appetizing people (men and women of all ages), new stimulations

Hobbies: Sports, martial arts, musical instruments, assessing prey

Rc Type: Kokaku

S H U T S U K I Y A M A

SUI ISHIDA was born in Fukuoka, Japan. He is the author of ***Tokyo Ghoul*** and several ***Tokyo Ghoul*** one-shots, including one that won him second place in the *Weekly Young Jump* 113th Grand Prix award in 2010. ***Tokyo Ghoul*** began serialization in *Weekly Young Jump* in 2011 and was adapted into an anime series in 2014.

東京喰種

TOKYO GHOUL

TOKYO GHOUL

SUI ISHIDA

T O K Y O G H O U L

sui ishida

4

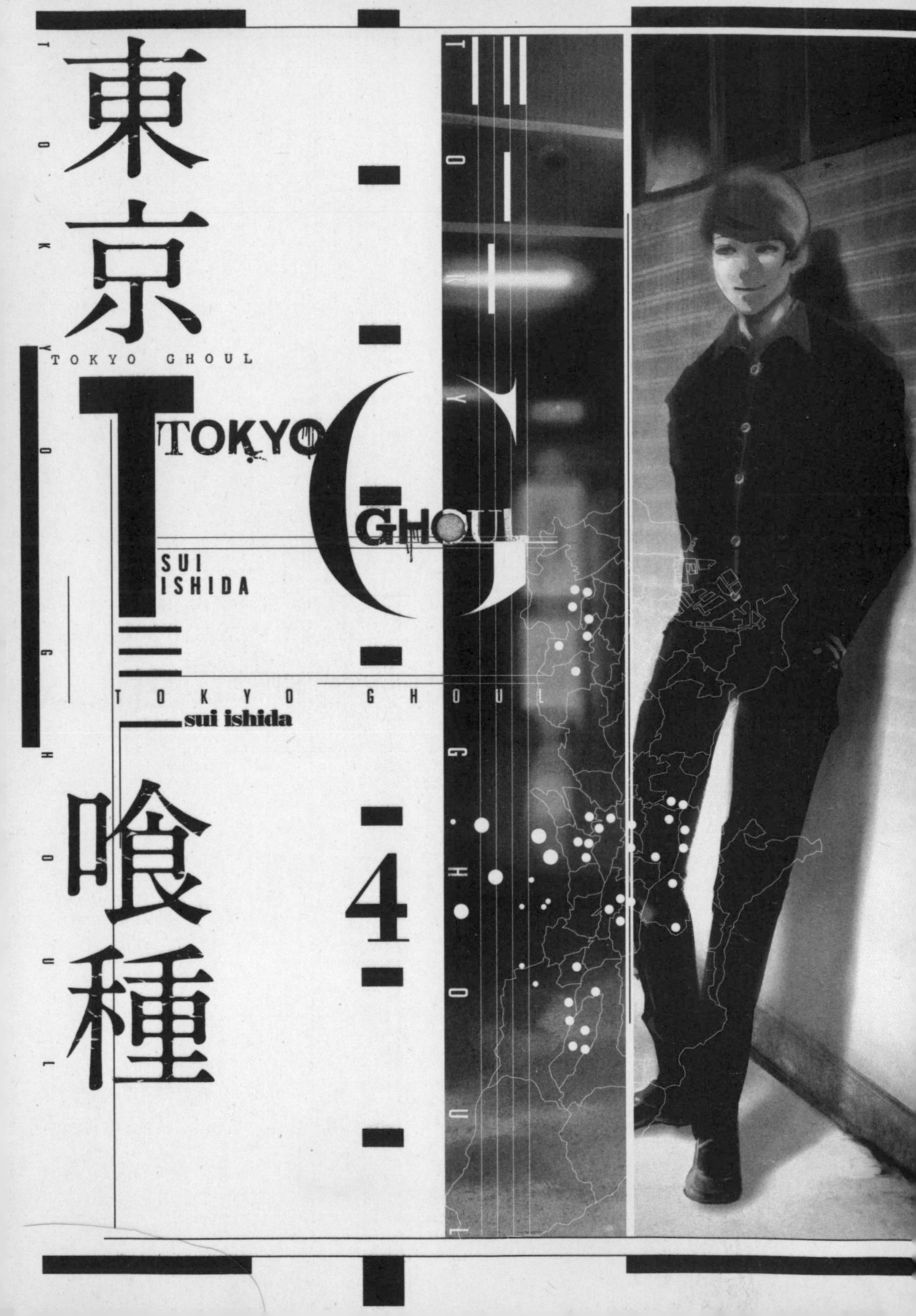
TOKYO GHOUL

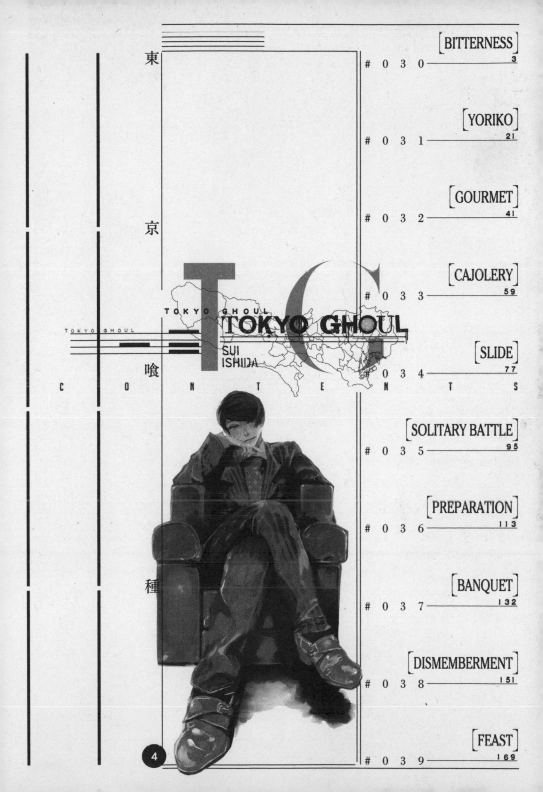

東

京

喰

種

TOKYO GHOUL

SUI ISHIDA

CONTENTS

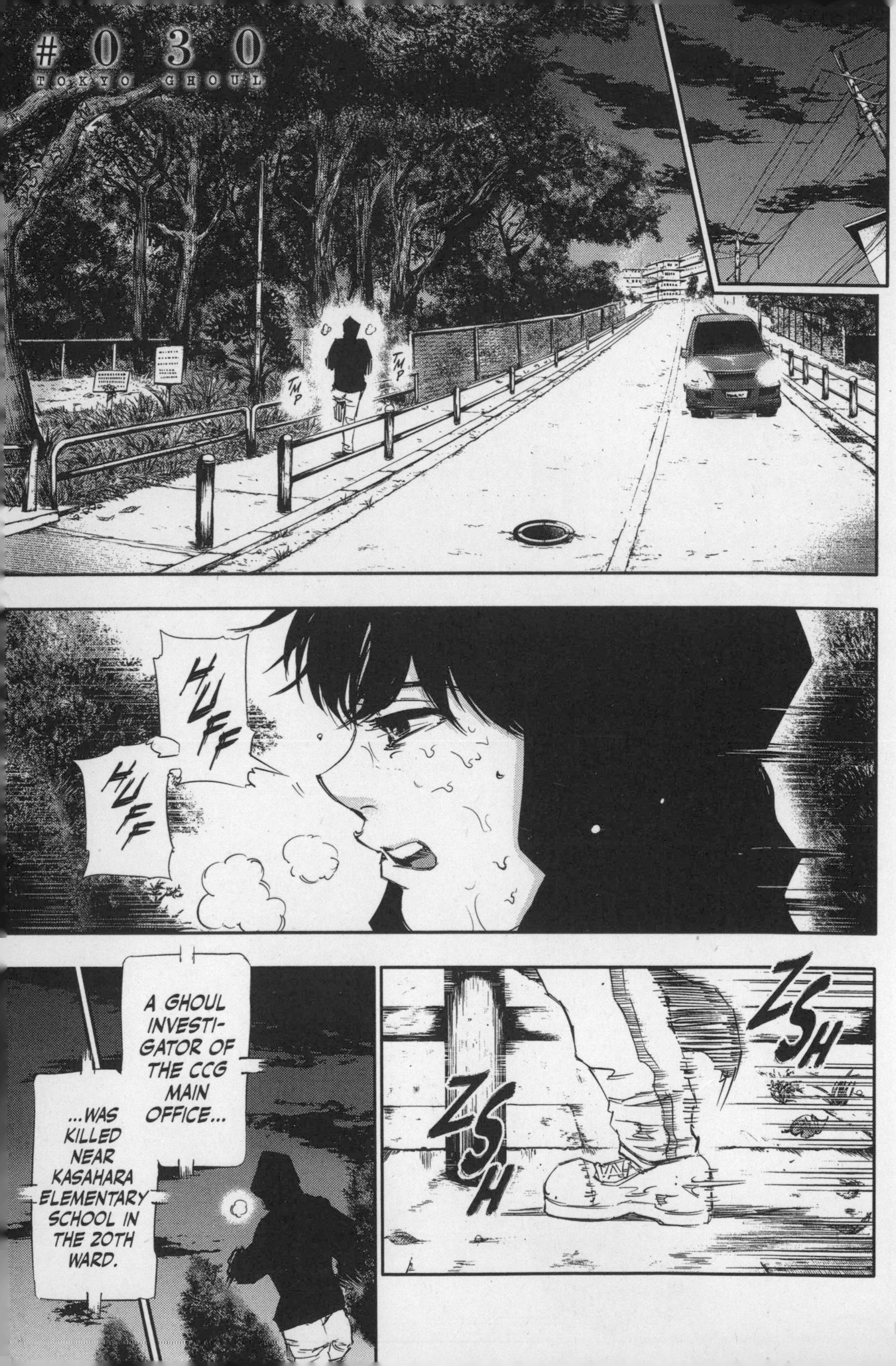
#030
TOKYO GHOUL
TMP
TMP
HUFF
HUFF
ZSH
ZSH
A GHOUL INVESTIGATOR OF THE CCG MAIN OFFICE...
...WAS KILLED NEAR KASAHARA ELEMENTARY SCHOOL IN THE 20TH WARD.

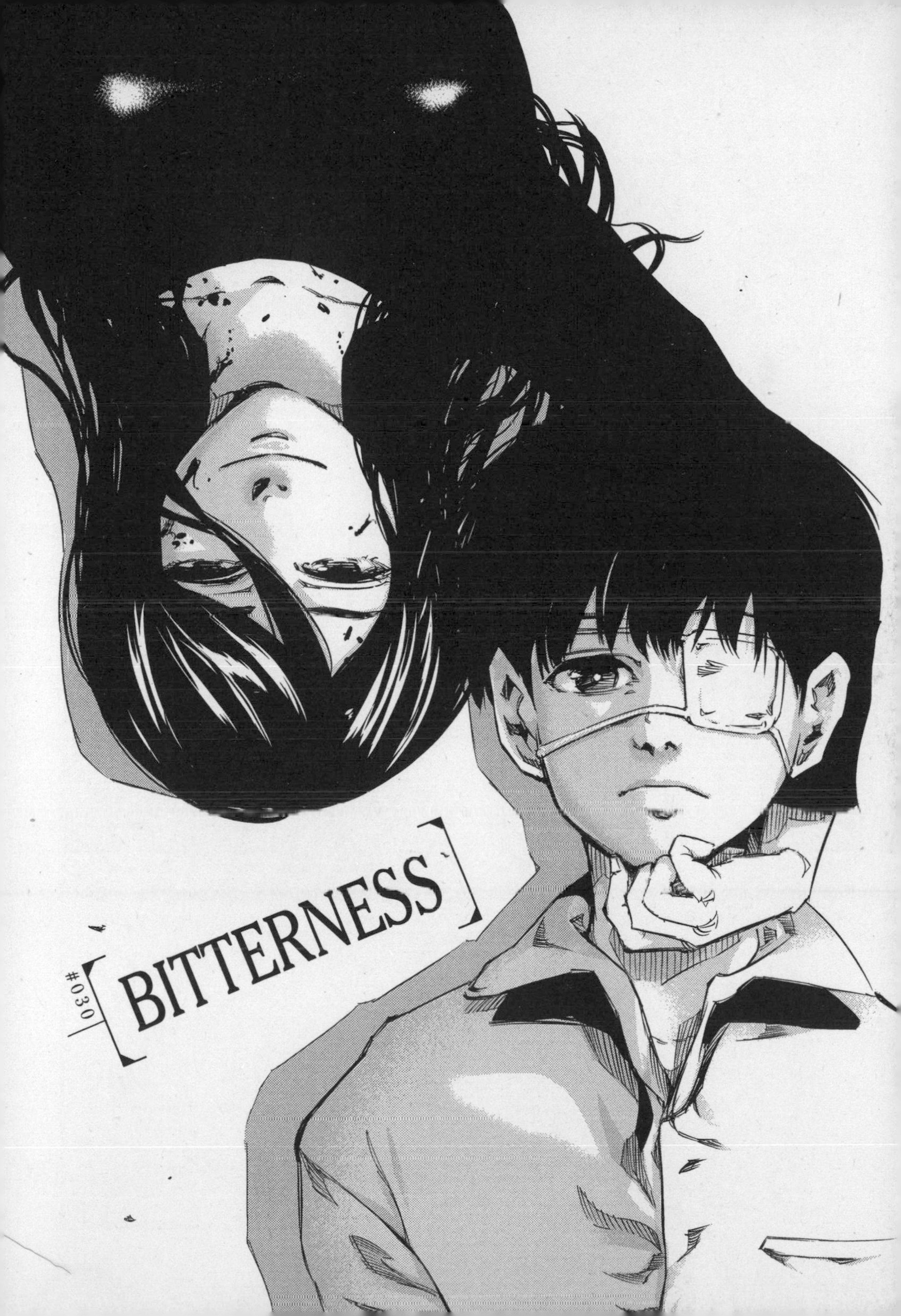
#030
BITTERNESS

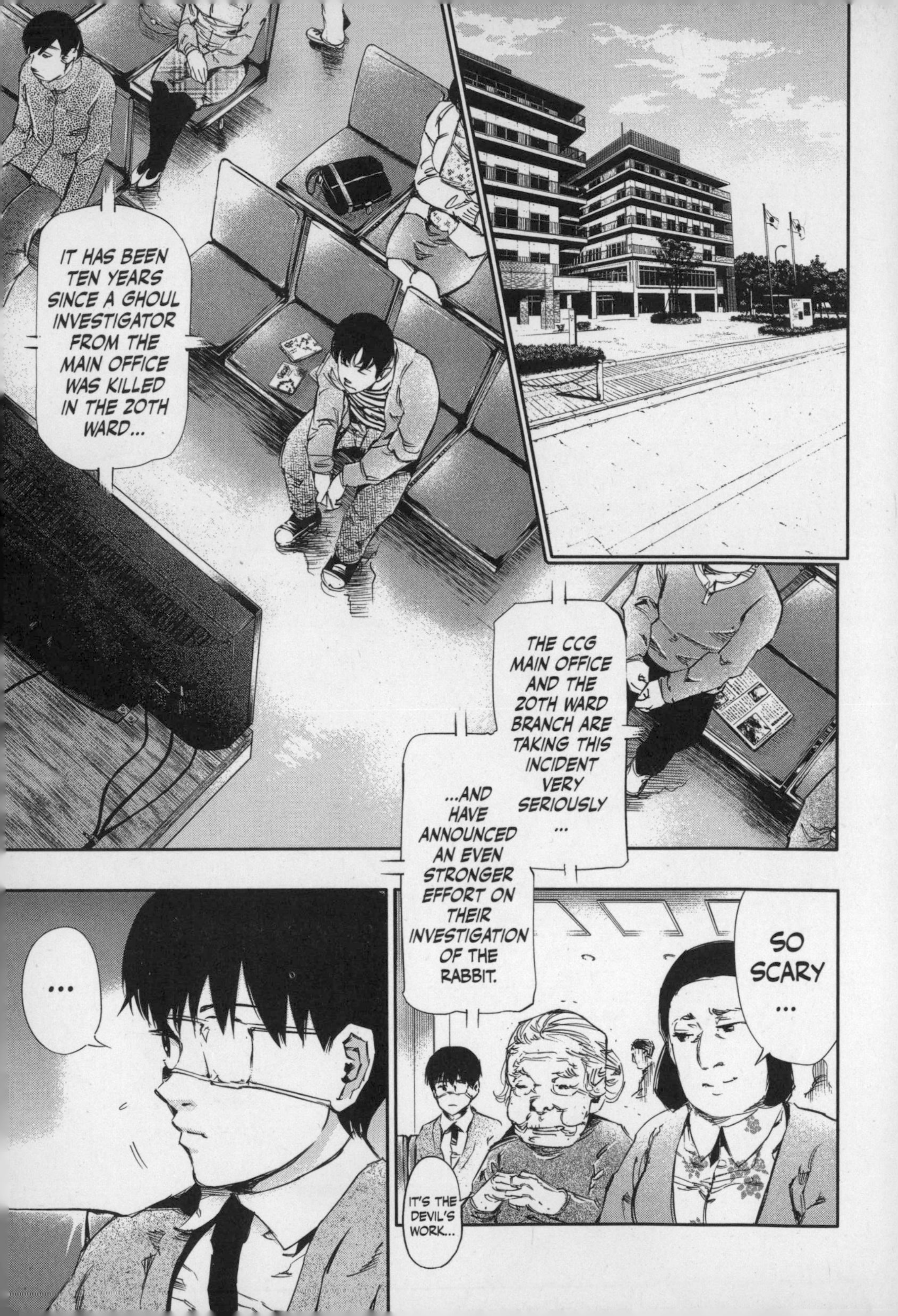
IT HAS BEEN TEN YEARS SINCE A GHOUL INVESTIGATOR FROM THE MAIN OFFICE WAS KILLED IN THE 20TH WARD...
THE CCG MAIN OFFICE AND THE 20TH WARD BRANCH ARE TAKING THIS INCIDENT VERY SERIOUSLY...
...AND HAVE ANNOUNCED AN EVEN STRONGER EFFORT ON THEIR INVESTIGATION OF THE RABBIT.
SO SCARY...
IT'S THE DEVIL'S WORK...
...

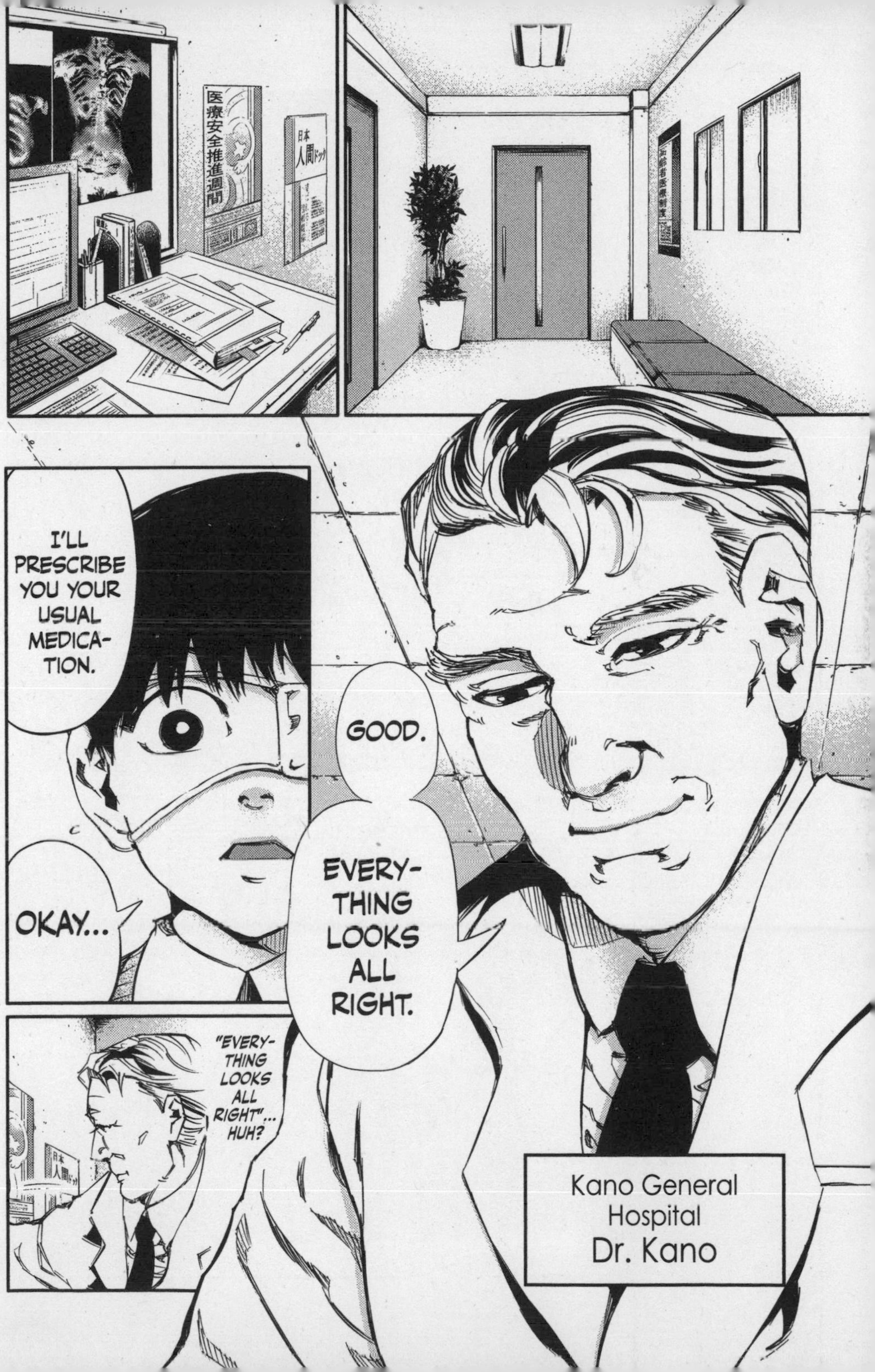
医療安全推進週間
日本人間ドック
GOOD.
EVERY-THING LOOKS ALL RIGHT.
Kano General Hospital Dr. Kano
I'LL PRESCRIBE YOU YOUR USUAL MEDICATION.
OKAY...
"EVERY-THING LOOKS ALL RIGHT"... HUH?

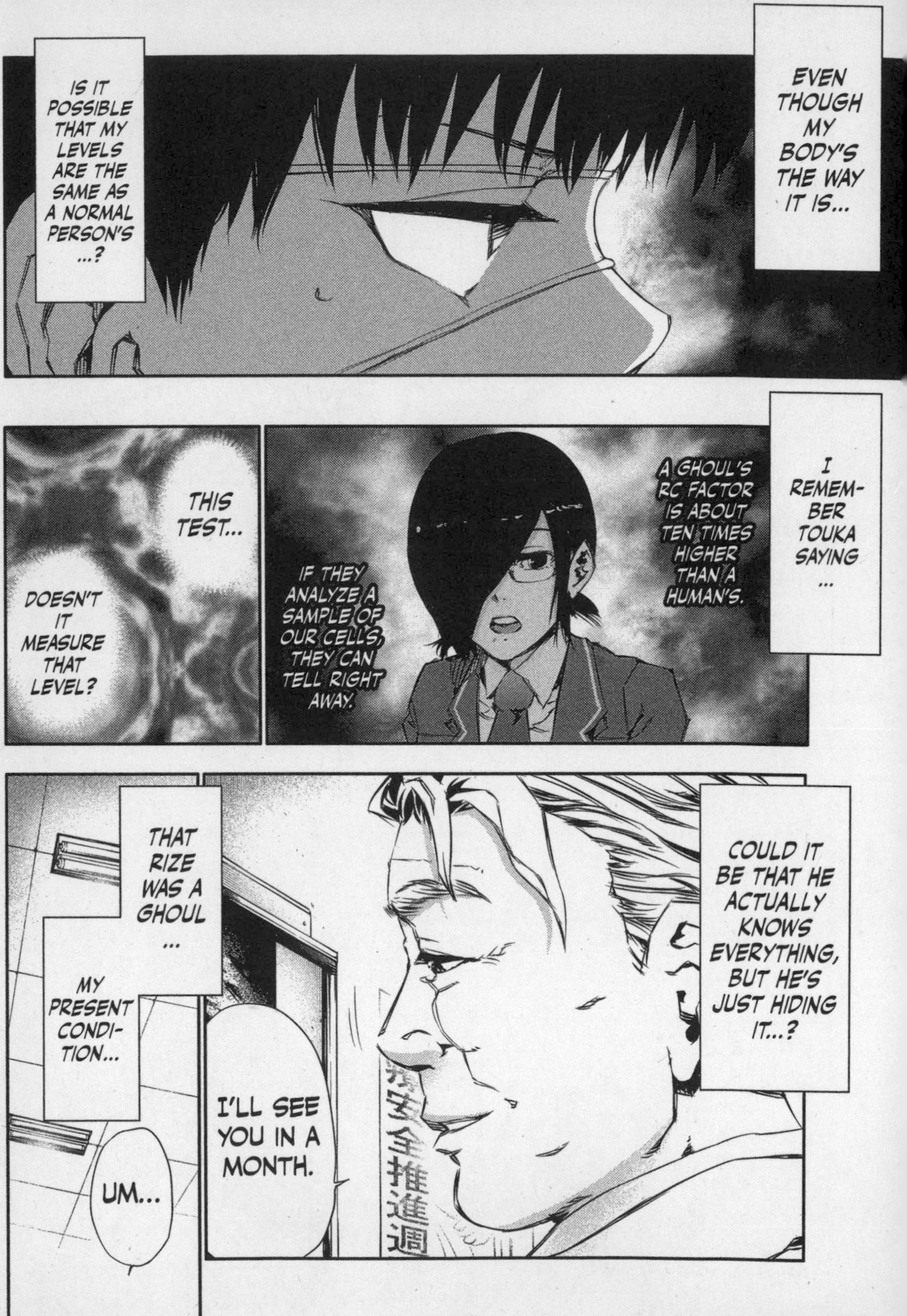
EVEN THOUGH MY BODY'S THE WAY IT IS...
IS IT POSSIBLE THAT MY LEVELS ARE THE SAME AS A NORMAL PERSON'S ...?
I REMEMBER TOUKA SAYING ...
A GHOUL'S RC FACTOR IS ABOUT TEN TIMES HIGHER THAN A HUMAN'S.
IF THEY ANALYZE A SAMPLE OF OUR CELLS, THEY CAN TELL RIGHT AWAY.
THIS TEST...
DOESN'T IT MEASURE THAT LEVEL?
COULD IT BE THAT HE ACTUALLY KNOWS EVERYTHING, BUT HE'S JUST HIDING IT...?
安全推進週
I'LL SEE YOU IN A MONTH.
THAT RIZE WAS A GHOUL ...
MY PRESENT CONDITION...
UM...

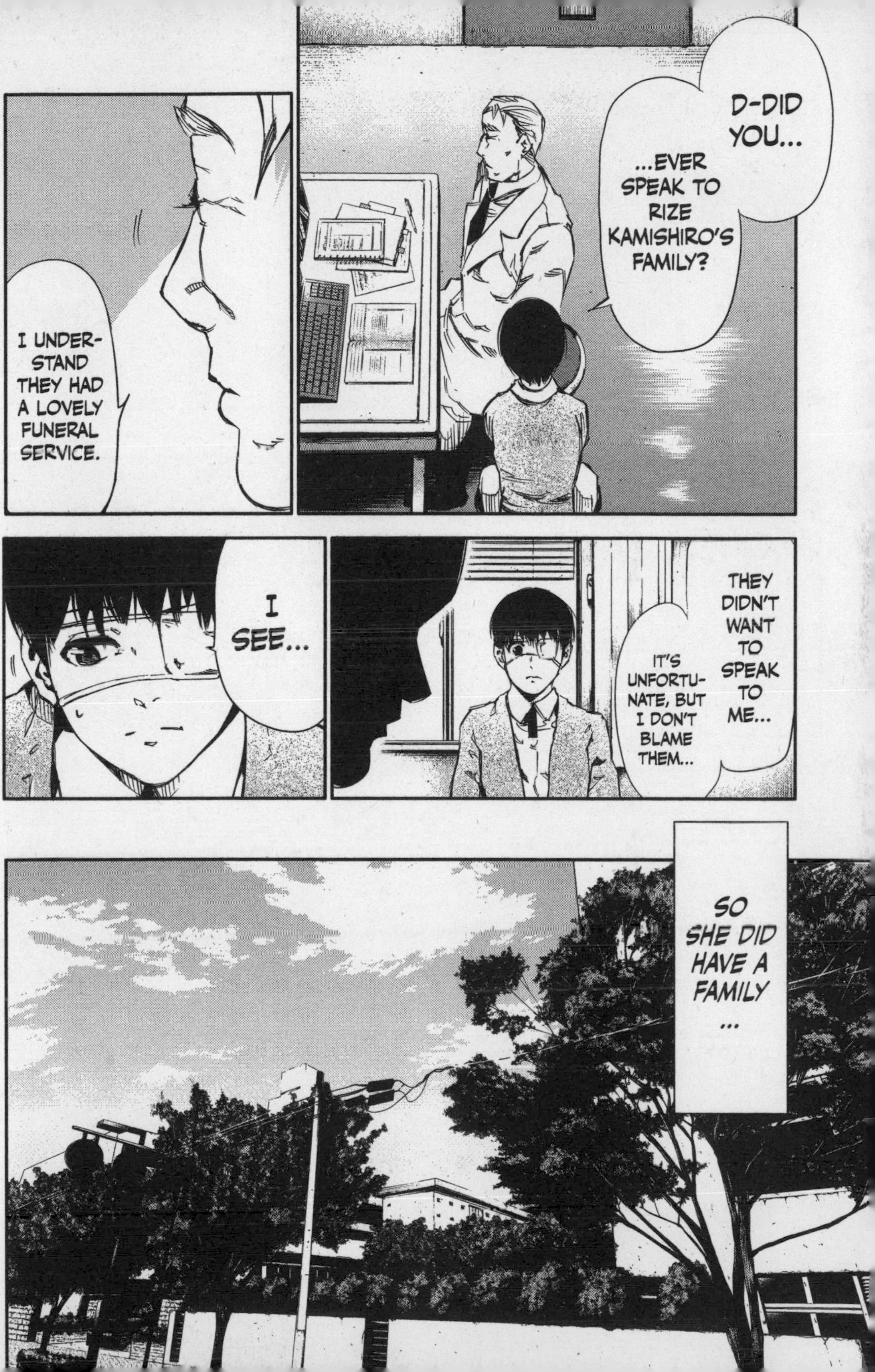
D-DID YOU...
...EVER SPEAK TO RIZE KAMISHIRO'S FAMILY?
I UNDER-STAND THEY HAD A LOVELY FUNERAL SERVICE.
THEY DIDN'T WANT TO SPEAK TO ME...
IT'S UNFORTU-NATE, BUT I DON'T BLAME THEM...
I SEE...
SO SHE DID HAVE A FAMILY...

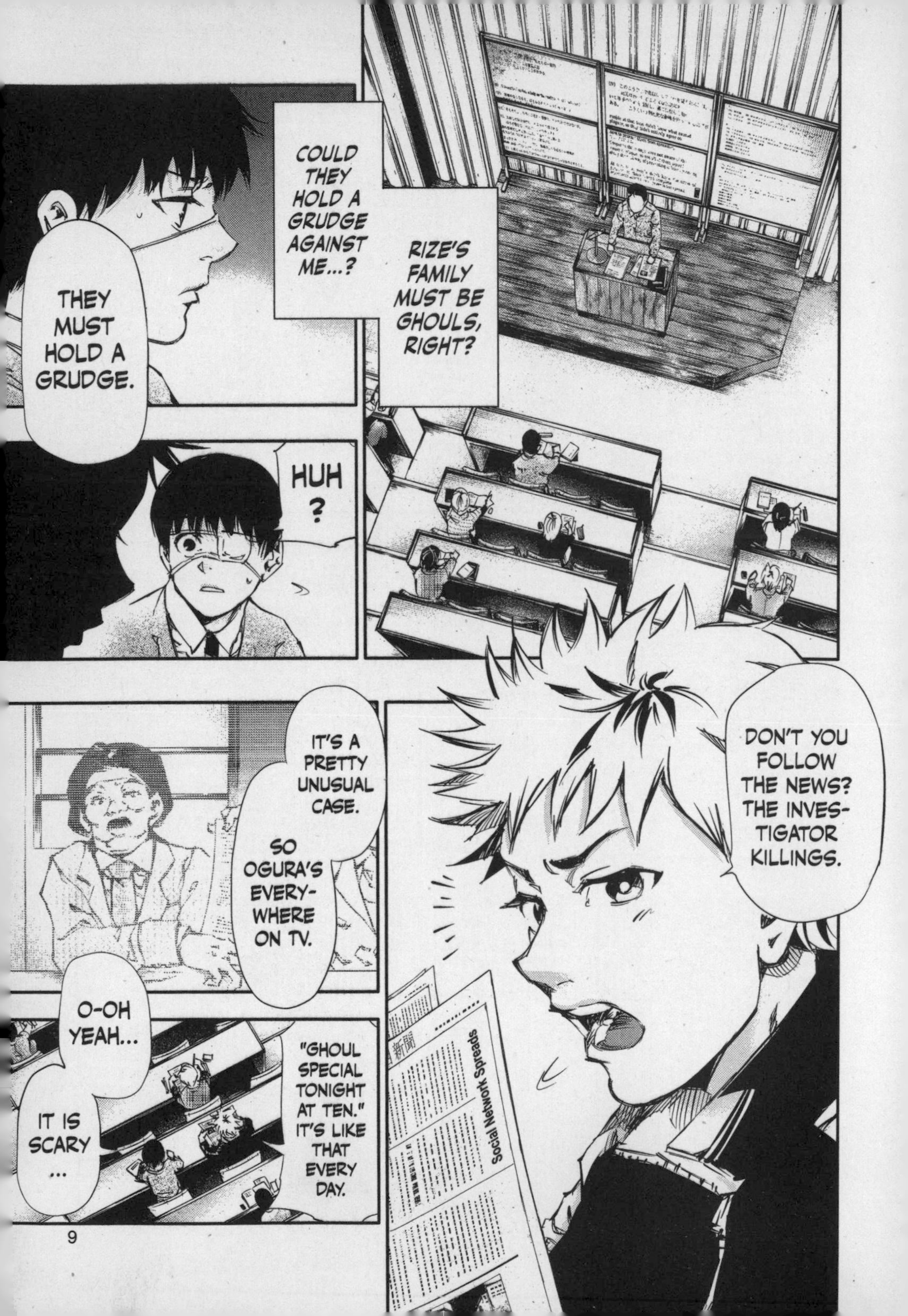
RIZE'S FAMILY MUST BE GHOULS, RIGHT?
COULD THEY HOLD A GRUDGE AGAINST ME...?
THEY MUST HOLD A GRUDGE.
HUH?
DON'T YOU FOLLOW THE NEWS? THE INVESTIGATOR KILLINGS.
新聞
Social Network Spreads
IT'S A PRETTY UNUSUAL CASE.
SO OGURA'S EVERYWHERE ON TV.
"GHOUL SPECIAL TONIGHT AT TEN." IT'S LIKE THAT EVERY DAY.
O-OH YEAH...
IT IS SCARY ...

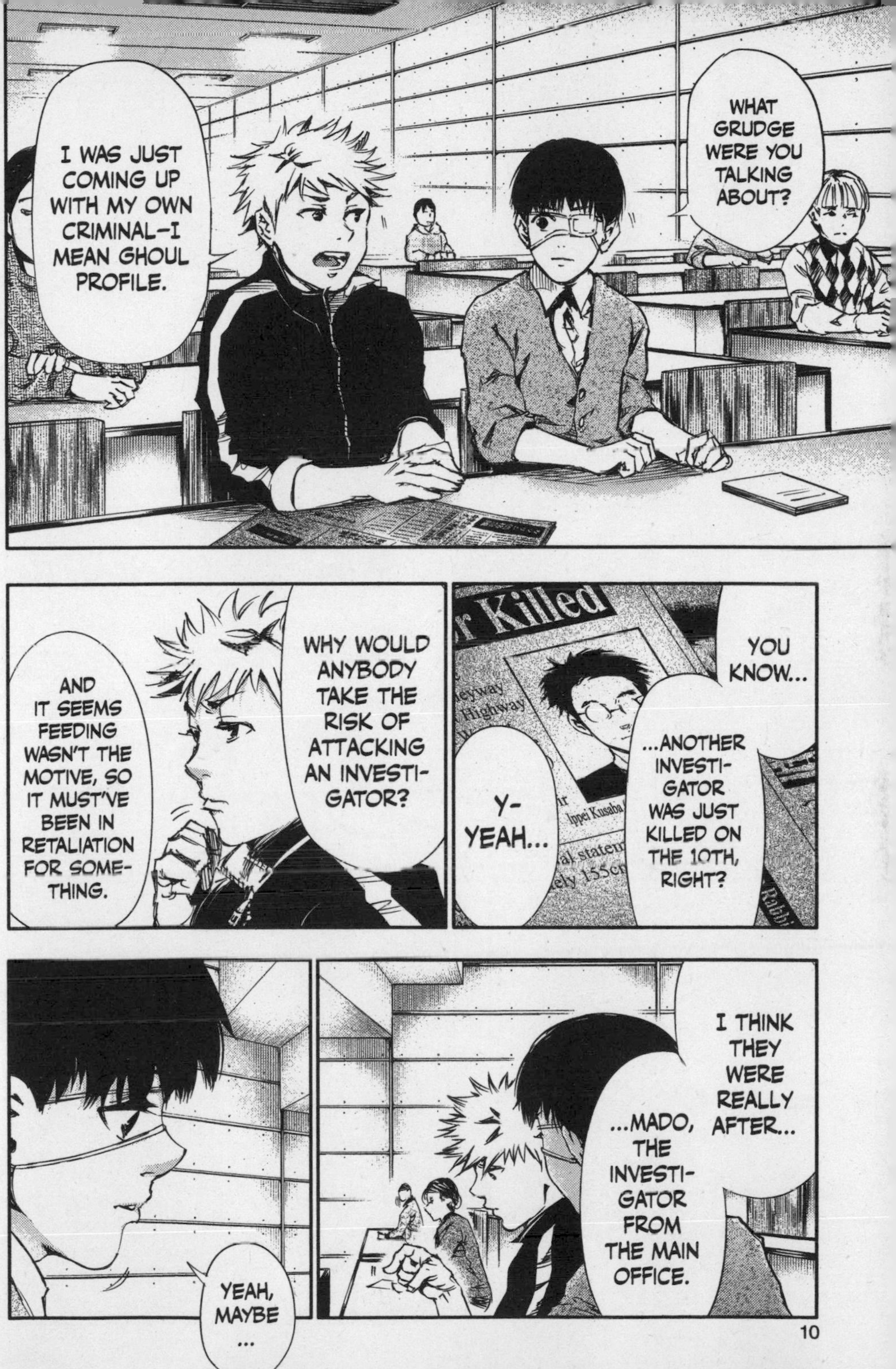
WHAT GRUDGE WERE YOU TALKING ABOUT?
I WAS JUST COMING UP WITH MY OWN CRIMINAL—I MEAN GHOUL PROFILE.
YOU KNOW...
...ANOTHER INVESTIGATOR WAS JUST KILLED ON THE 10TH, RIGHT?
Y-YEAH...
WHY WOULD ANYBODY TAKE THE RISK OF ATTACKING AN INVESTIGATOR?
AND IT SEEMS FEEDING WASN'T THE MOTIVE, SO IT MUST'VE BEEN IN RETALIATION FOR SOMETHING.
I THINK THEY WERE REALLY AFTER...
...MADO, THE INVESTIGATOR FROM THE MAIN OFFICE.
YEAH, MAYBE...

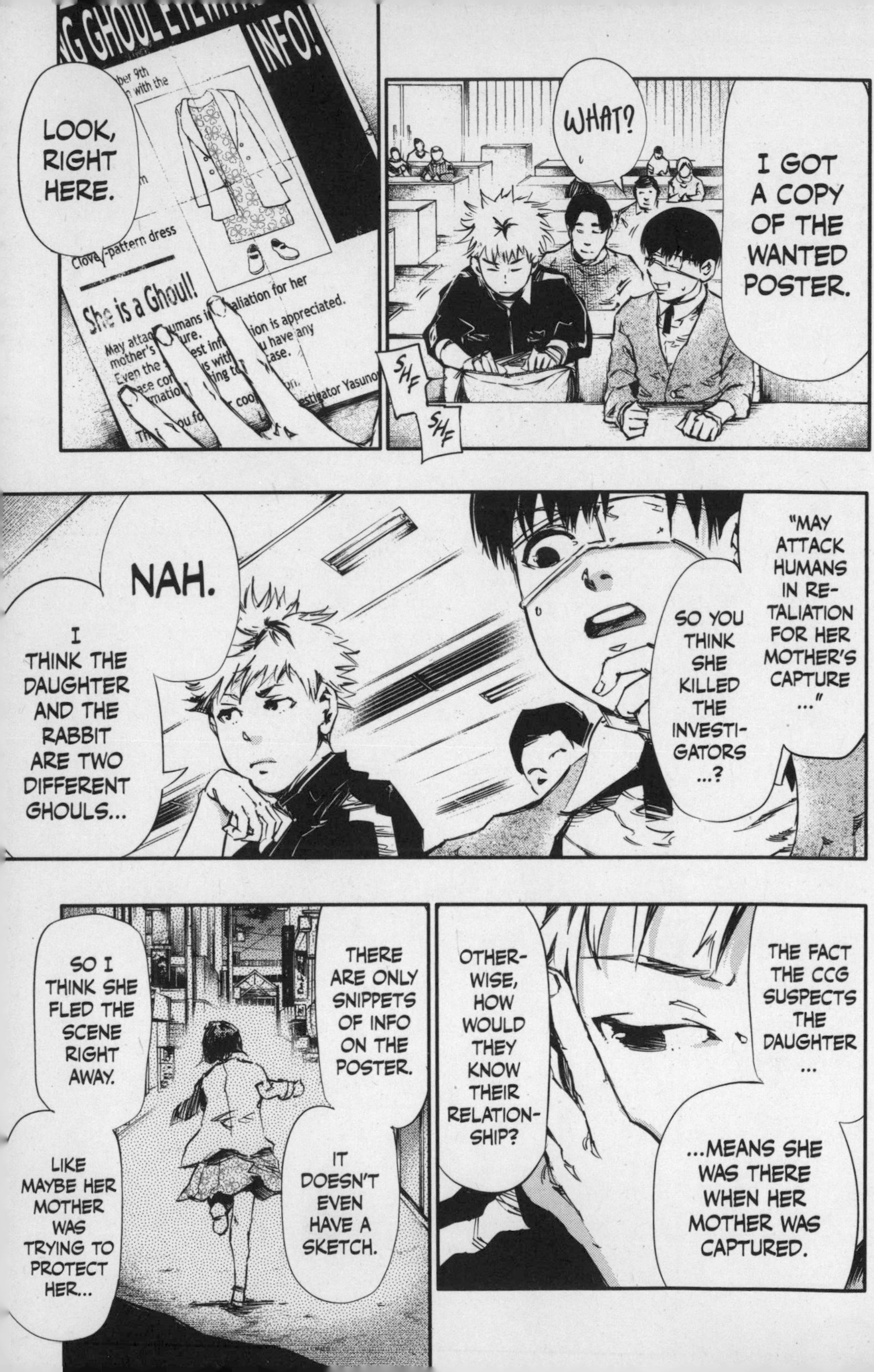
I GOT A COPY OF THE WANTED POSTER.
WHAT?
SHF
SHF
INFO!
She is a Ghoul!
LOOK, RIGHT HERE.
"MAY ATTACK HUMANS IN RETALIATION FOR HER MOTHER'S CAPTURE..."
SO YOU THINK SHE KILLED THE INVESTIGATORS...?
NAH.
I THINK THE DAUGHTER AND THE RABBIT ARE TWO DIFFERENT GHOULS...
THE FACT THE CCG SUSPECTS THE DAUGHTER...
...MEANS SHE WAS THERE WHEN HER MOTHER WAS CAPTURED.
OTHERWISE, HOW WOULD THEY KNOW THEIR RELATIONSHIP?
THERE ARE ONLY SNIPPETS OF INFO ON THE POSTER.
IT DOESN'T EVEN HAVE A SKETCH.
SO I THINK SHE FLED THE SCENE RIGHT AWAY.
LIKE MAYBE HER MOTHER WAS TRYING TO PROTECT HER...

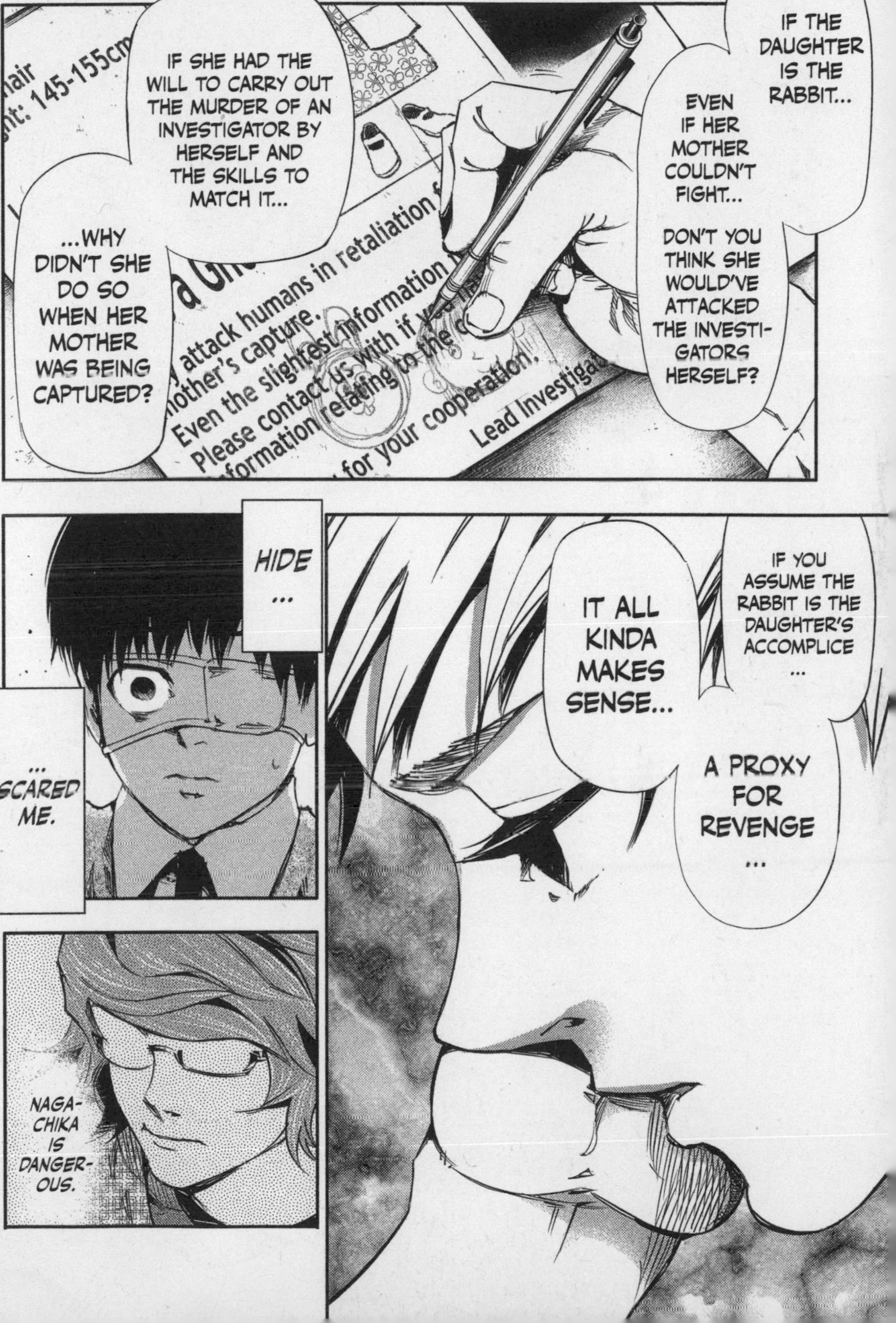
IF THE DAUGHTER IS THE RABBIT...
EVEN IF HER MOTHER COULDN'T FIGHT...
DON'T YOU THINK SHE WOULD'VE ATTACKED THE INVESTI-GATORS HERSELF?
IF SHE HAD THE WILL TO CARRY OUT THE MURDER OF AN INVESTIGATOR BY HERSELF AND THE SKILLS TO MATCH IT...
...WHY DIDN'T SHE DO SO WHEN HER MOTHER WAS BEING CAPTURED?
IF YOU ASSUME THE RABBIT IS THE DAUGHTER'S ACCOMPLICE ...
A PROXY FOR REVENGE ...
IT ALL KINDA MAKES SENSE...
HIDE ...
... SCARED ME.
NAGA-CHIKA IS DANGER-OUS.

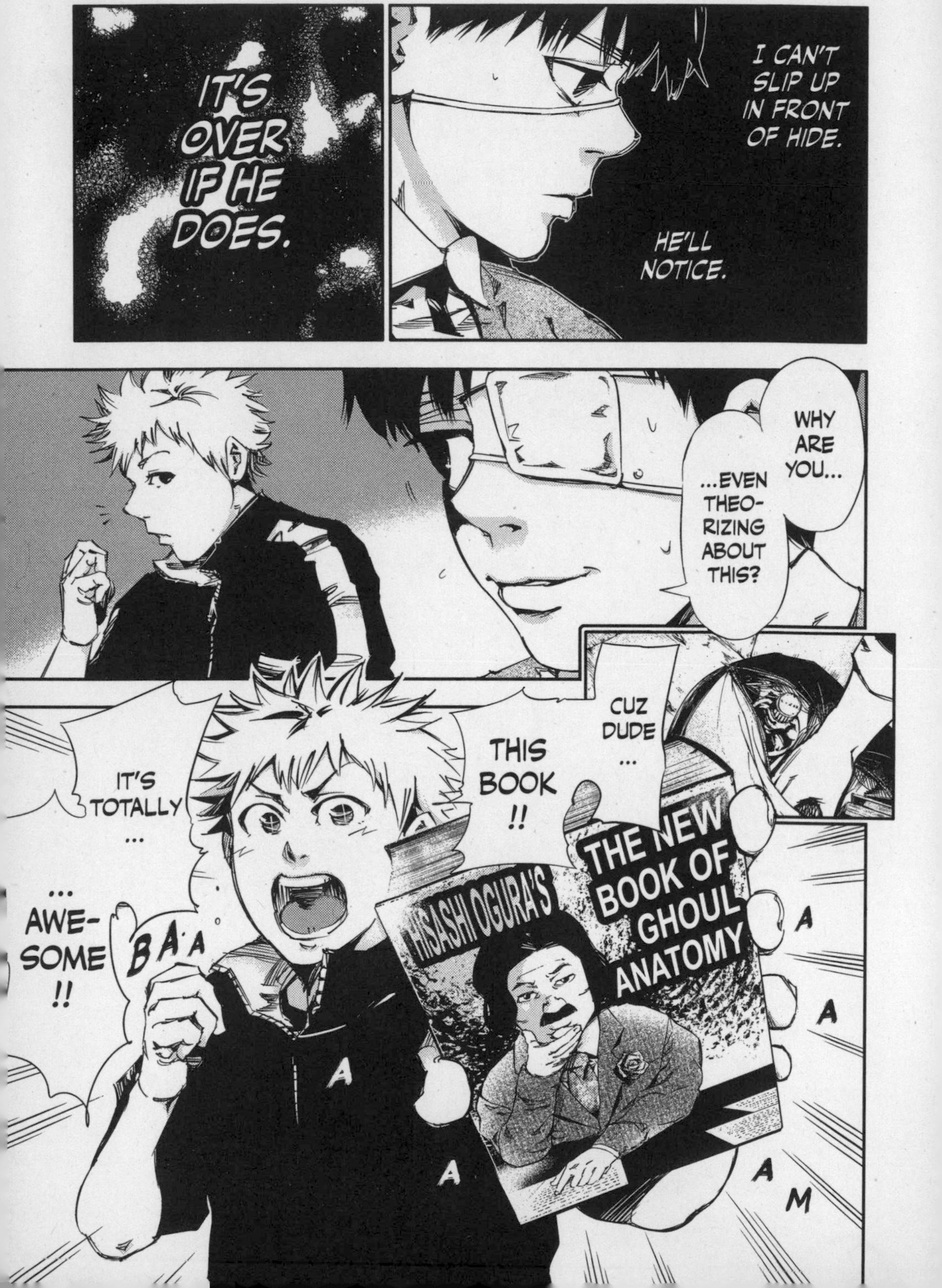
I CAN'T SLIP UP IN FRONT OF HIDE.
HE'LL NOTICE.
IT'S OVER IF HE DOES.
WHY ARE YOU...
...EVEN THEO-RIZING ABOUT THIS?
CUZ DUDE ...
THIS BOOK !!
IT'S TOTALLY ...
... AWE-SOME !!
HISASHI OGURA'S
THE NEW BOOK OF GHOUL ANATOMY
BAA
AAAAAM

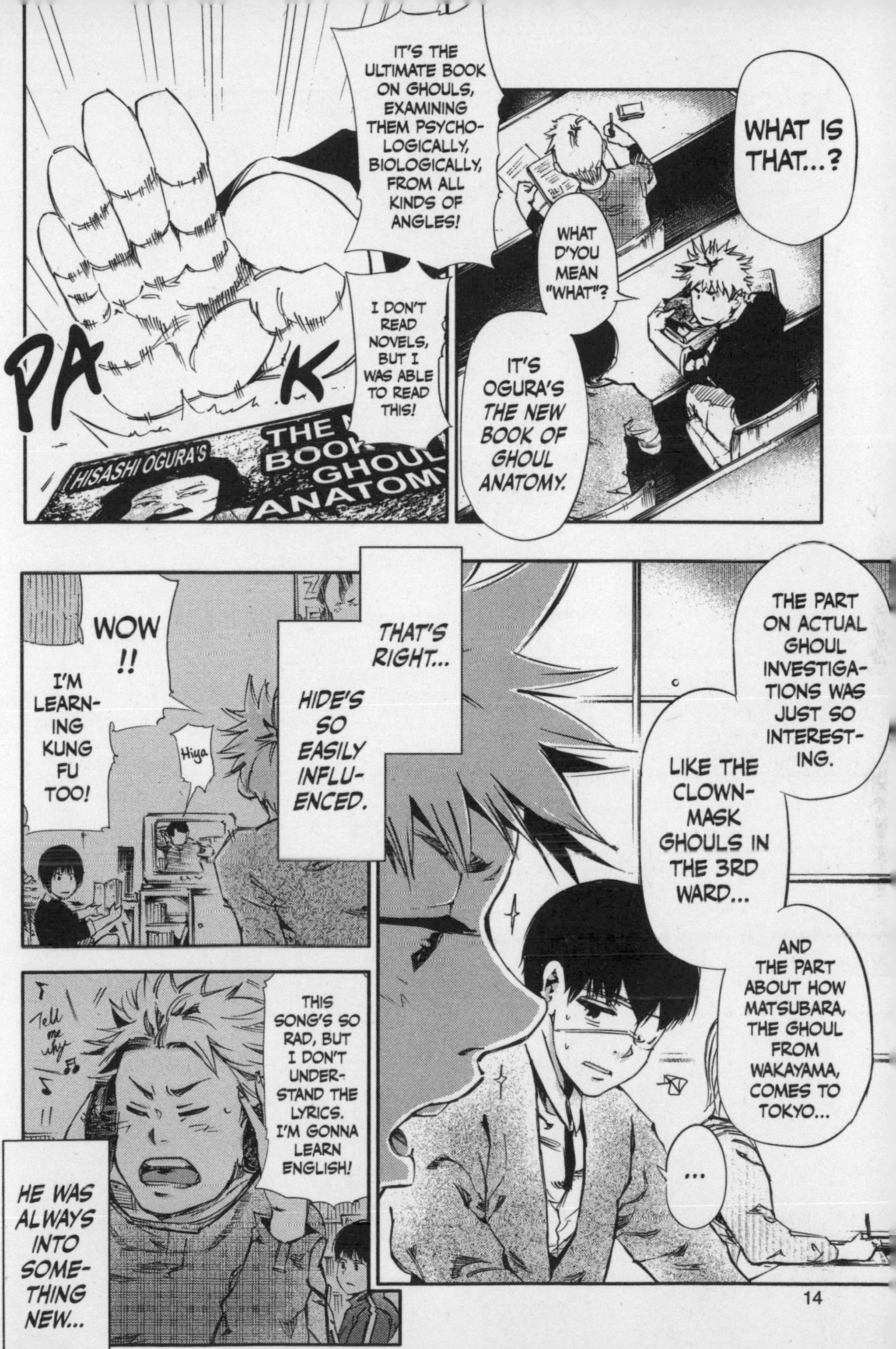
WHAT IS THAT...?
WHAT D'YOU MEAN "WHAT"?
IT'S OGURA'S THE NEW BOOK OF GHOUL ANATOMY.
PAK
IT'S THE ULTIMATE BOOK ON GHOULS, EXAMINING THEM PSYCHOLOGICALLY, BIOLOGICALLY, FROM ALL KINDS OF ANGLES!
I DON'T READ NOVELS, BUT I WAS ABLE TO READ THIS!
HISASHI OGURA'S
ANATOMY
THE PART ON ACTUAL GHOUL INVESTIGATIONS WAS JUST SO INTERESTING.
LIKE THE CLOWN-MASK GHOULS IN THE 3RD WARD...
AND THE PART ABOUT HOW MATSUBARA, THE GHOUL FROM WAKAYAMA, COMES TO TOKYO...
...
THAT'S RIGHT...
HIDE'S SO EASILY INFLUENCED.
WOW!!
I'M LEARNING KUNG FU TOO!
Hiya
THIS SONG'S SO RAD, BUT I DON'T UNDERSTAND THE LYRICS. I'M GONNA LEARN ENGLISH!
Tell me why
HE WAS ALWAYS INTO SOMETHING NEW...

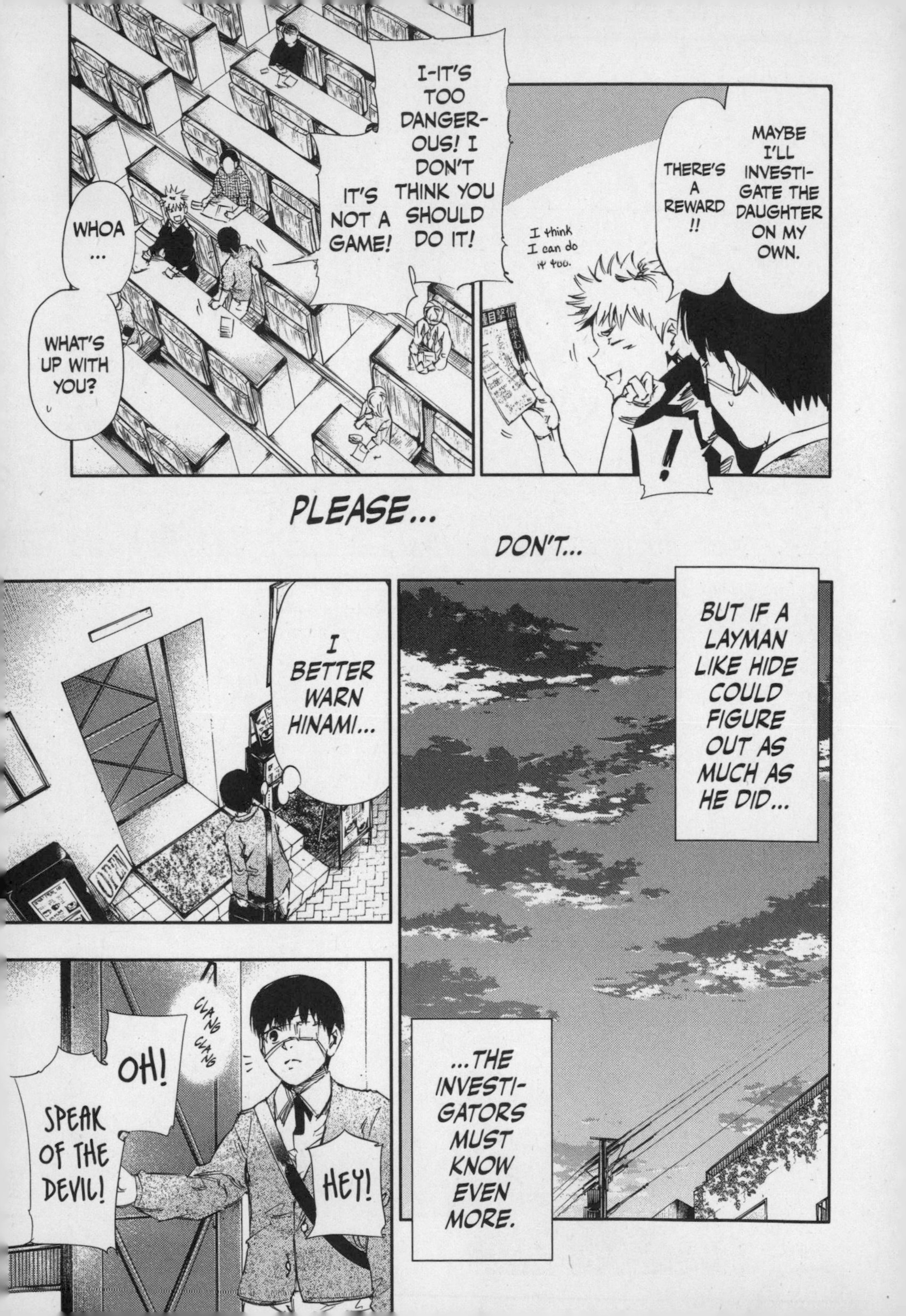
MAYBE I'LL INVESTI-GATE THE DAUGHTER ON MY OWN.
THERE'S A REWARD !!
I think I can do it too.
I-IT'S TOO DANGER-OUS! I DON'T THINK YOU SHOULD DO IT!
IT'S NOT A GAME!
WHOA ...
WHAT'S UP WITH YOU?
PLEASE...
DON'T...
BUT IF A LAYMAN LIKE HIDE COULD FIGURE OUT AS MUCH AS HE DID...
...THE INVESTI-GATORS MUST KNOW EVEN MORE.
I BETTER WARN HINAMI...
OPEN
CLANG CLANG
OH!
SPEAK OF THE DEVIL!
HEY!

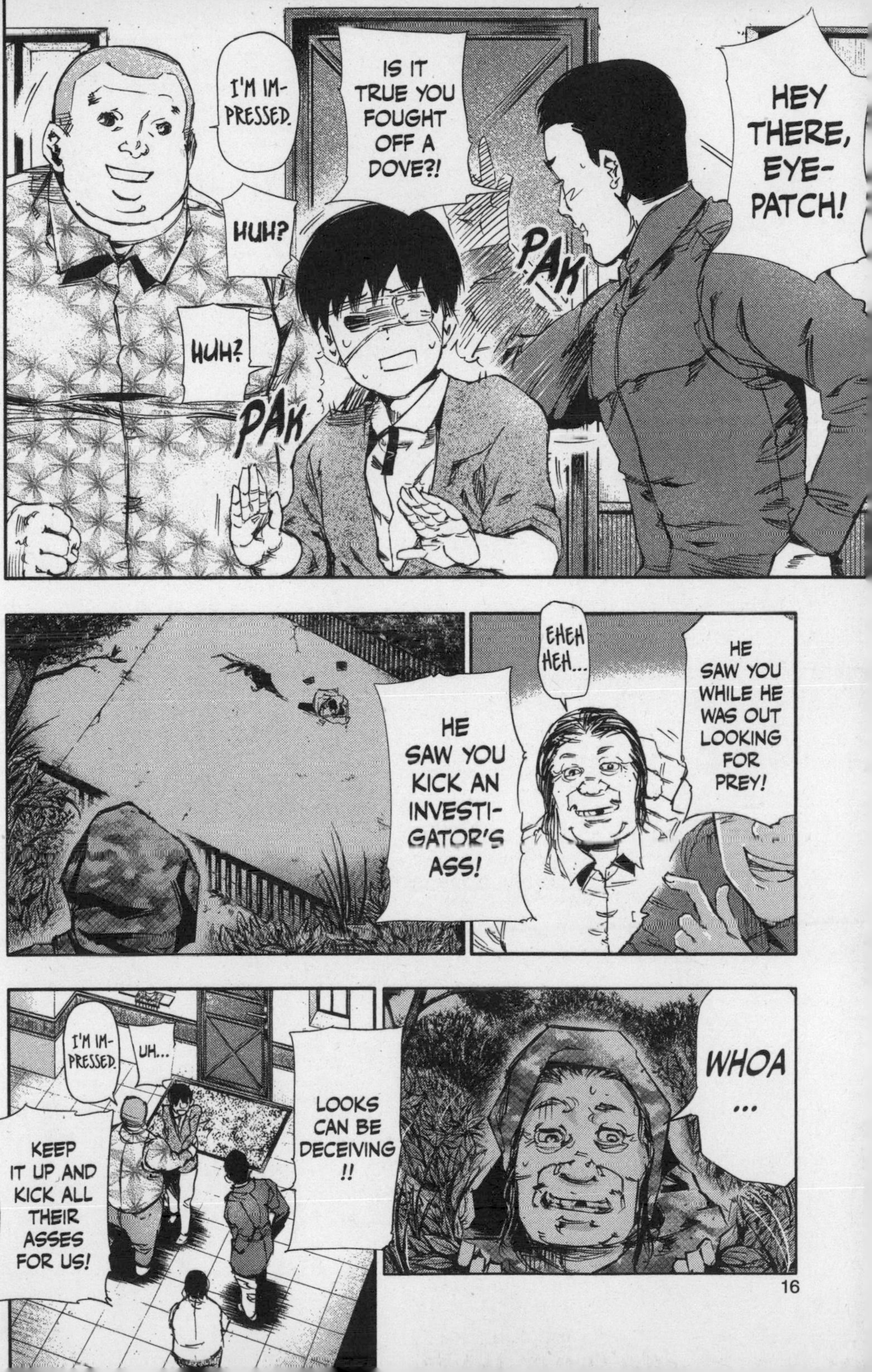
HEY THERE, EYE-PATCH!
PAK
IS IT TRUE YOU FOUGHT OFF A DOVE?!
I'M IM-PRESSED.
HUH?
HUH?
PAK
HE SAW YOU WHILE HE WAS OUT LOOKING FOR PREY!
EHEH HEH...
HE SAW YOU KICK AN INVESTI-GATOR'S ASS!
WHOA ...
LOOKS CAN BE DECEIVING !!
UH...
I'M IM-PRESSED.
KEEP IT UP AND KICK ALL THEIR ASSES FOR US!

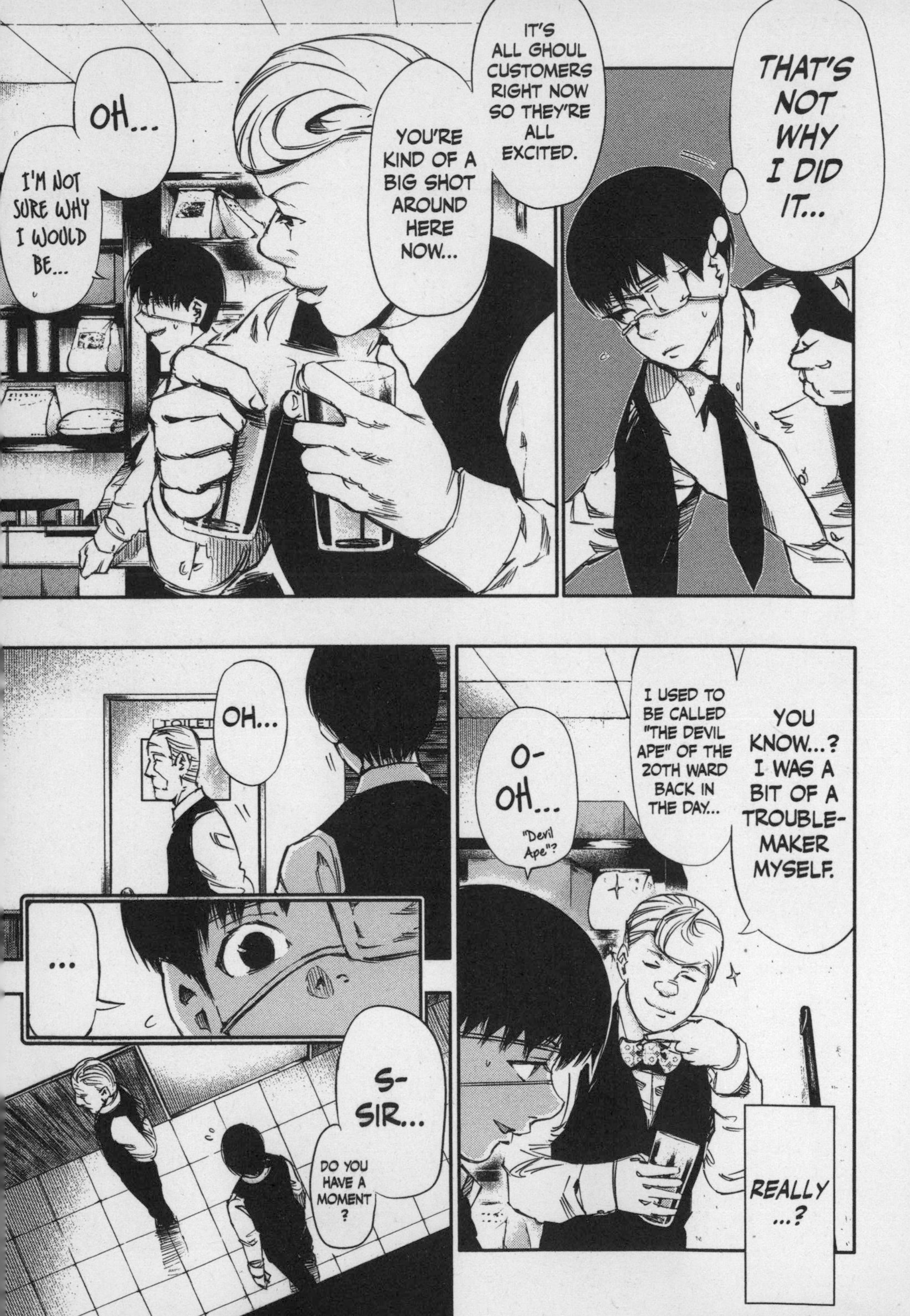
THAT'S NOT WHY I DID IT...
IT'S ALL GHOUL CUSTOMERS RIGHT NOW SO THEY'RE ALL EXCITED.
YOU'RE KIND OF A BIG SHOT AROUND HERE NOW...
OH...
I'M NOT SURE WHY I WOULD BE...
YOU KNOW...? I WAS A BIT OF A TROUBLE-MAKER MYSELF.
I USED TO BE CALLED "THE DEVIL APE" OF THE 20TH WARD BACK IN THE DAY...
O-OH...
"Devil Ape"?
REALLY...?
TOILET
OH...
...
S-SIR...
DO YOU HAVE A MOMENT?

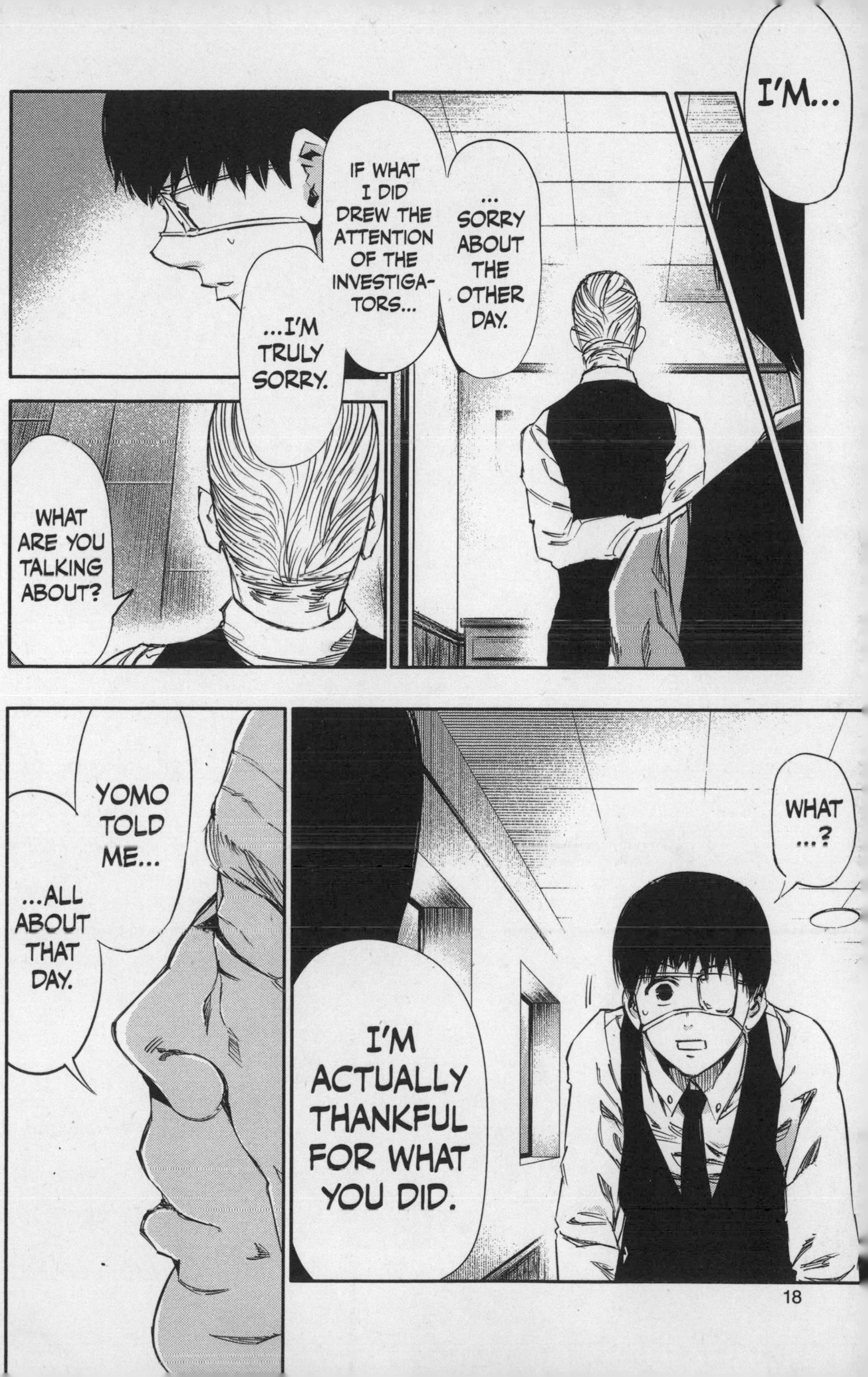
I'M...
... SORRY ABOUT THE OTHER DAY.
IF WHAT I DID DREW THE ATTENTION OF THE INVESTIGATORS...
...I'M TRULY SORRY.
WHAT ARE YOU TALKING ABOUT?
WHAT ...?
I'M ACTUALLY THANKFUL FOR WHAT YOU DID.
YOMO TOLD ME...
...ALL ABOUT THAT DAY.

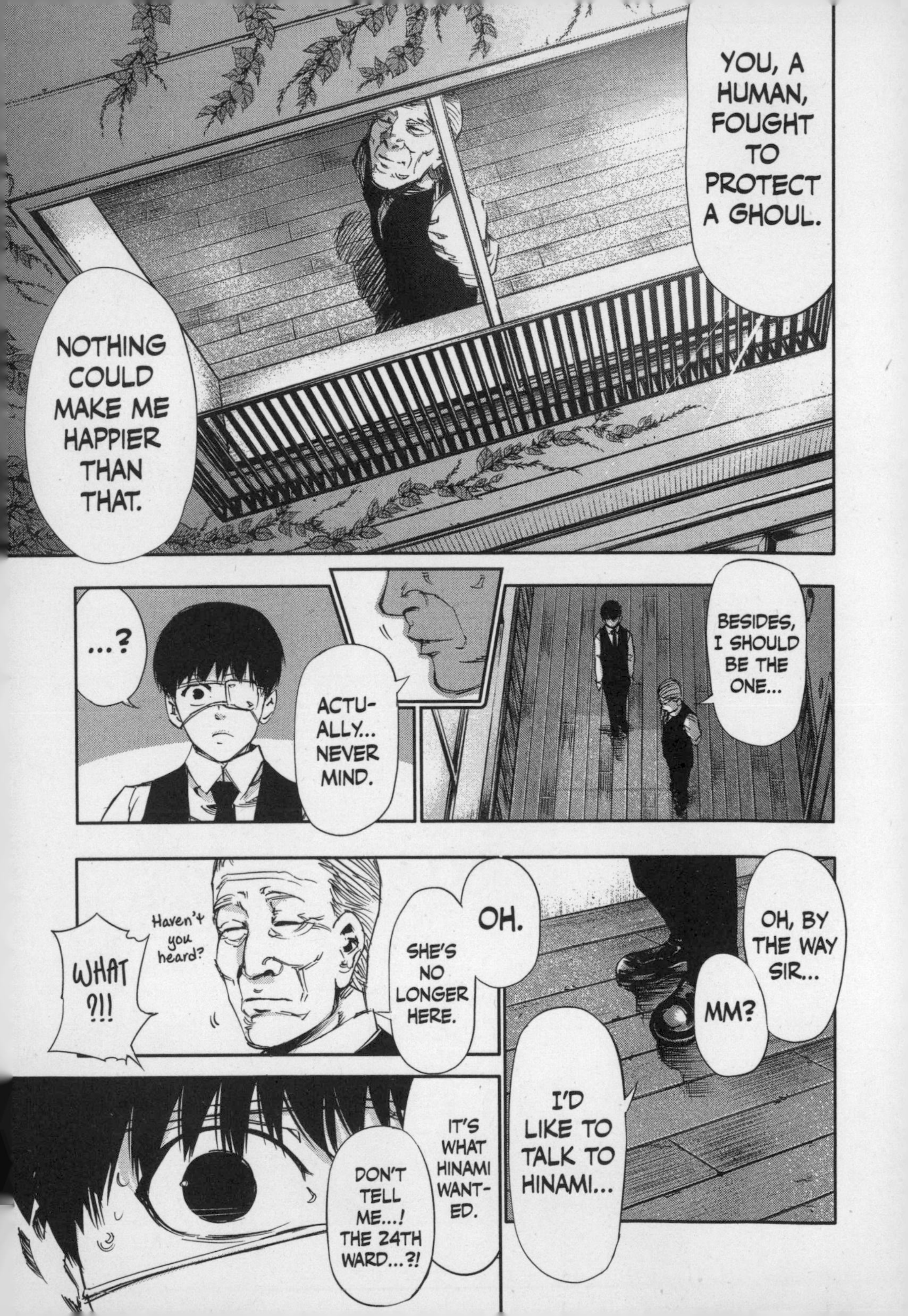
YOU, A HUMAN, FOUGHT TO PROTECT A GHOUL.
NOTHING COULD MAKE ME HAPPIER THAN THAT.
BESIDES, I SHOULD BE THE ONE...
ACTU-ALLY... NEVER MIND.
...?
OH, BY THE WAY SIR...
MM?
I'D LIKE TO TALK TO HINAMI...
OH.
SHE'S NO LONGER HERE.
Haven't you heard?
WHAT ?!!
IT'S WHAT HINAMI WANT-ED.
DON'T TELL ME...! THE 24TH WARD...?!

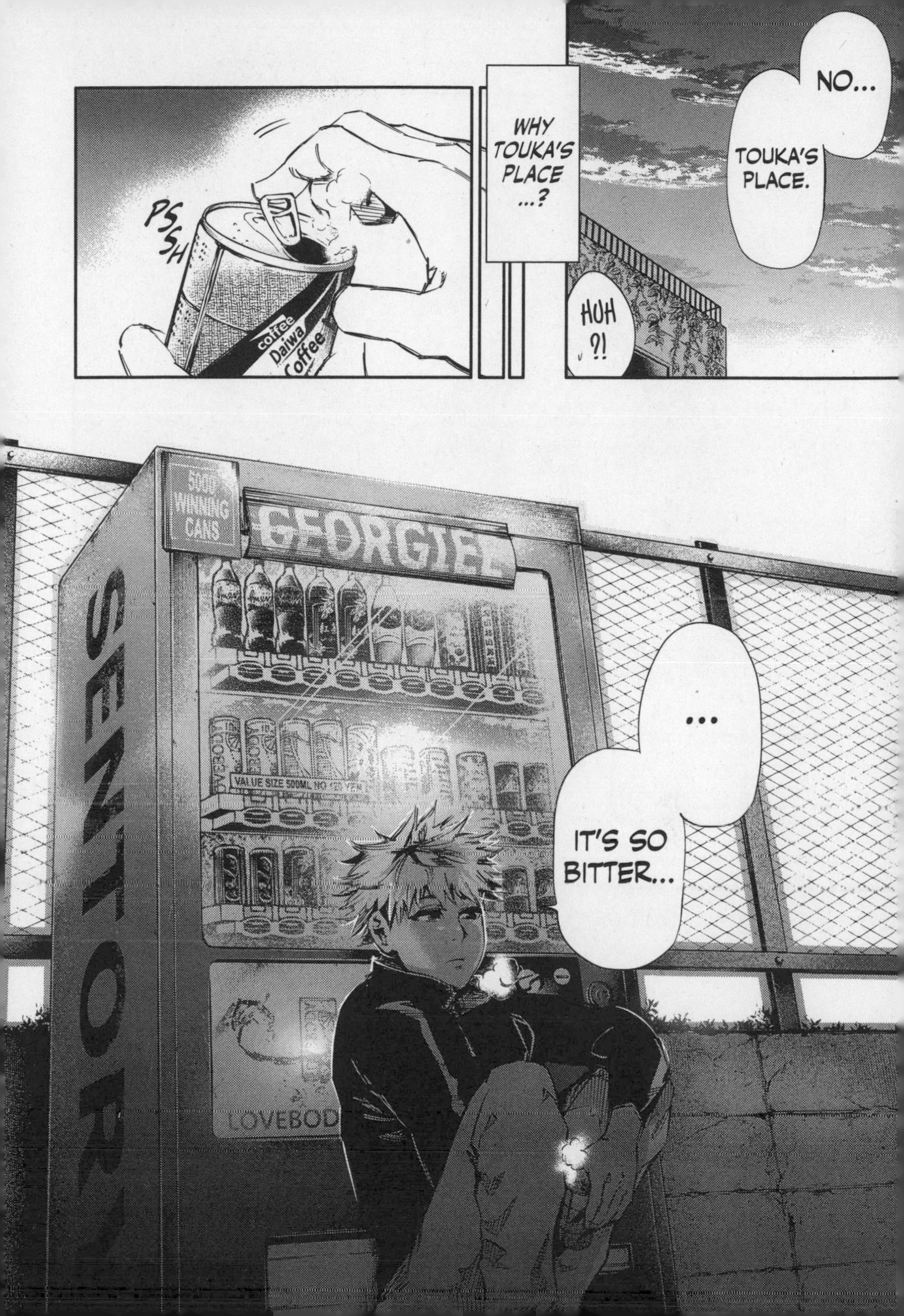
NO...
TOUKA'S PLACE.
HUH ?!
WHY TOUKA'S PLACE ...?
PSSH
coffee Daiwa Coffee
5000 WINNING CANS
...
IT'S SO BITTER...

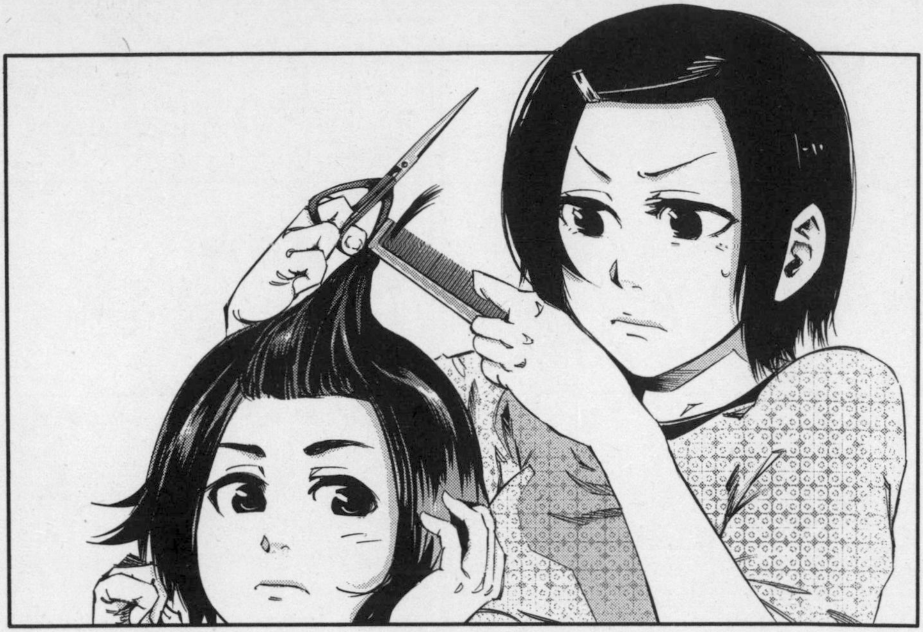

#031 TOKYO GHOUL [YORIKO]

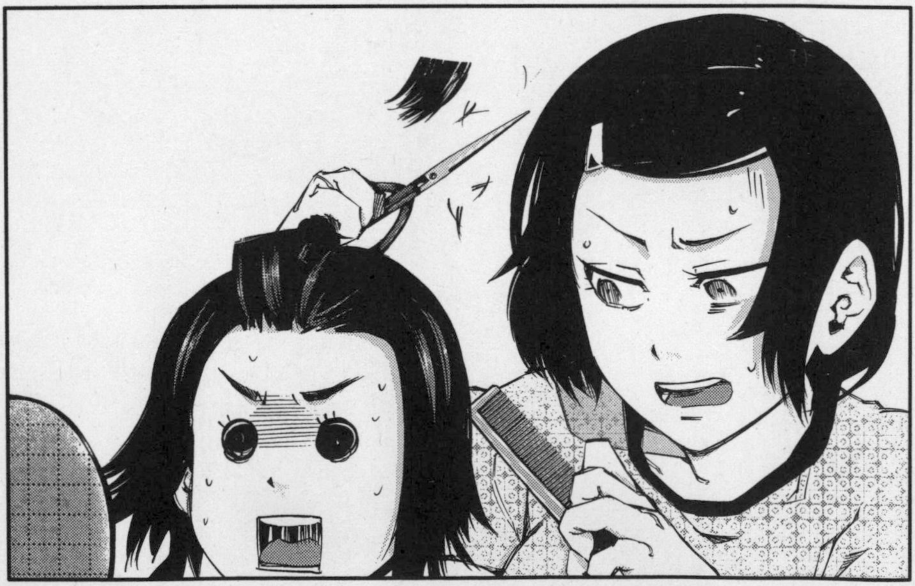

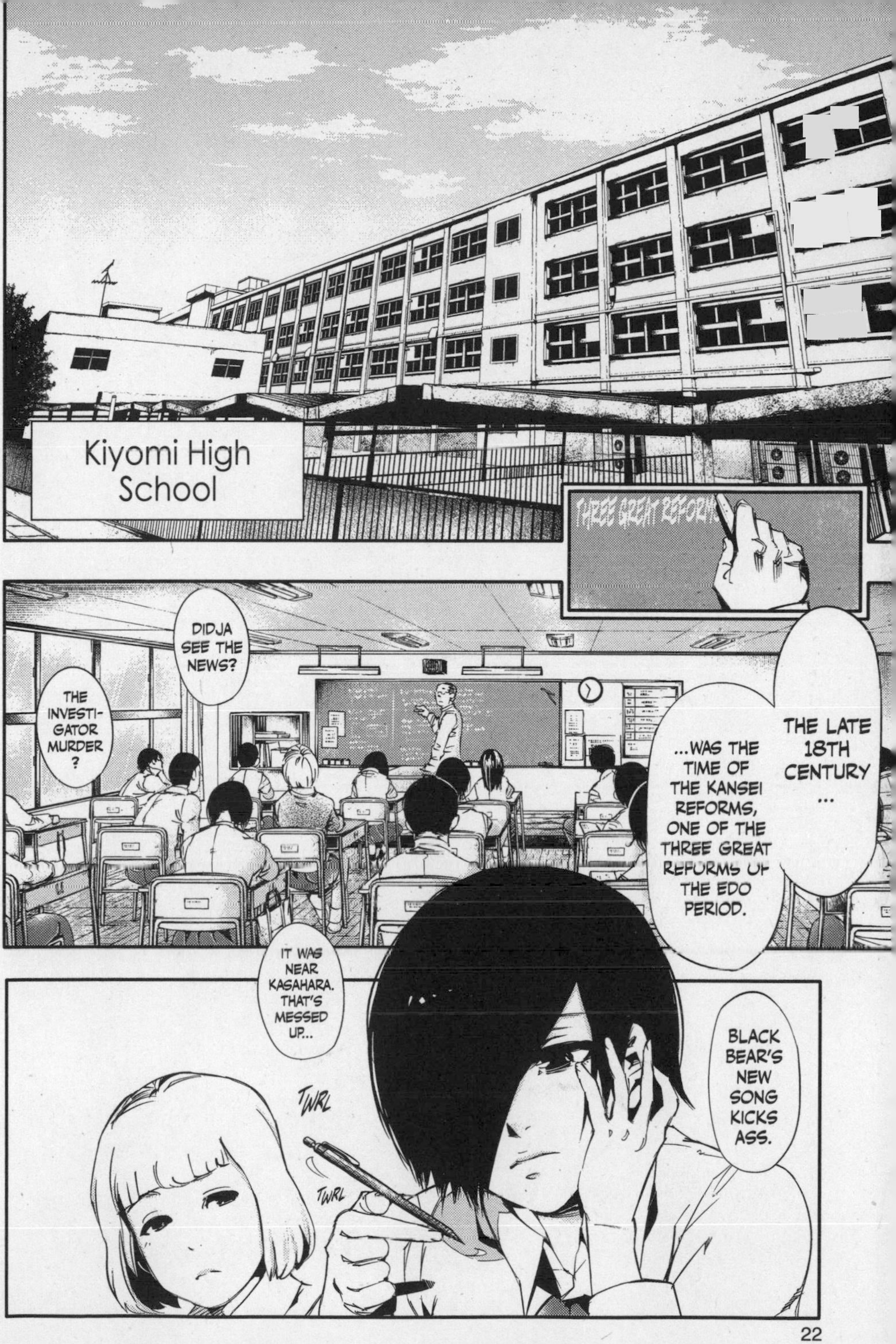
Kiyomi High School
THREE GREAT REFORM
THE LATE 18TH CENTURY ...
...WAS THE TIME OF THE KANSEI REFORMS, ONE OF THE THREE GREAT REFORMS OF THE EDO PERIOD.
DIDJA SEE THE NEWS?
THE INVESTIGATOR MURDER?
BLACK BEAR'S NEW SONG KICKS ASS.
IT WAS NEAR KASAHARA. THAT'S MESSED UP...
TWRL
TWRL

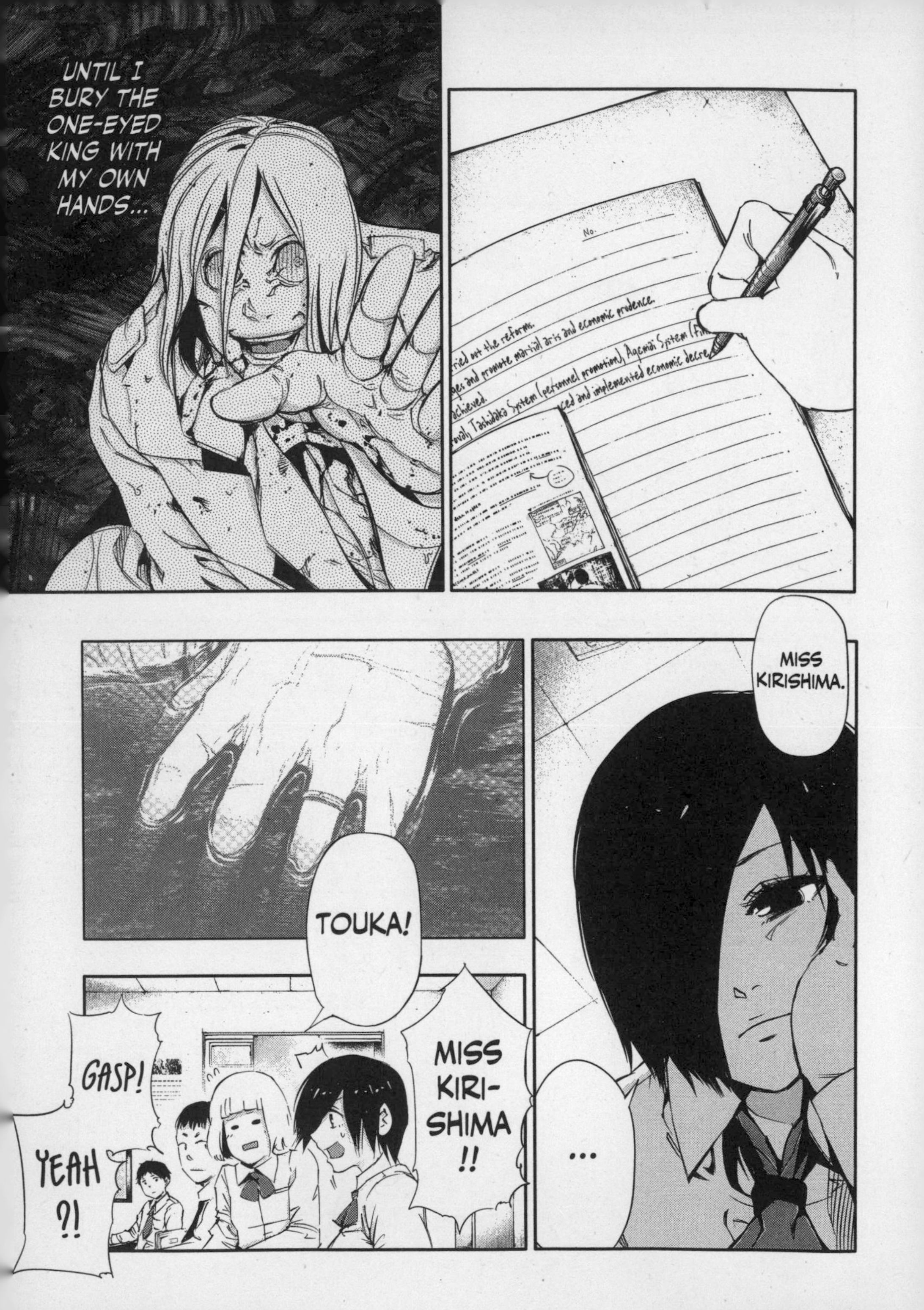
No.
ried out the reforms.
ges and promote martial arts and economic prudence.
achieved.
ovd, Tashidaka System (personnel promotion), Agemai System (Fi
ced and implemented economic decre
UNTIL I BURY THE ONE-EYED KING WITH MY OWN HANDS...
MISS KIRISHIMA.
...
TOUKA!
MISS KIRI-SHIMA!!
GASP!
YEAH?!

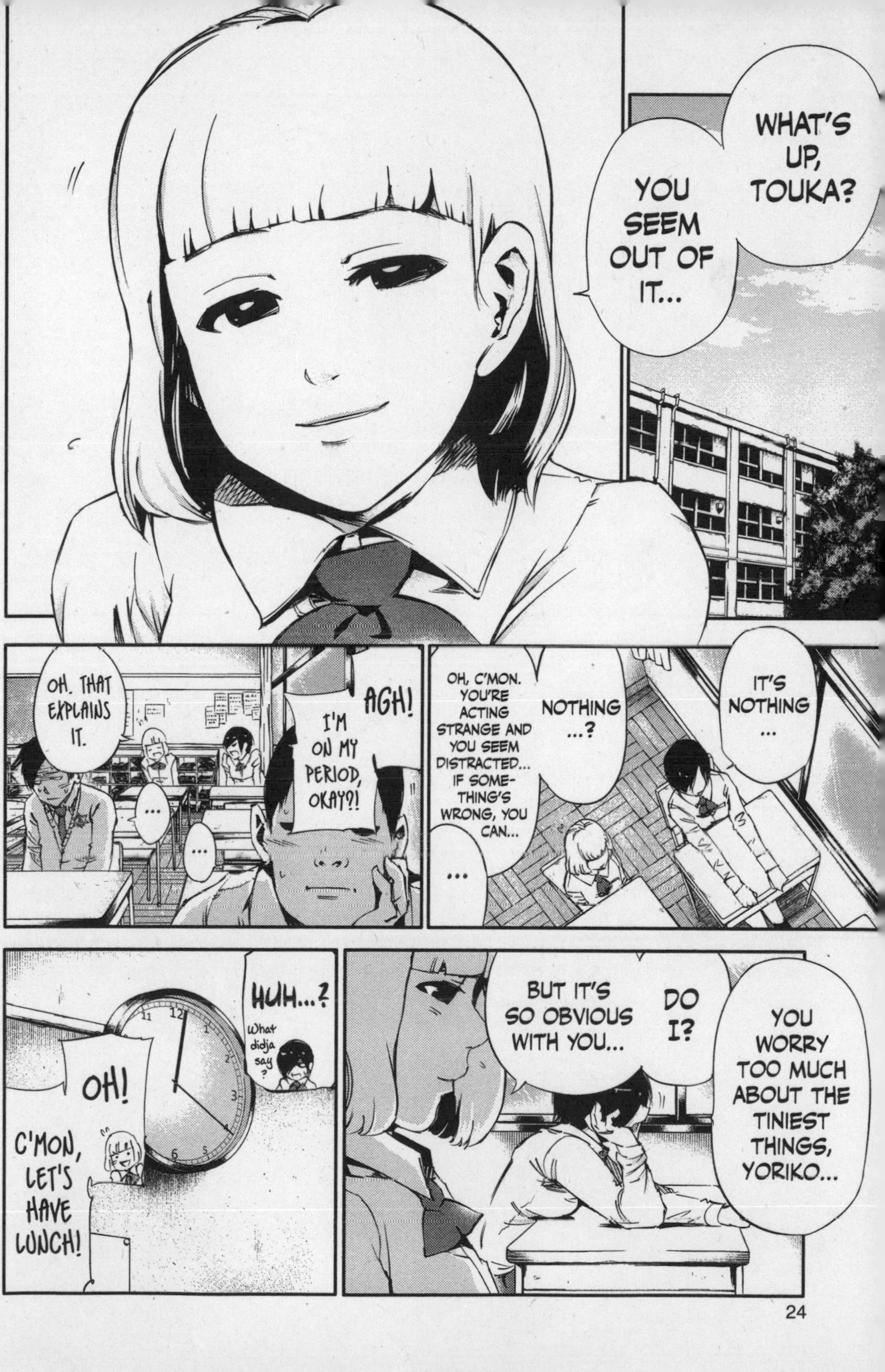
WHAT'S UP, TOUKA?
YOU SEEM OUT OF IT...
IT'S NOTHING ...
NOTHING ...?
OH, C'MON. YOU'RE ACTING STRANGE AND YOU SEEM DISTRACTED... IF SOME-THING'S WRONG, YOU CAN...
...
AGH!
I'M ON MY PERIOD, OKAY?!
OH. THAT EXPLAINS IT.
...
...
YOU WORRY TOO MUCH ABOUT THE TINIEST THINGS, YORIKO...
DO I?
BUT IT'S SO OBVIOUS WITH YOU...
HUH...?
What didja say?
OH!
C'MON, LET'S HAVE LUNCH!

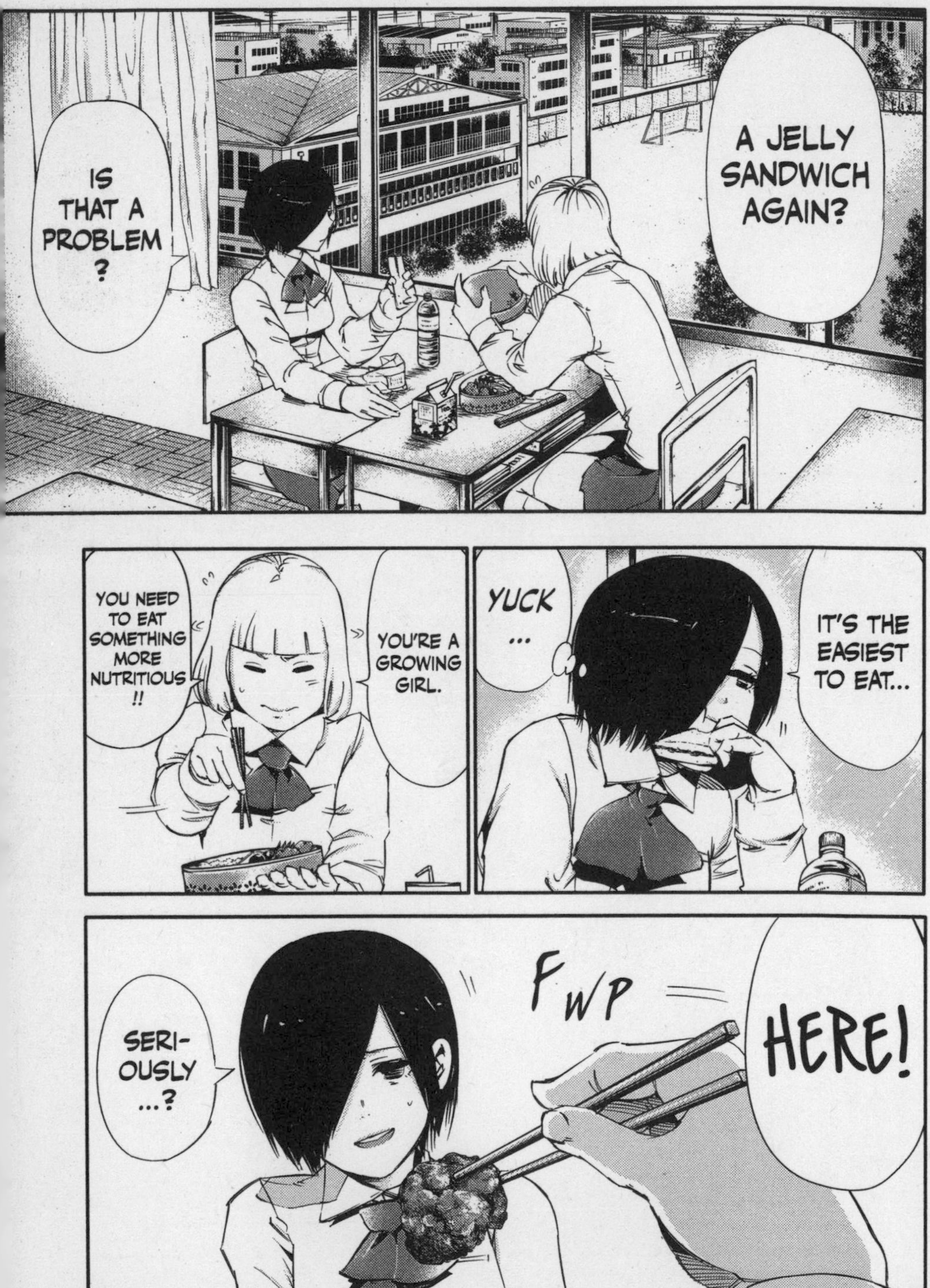
A JELLY SANDWICH AGAIN?
IS THAT A PROBLEM?
IT'S THE EASIEST TO EAT...
YUCK ...
YOU'RE A GROWING GIRL.
YOU NEED TO EAT SOMETHING MORE NUTRITIOUS!!
HERE!
FWP
SERI-OUSLY ...?

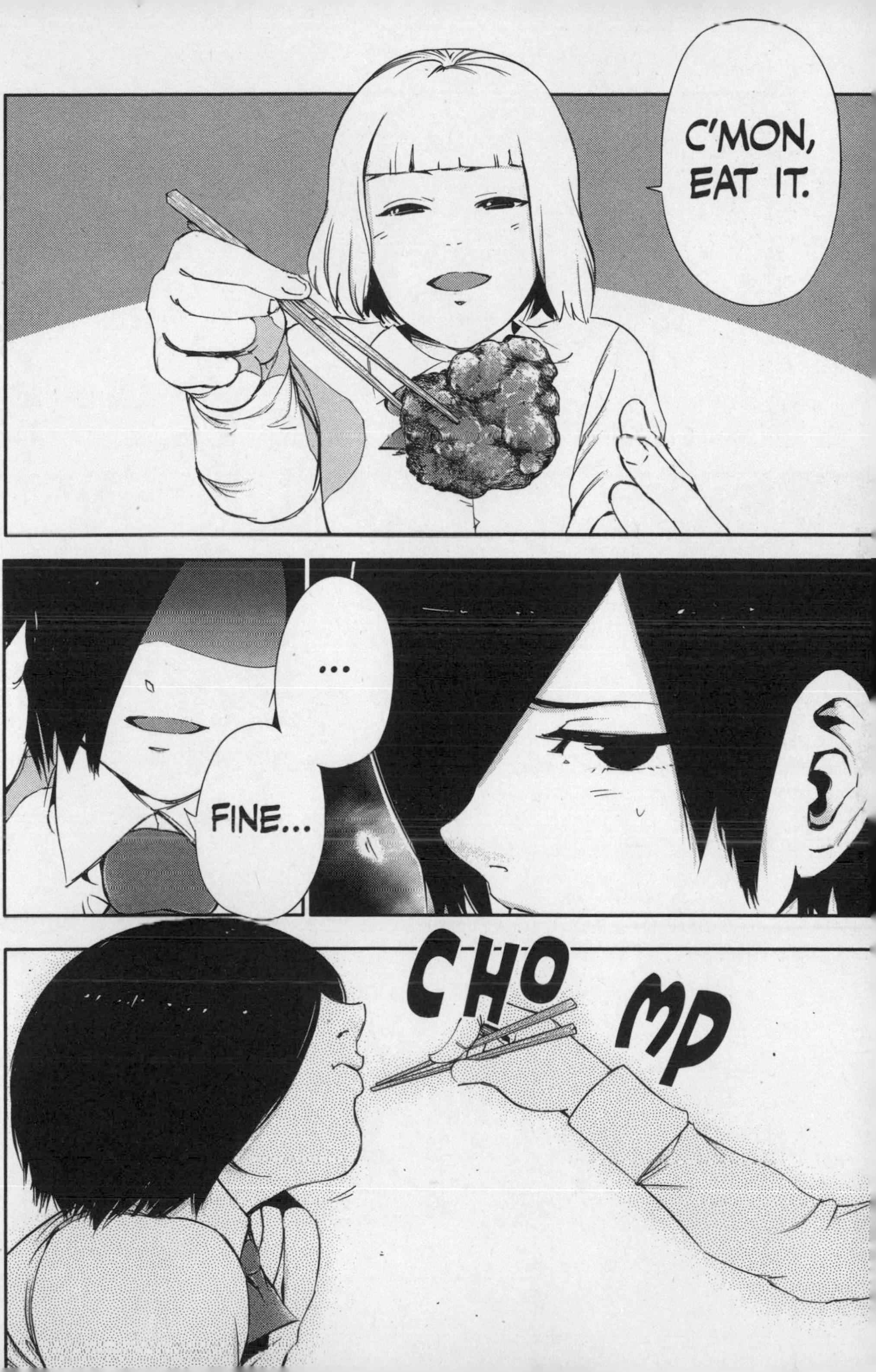
C'MON, EAT IT.
...
FINE...
CHO MP

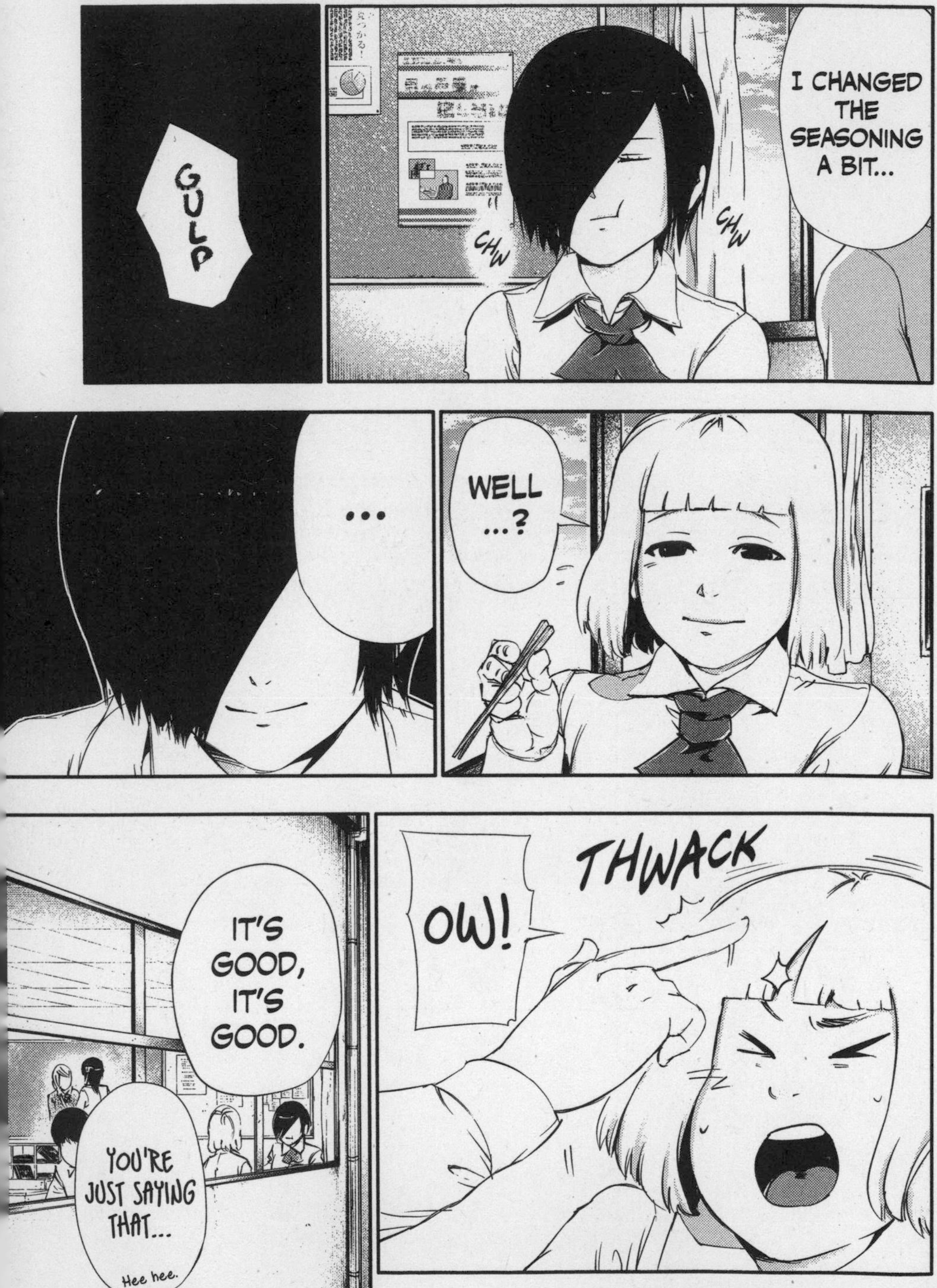
I CHANGED THE SEASONING A BIT...
CHW
CHW
GULP
WELL ...?
...
THWACK
OW!
IT'S GOOD, IT'S GOOD.
YOU'RE JUST SAYING THAT...
Hee hee.

URGH ...
...
...
URP...

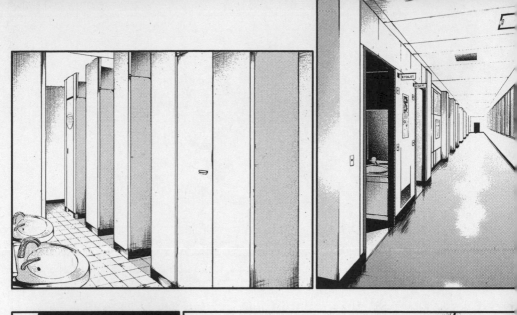

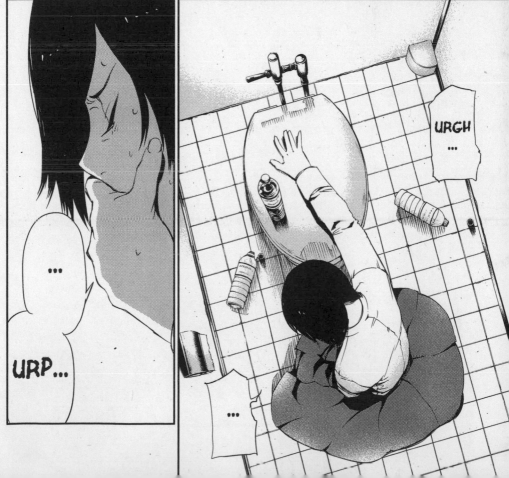

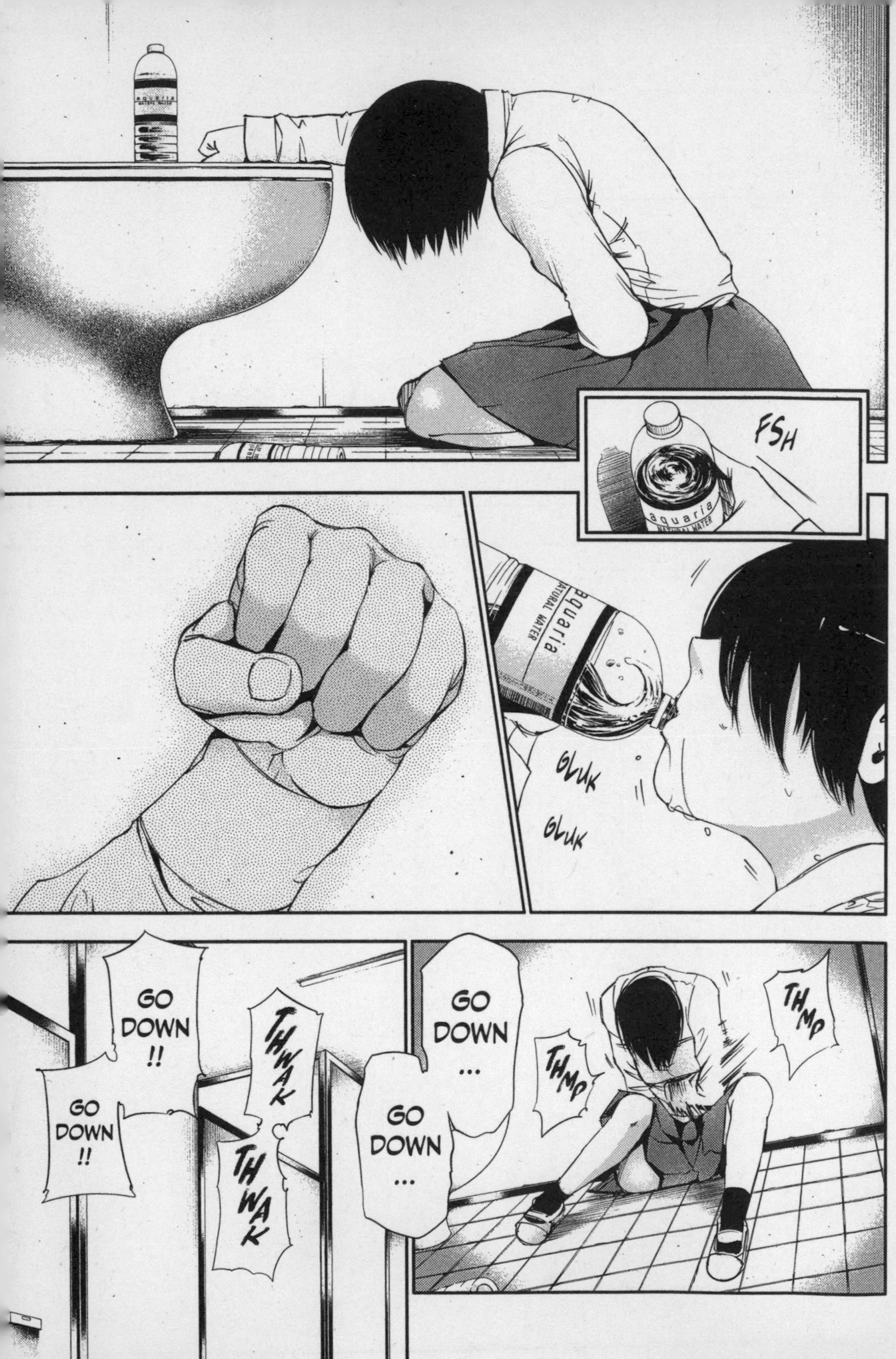
FSH
aquaria NATURAL WATER
GLUK
GLUK
THMP
THMP
GO DOWN ...
GO DOWN ...
GO DOWN !!
THWAK
GO DOWN !!
THWAK

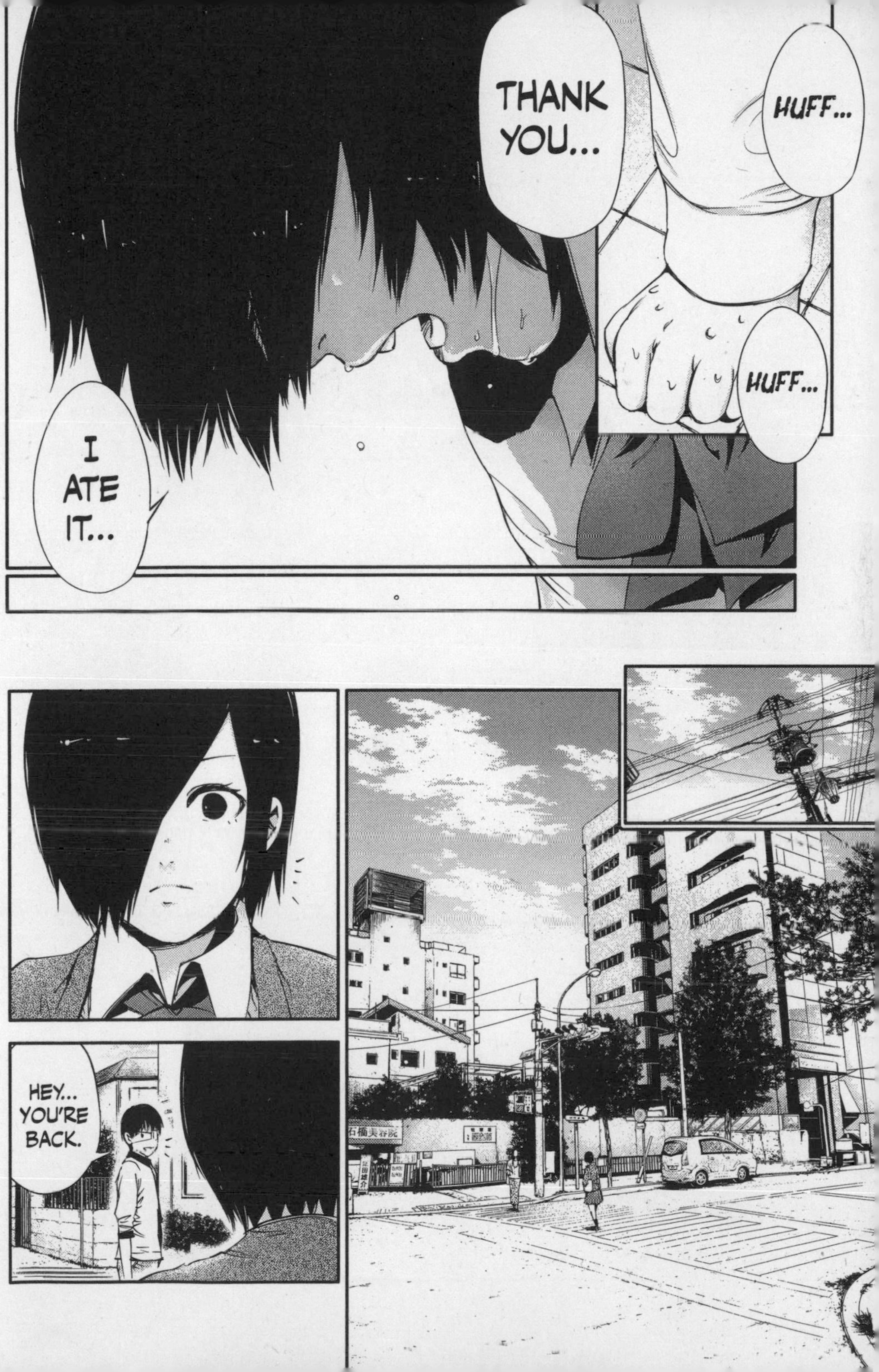
HUFF...
THANK YOU...
HUFF...
I ATE IT...
HEY... YOU'RE BACK.

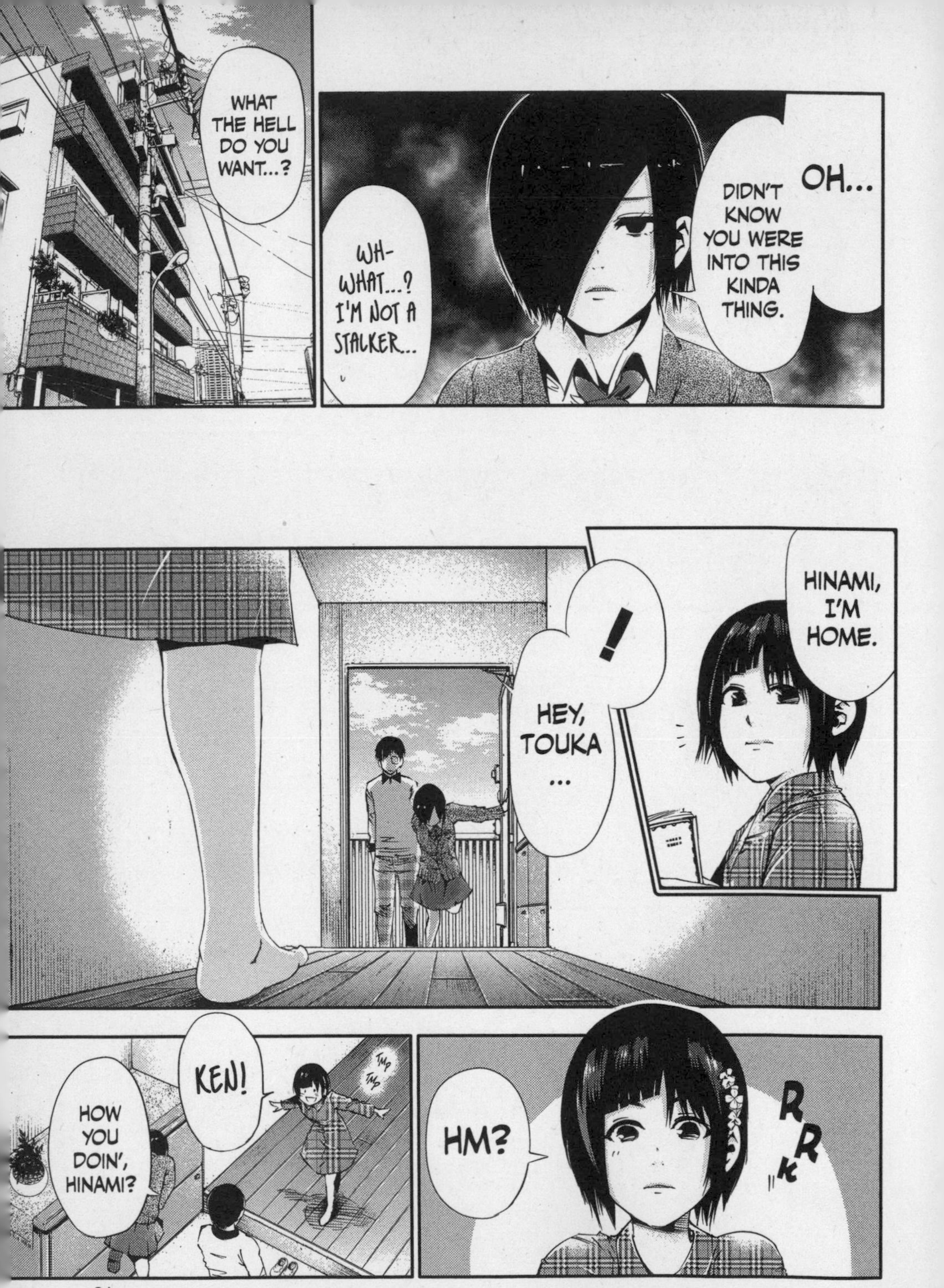
OH...
DIDN'T KNOW YOU WERE INTO THIS KINDA THING.
WH- WHAT...? I'M NOT A STALKER...
WHAT THE HELL DO YOU WANT...?
HINAMI, I'M HOME.
!
HEY, TOUKA ...
HM?
RRK
KEN!
TMP TMP
HOW YOU DOIN', HINAMI?

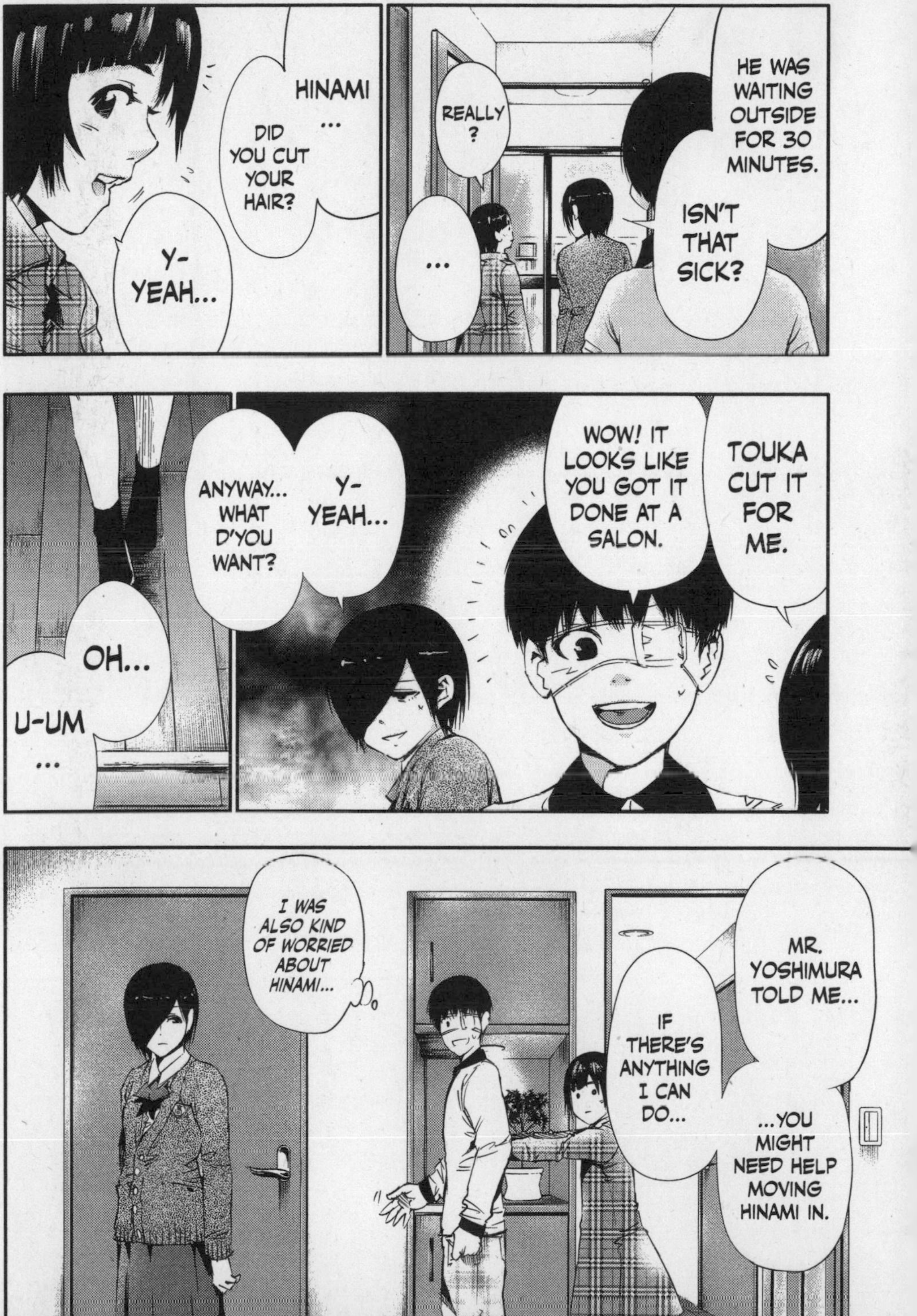
HE WAS WAITING OUTSIDE FOR 30 MINUTES.
ISN'T THAT SICK?
REALLY?
...
HINAMI... DID YOU CUT YOUR HAIR?
Y-YEAH...
TOUKA CUT IT FOR ME.
WOW! IT LOOKS LIKE YOU GOT IT DONE AT A SALON.
Y-YEAH...
ANYWAY... WHAT D'YOU WANT?
OH...
U-UM...
MR. YOSHIMURA TOLD ME...
IF THERE'S ANYTHING I CAN DO...
...YOU MIGHT NEED HELP MOVING HINAMI IN.
I WAS ALSO KIND OF WORRIED ABOUT HINAMI...

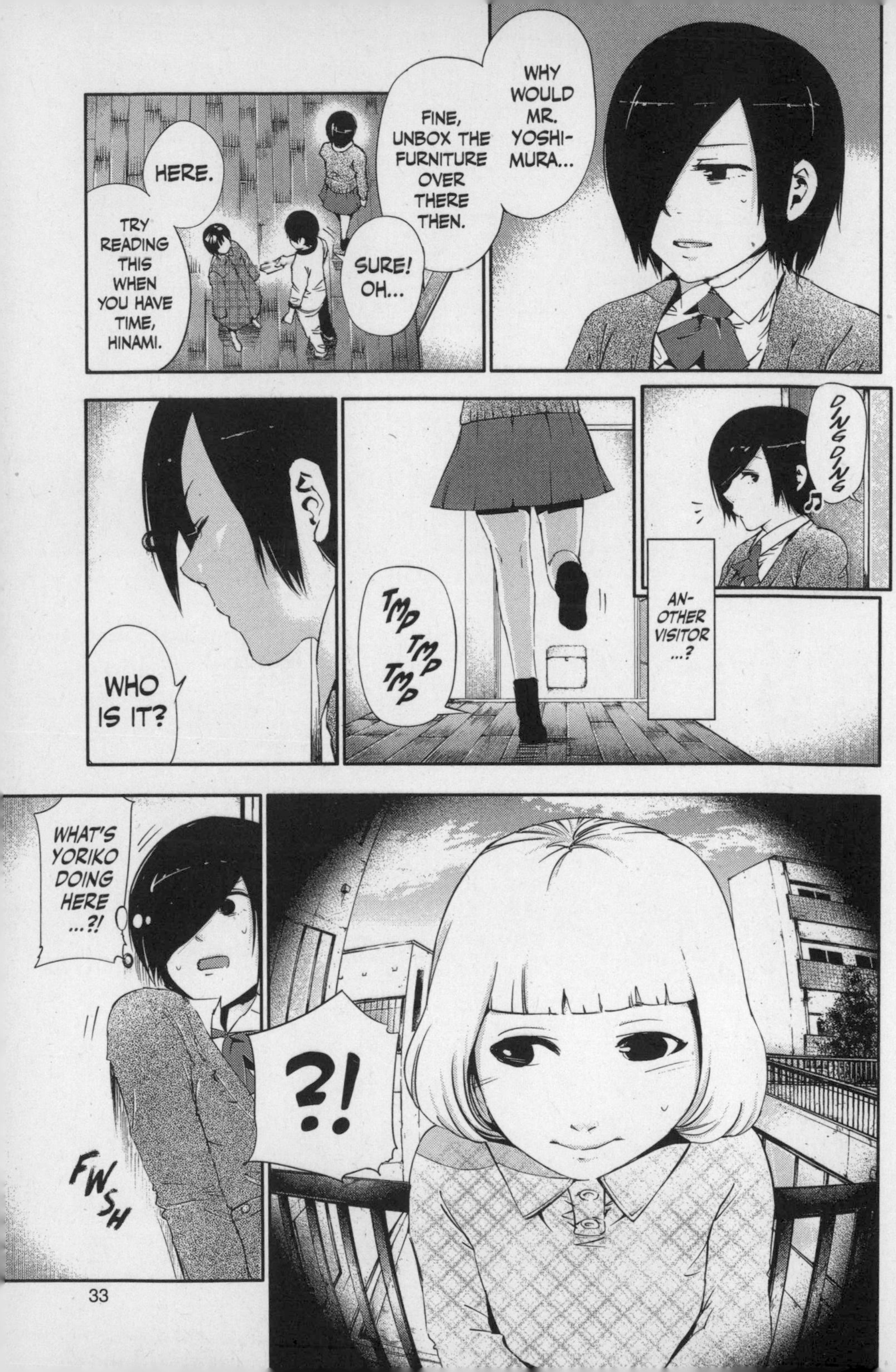
WHY WOULD MR. YOSHIMURA...
FINE, UNBOX THE FURNITURE OVER THERE THEN.
SURE! OH...
HERE.
TRY READING THIS WHEN YOU HAVE TIME, HINAMI.
DING DING
AN-OTHER VISITOR ...?
TMP TMP TMP
WHO IS IT?
?!
WHAT'S YORIKO DOING HERE ...?!
FWSH

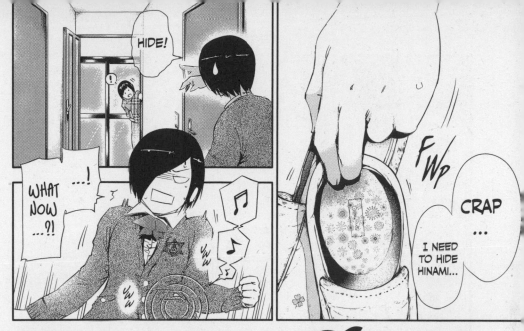

HIDE!

WHAT NOW ...?!

...!

CRAP ...

I NEED TO HIDE HINAMI...

...!

WHAT'S UP...?

I'M SORRY...

...FOR SHOWING UP LIKE THIS.

34

NO.

TOUKA.

YOU WERE ACTING STRANGE AT SCHOOL SO...

I GOT KINDA WORRIED...

HUH?

I'M FINE... YOU WORRY TOO MUCH.

LIKE WHEN YOUR DAD MOVED OVERSEAS FOR WORK...

YOU HAD THAT SAD LOOK ON YOUR FACE.

I'M SORRY IF I'M WRONG...

...

Ayato...?

HEY?!

...

OH... AYATO'S HOME...?

Gasp

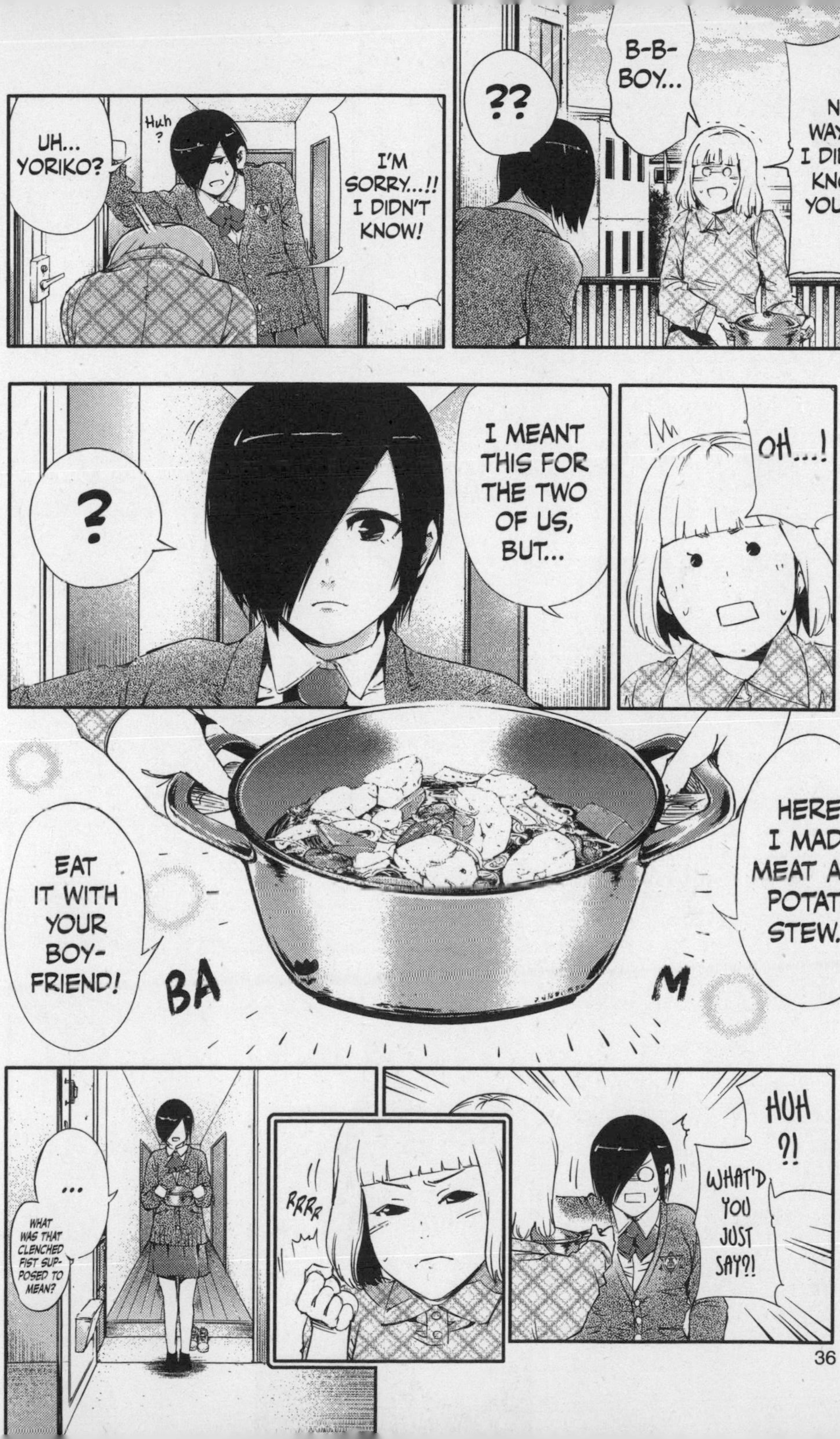
B-B-BOY...
NO WAY...? I DIDN'T KNOW YOUR...
??
I'M SORRY...!! I DIDN'T KNOW!
Huh ?
UH... YORIKO?
OH...!
I MEANT THIS FOR THE TWO OF US, BUT...
?
HERE! I MADE MEAT AND POTATO STEW...
BAM
EAT IT WITH YOUR BOY-FRIEND!
HUH ?!
WHAT'D YOU JUST SAY?!
RRRR
...
WHAT WAS THAT CLENCHED FIST SUP-POSED TO MEAN?

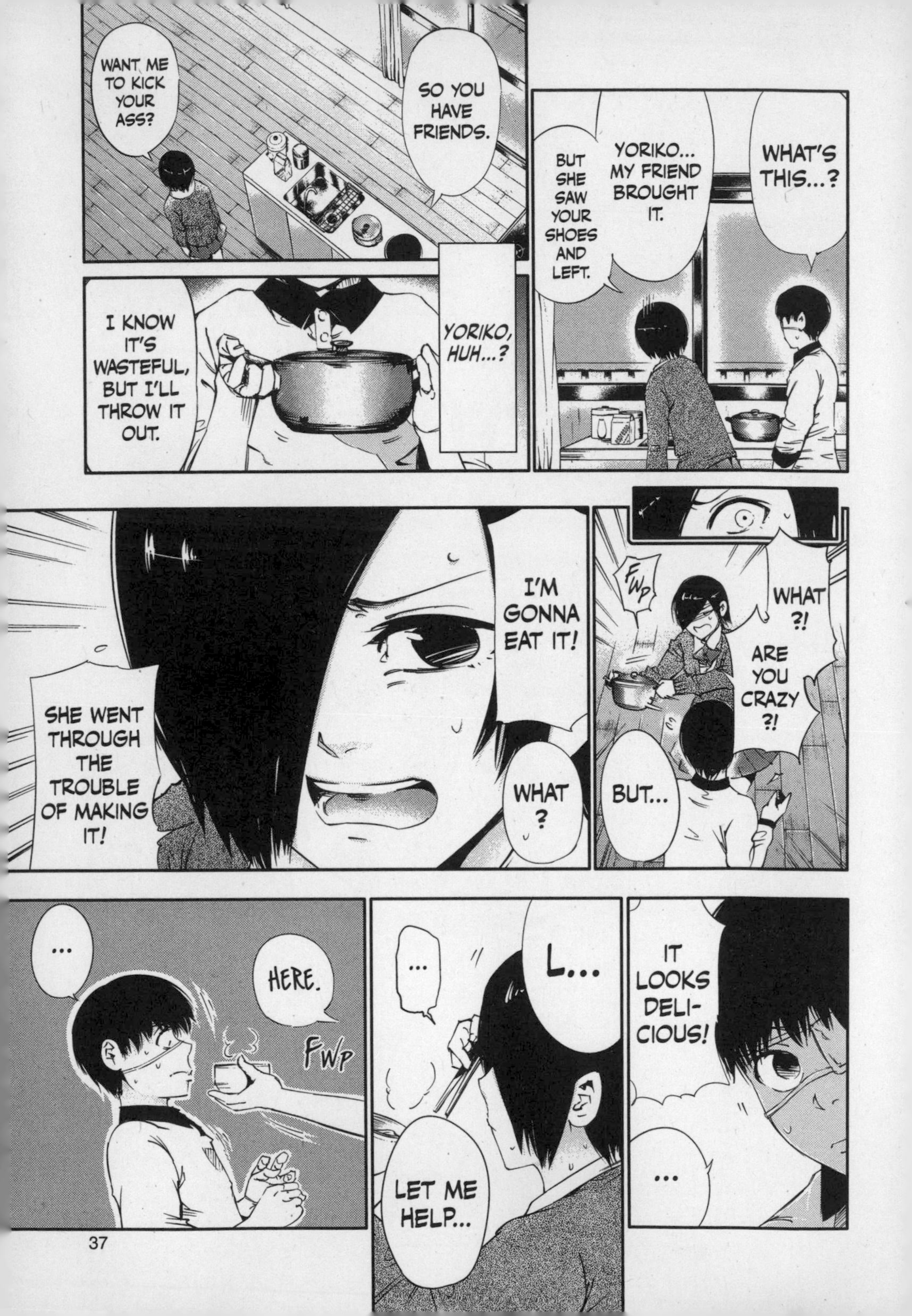
WHAT'S THIS...?
YORIKO... MY FRIEND BROUGHT IT.
BUT SHE SAW YOUR SHOES AND LEFT.
SO YOU HAVE FRIENDS.
WANT ME TO KICK YOUR ASS?
YORIKO, HUH...?
I KNOW IT'S WASTEFUL, BUT I'LL THROW IT OUT.
FWP
WHAT?!
ARE YOU CRAZY?!
BUT...
I'M GONNA EAT IT!
WHAT?
SHE WENT THROUGH THE TROUBLE OF MAKING IT!
IT LOOKS DELICIOUS!
...
L...
...
LET ME HELP...
HERE.
...
FWP

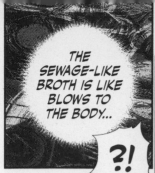

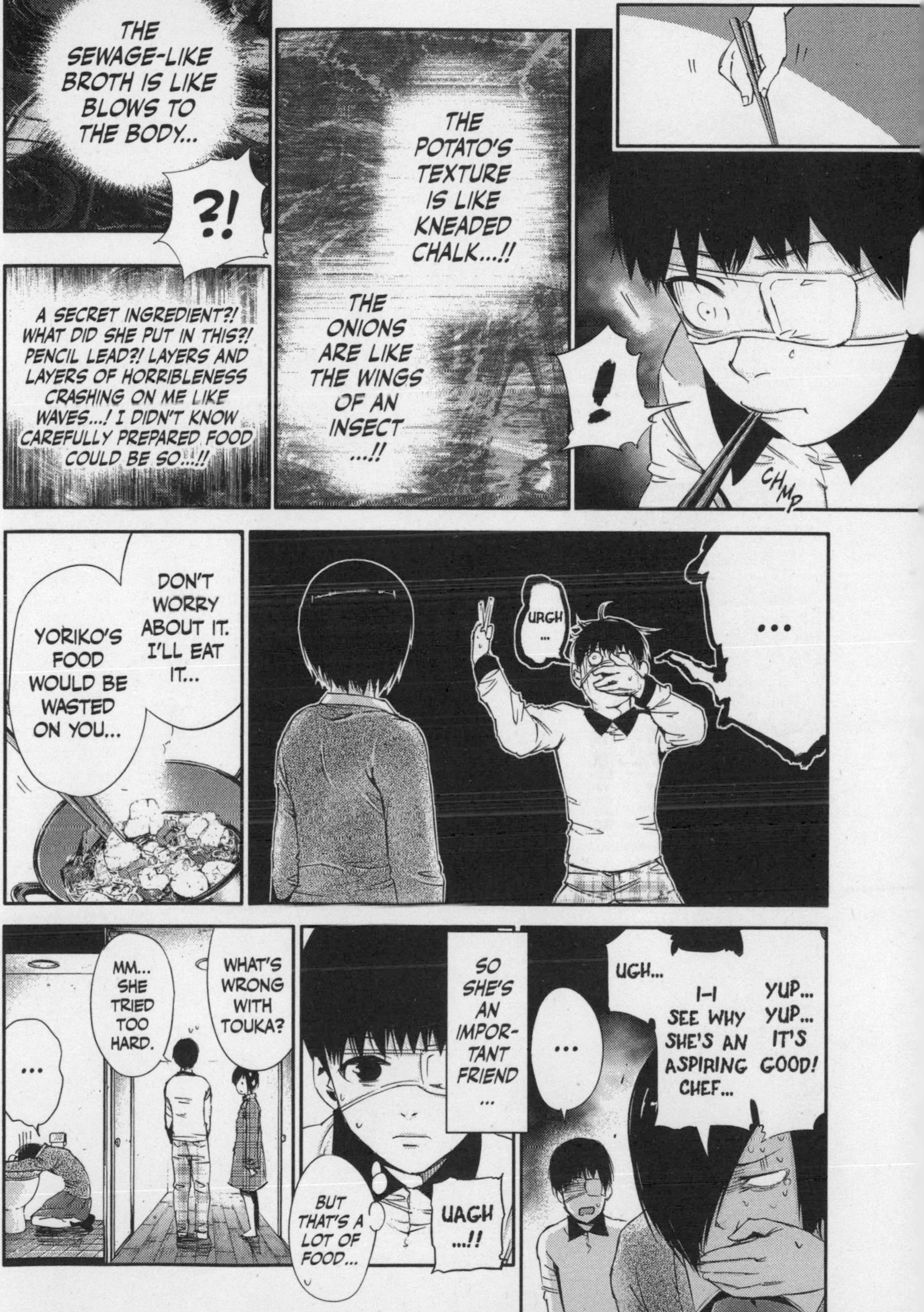
!
CHMP
THE POTATO'S TEXTURE IS LIKE KNEADED CHALK...!!
THE ONIONS ARE LIKE THE WINGS OF AN INSECT ...!!
THE SEWAGE-LIKE BROTH IS LIKE BLOWS TO THE BODY...
?!
A SECRET INGREDIENT?! WHAT DID SHE PUT IN THIS?! PENCIL LEAD?! LAYERS AND LAYERS OF HORRIBLENESS CRASHING ON ME LIKE WAVES...! I DIDN'T KNOW CAREFULLY PREPARED FOOD COULD BE SO...!!
...
URGH ...
DON'T WORRY ABOUT IT. I'LL EAT IT...
YORIKO'S FOOD WOULD BE WASTED ON YOU...
UGH...
YUP... YUP... IT'S GOOD!
I-I SEE WHY SHE'S AN ASPIRING CHEF...
...
SO SHE'S AN IMPOR-TANT FRIEND ...
UAGH ...!!
BUT THAT'S A LOT OF FOOD...
WHAT'S WRONG WITH TOUKA?
MM... SHE TRIED TOO HARD.
...

Fried egg

Sausage

Fried chicken

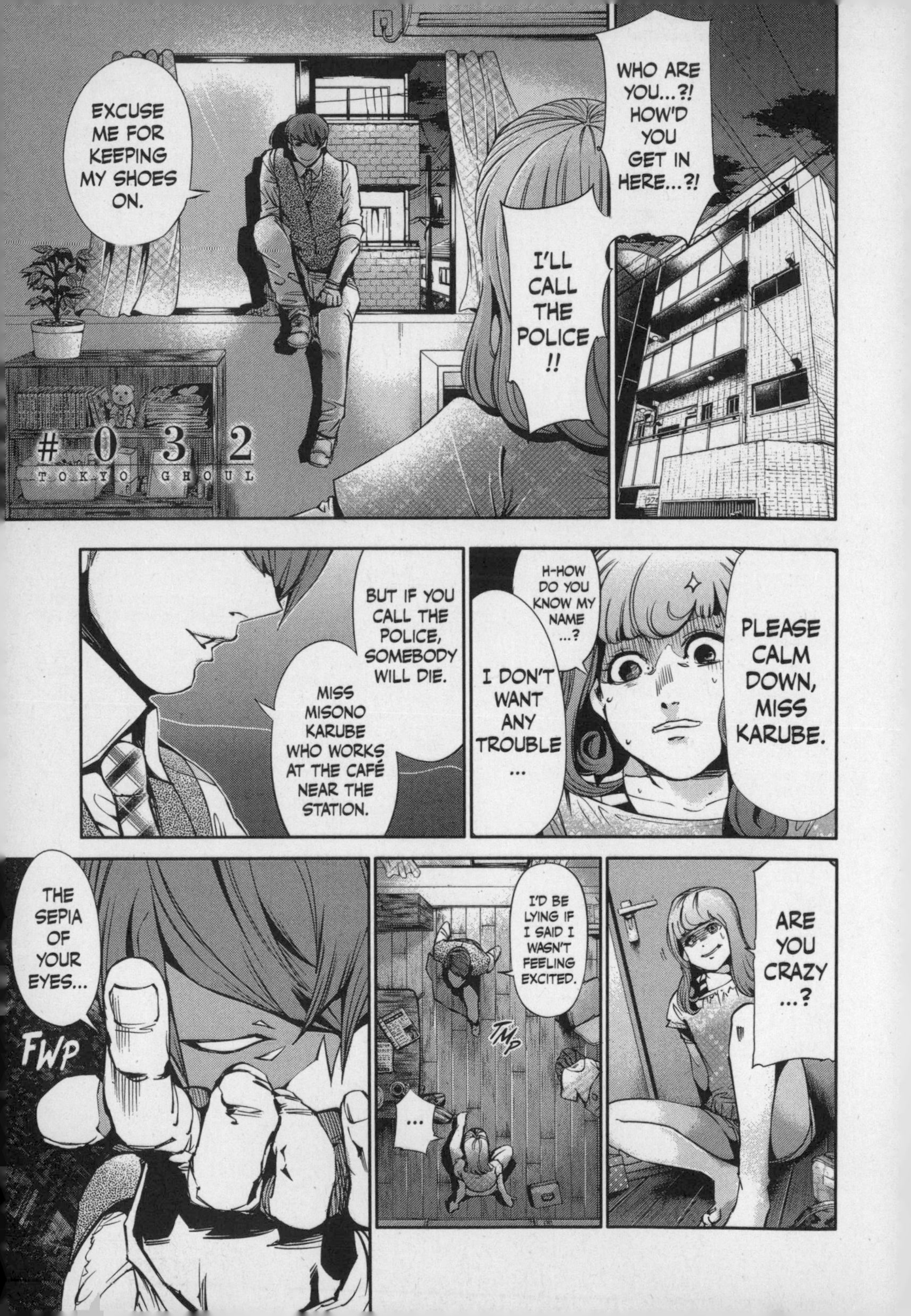

WHO ARE YOU...?! HOW'D YOU GET IN HERE...?!
I'LL CALL THE POLICE !!
EXCUSE ME FOR KEEPING MY SHOES ON.
#032
TOKYO GHOUL
PLEASE CALM DOWN, MISS KARUBE.
H-HOW DO YOU KNOW MY NAME ...?
I DON'T WANT ANY TROUBLE ...
BUT IF YOU CALL THE POLICE, SOMEBODY WILL DIE.
MISS MISONO KARUBE WHO WORKS AT THE CAFÉ NEAR THE STATION.
ARE YOU CRAZY ...?
I'D BE LYING IF I SAID I WASN'T FEELING EXCITED.
TMP
...
THE SEPIA OF YOUR EYES...
FWP

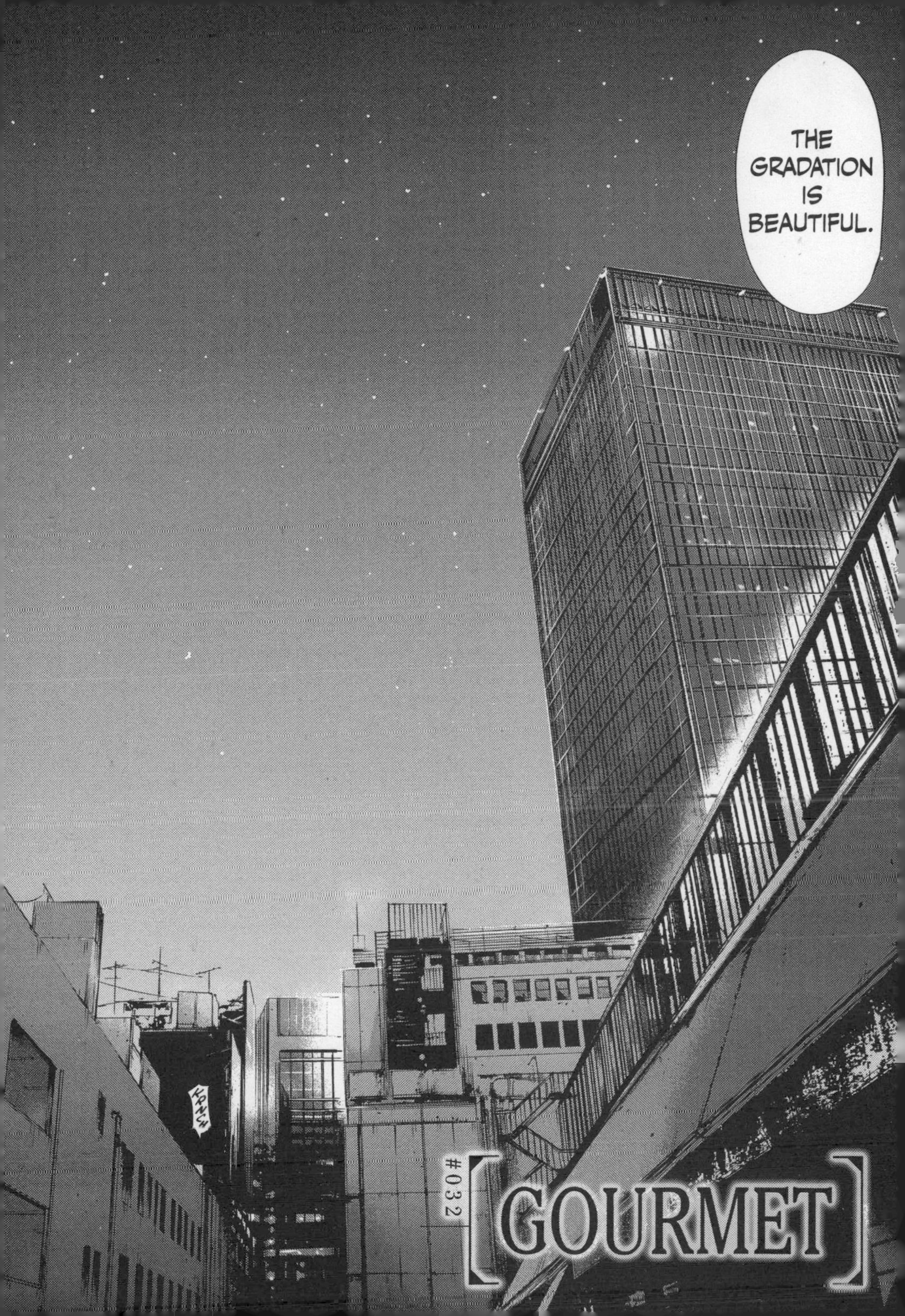
THE GRADATION IS BEAUTIFUL.
#032
[GOURMET]

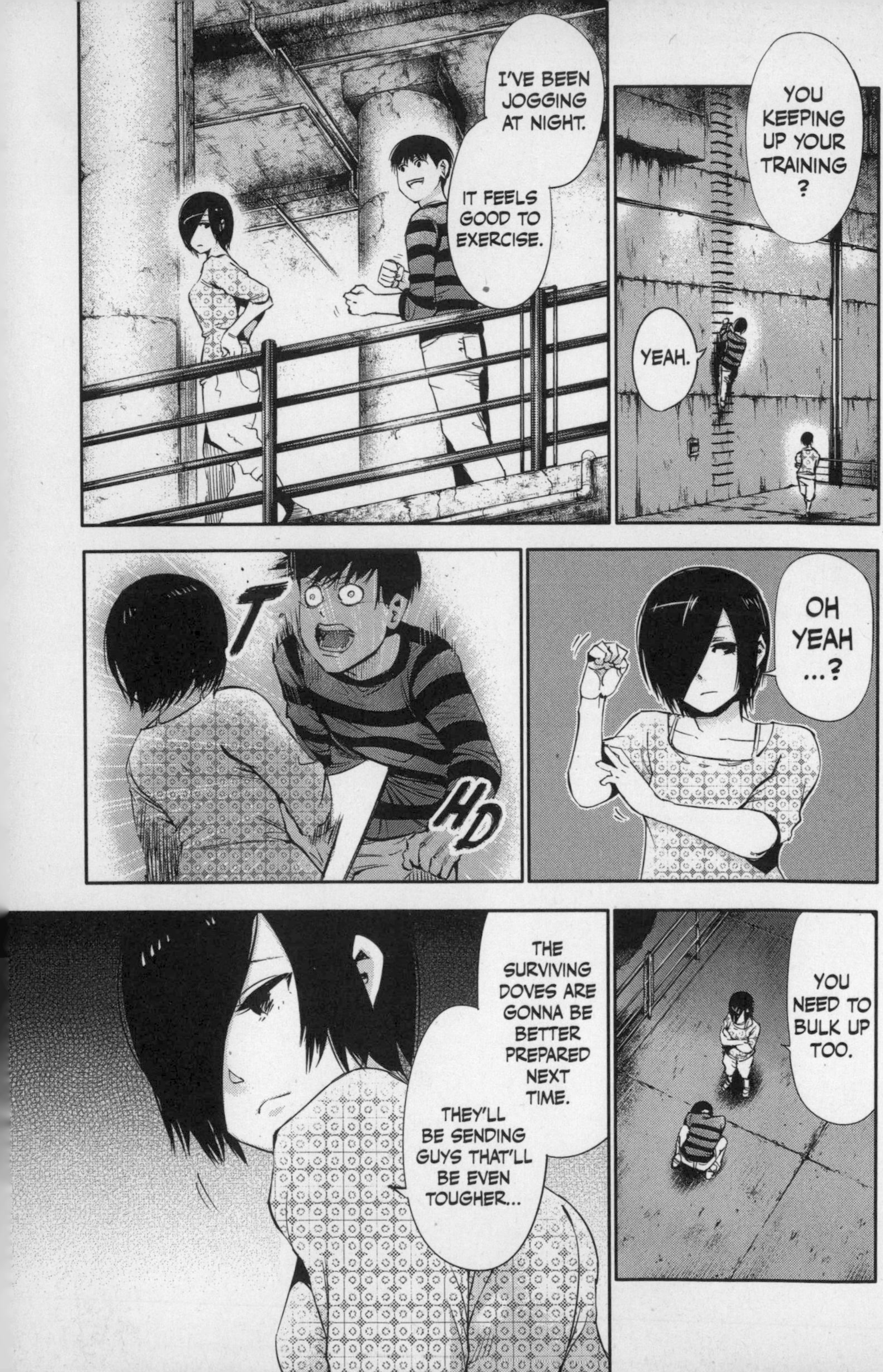
YOU KEEPING UP YOUR TRAINING?
YEAH.
I'VE BEEN JOGGING AT NIGHT.
IT FEELS GOOD TO EXERCISE.
OH YEAH...?
T
HD
YOU NEED TO BULK UP TOO.
THE SURVIVING DOVES ARE GONNA BE BETTER PREPARED NEXT TIME.
THEY'LL BE SENDING GUYS THAT'LL BE EVEN TOUGHER...

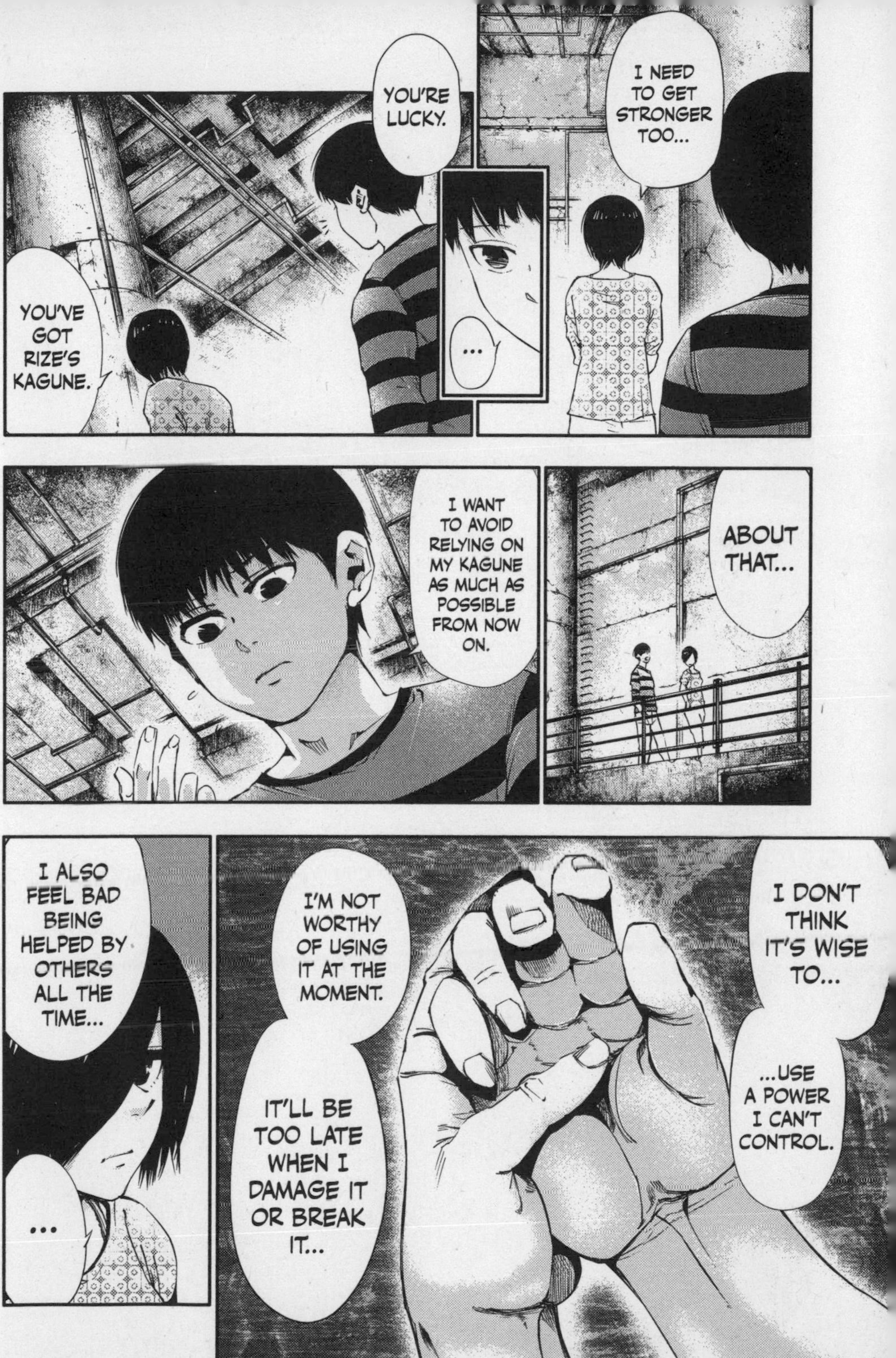
I NEED TO GET STRONGER TOO...
...
YOU'RE LUCKY.
YOU'VE GOT RIZE'S KAGUNE.
ABOUT THAT...
I WANT TO AVOID RELYING ON MY KAGUNE AS MUCH AS POSSIBLE FROM NOW ON.
I DON'T THINK IT'S WISE TO...
...USE A POWER I CAN'T CONTROL.
I'M NOT WORTHY OF USING IT AT THE MOMENT.
IT'LL BE TOO LATE WHEN I DAMAGE IT OR BREAK IT...
I ALSO FEEL BAD BEING HELPED BY OTHERS ALL THE TIME...
...

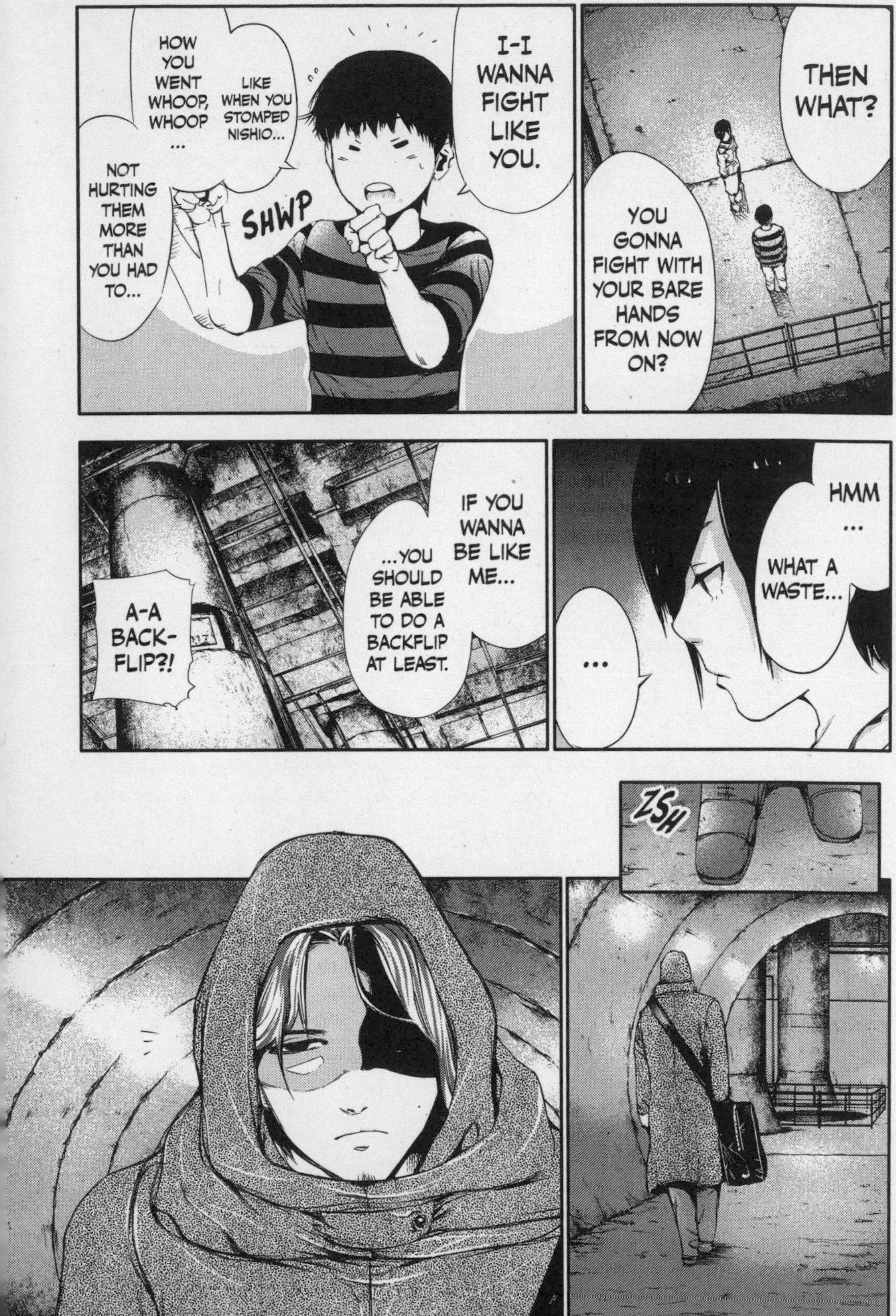
THEN WHAT?
YOU GONNA FIGHT WITH YOUR BARE HANDS FROM NOW ON?
I-I WANNA FIGHT LIKE YOU.
LIKE WHEN YOU STOMPED NISHIO...
HOW YOU WENT WHOOP, WHOOP ...
NOT HURTING THEM MORE THAN YOU HAD TO...
SHWP
HMM ...
WHAT A WASTE...
...
IF YOU WANNA BE LIKE ME...
...YOU SHOULD BE ABLE TO DO A BACKFLIP AT LEAST.
A-A BACK-FLIP?!
ZSH

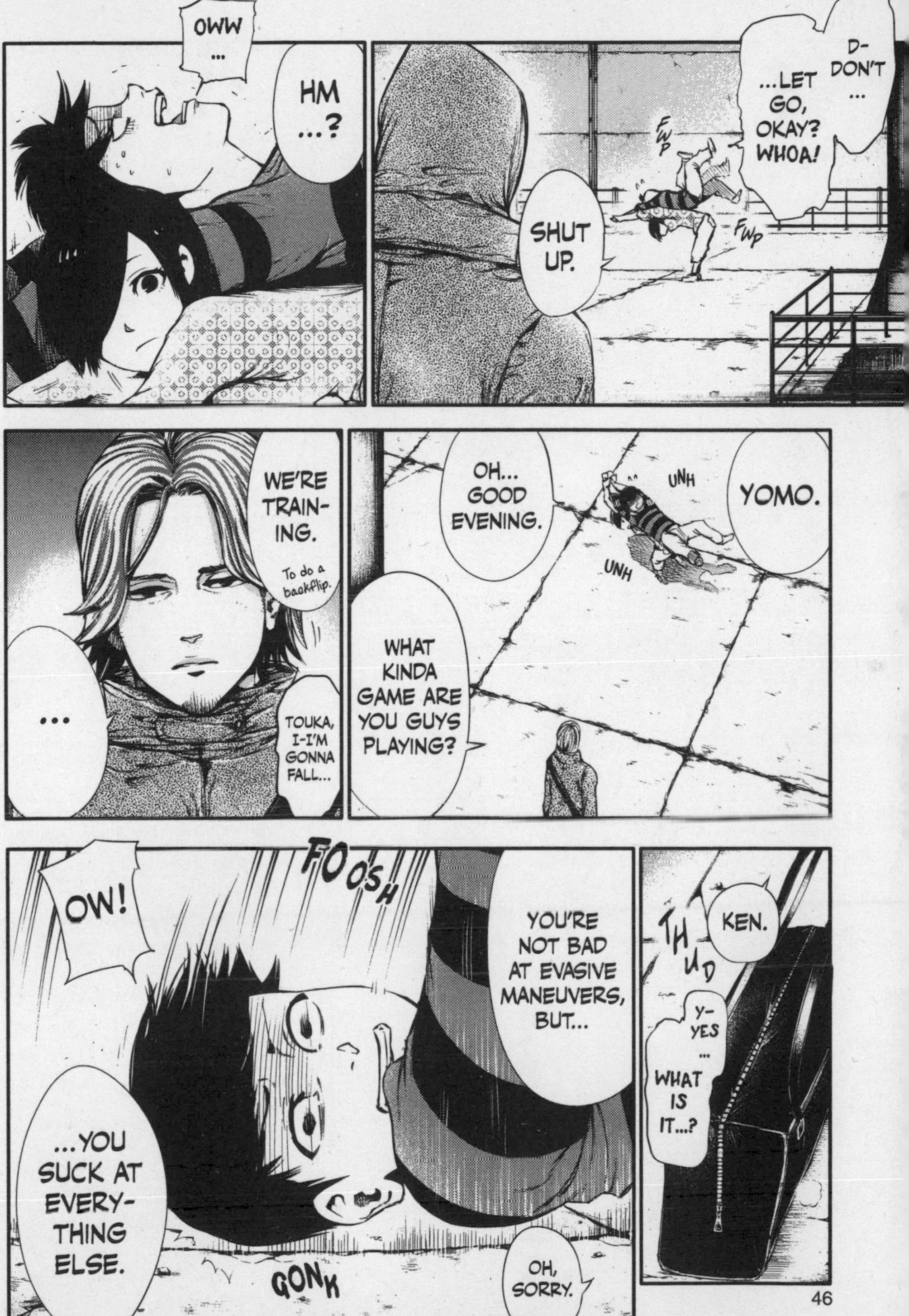
D-DON'T ...
...LET GO, OKAY? WHOA!
FWP
FWP
SHUT UP.
OWW ...
HM ...?
YOMO.
OH... GOOD EVENING.
UNH
UNH
WHAT KINDA GAME ARE YOU GUYS PLAYING?
WE'RE TRAINING.
To do a backflip.
...
TOUKA, I-I'M GONNA FALL...
KEN.
THUD
Y-YES ... WHAT IS IT...?
FOOSH
YOU'RE NOT BAD AT EVASIVE MANEUVERS, BUT...
OW!
...YOU SUCK AT EVERYTHING ELSE.
GONK
OH, SORRY.

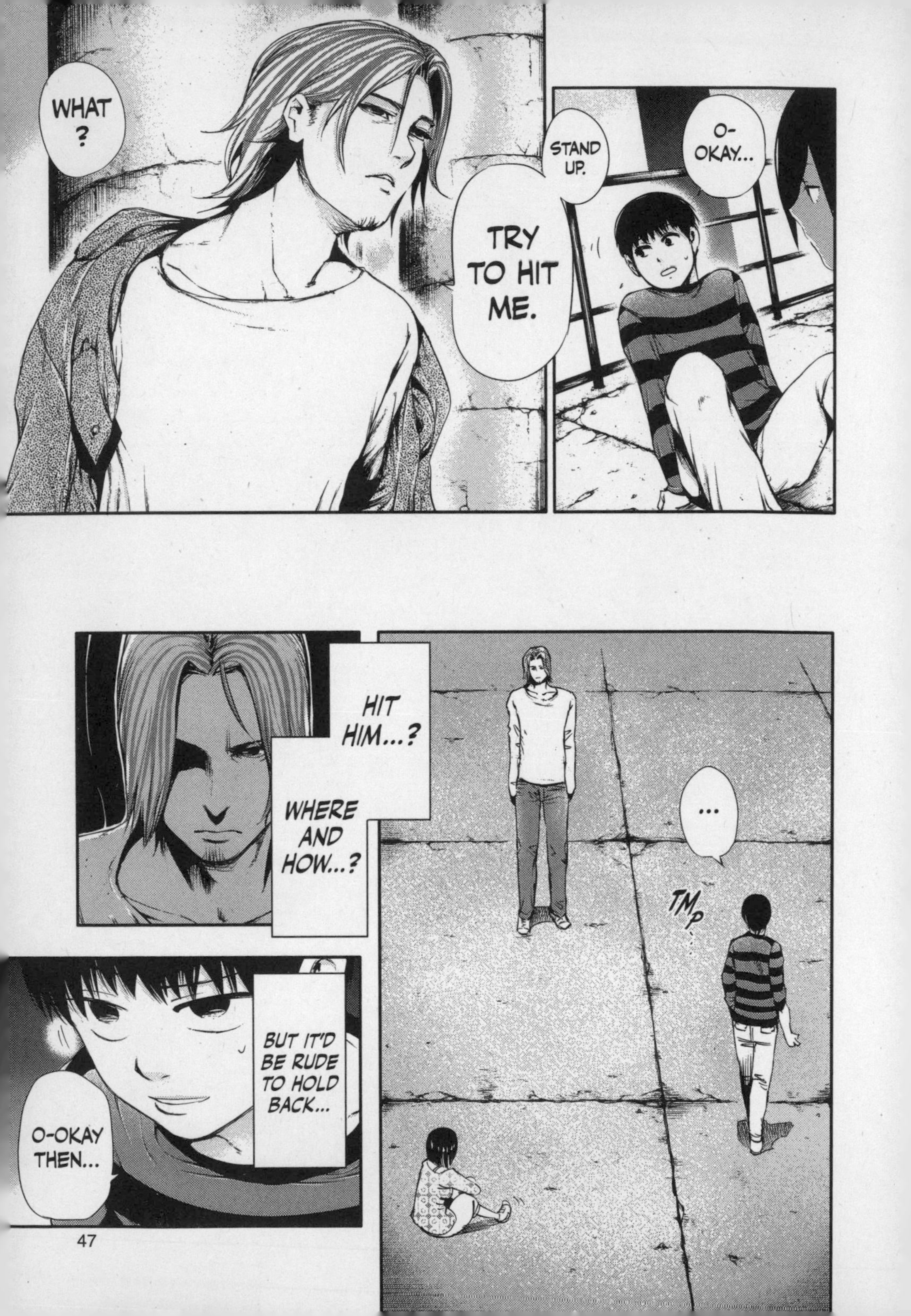
STAND UP.
O-OKAY...
TRY TO HIT ME.
WHAT ?
...
TMP...
HIT HIM...?
WHERE AND HOW...?
BUT IT'D BE RUDE TO HOLD BACK...
O-OKAY THEN...

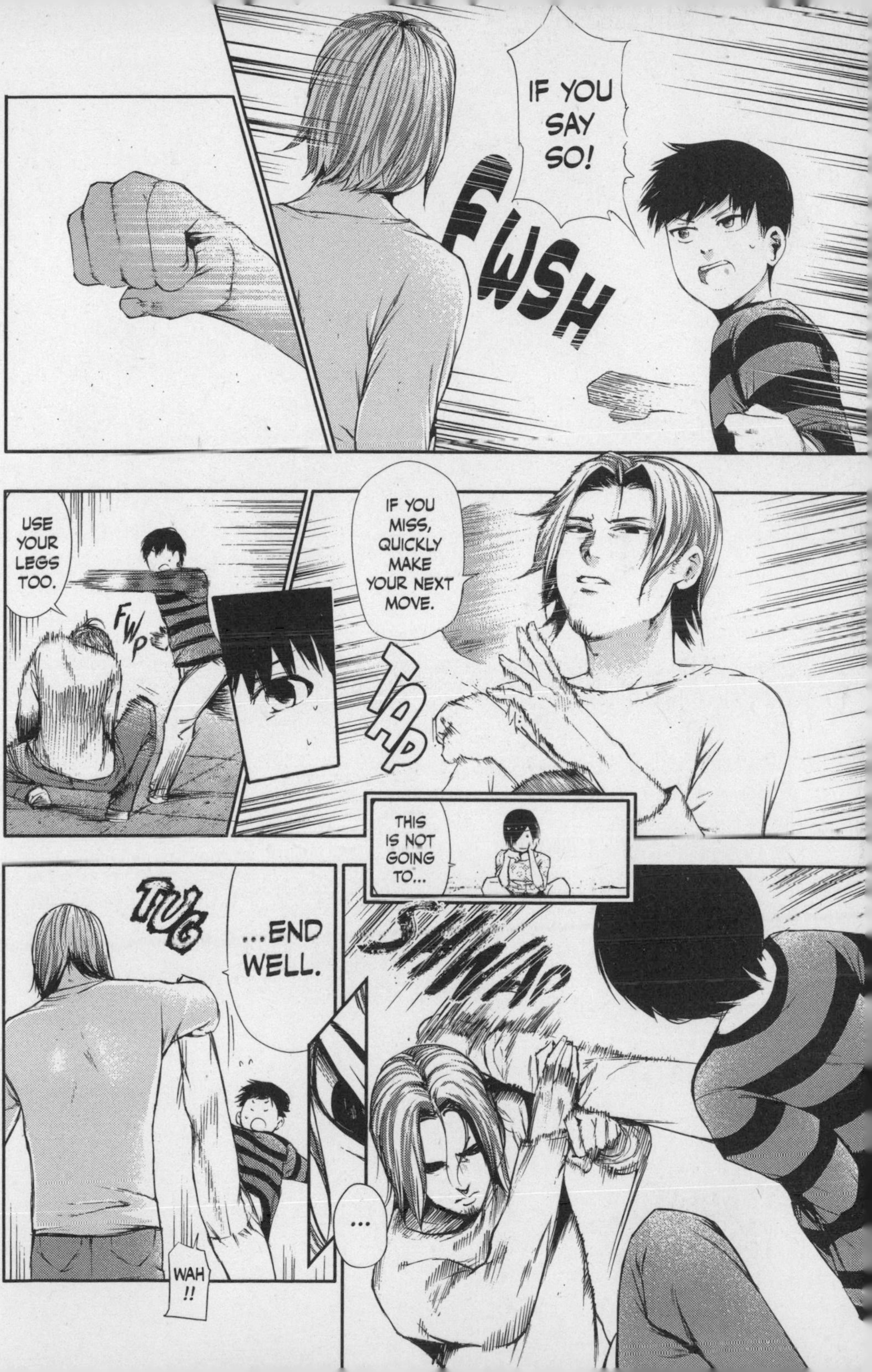
IF YOU SAY SO!
FWSH
IF YOU MISS, QUICKLY MAKE YOUR NEXT MOVE.
TAP
USE YOUR LEGS TOO.
FWP
THIS IS NOT GOING TO...
SHWAP
...
TUG
...END WELL.
WAH!!

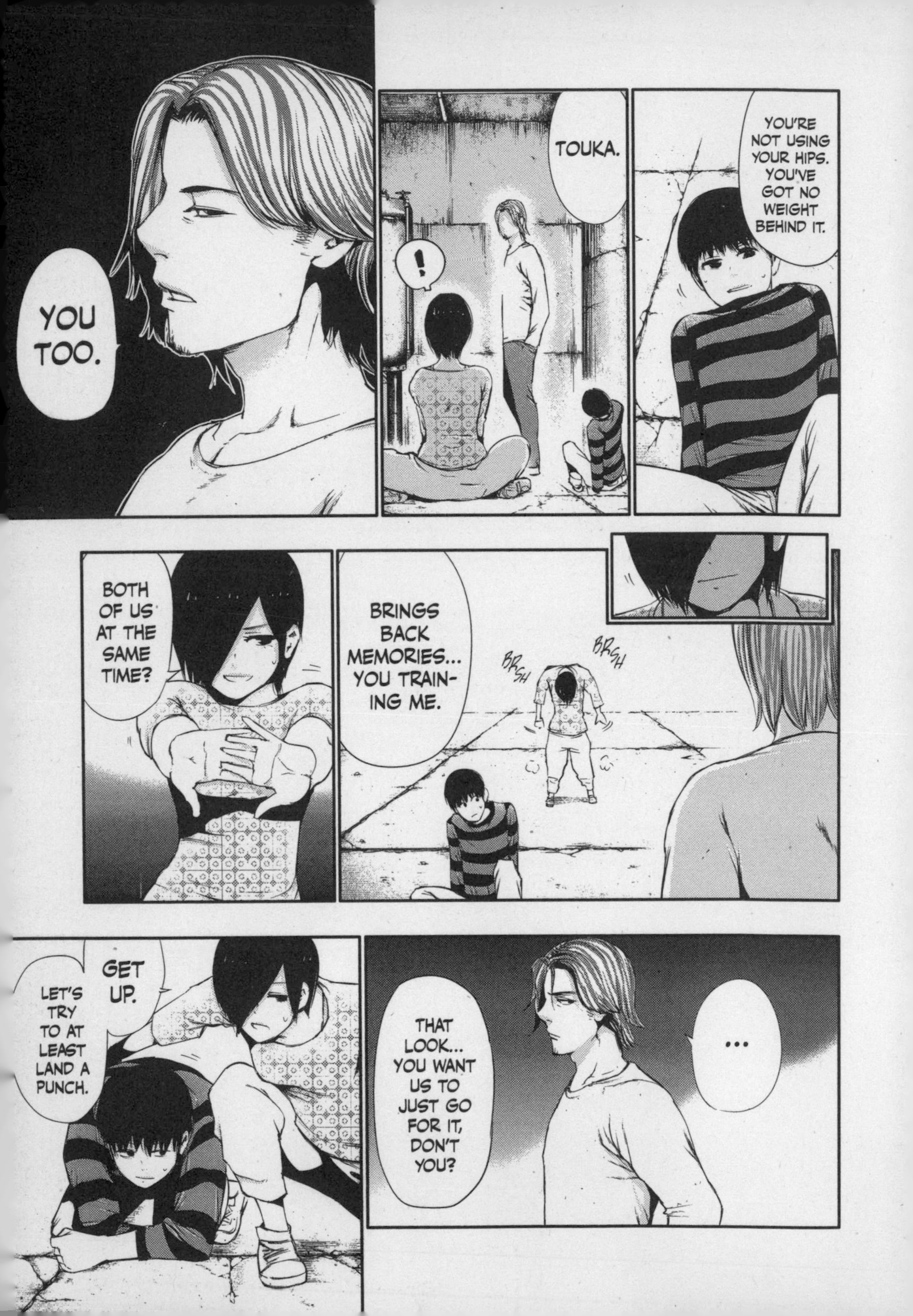
YOU'RE NOT USING YOUR HIPS. YOU'VE GOT NO WEIGHT BEHIND IT.
TOUKA.
!
YOU TOO.
BRINGS BACK MEMORIES... YOU TRAINING ME.
BRSH
BRSH
BOTH OF US AT THE SAME TIME?
...
THAT LOOK... YOU WANT US TO JUST GO FOR IT, DON'T YOU?
GET UP.
LET'S TRY TO AT LEAST LAND A PUNCH.

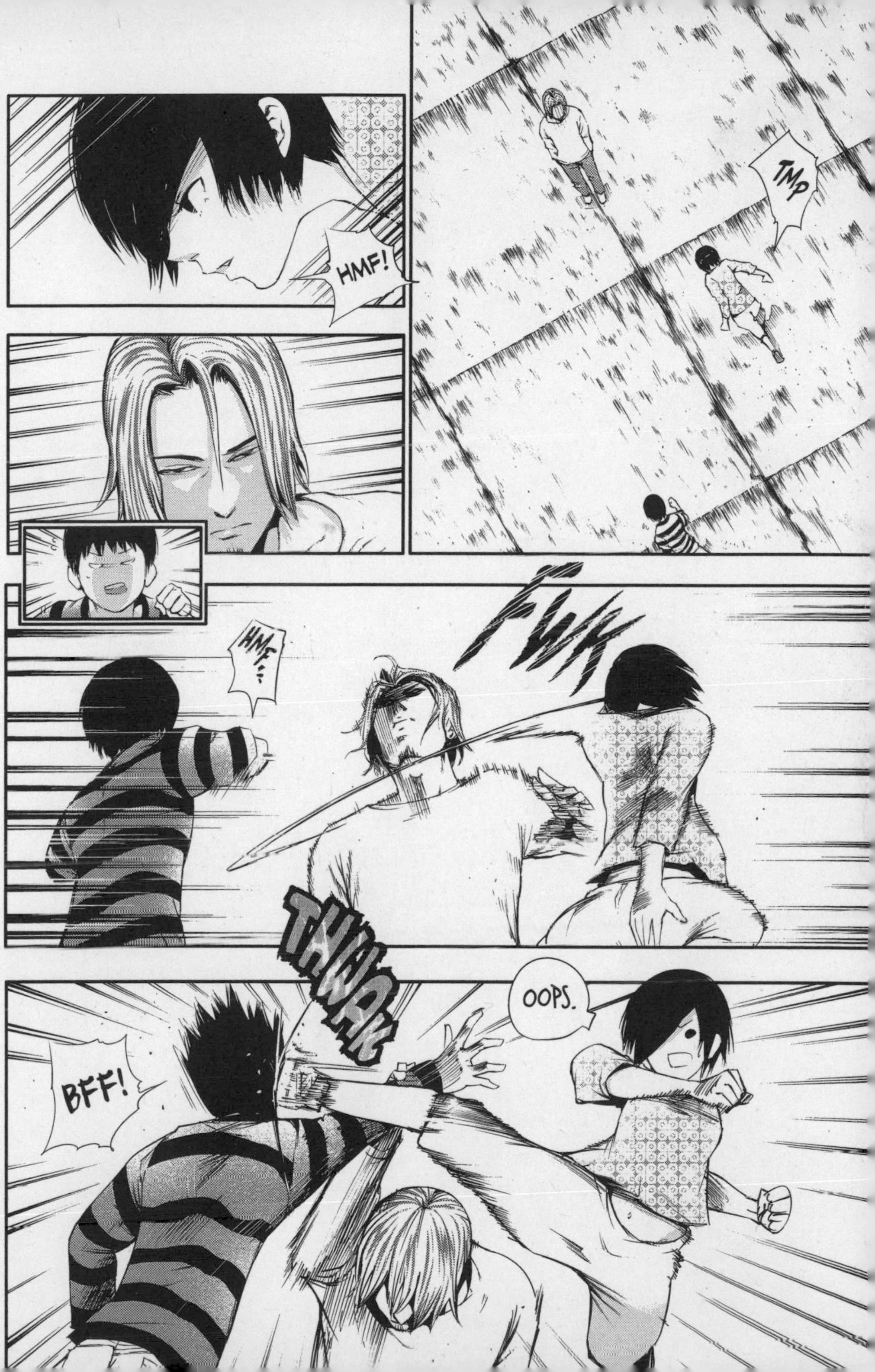
TMP
HMF!
FWK
HMF...
THWAK
OOPS.
BFF!

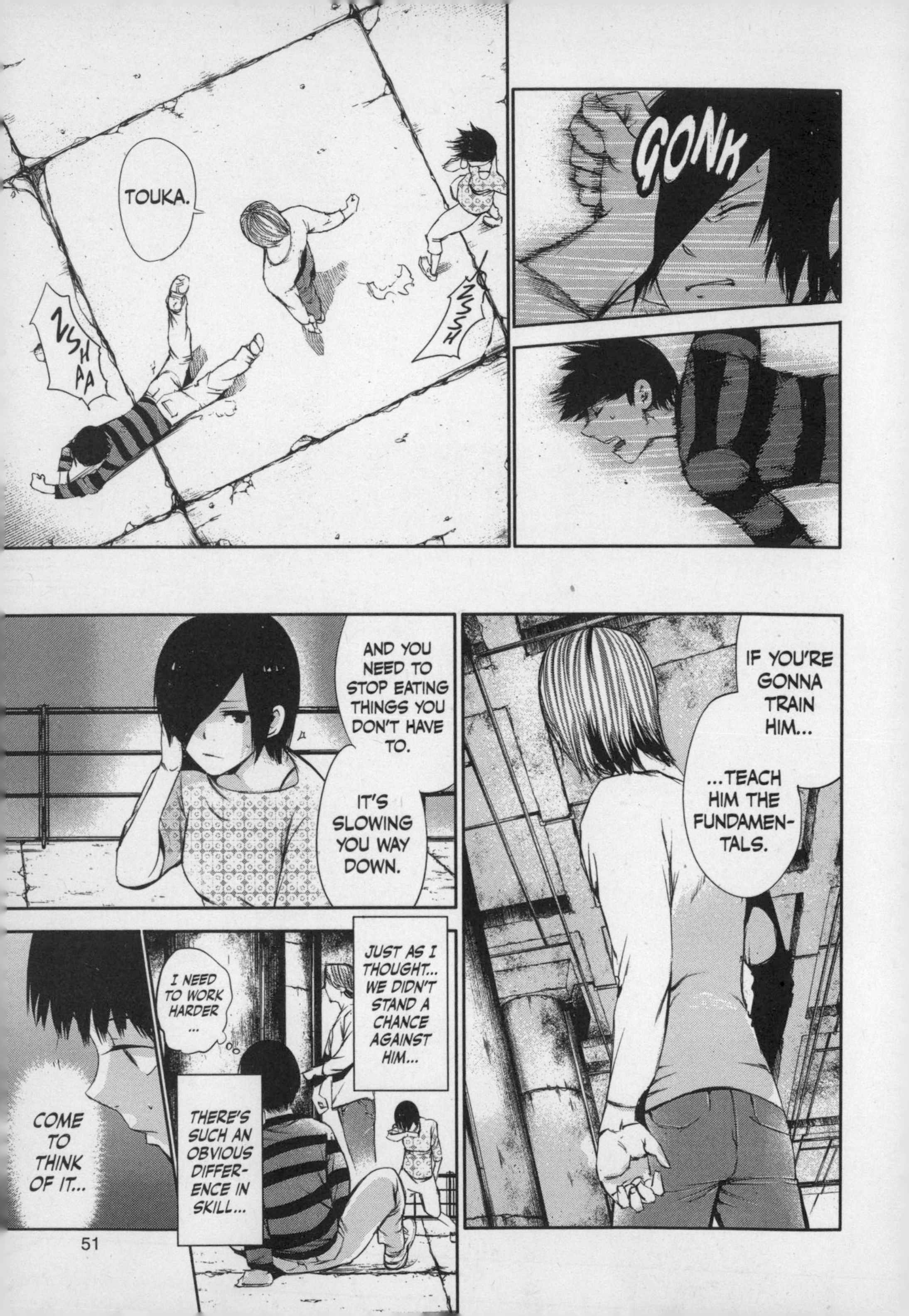
GONK
TOUKA.
ZSSH
ZSHAA
IF YOU'RE GONNA TRAIN HIM...
...TEACH HIM THE FUNDAMENTALS.
AND YOU NEED TO STOP EATING THINGS YOU DON'T HAVE TO.
IT'S SLOWING YOU WAY DOWN.
JUST AS I THOUGHT... WE DIDN'T STAND A CHANCE AGAINST HIM...
I NEED TO WORK HARDER...
THERE'S SUCH AN OBVIOUS DIFFERENCE IN SKILL...
COME TO THINK OF IT...

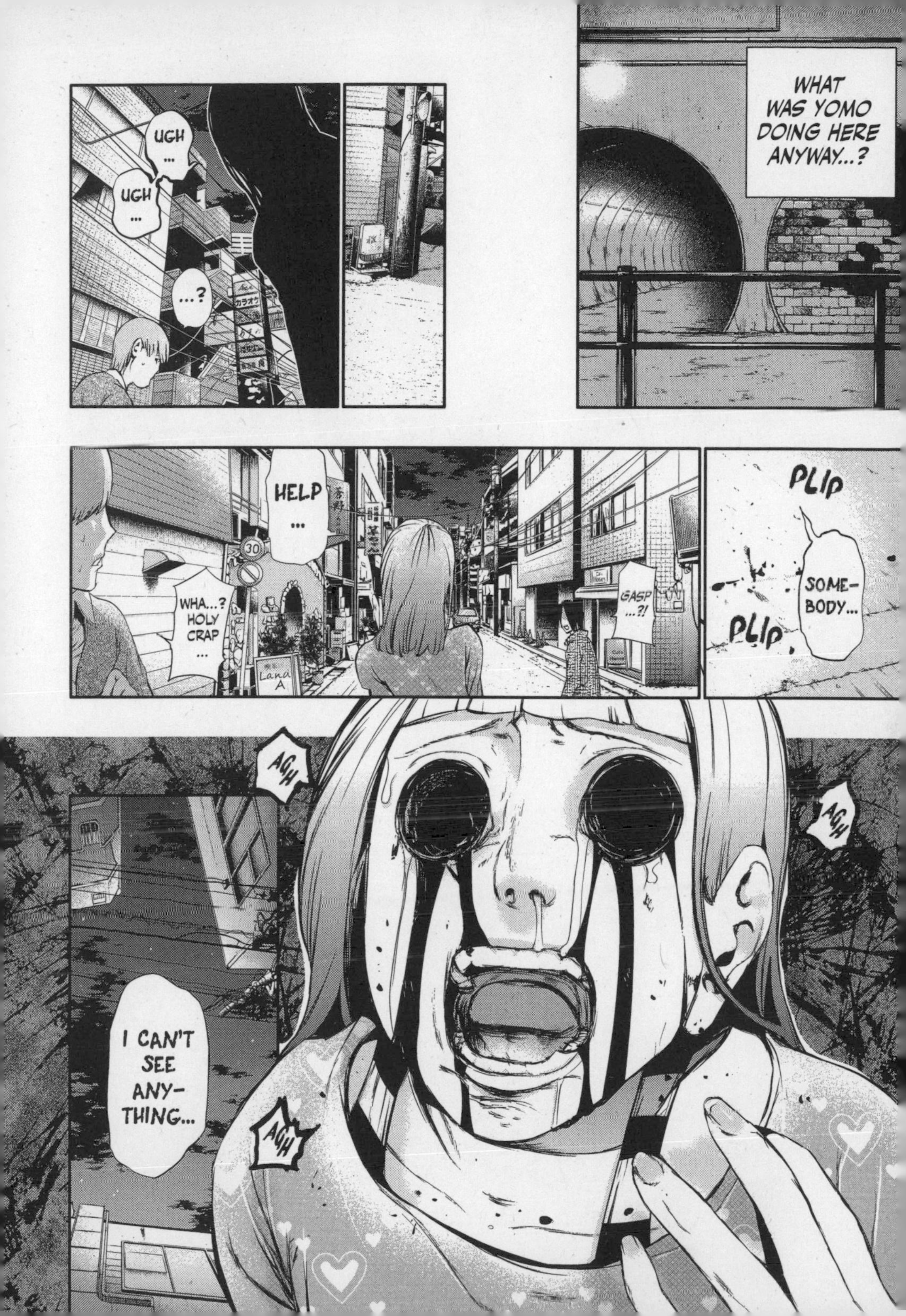
WHAT WAS YOMO DOING HERE ANYWAY...?
UGH ...
UGH ...
...?
PLIP
SOMEBODY...
PLIP
HELP ...
GASP ...?!
WHA...? HOLY CRAP ...
AGH
AGH
I CAN'T SEE ANYTHING...
AGH

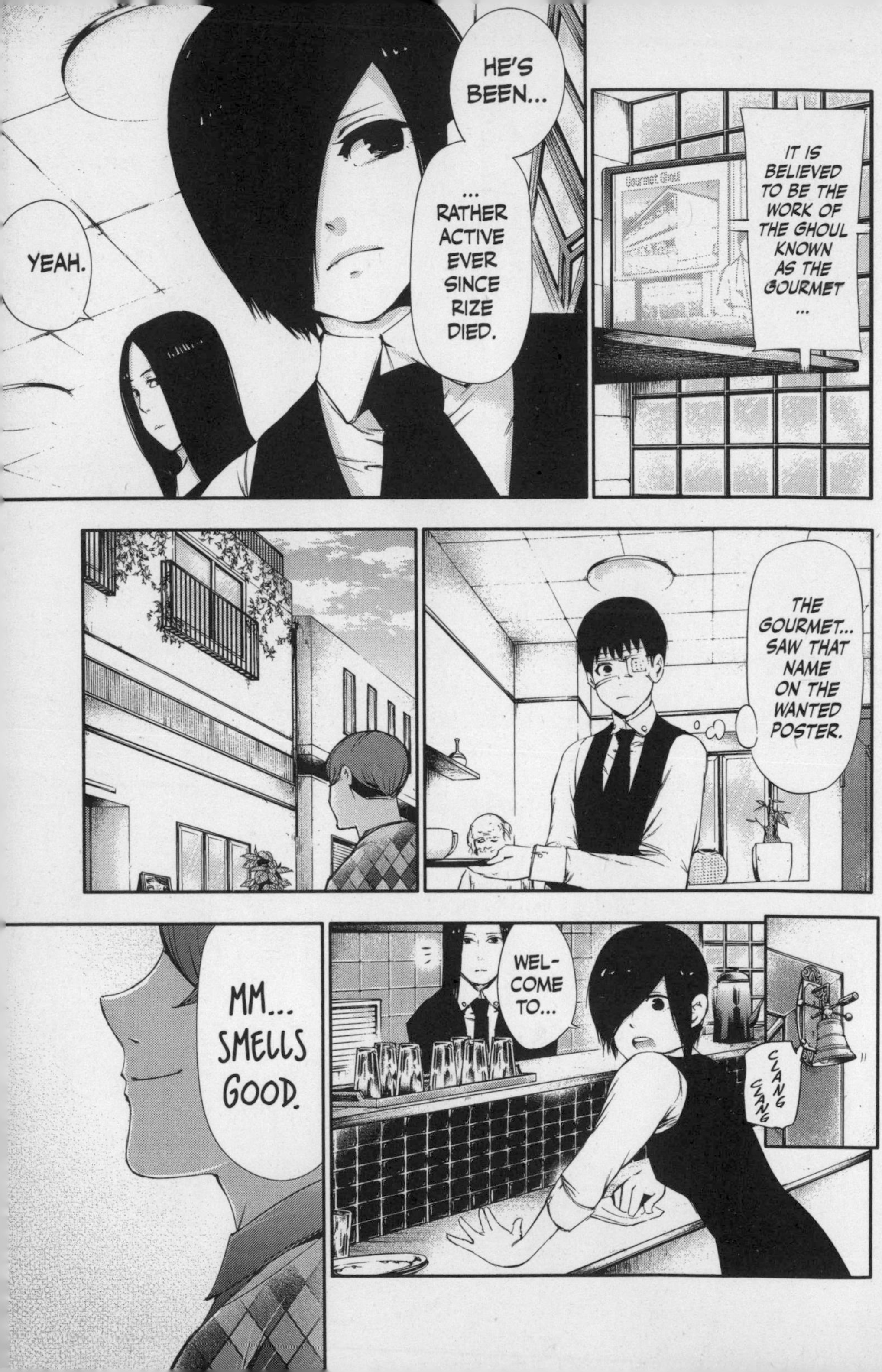
Gourmet Ghoul
IT IS BELIEVED TO BE THE WORK OF THE GHOUL KNOWN AS THE GOURMET ...
HE'S BEEN...
... RATHER ACTIVE EVER SINCE RIZE DIED.
YEAH.
THE GOURMET... SAW THAT NAME ON THE WANTED POSTER.
WEL- COME TO...
CLANG CLANG
MM... SMELLS GOOD.

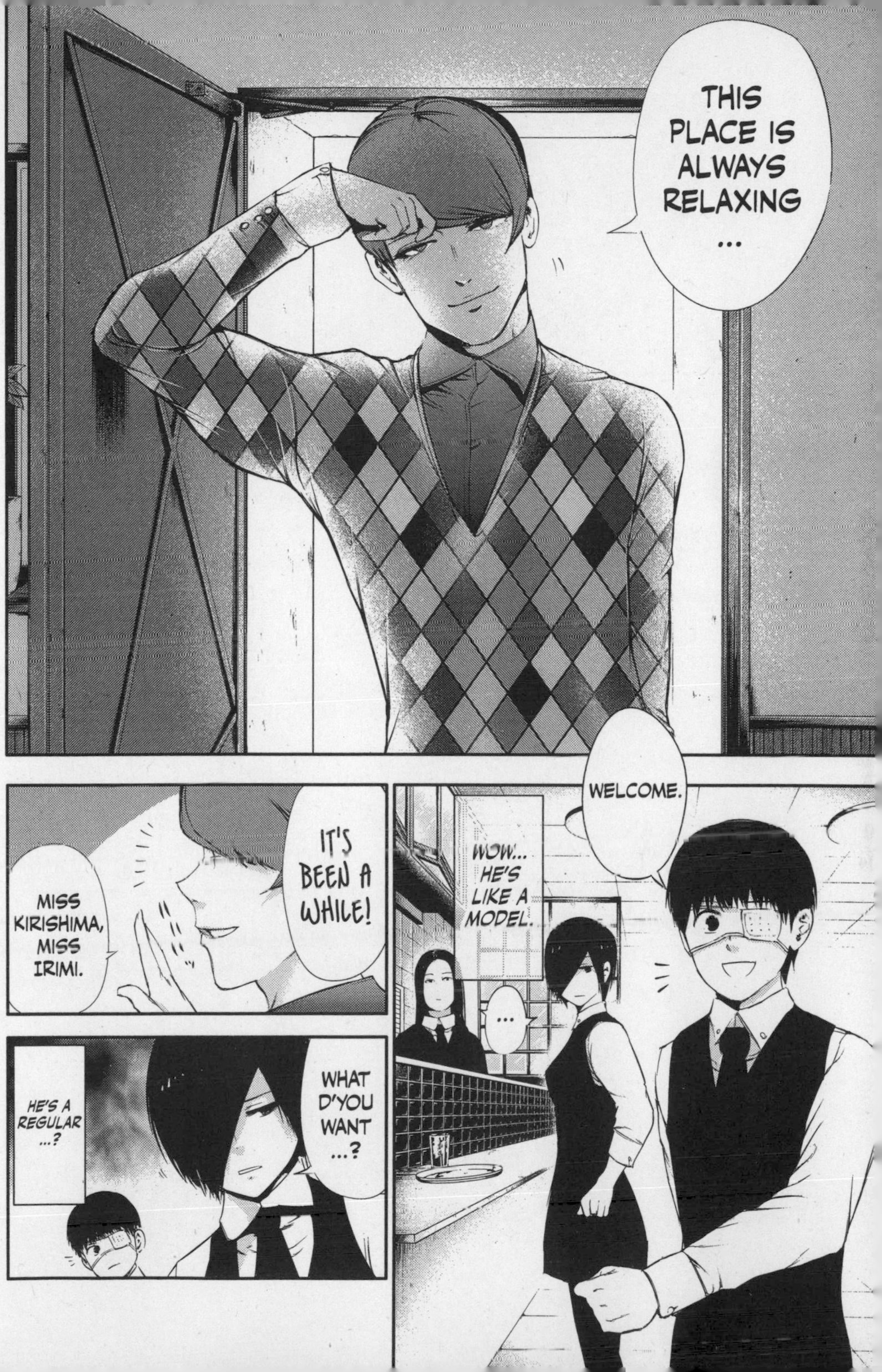
THIS PLACE IS ALWAYS RELAXING ...
WELCOME.
WOW... HE'S LIKE A MODEL.
...
IT'S BEEN A WHILE!
MISS KIRISHIMA, MISS IRIMI.
WHAT D'YOU WANT ...?
HE'S A REGULAR ...?

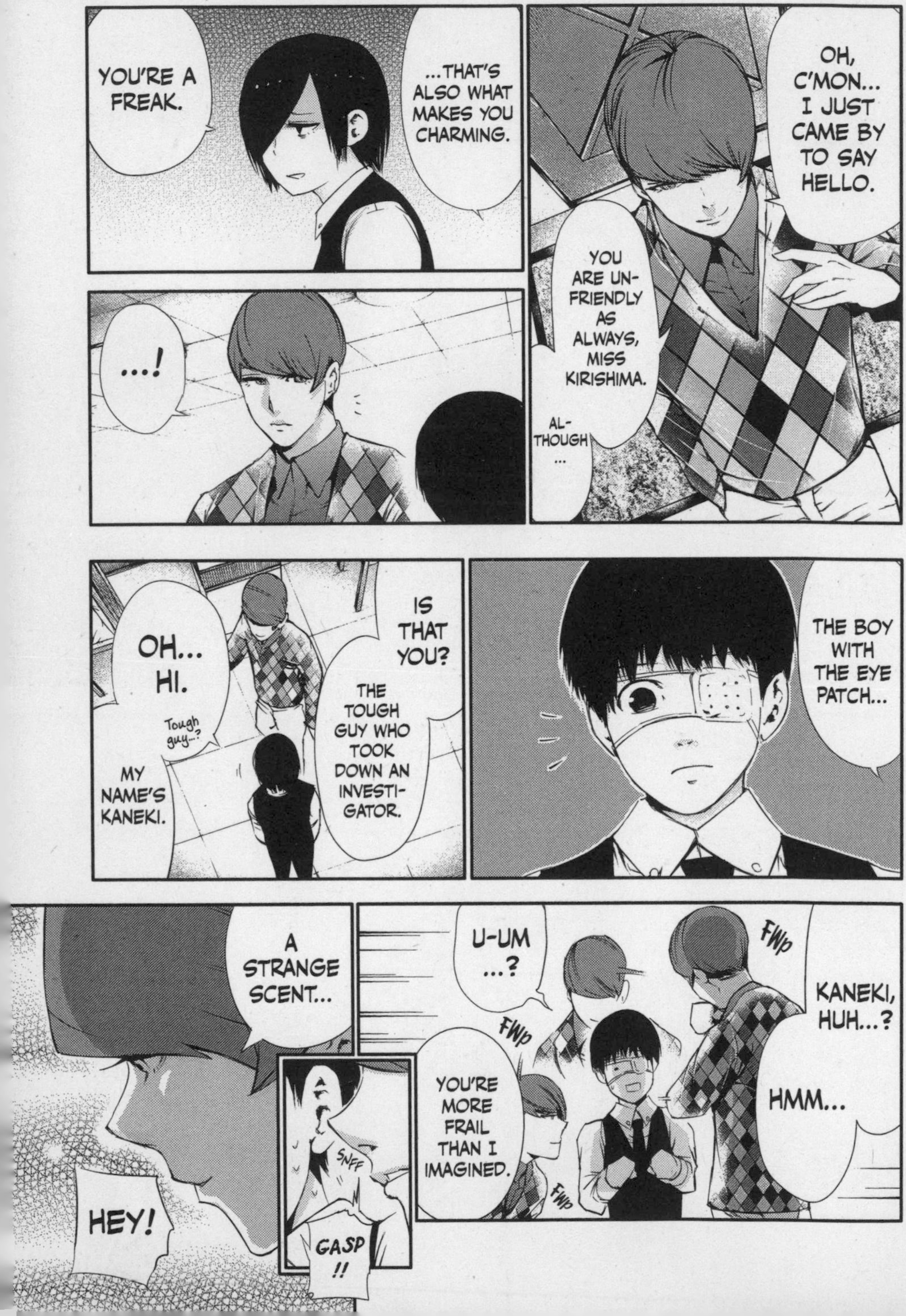

OH, C'MON... I JUST CAME BY TO SAY HELLO.
YOU ARE UN-FRIENDLY AS ALWAYS, MISS KIRISHIMA.
AL-THOUGH ...
...THAT'S ALSO WHAT MAKES YOU CHARMING.
YOU'RE A FREAK.
...!
THE BOY WITH THE EYE PATCH...
IS THAT YOU?
THE TOUGH GUY WHO TOOK DOWN AN INVESTI-GATOR.
OH... HI.
Tough guy...?
MY NAME'S KANEKI.
FWP
KANEKI, HUH...?
HMM...
U-UM ...?
FWP
YOU'RE MORE FRAIL THAN I IMAGINED.
FWP
A STRANGE SCENT...
SNFF
HEY!
GASP !!

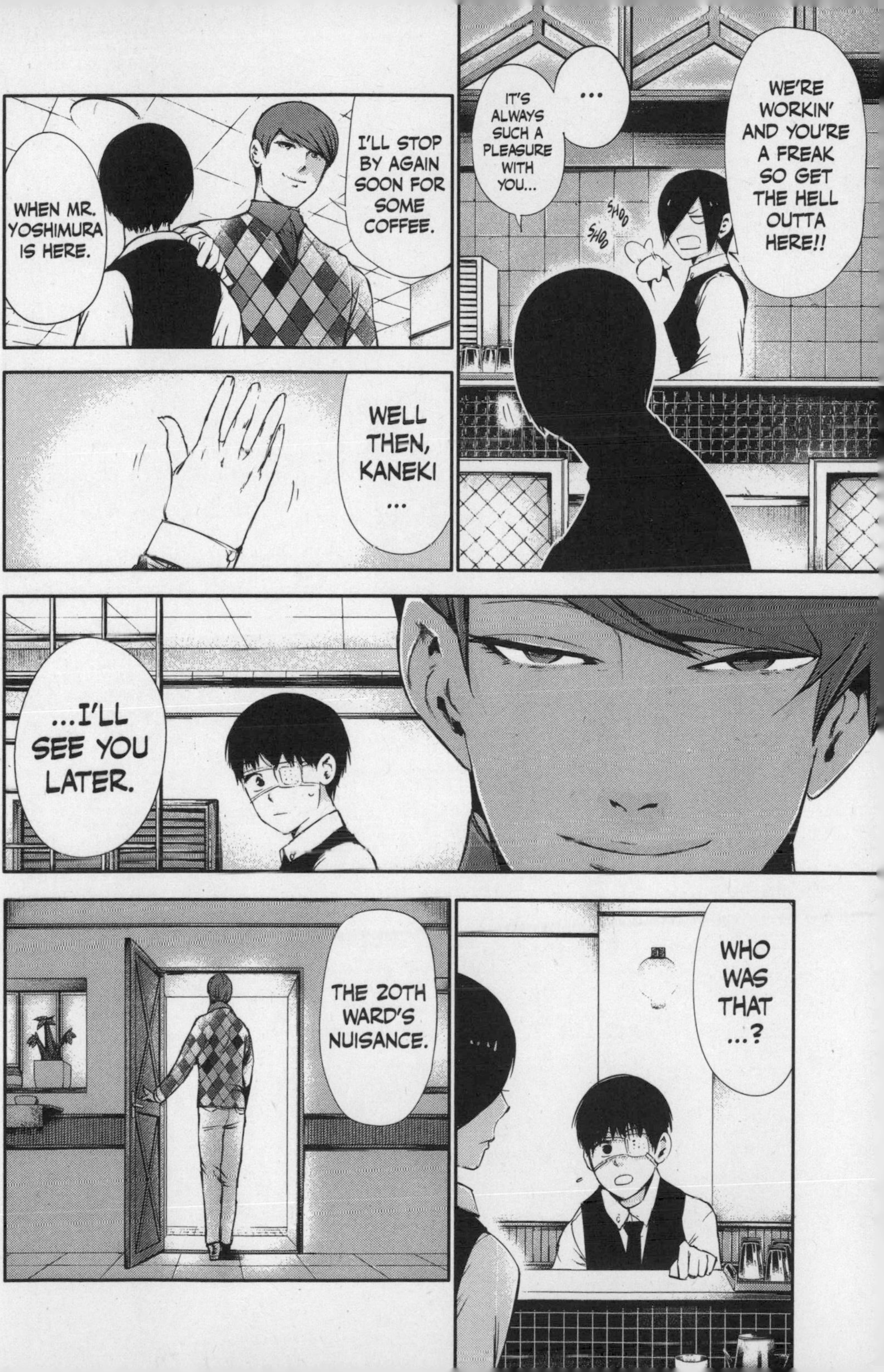
WE'RE WORKIN' AND YOU'RE A FREAK SO GET THE HELL OUTTA HERE!!
SHOO SHOO
...
IT'S ALWAYS SUCH A PLEASURE WITH YOU...
I'LL STOP BY AGAIN SOON FOR SOME COFFEE.
WHEN MR. YOSHIMURA IS HERE.
WELL THEN, KANEKI ...
...I'LL SEE YOU LATER.
WHO WAS THAT ...?
THE 20TH WARD'S NUISANCE.

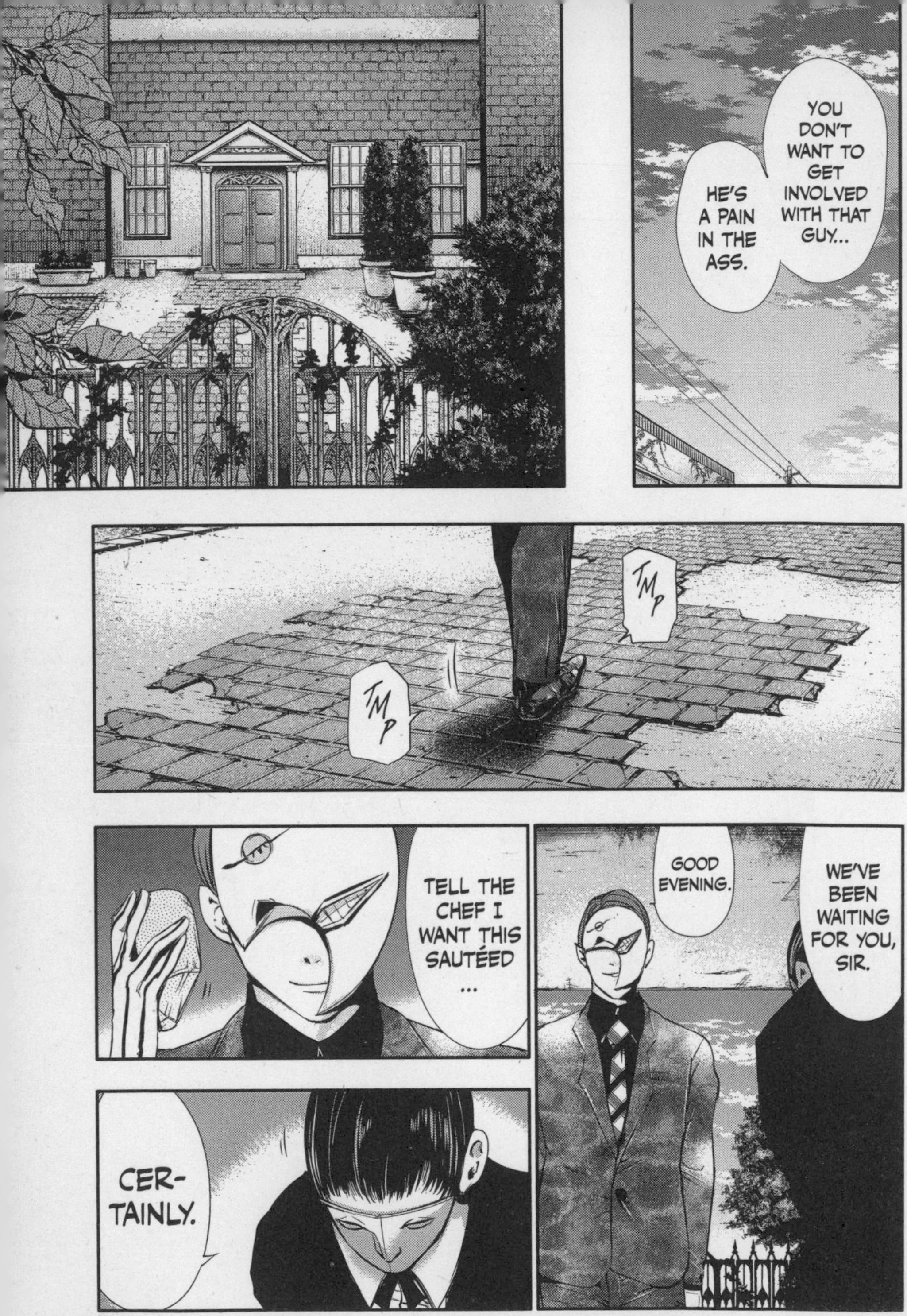
YOU DON'T WANT TO GET INVOLVED WITH THAT GUY...
HE'S A PAIN IN THE ASS.
TMP
TMP
WE'VE BEEN WAITING FOR YOU, SIR.
GOOD EVENING.
TELL THE CHEF I WANT THIS SAUTÉED ...
CER-TAINLY.

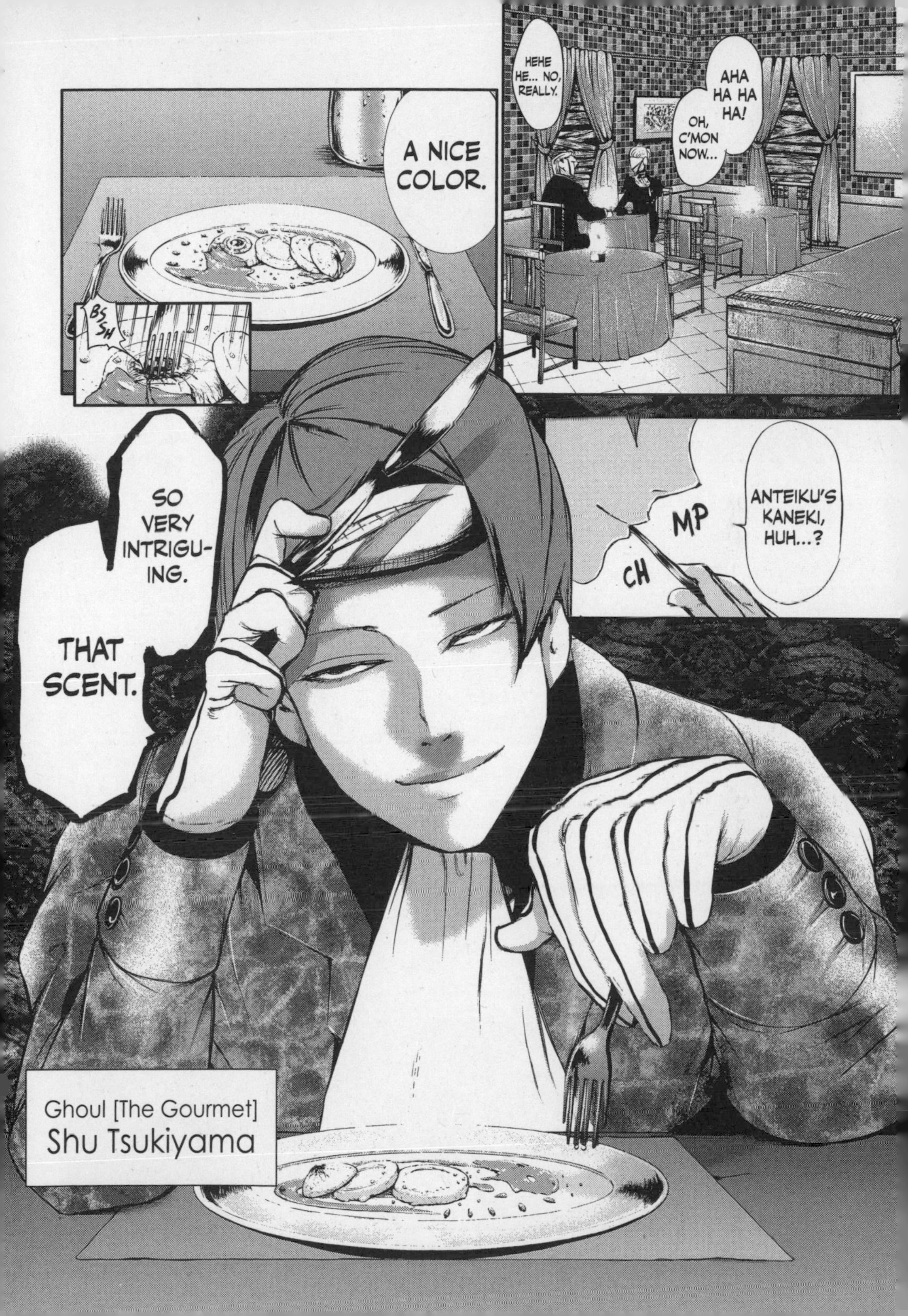
AHA HA HA HA!
OH, C'MON NOW...
HEHE HE... NO, REALLY.
A NICE COLOR.
BSSH
ANTEIKU'S KANEKI, HUH...?
CH MP
SO VERY INTRIGUING.
THAT SCENT.
Ghoul [The Gourmet]
Shu Tsukiyama

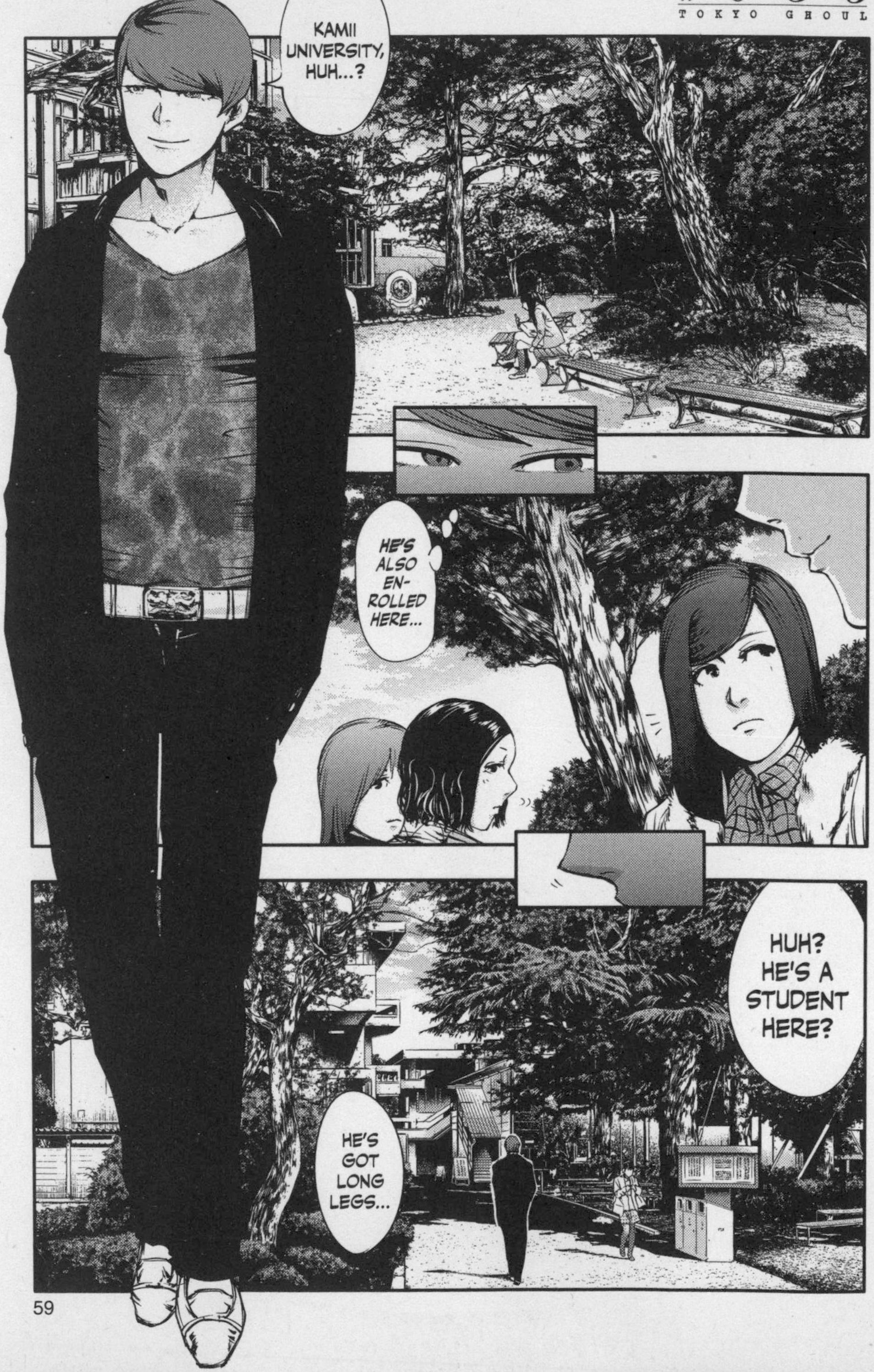
KAMII UNIVERSITY, HUH...?
HE'S ALSO EN-ROLLED HERE...
HUH? HE'S A STUDENT HERE?
HE'S GOT LONG LEGS...

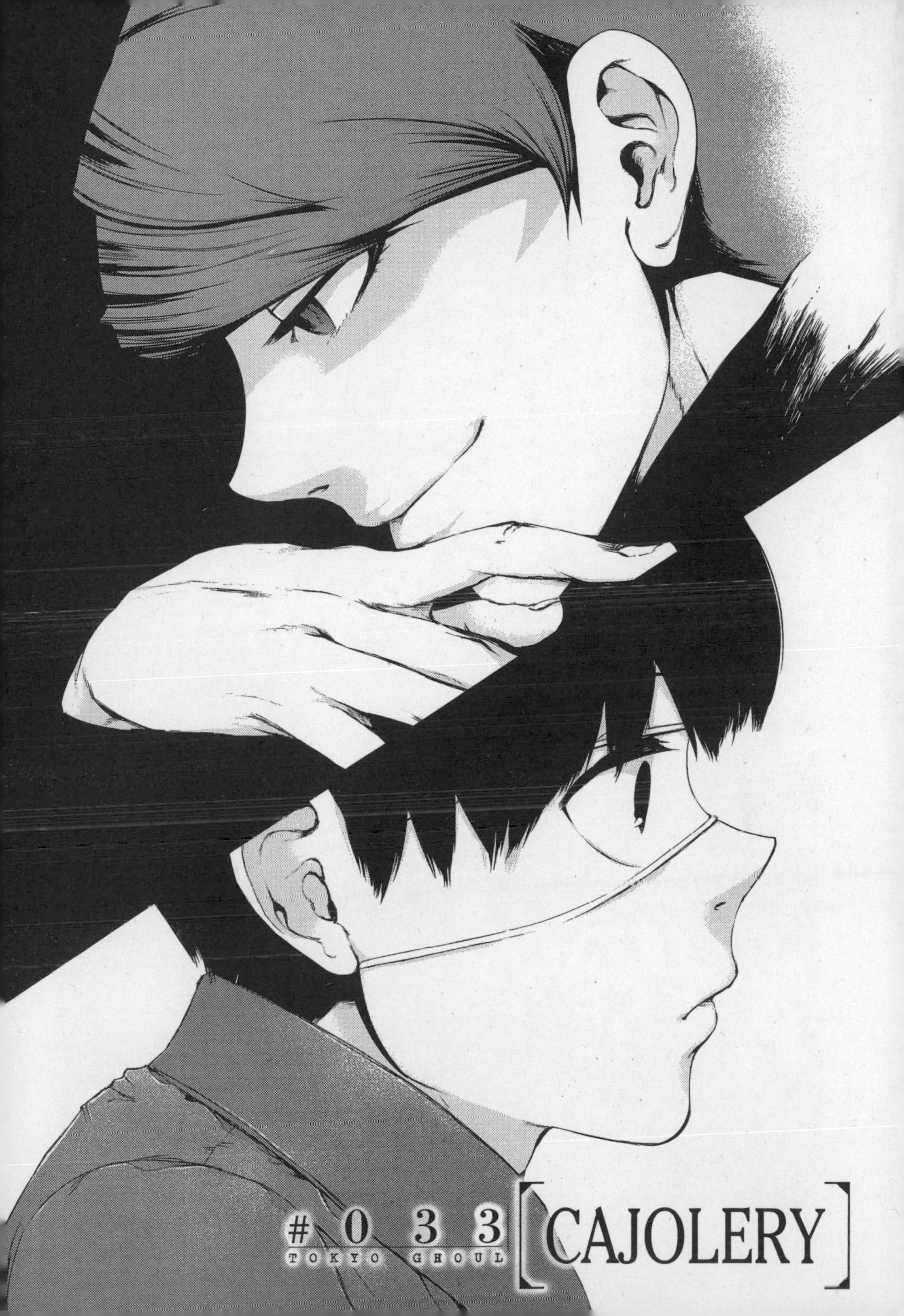
#033
TOKYO GHOUL
[CAJOLERY]

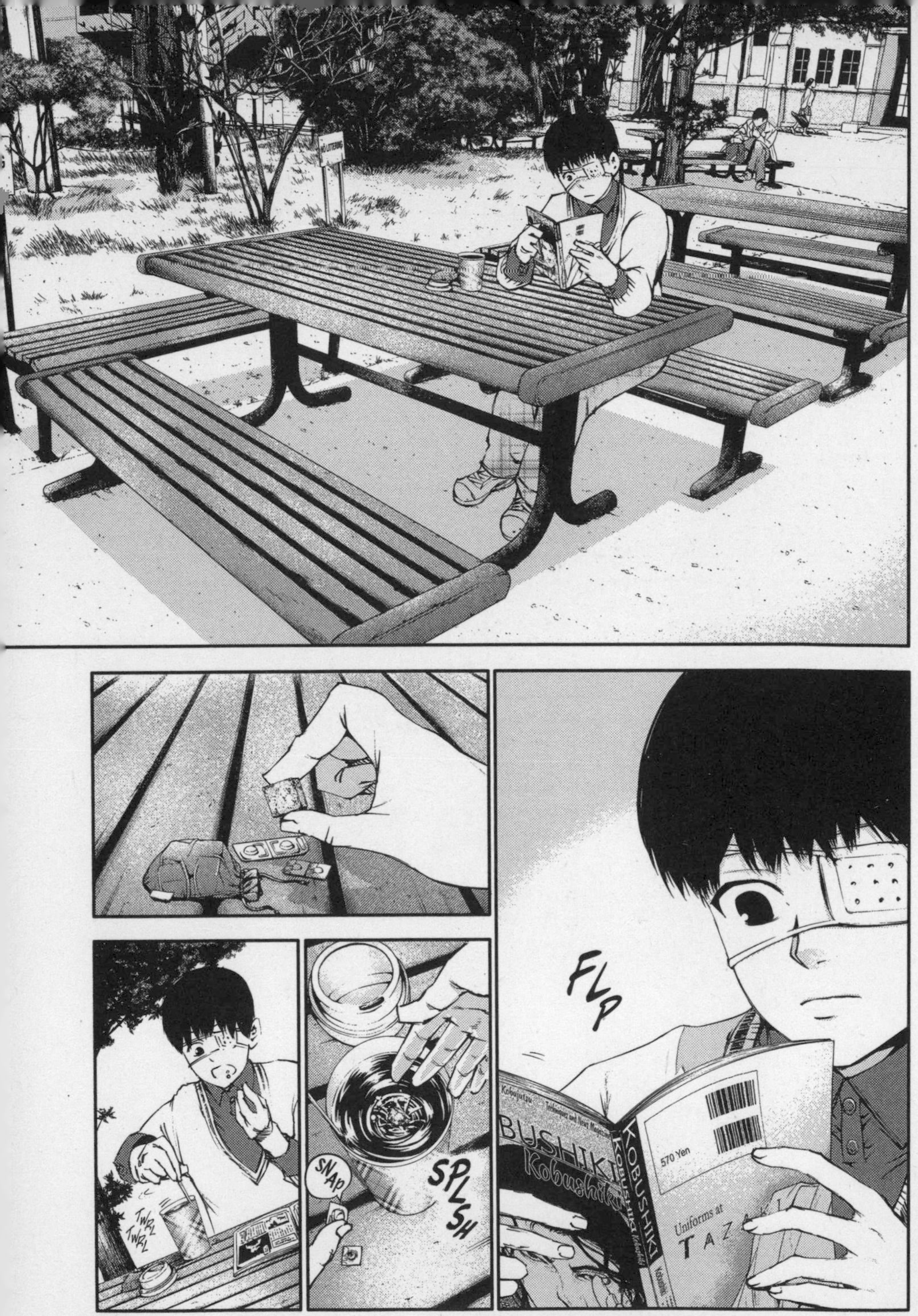
FLIP
Kobujutsu Techniques and News Magazine
BUSHIKI
Kobushiki
KOBUSHIKI
570 Yen
Uniforms at
TAZA
SNAP
SPLSH
TWRL TWRL

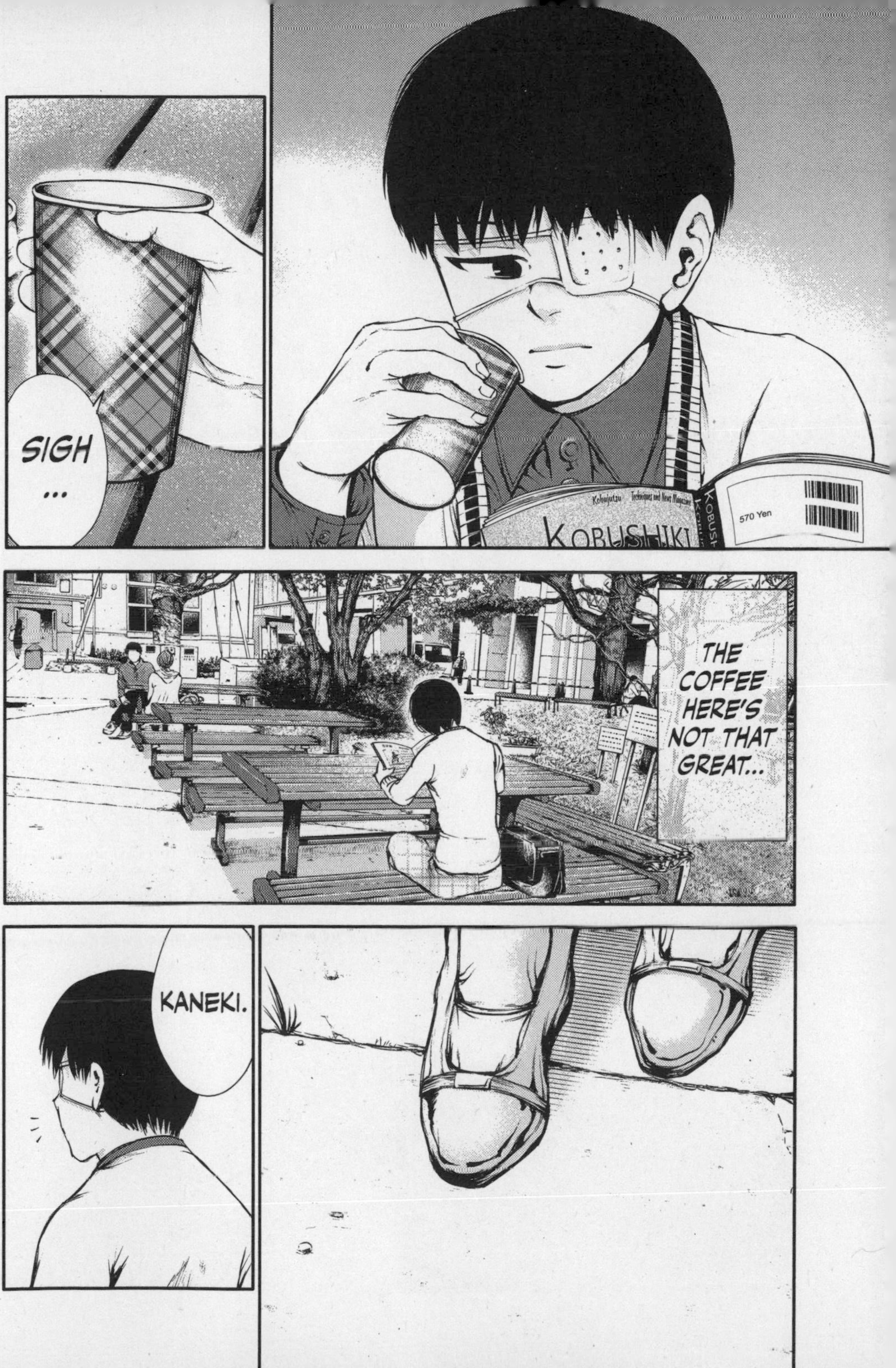
Kobujutsu Techniques and News Magazine
KOBUSHIKI
570 Yen
SIGH ...
THE COFFEE HERE'S NOT THAT GREAT...
KANEKI.

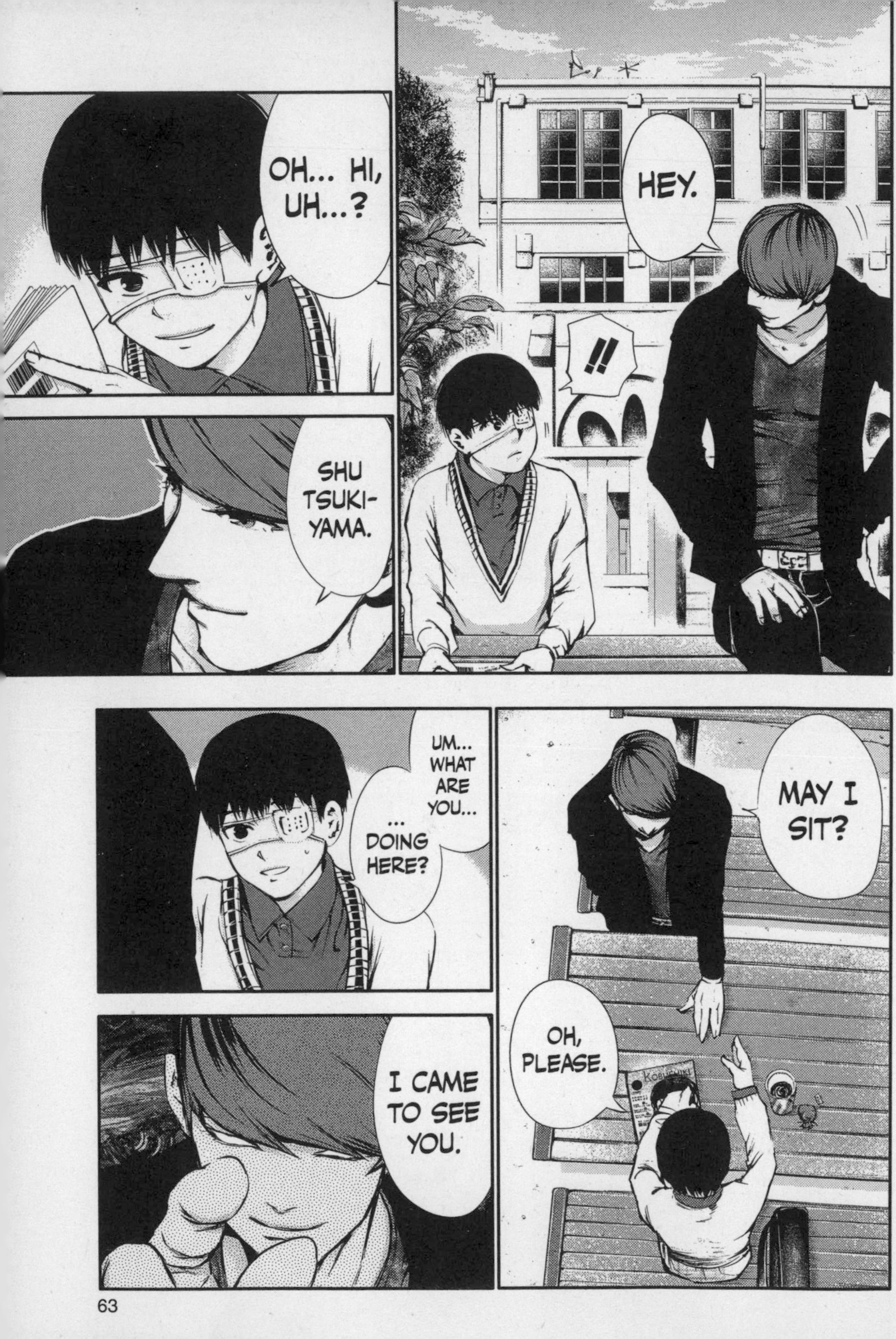
HEY.
!!
OH... HI, UH...?
SHU TSUKI-YAMA.
MAY I SIT?
OH, PLEASE.
UM... WHAT ARE YOU...
... DOING HERE?
I CAME TO SEE YOU.

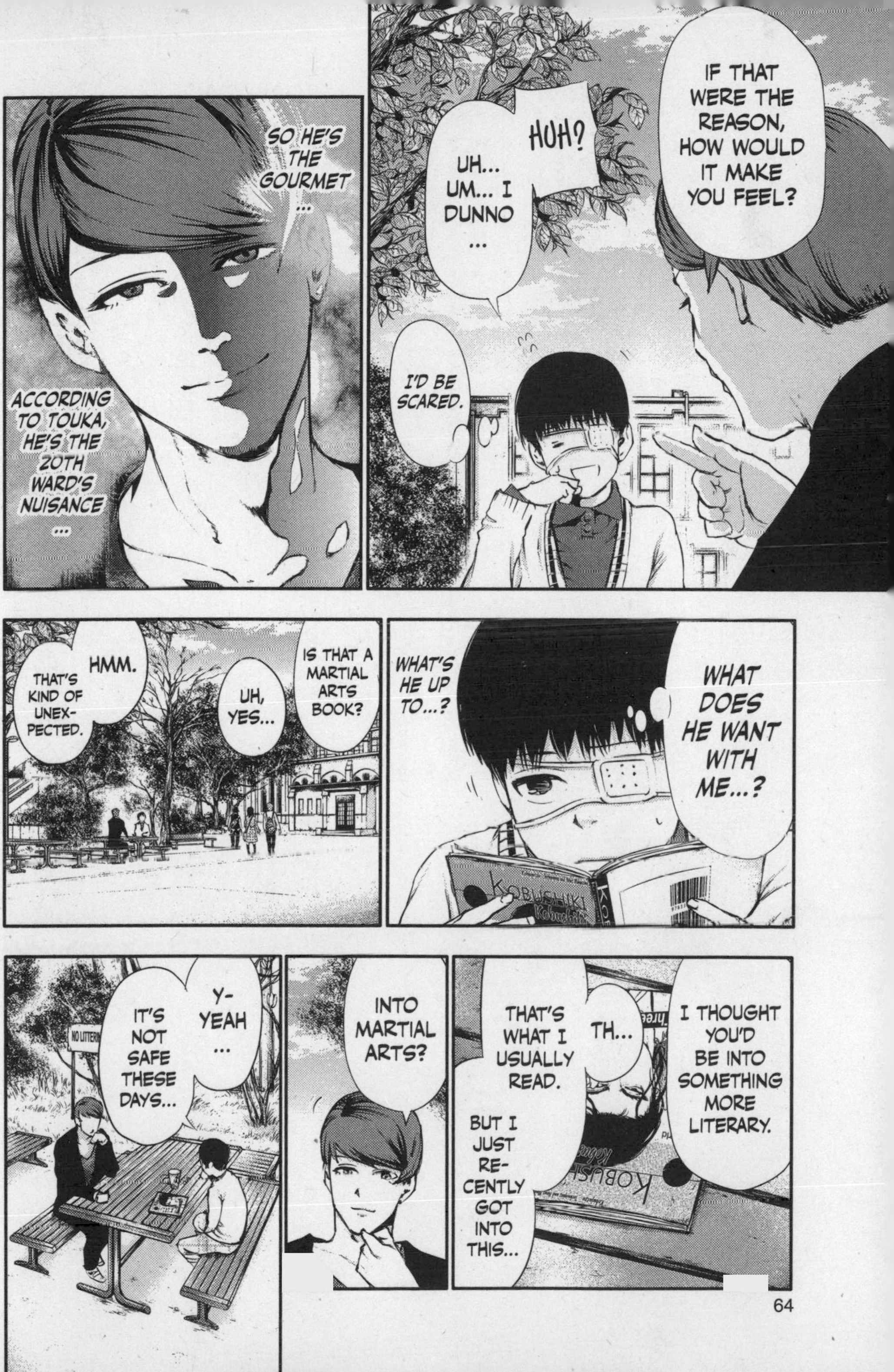
IF THAT WERE THE REASON, HOW WOULD IT MAKE YOU FEEL?
HUH?
UH... UM... I DUNNO ...
I'D BE SCARED.
SO HE'S THE GOURMET ...
ACCORDING TO TOUKA, HE'S THE 20TH WARD'S NUISANCE ...
WHAT DOES HE WANT WITH ME...?
WHAT'S HE UP TO...?
IS THAT A MARTIAL ARTS BOOK?
UH, YES...
HMM.
THAT'S KIND OF UNEXPECTED.
I THOUGHT YOU'D BE INTO SOMETHING MORE LITERARY.
TH...
THAT'S WHAT I USUALLY READ.
BUT I JUST RE-CENTLY GOT INTO THIS...
INTO MARTIAL ARTS?
Y-YEAH ...
IT'S NOT SAFE THESE DAYS...

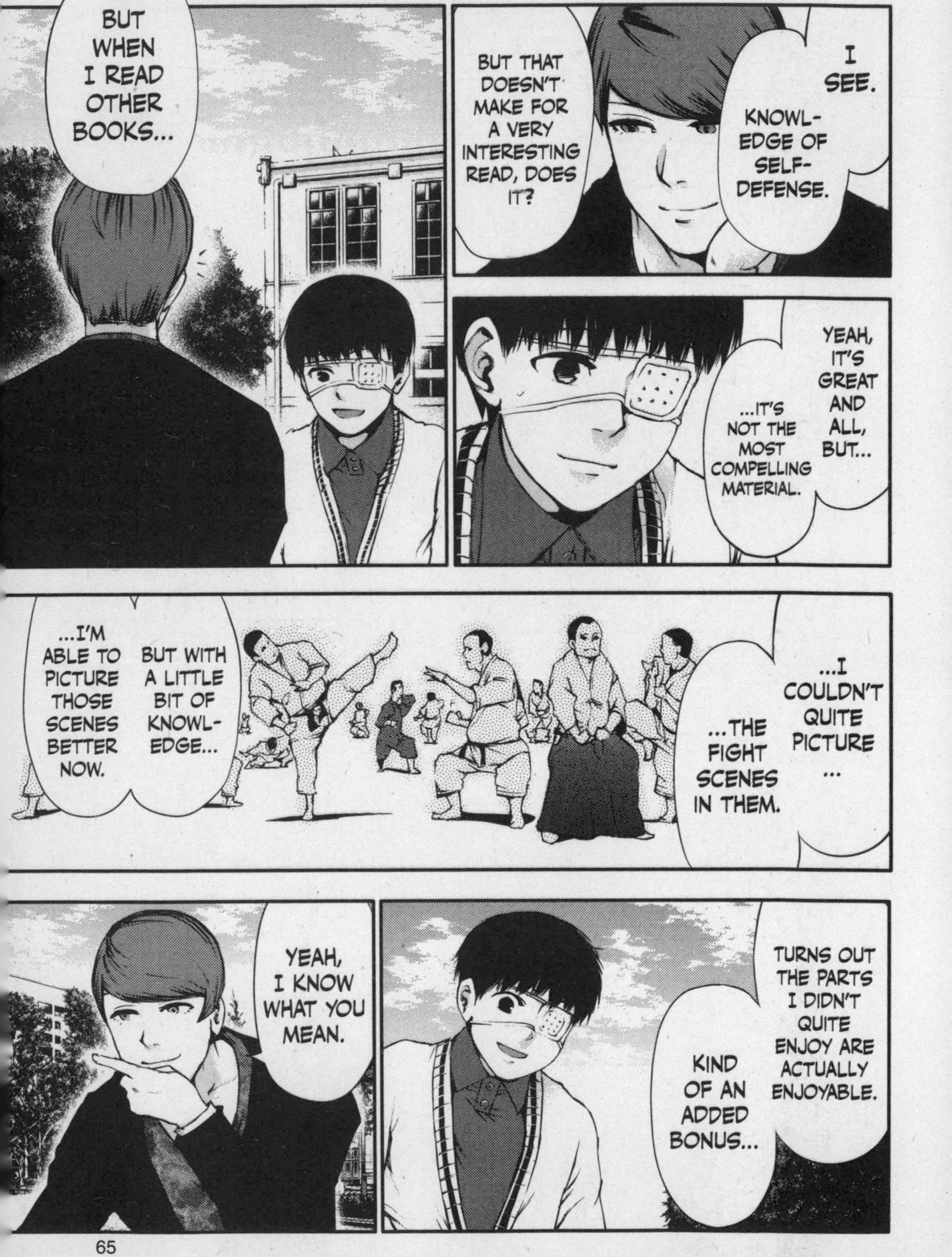
I SEE.
KNOWL-EDGE OF SELF-DEFENSE.
BUT THAT DOESN'T MAKE FOR A VERY INTERESTING READ, DOES IT?
YEAH, IT'S GREAT AND ALL, BUT...
...IT'S NOT THE MOST COMPELLING MATERIAL.
BUT WHEN I READ OTHER BOOKS...
...I COULDN'T QUITE PICTURE...
...THE FIGHT SCENES IN THEM.
BUT WITH A LITTLE BIT OF KNOWL-EDGE...
...I'M ABLE TO PICTURE THOSE SCENES BETTER NOW.
TURNS OUT THE PARTS I DIDN'T QUITE ENJOY ARE ACTUALLY ENJOYABLE.
KIND OF AN ADDED BONUS...
YEAH, I KNOW WHAT YOU MEAN.

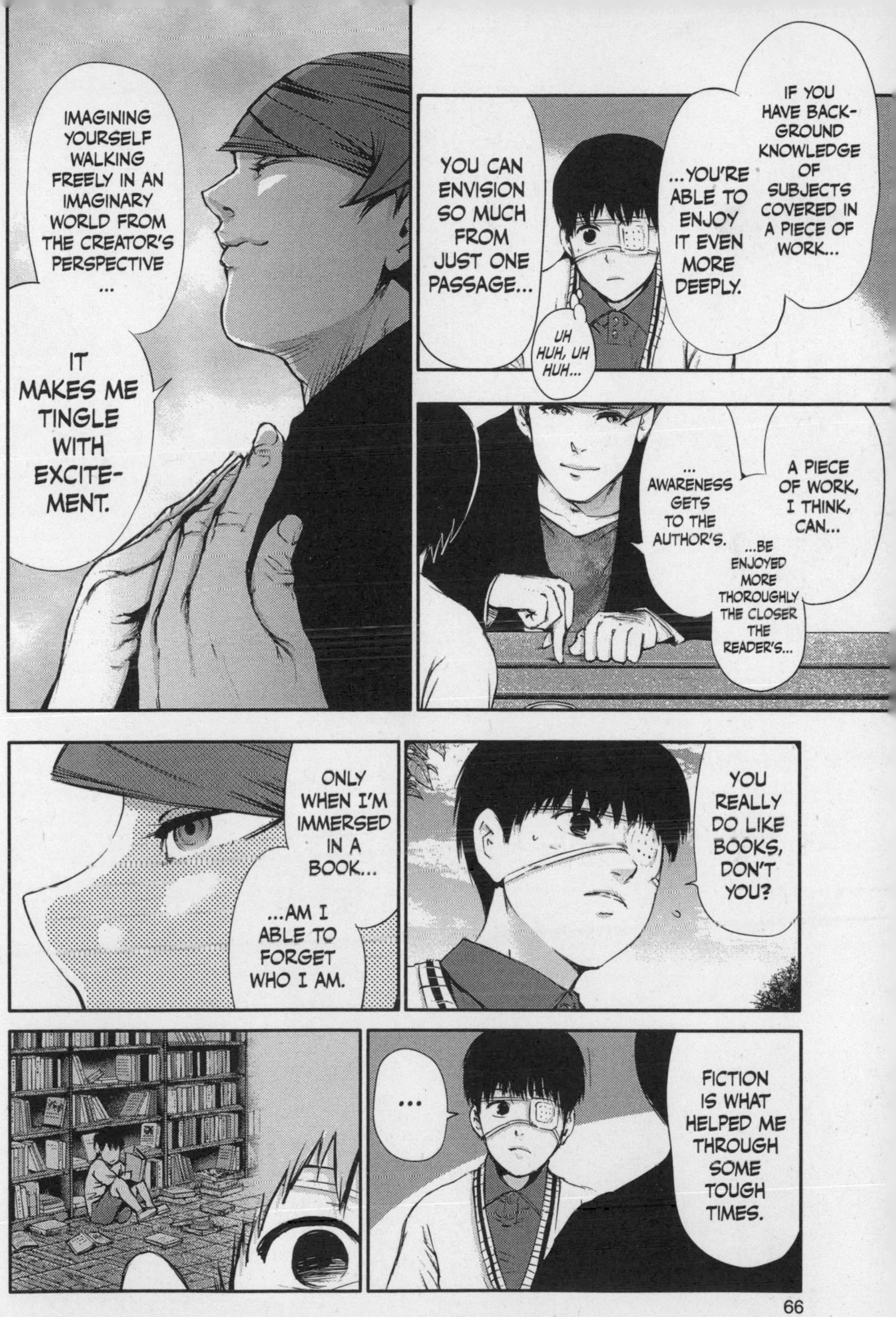
IF YOU HAVE BACK-GROUND KNOWLEDGE OF SUBJECTS COVERED IN A PIECE OF WORK...
...YOU'RE ABLE TO ENJOY IT EVEN MORE DEEPLY.
YOU CAN ENVISION SO MUCH FROM JUST ONE PASSAGE...
UH HUH, UH HUH...
A PIECE OF WORK, I THINK, CAN...
...BE ENJOYED MORE THOROUGHLY THE CLOSER THE READER'S...
...AWARENESS GETS TO THE AUTHOR'S.
IMAGINING YOURSELF WALKING FREELY IN AN IMAGINARY WORLD FROM THE CREATOR'S PERSPECTIVE ...
IT MAKES ME TINGLE WITH EXCITE-MENT.
YOU REALLY DO LIKE BOOKS, DON'T YOU?
ONLY WHEN I'M IMMERSED IN A BOOK...
...AM I ABLE TO FORGET WHO I AM.
FICTION IS WHAT HELPED ME THROUGH SOME TOUGH TIMES.
...

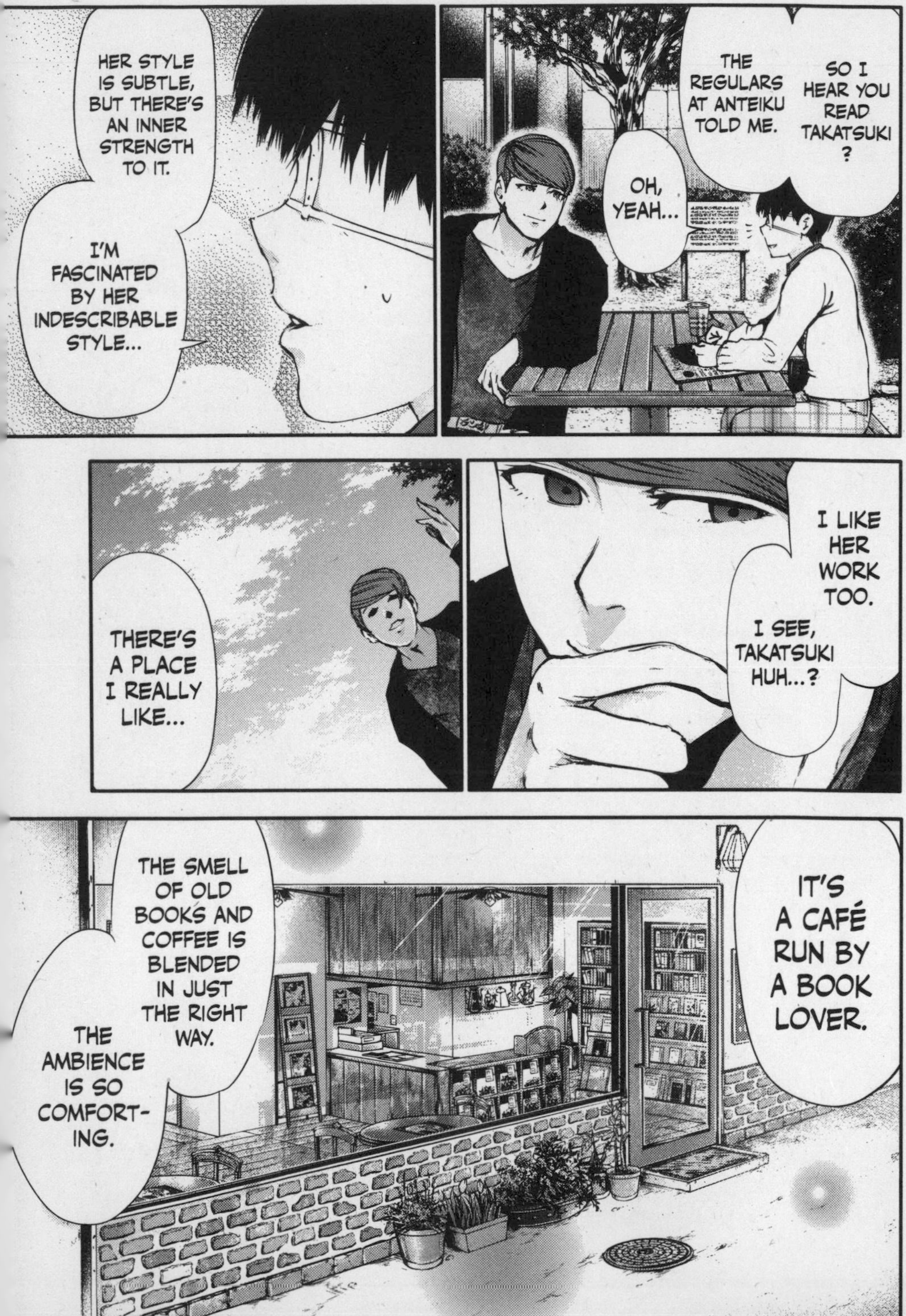
SO I HEAR YOU READ TAKATSUKI?
THE REGULARS AT ANTEIKU TOLD ME.
OH, YEAH...
HER STYLE IS SUBTLE, BUT THERE'S AN INNER STRENGTH TO IT.
I'M FASCINATED BY HER INDESCRIBABLE STYLE...
I LIKE HER WORK TOO.
I SEE, TAKATSUKI HUH...?
THERE'S A PLACE I REALLY LIKE...
IT'S A CAFÉ RUN BY A BOOK LOVER.
THE SMELL OF OLD BOOKS AND COFFEE IS BLENDED IN JUST THE RIGHT WAY.
THE AMBIENCE IS SO COMFORT-ING.

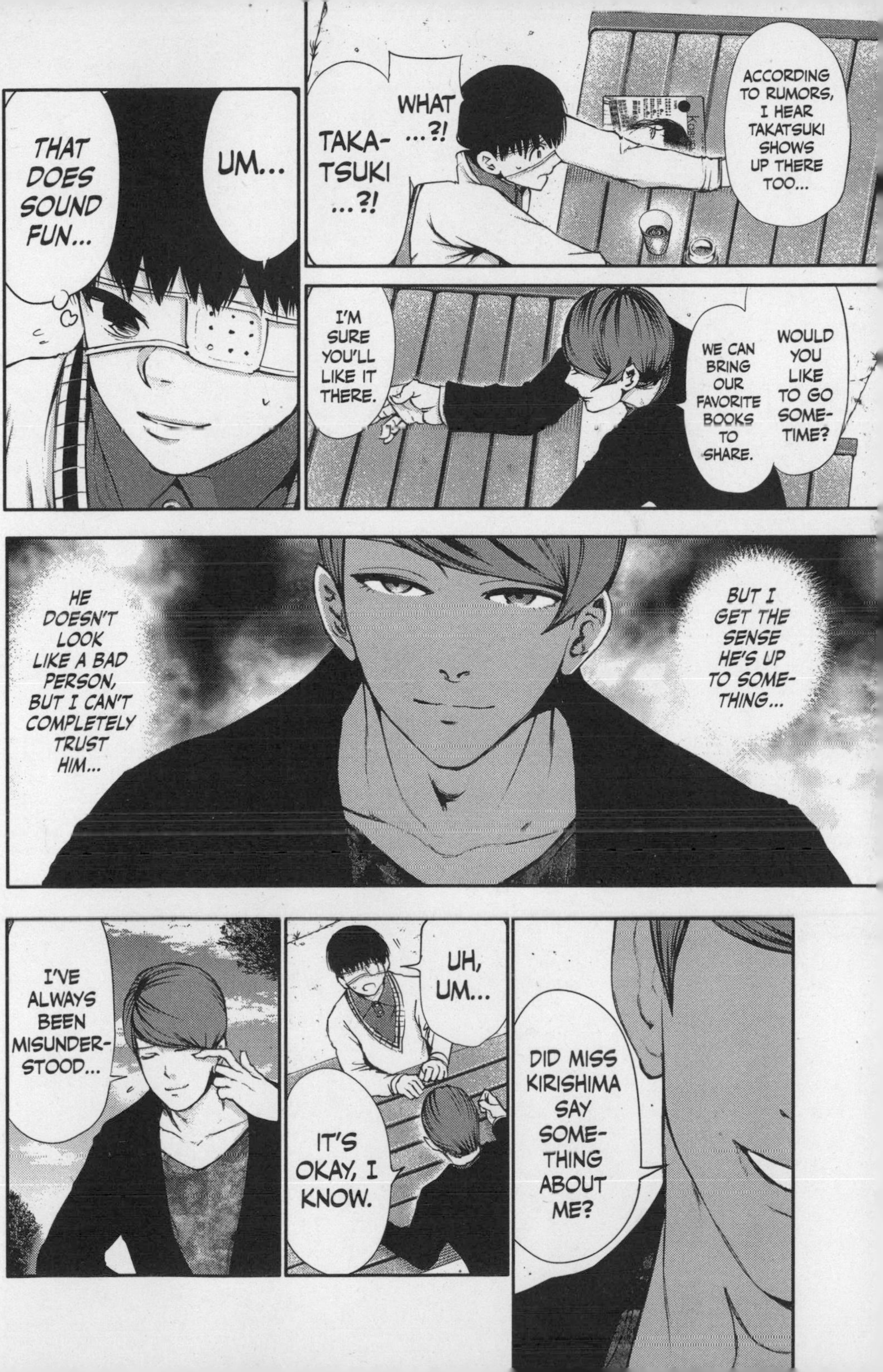
ACCORDING TO RUMORS, I HEAR TAKATSUKI SHOWS UP THERE TOO...
WHAT ...?!
TAKA-TSUKI ...?!
WOULD YOU LIKE TO GO SOME-TIME?
WE CAN BRING OUR FAVORITE BOOKS TO SHARE.
I'M SURE YOU'LL LIKE IT THERE.
UM...
THAT DOES SOUND FUN...
BUT I GET THE SENSE HE'S UP TO SOME-THING...
HE DOESN'T LOOK LIKE A BAD PERSON, BUT I CAN'T COMPLETELY TRUST HIM...
DID MISS KIRISHIMA SAY SOME-THING ABOUT ME?
UH, UM...
IT'S OKAY, I KNOW.
I'VE ALWAYS BEEN MISUNDER-STOOD...

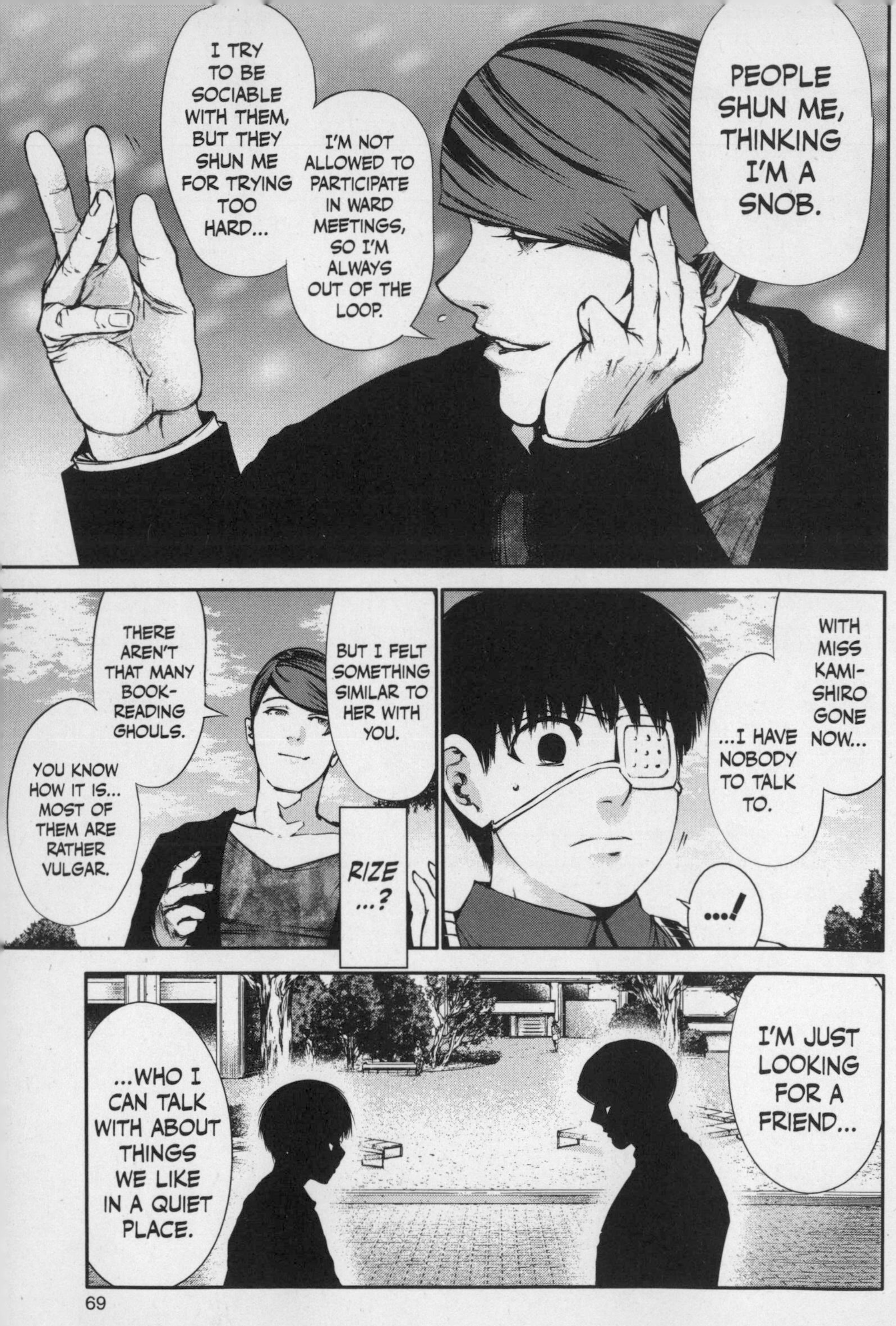
PEOPLE SHUN ME, THINKING I'M A SNOB.
I'M NOT ALLOWED TO PARTICIPATE IN WARD MEETINGS, SO I'M ALWAYS OUT OF THE LOOP.
I TRY TO BE SOCIABLE WITH THEM, BUT THEY SHUN ME FOR TRYING TOO HARD...
WITH MISS KAMI-SHIRO GONE NOW...
...I HAVE NOBODY TO TALK TO.
...!
BUT I FELT SOMETHING SIMILAR TO HER WITH YOU.
THERE AREN'T THAT MANY BOOK-READING GHOULS.
YOU KNOW HOW IT IS... MOST OF THEM ARE RATHER VULGAR.
RIZE ...?
I'M JUST LOOKING FOR A FRIEND...
...WHO I CAN TALK WITH ABOUT THINGS WE LIKE IN A QUIET PLACE.

...

I'VE BOTHERED YOU, HAVEN'T I? I'M SORRY...

I'LL LEAVE YOU...

UH...

IF...

UM...

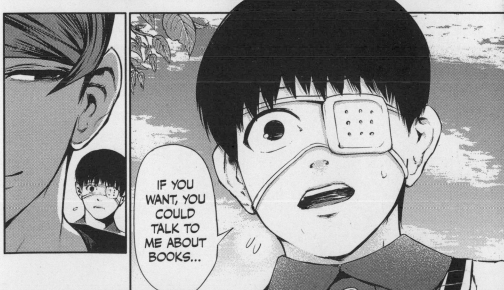

IF YOU WANT, YOU COULD TALK TO ME ABOUT BOOKS...

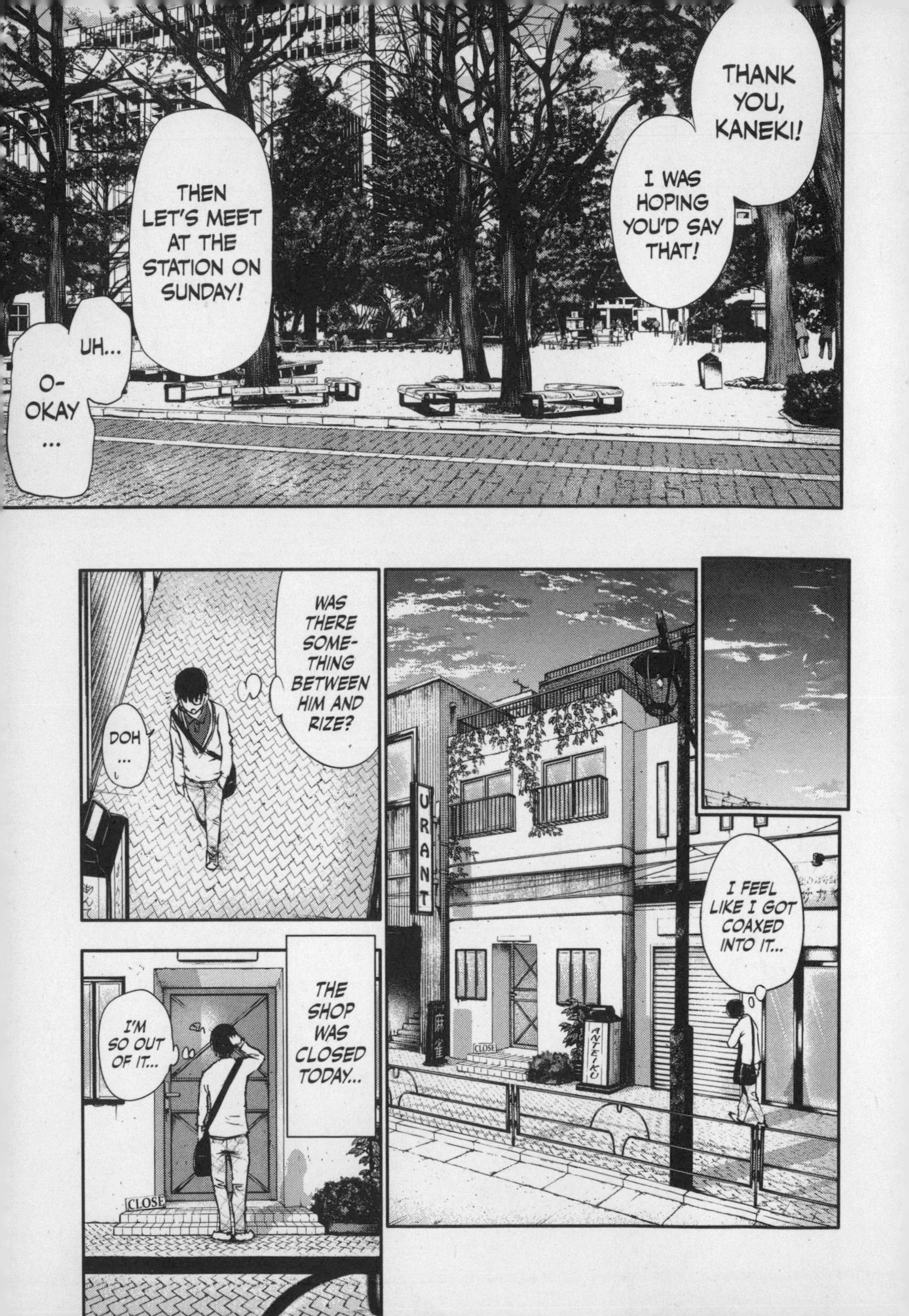
THANK YOU, KANEKI!
I WAS HOPING YOU'D SAY THAT!
THEN LET'S MEET AT THE STATION ON SUNDAY!
UH... O-OKAY ...
URANT
CLOSE
ANTEIKU
I FEEL LIKE I GOT COAXED INTO IT...
WAS THERE SOME-THING BETWEEN HIM AND RIZE?
DOH ...
THE SHOP WAS CLOSED TODAY...
I'M SO OUT OF IT...
CLOSE

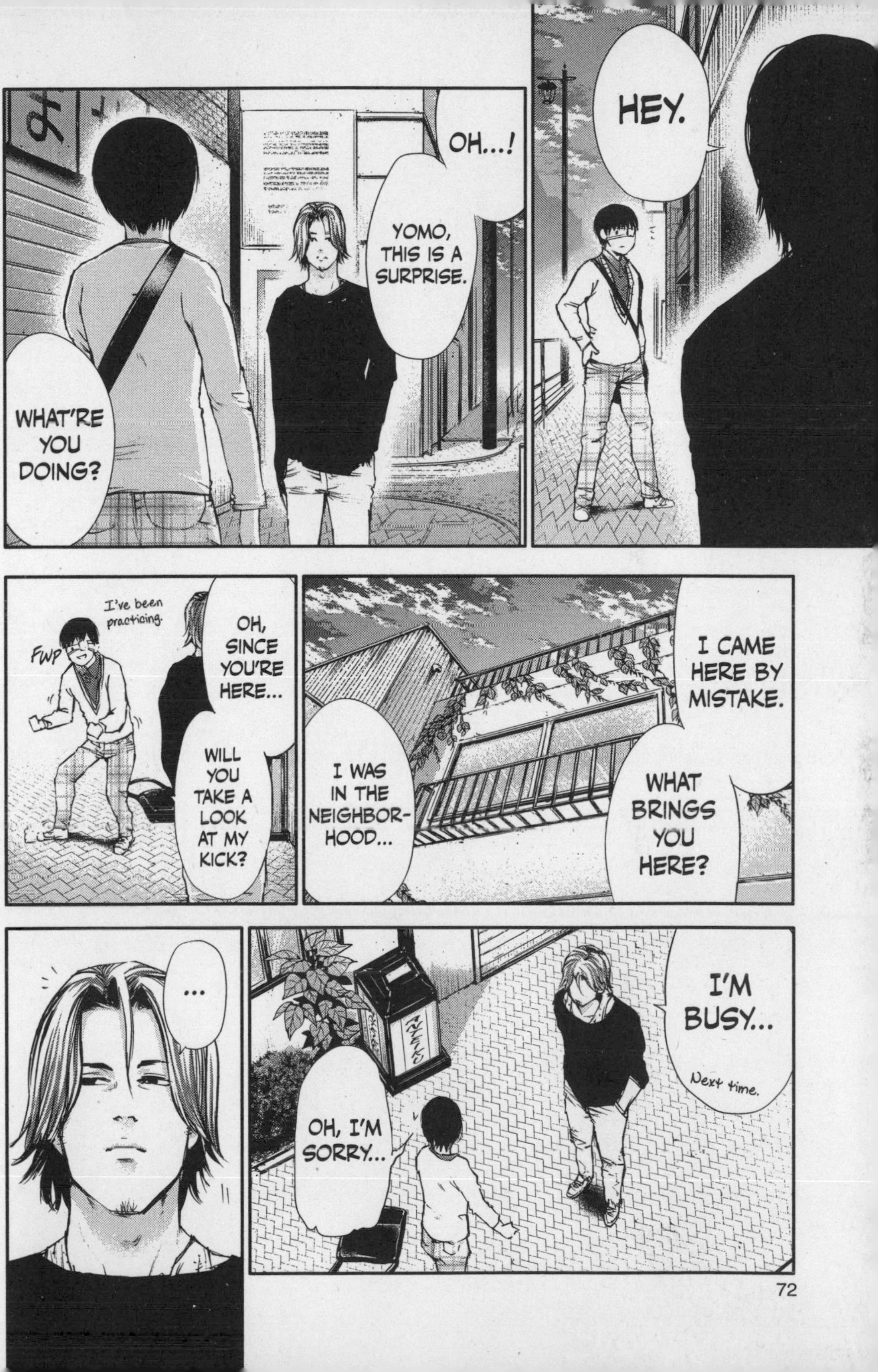
HEY.
OH...!
YOMO, THIS IS A SURPRISE.
WHAT'RE YOU DOING?
I CAME HERE BY MISTAKE.
WHAT BRINGS YOU HERE?
I WAS IN THE NEIGHBOR-HOOD...
OH, SINCE YOU'RE HERE...
I've been practicing.
FWP
WILL YOU TAKE A LOOK AT MY KICK?
I'M BUSY...
Next time.
OH, I'M SORRY...
...

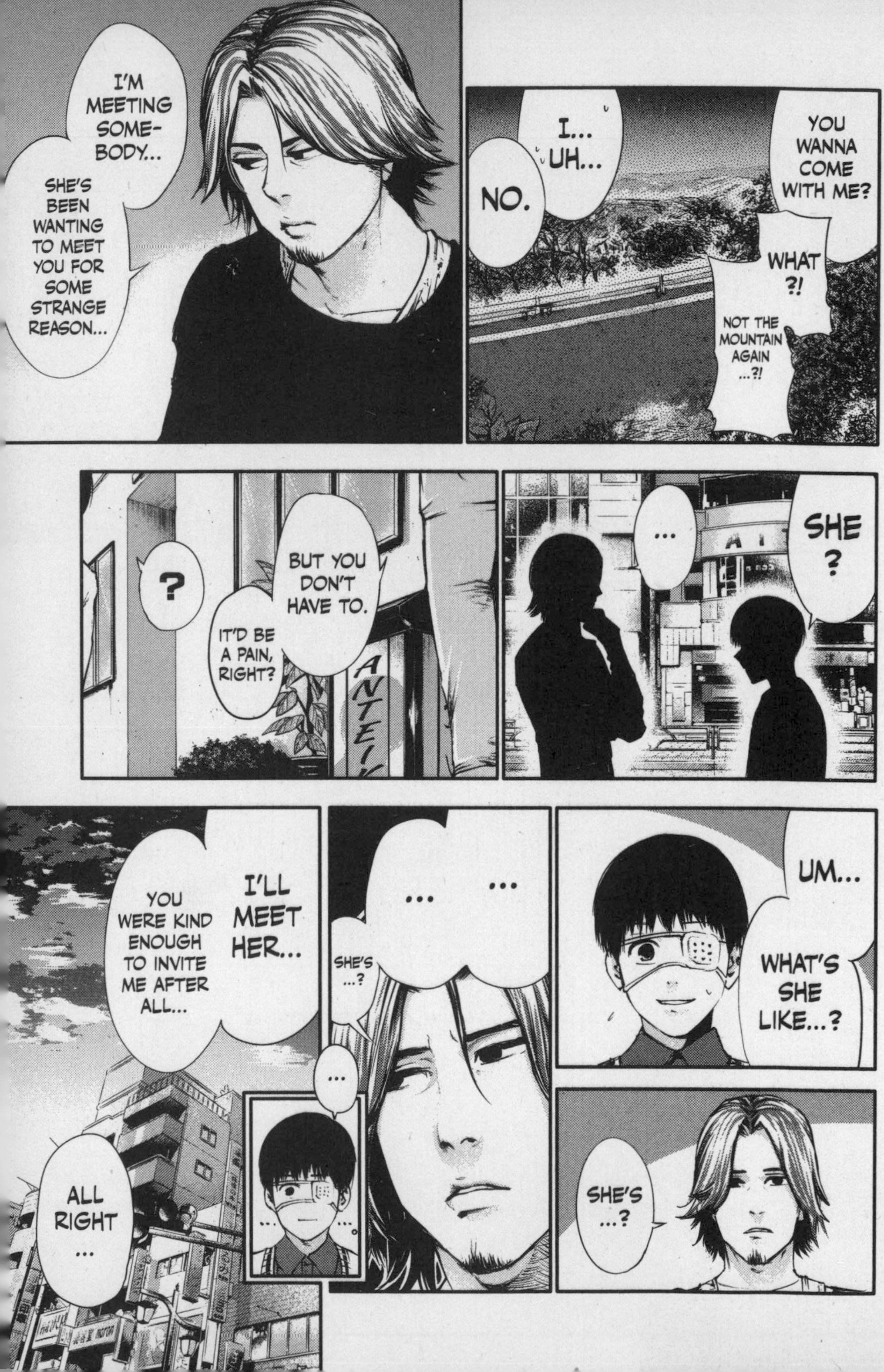
YOU WANNA COME WITH ME?
I... UH...
NO.
WHAT ?!
NOT THE MOUNTAIN AGAIN ...?!
I'M MEETING SOMEBODY...
SHE'S BEEN WANTING TO MEET YOU FOR SOME STRANGE REASON...
SHE ?
...
BUT YOU DON'T HAVE TO.
IT'D BE A PAIN, RIGHT?
?
ANTEI
UM...
WHAT'S SHE LIKE...?
SHE'S ...?
... ...
SHE'S ...?
...
... ...
I'LL MEET HER...
YOU WERE KIND ENOUGH TO INVITE ME AFTER ALL...
ALL RIGHT ...

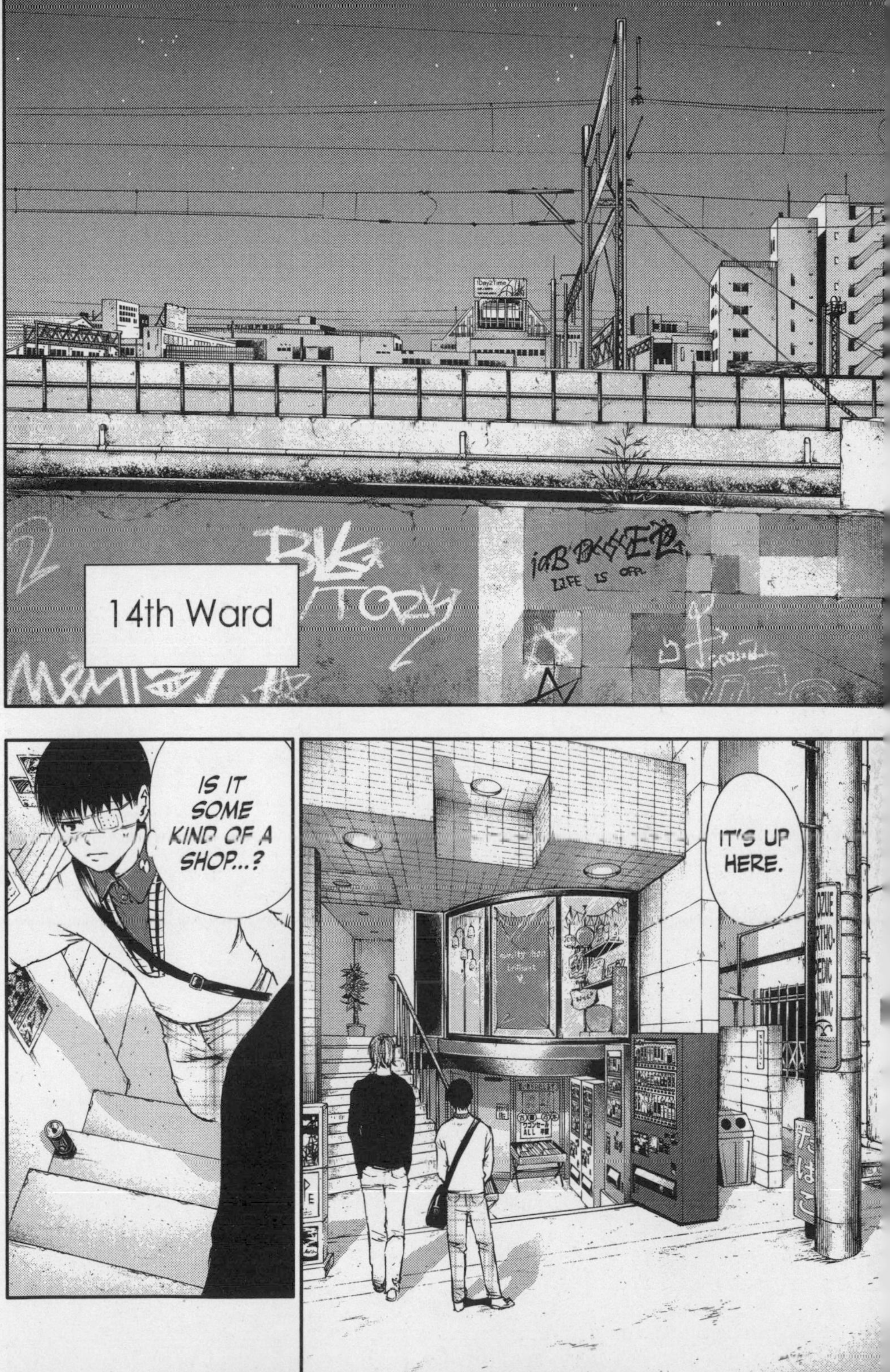
14th Ward
IT'S UP HERE.
IS IT SOME KIND OF A SHOP...?

EXCUSE ME...

GGH

VWSH

?!

IS IT A BAR...?

I'M ACTUALLY UNDER-AGE...

SHE'S PROBABLY INSIDE.

OH. I SEE.

IT'S CLOSED.

WAIT...?

CLOSED

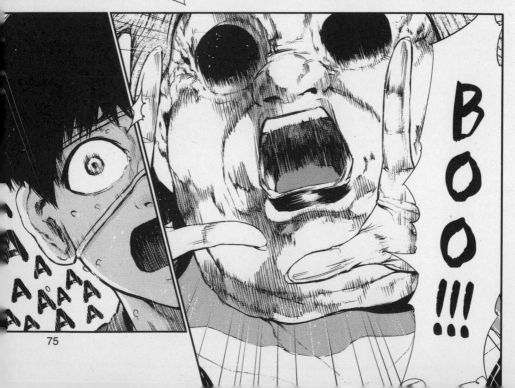

BOO!!!

AAAAAAAAAAAAA

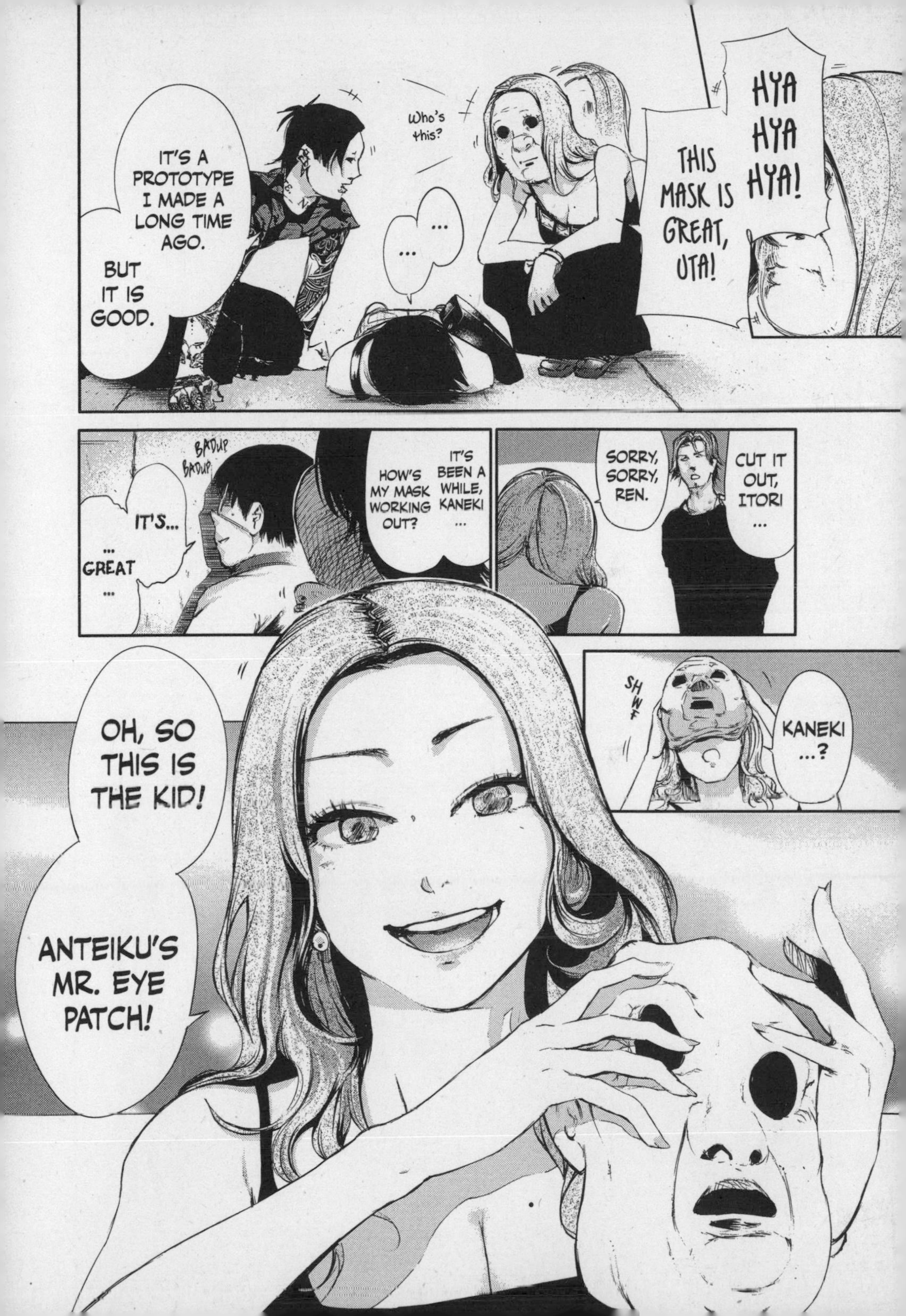
HYA HYA HYA!
THIS MASK IS GREAT, UTA!
Who's this?
...
...
IT'S A PROTOTYPE I MADE A LONG TIME AGO.
BUT IT IS GOOD.
CUT IT OUT, ITORI ...
SORRY, SORRY, REN.
IT'S BEEN A WHILE, KANEKI ...
HOW'S MY MASK WORKING OUT?
BADUP BADUP
IT'S...
... GREAT ...
KANEKI ...?
SHWF
OH, SO THIS IS THE KID!
ANTEIKU'S MR. EYE PATCH!

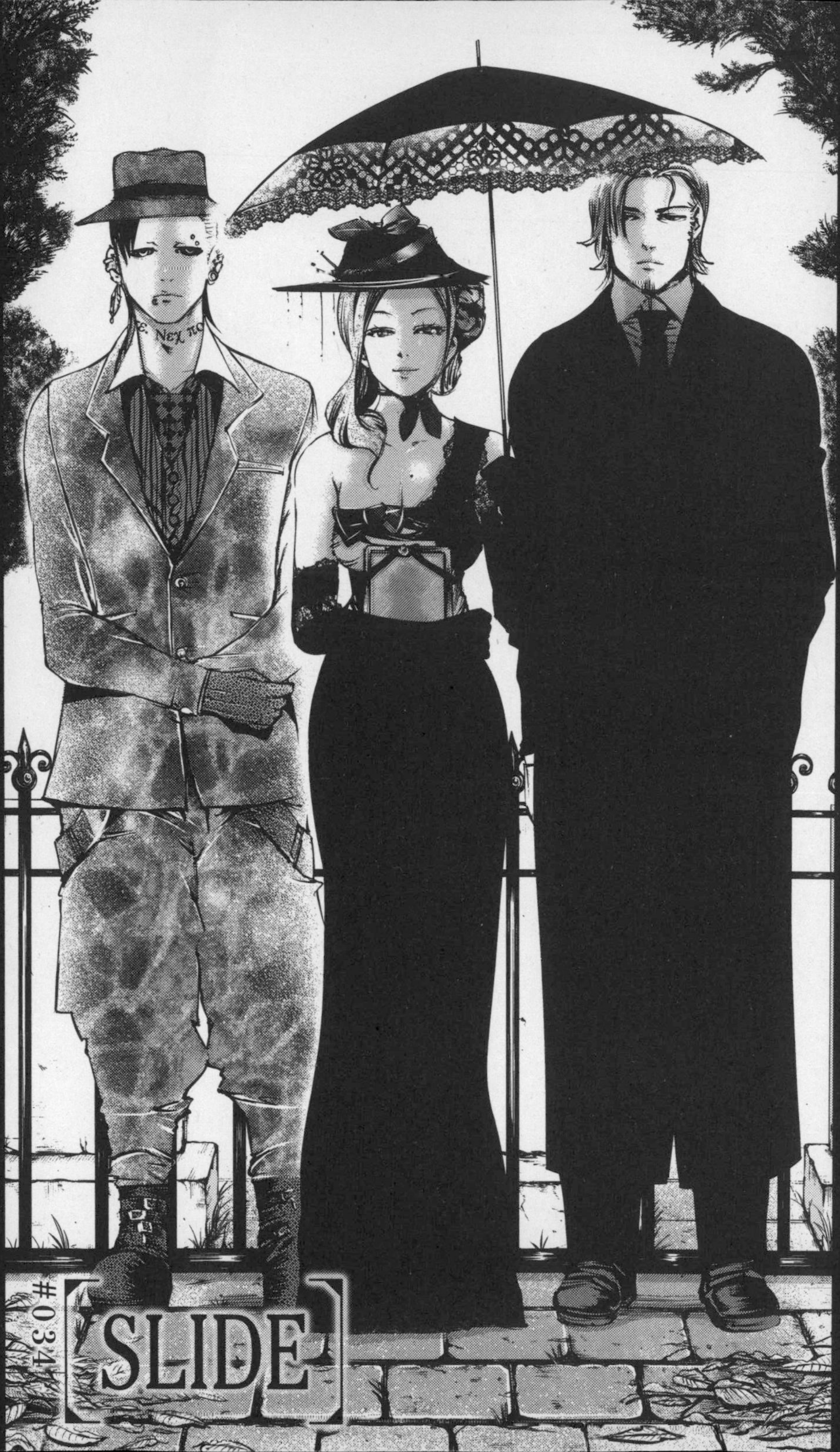
#034
SLIDE

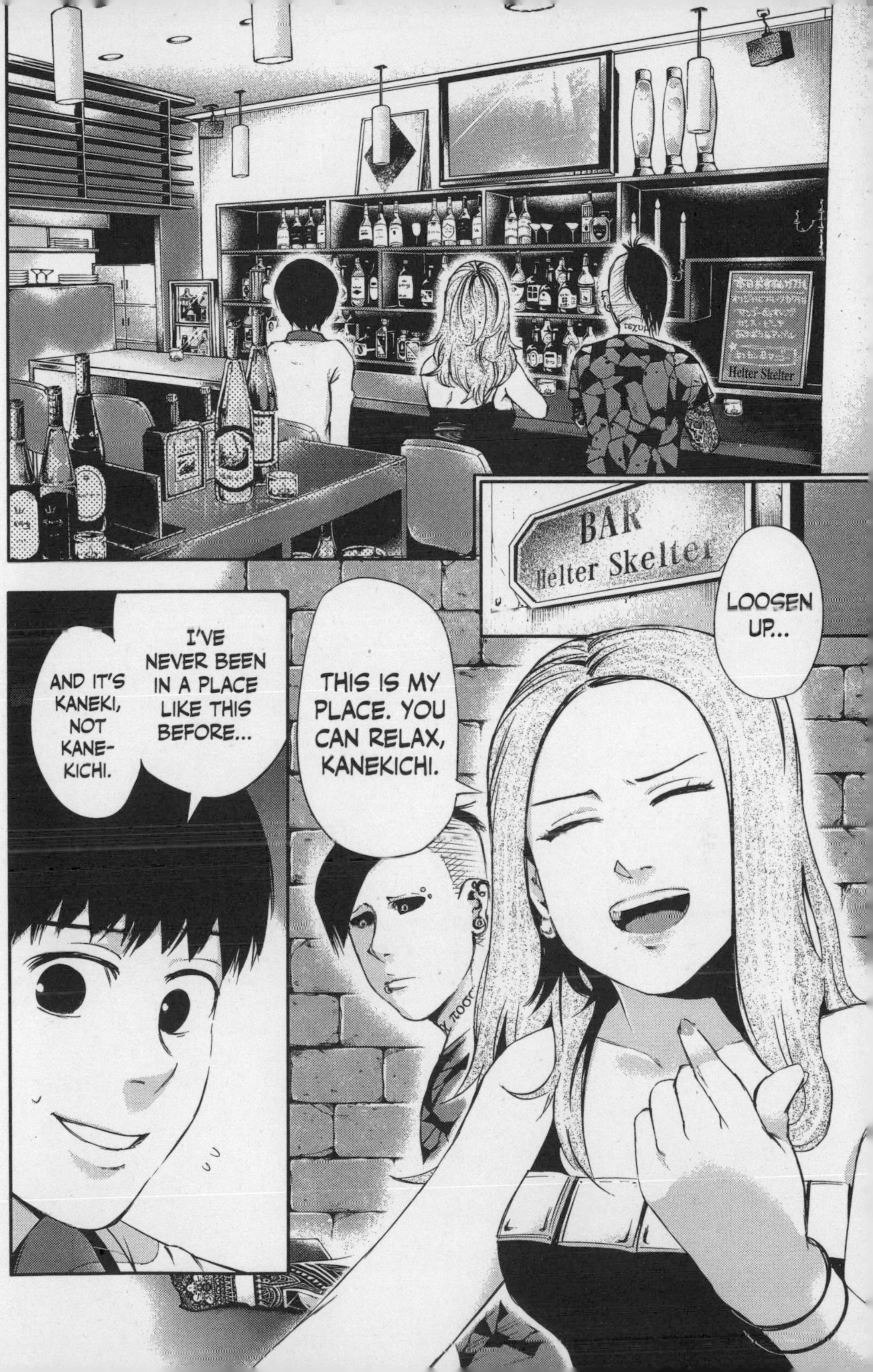
Helter Skelter
BAR
Helter Skelter
LOOSEN UP...
THIS IS MY PLACE. YOU CAN RELAX, KANEKICHI.
I'VE NEVER BEEN IN A PLACE LIKE THIS BEFORE...
AND IT'S KANEKI, NOT KANE-KICHI.

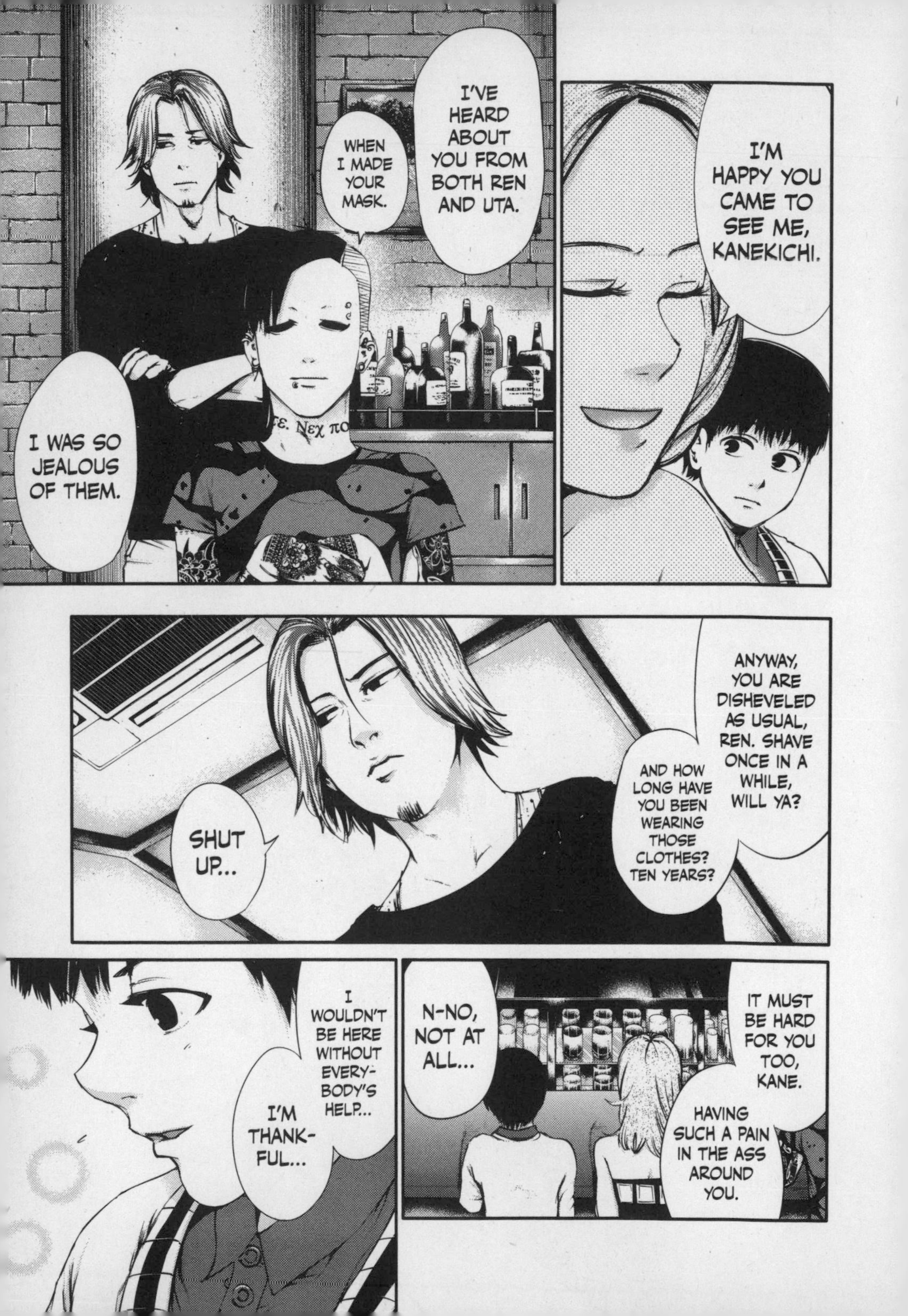
I'M HAPPY YOU CAME TO SEE ME, KANEKICHI.
I'VE HEARD ABOUT YOU FROM BOTH REN AND UTA.
WHEN I MADE YOUR MASK.
I WAS SO JEALOUS OF THEM.
ANYWAY, YOU ARE DISHEVELED AS USUAL, REN. SHAVE ONCE IN A WHILE, WILL YA?
AND HOW LONG HAVE YOU BEEN WEARING THOSE CLOTHES? TEN YEARS?
SHUT UP...
IT MUST BE HARD FOR YOU TOO, KANE.
HAVING SUCH A PAIN IN THE ASS AROUND YOU.
N-NO, NOT AT ALL...
I WOULDN'T BE HERE WITHOUT EVERY-BODY'S HELP...
I'M THANK-FUL...

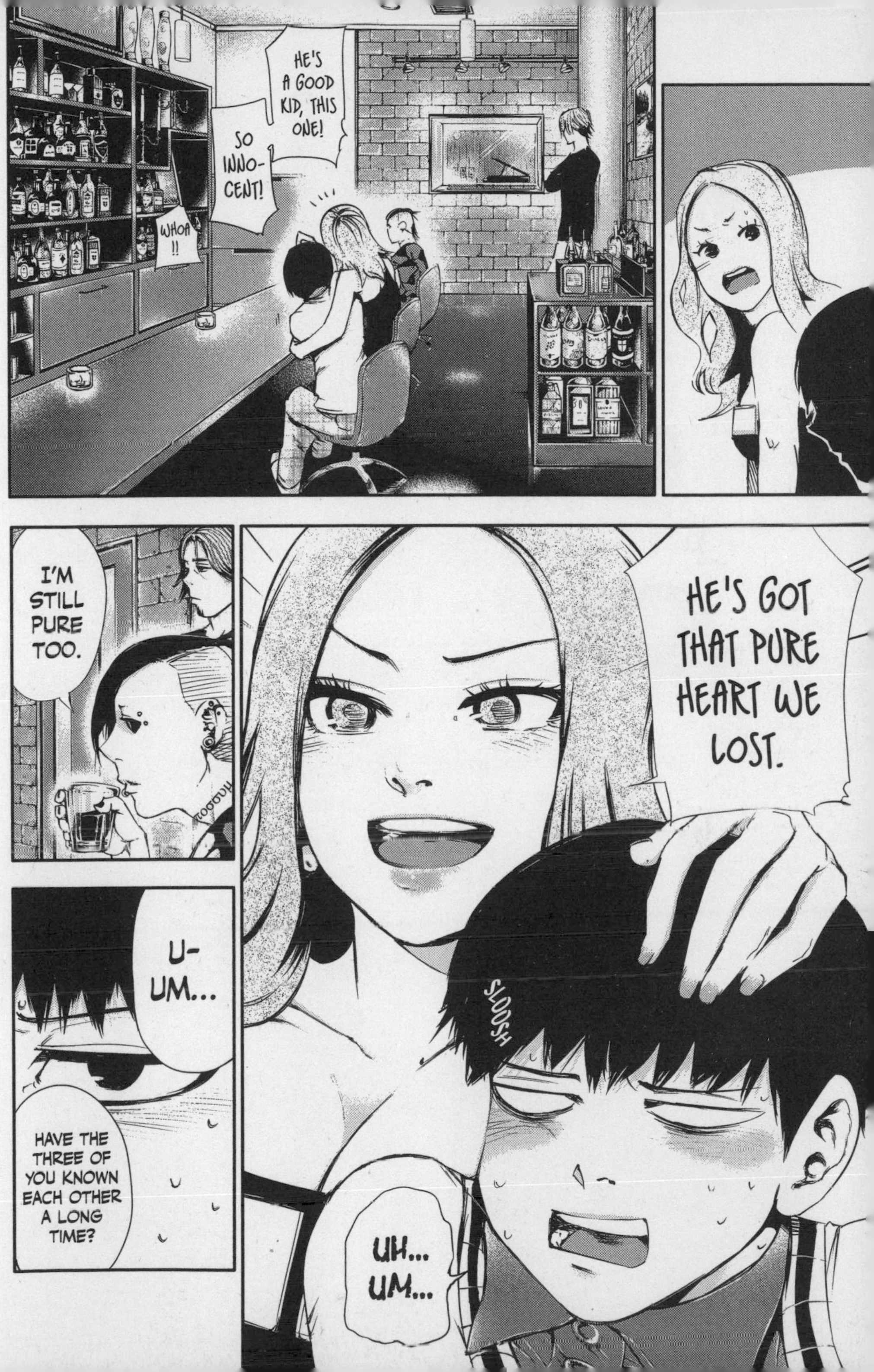
HE'S A GOOD KID, THIS ONE!
SO INNO-CENT!
WHOA!!
HE'S GOT THAT PURE HEART WE LOST.
SLOOSH
UH... UM...
I'M STILL PURE TOO.
U- UM...
HAVE THE THREE OF YOU KNOWN EACH OTHER A LONG TIME?

WARDS 1 THROUGH 4 ARE BASICALLY UNLIVABLE...

I REMEMBER UTA SAYING...

REALLY...?

REN AND UTA HATED EACH OTHER BACK THEN.

THE 4TH WARD?

YEAH. I'VE UNFORTUNATELY BEEN INSEPARABLE FROM REN SINCE HE SHOWED UP IN THE 4TH WARD.

THE 4TH WARD WAS EVEN CRAZIER THAN IT IS NOW BECAUSE OF THESE TWO.

THE PROBLEMS THEY CAUSED US...

WHO CARES ABOUT OTHER PEOPLE...

I'M SORRY, YOU KNOW HOW TEENAGERS ARE.

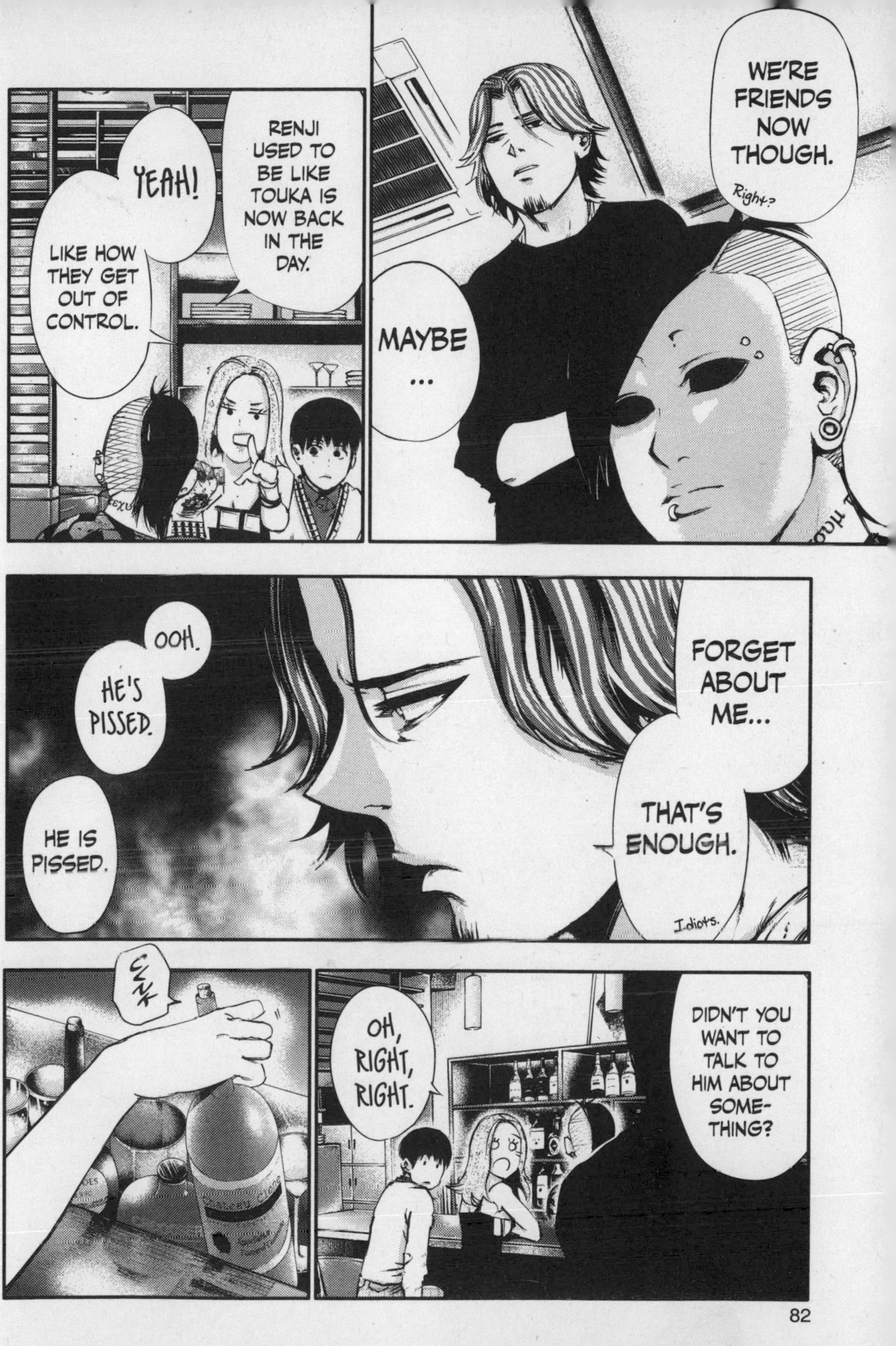
WE'RE FRIENDS NOW THOUGH.
Right?
MAYBE...
RENJI USED TO BE LIKE TOUKA IS NOW BACK IN THE DAY.
YEAH!
LIKE HOW THEY GET OUT OF CONTROL.
FORGET ABOUT ME...
THAT'S ENOUGH.
Idiots.
OOH.
HE'S PISSED.
HE IS PISSED.
DIDN'T YOU WANT TO TALK TO HIM ABOUT SOME-THING?
OH, RIGHT, RIGHT.
CLINK

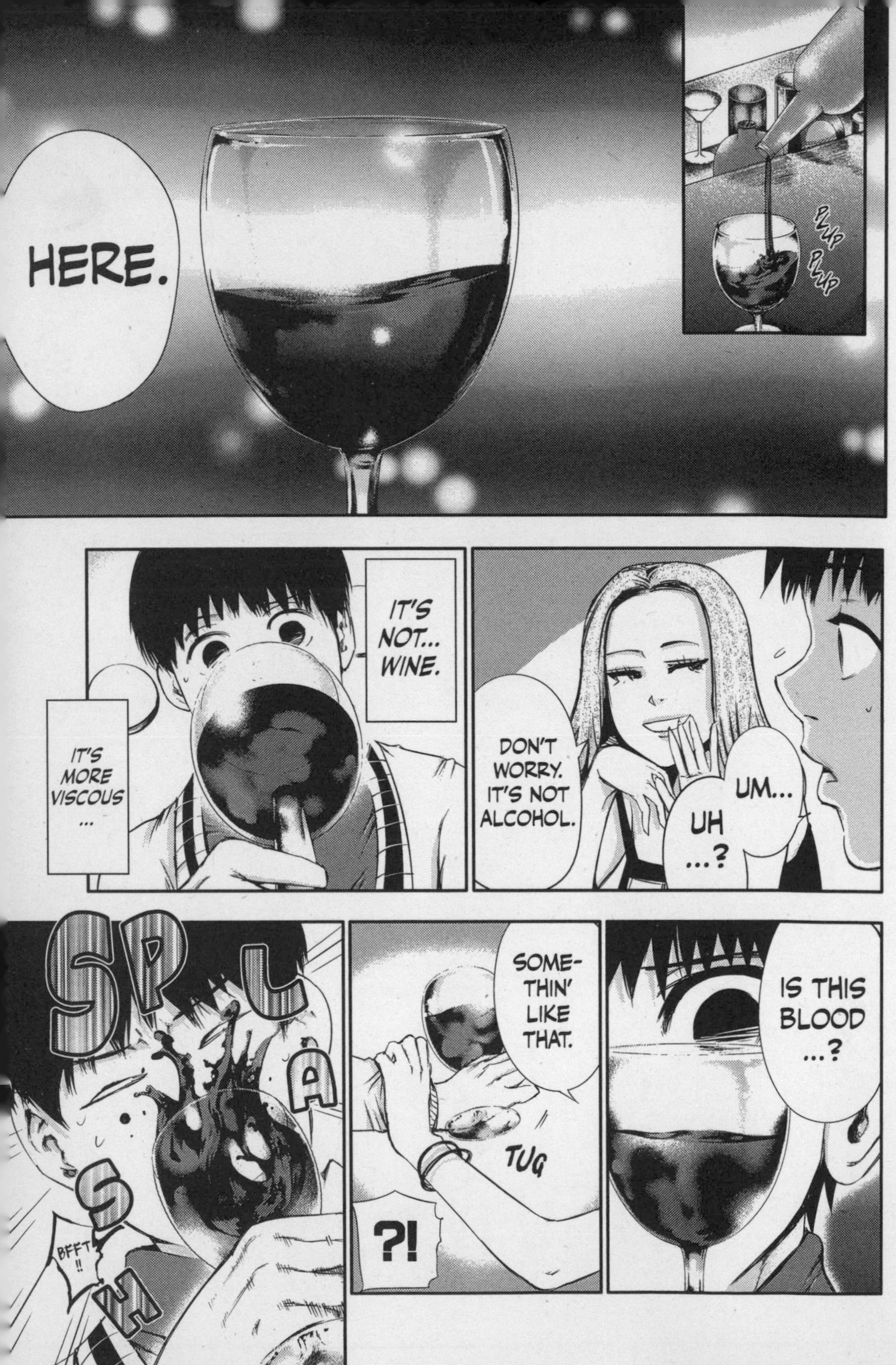
PLUP PLUP
HERE.
UM...
UH ...?
DON'T WORRY. IT'S NOT ALCOHOL.
IT'S NOT... WINE.
IT'S MORE VISCOUS ...
IS THIS BLOOD ...?
SOME-THIN' LIKE THAT.
TUG
?!
SPLASH
BFFT !!

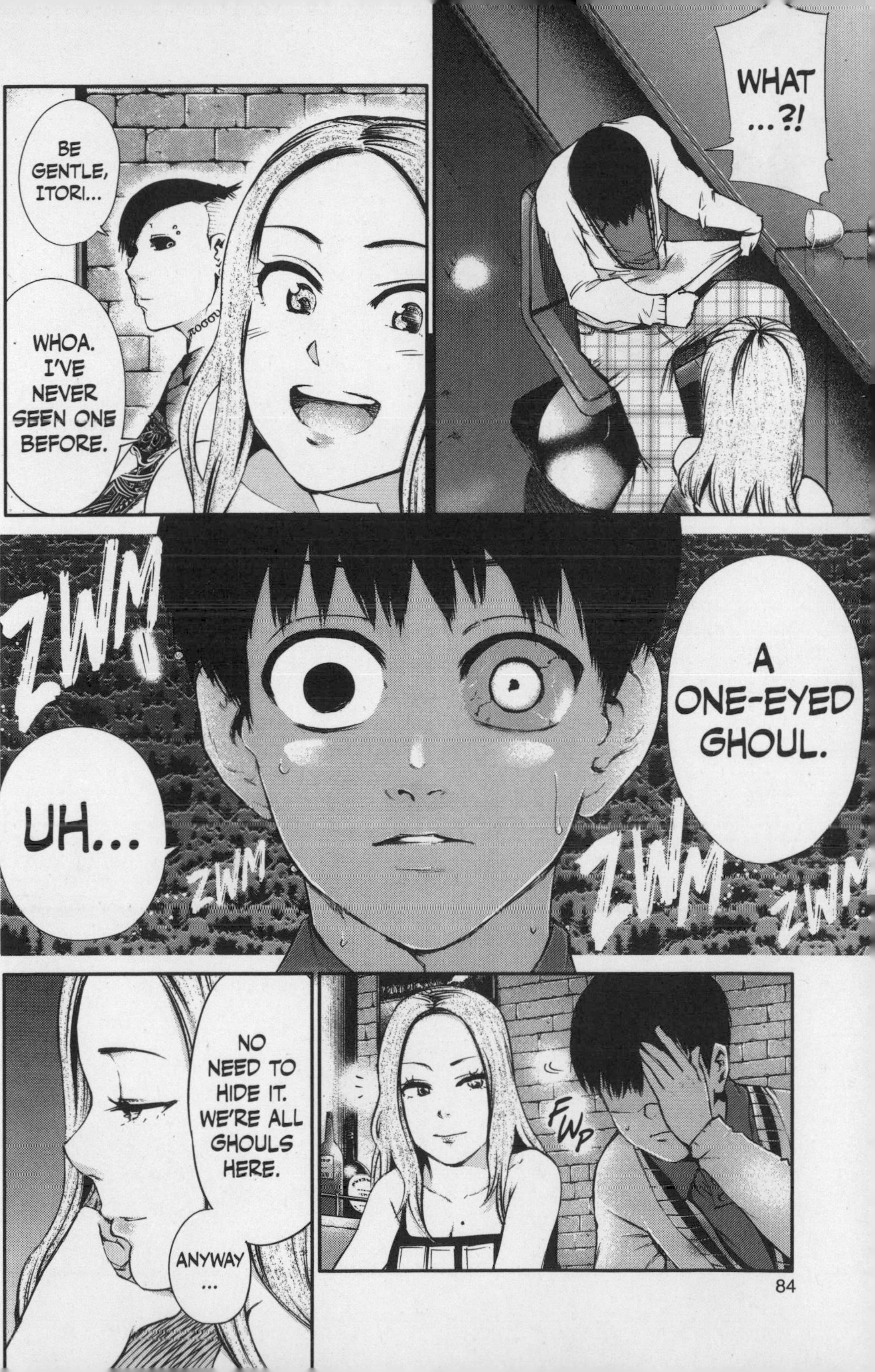
WHAT ...?!
BE GENTLE, ITORI...
WHOA. I'VE NEVER SEEN ONE BEFORE.
A ONE-EYED GHOUL.
ZWM
ZWM
ZWM!
UH...
ZWM
FWP
NO NEED TO HIDE IT. WE'RE ALL GHOULS HERE.
ANYWAY ...

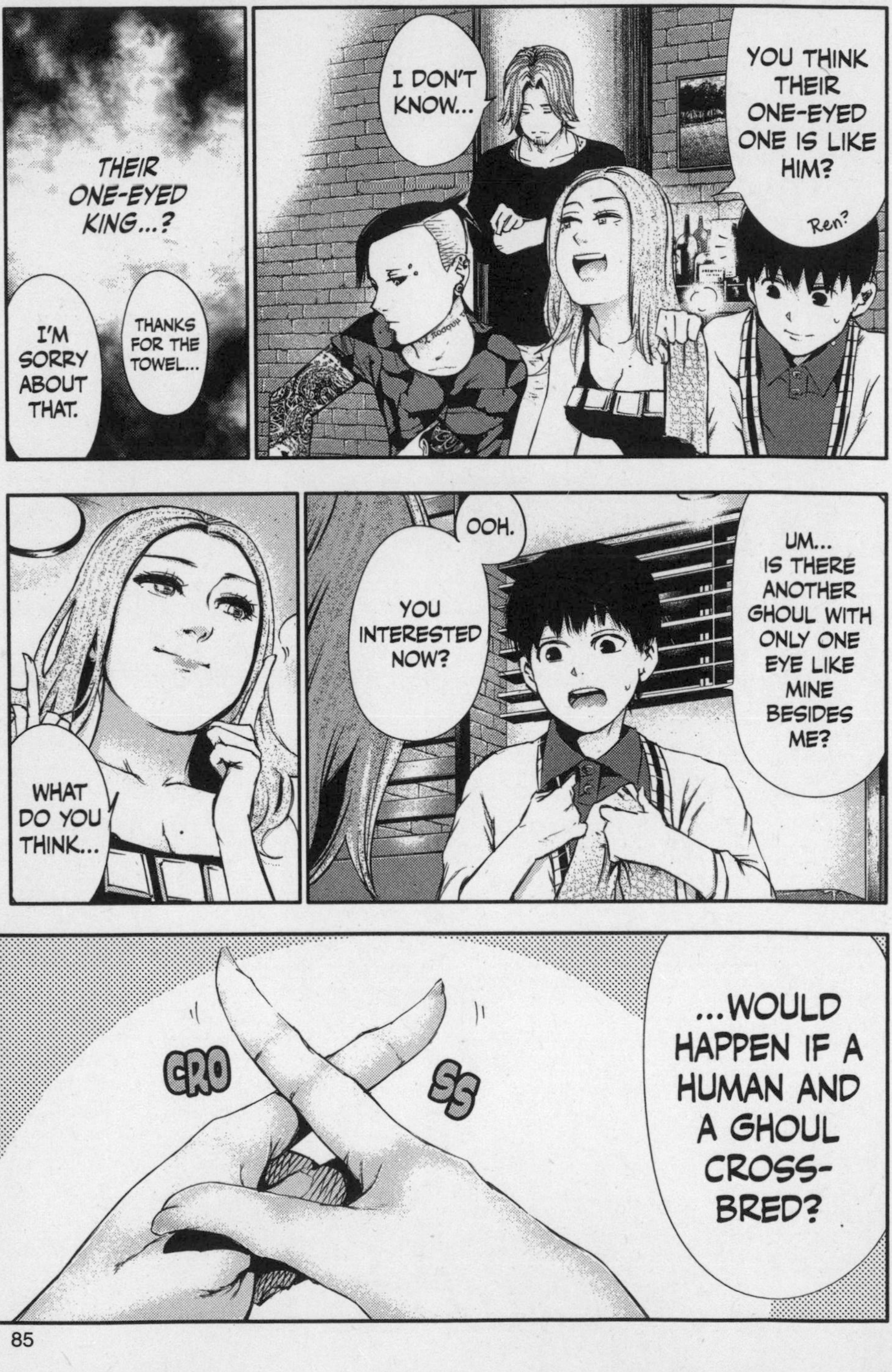
YOU THINK THEIR ONE-EYED ONE IS LIKE HIM?
Ren?
I DON'T KNOW...
THEIR ONE-EYED KING...?
THANKS FOR THE TOWEL...
I'M SORRY ABOUT THAT.
UM... IS THERE ANOTHER GHOUL WITH ONLY ONE EYE LIKE MINE BESIDES ME?
OOH.
YOU INTERESTED NOW?
WHAT DO YOU THINK...
...WOULD HAPPEN IF A HUMAN AND A GHOUL CROSS-BRED?
SS
CRO

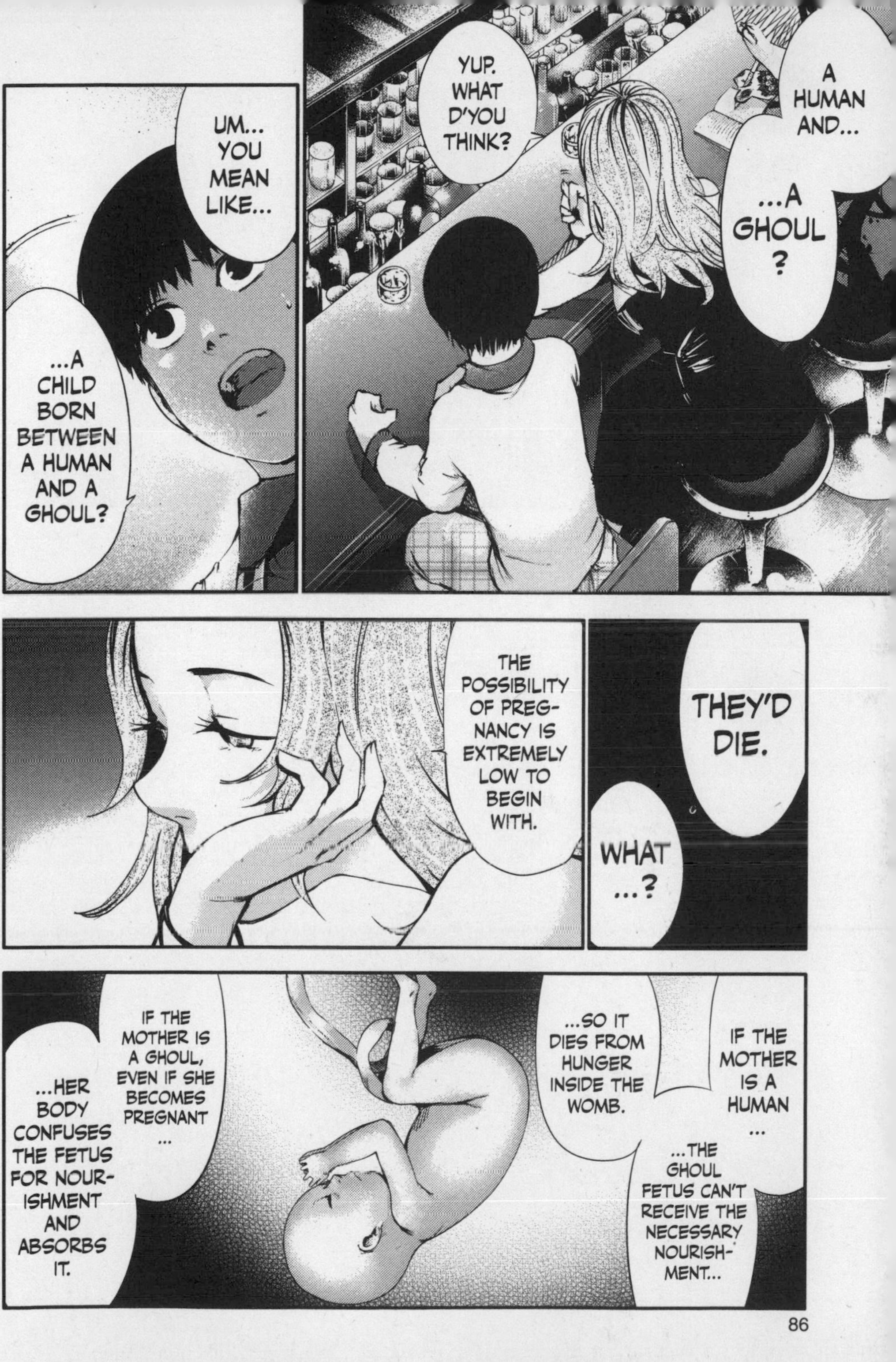
A HUMAN AND...
...A GHOUL?
YUP. WHAT D'YOU THINK?
UM... YOU MEAN LIKE...
...A CHILD BORN BETWEEN A HUMAN AND A GHOUL?
THEY'D DIE.
WHAT ...?
THE POSSIBILITY OF PREGNANCY IS EXTREMELY LOW TO BEGIN WITH.
IF THE MOTHER IS A HUMAN ...
...THE GHOUL FETUS CAN'T RECEIVE THE NECESSARY NOURISHMENT...
...SO IT DIES FROM HUNGER INSIDE THE WOMB.
IF THE MOTHER IS A GHOUL, EVEN IF SHE BECOMES PREGNANT ...
...HER BODY CONFUSES THE FETUS FOR NOURISHMENT AND ABSORBS IT.

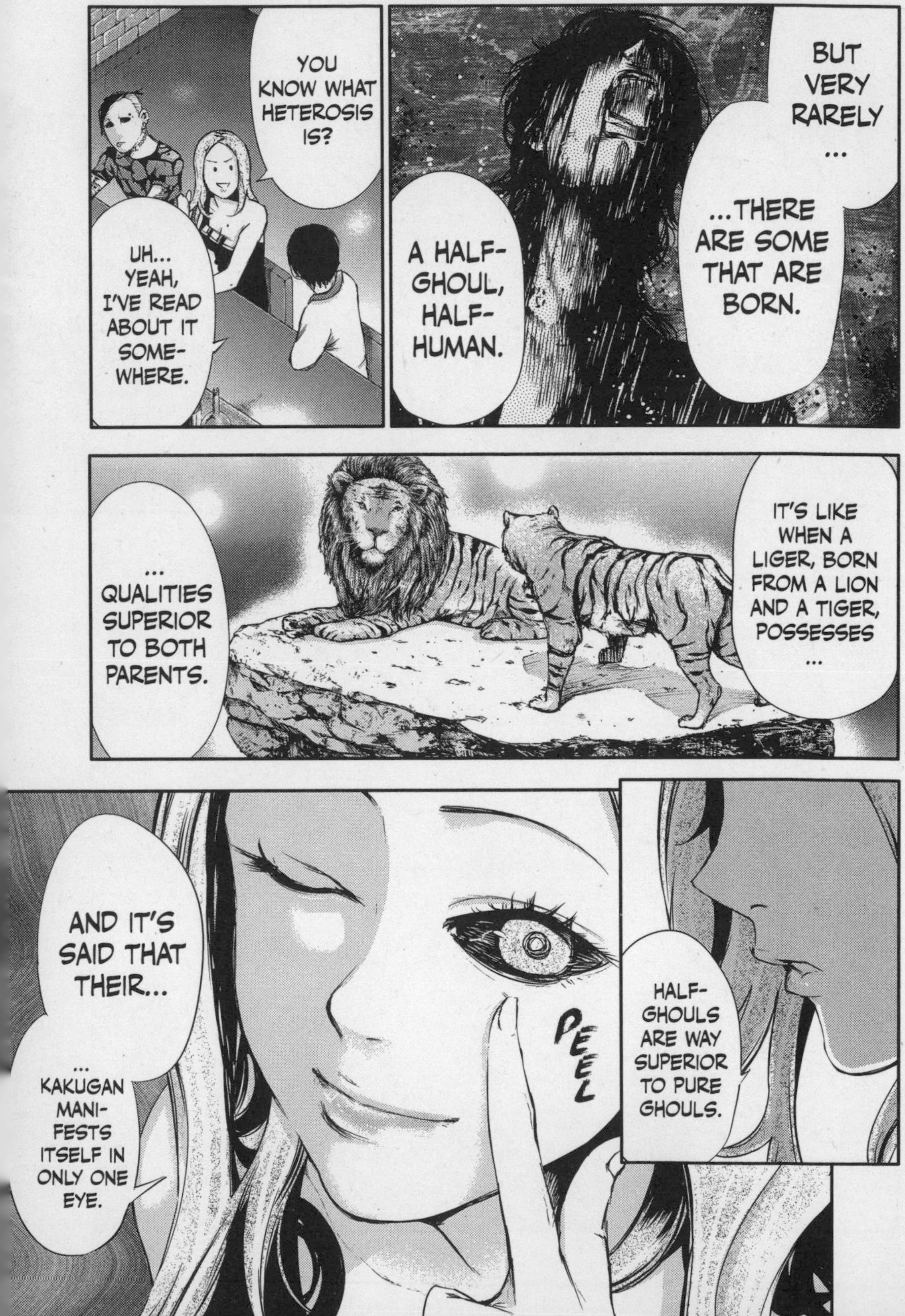
BUT VERY RARELY ...
...THERE ARE SOME THAT ARE BORN.
A HALF-GHOUL, HALF-HUMAN.
YOU KNOW WHAT HETEROSIS IS?
UH... YEAH, I'VE READ ABOUT IT SOMEWHERE.
IT'S LIKE WHEN A LIGER, BORN FROM A LION AND A TIGER, POSSESSES ...
... QUALITIES SUPERIOR TO BOTH PARENTS.
HALF-GHOULS ARE WAY SUPERIOR TO PURE GHOULS.
AND IT'S SAID THAT THEIR...
PEEL
... KAKUGAN MANIFESTS ITSELF IN ONLY ONE EYE.

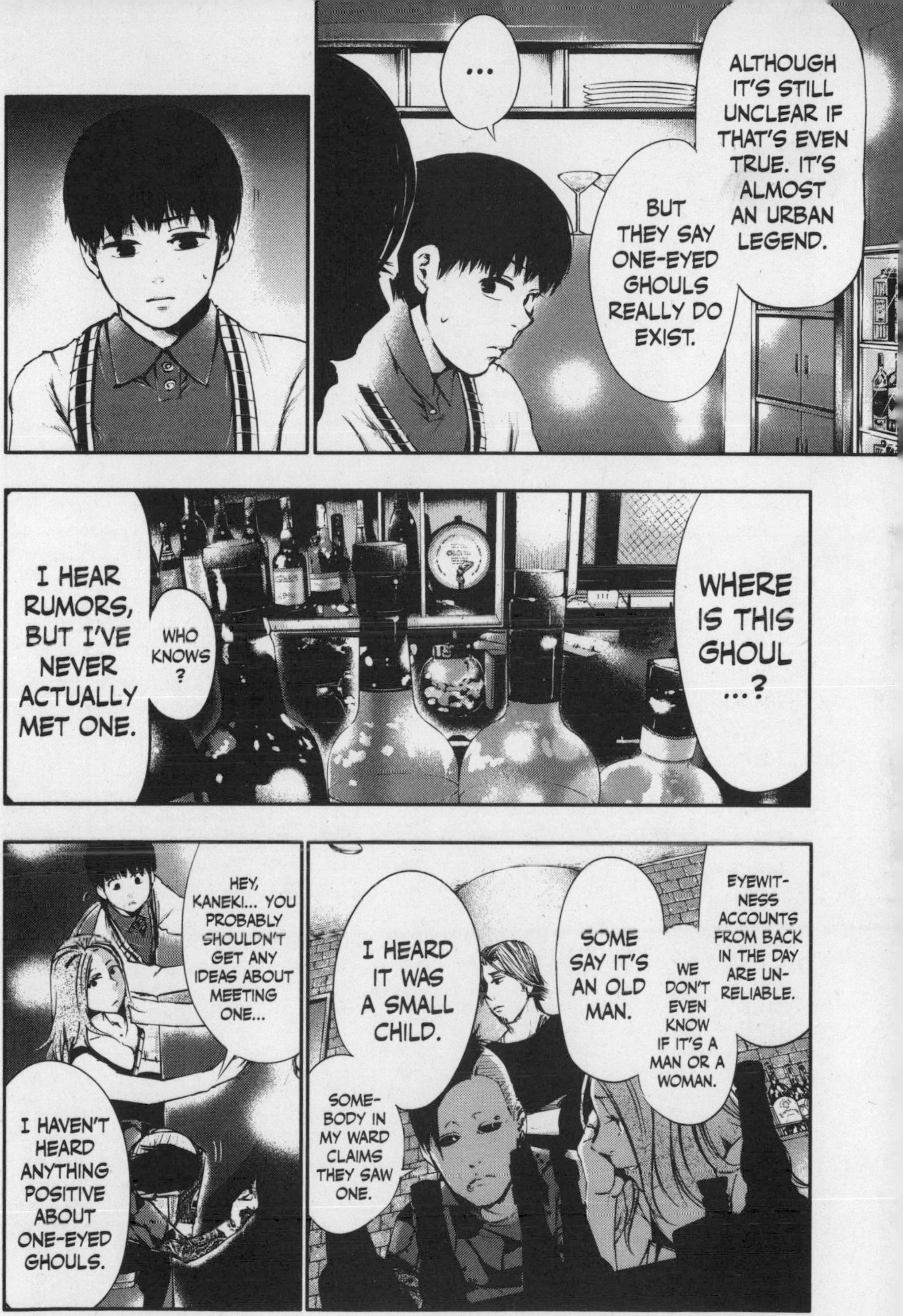
BUT THEY SAY ONE-EYED GHOULS REALLY DO EXIST.
ALTHOUGH IT'S STILL UNCLEAR IF THAT'S EVEN TRUE. IT'S ALMOST AN URBAN LEGEND.
...
WHERE IS THIS GHOUL ...?
WHO KNOWS?
I HEAR RUMORS, BUT I'VE NEVER ACTUALLY MET ONE.
EYEWIT-NESS ACCOUNTS FROM BACK IN THE DAY ARE UN-RELIABLE.
WE DON'T EVEN KNOW IF IT'S A MAN OR A WOMAN.
SOME SAY IT'S AN OLD MAN.
I HEARD IT WAS A SMALL CHILD.
SOME-BODY IN MY WARD CLAIMS THEY SAW ONE.
HEY, KANEKI... YOU PROBABLY SHOULDN'T GET ANY IDEAS ABOUT MEETING ONE...
I HAVEN'T HEARD ANYTHING POSITIVE ABOUT ONE-EYED GHOULS.

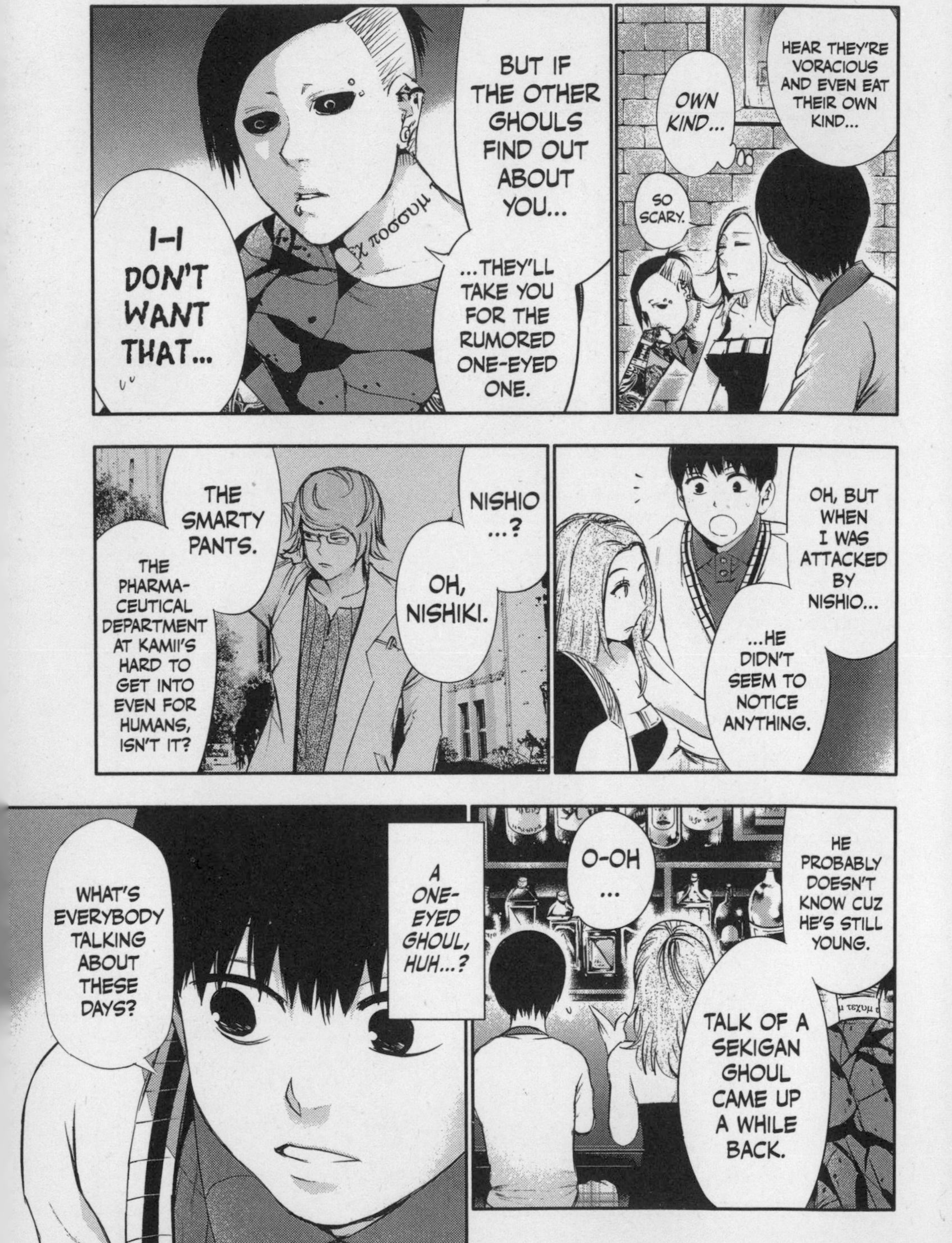
HEAR THEY'RE VORACIOUS AND EVEN EAT THEIR OWN KIND...
OWN KIND...
SO SCARY.
BUT IF THE OTHER GHOULS FIND OUT ABOUT YOU...
...THEY'LL TAKE YOU FOR THE RUMORED ONE-EYED ONE.
I-I DON'T WANT THAT...
OH, BUT WHEN I WAS ATTACKED BY NISHIO...
...HE DIDN'T SEEM TO NOTICE ANYTHING.
NISHIO ...?
OH, NISHIKI.
THE SMARTY PANTS.
THE PHARMACEUTICAL DEPARTMENT AT KAMII'S HARD TO GET INTO EVEN FOR HUMANS, ISN'T IT?
HE PROBABLY DOESN'T KNOW CUZ HE'S STILL YOUNG.
O-OH ...
TALK OF A SEKIGAN GHOUL CAME UP A WHILE BACK.
A ONE-EYED GHOUL, HUH...?
WHAT'S EVERYBODY TALKING ABOUT THESE DAYS?

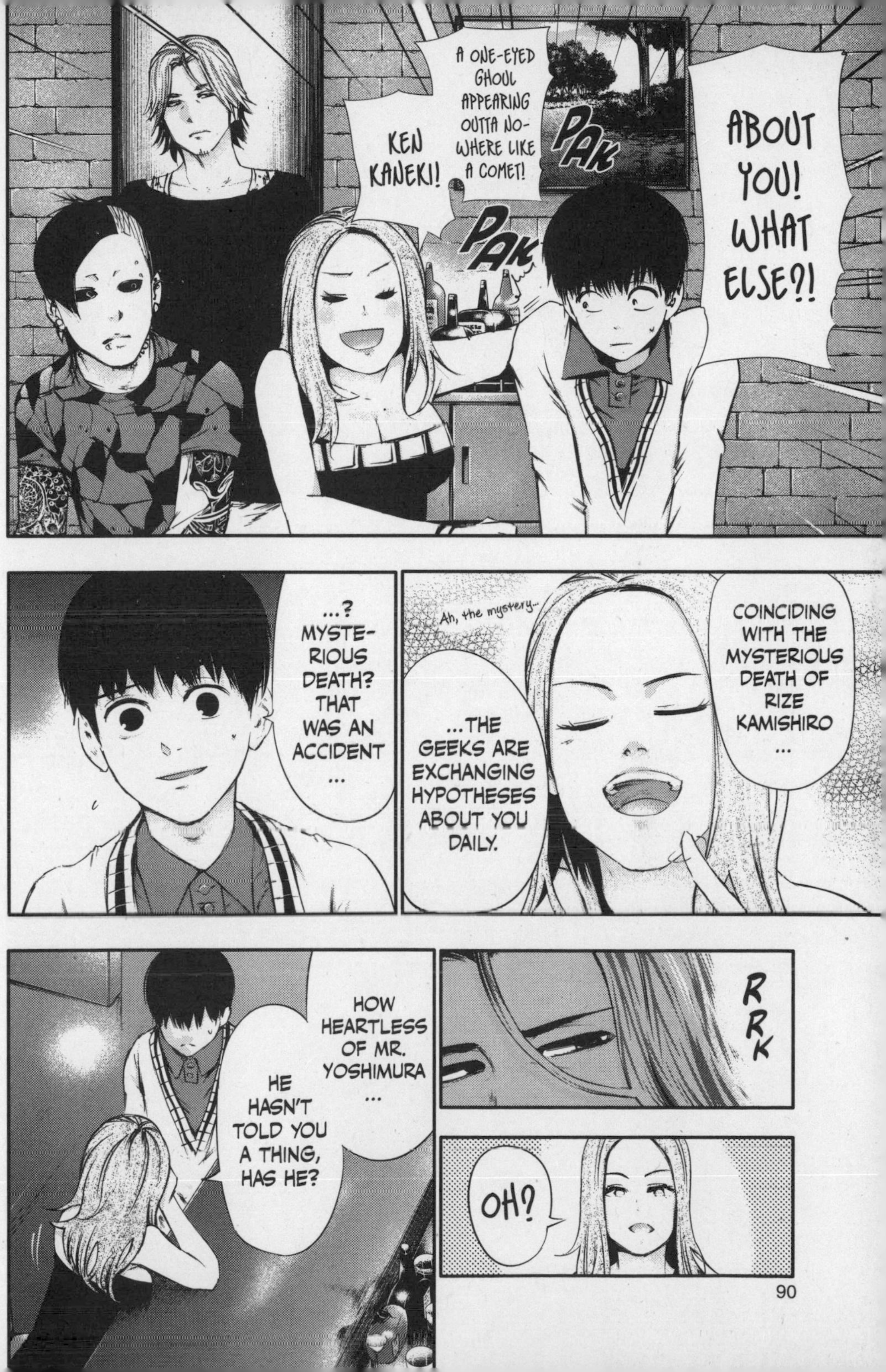
ABOUT YOU! WHAT ELSE?!
PAK
A ONE-EYED GHOUL APPEARING OUTTA NOWHERE LIKE A COMET!
KEN KANEKI!
PAK
COINCIDING WITH THE MYSTERIOUS DEATH OF RIZE KAMISHIRO ...
Ah, the mystery...
...THE GEEKS ARE EXCHANGING HYPOTHESES ABOUT YOU DAILY.
...? MYSTERIOUS DEATH? THAT WAS AN ACCIDENT ...
RRK
OH?
HOW HEARTLESS OF MR. YOSHIMURA ...
HE HASN'T TOLD YOU A THING, HAS HE?

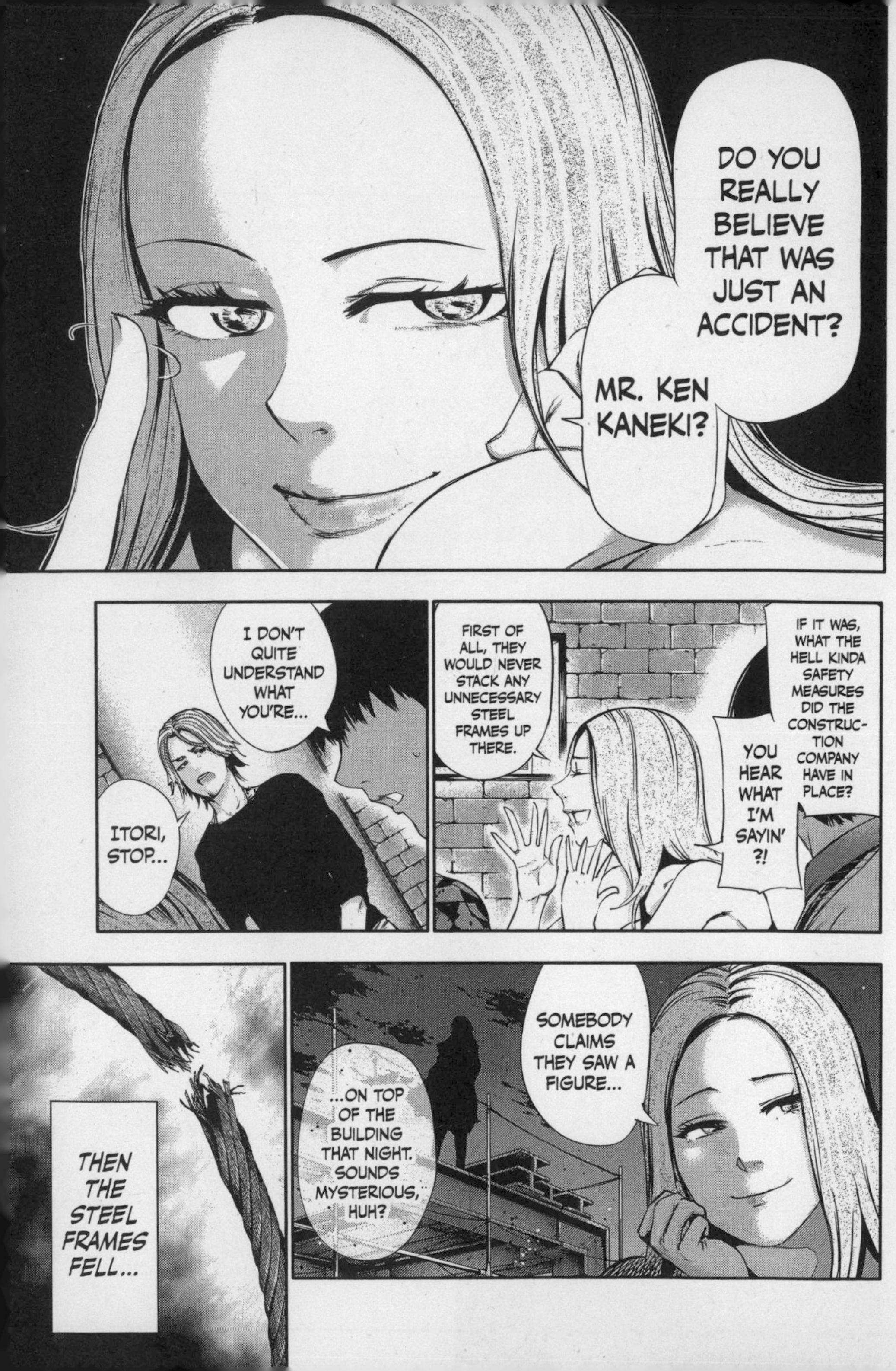
DO YOU REALLY BELIEVE THAT WAS JUST AN ACCIDENT?
MR. KEN KANEKI?
IF IT WAS, WHAT THE HELL KINDA SAFETY MEASURES DID THE CONSTRUCTION COMPANY HAVE IN PLACE?
FIRST OF ALL, THEY WOULD NEVER STACK ANY UNNECESSARY STEEL FRAMES UP THERE.
YOU HEAR WHAT I'M SAYIN'?!
I DON'T QUITE UNDERSTAND WHAT YOU'RE...
ITORI, STOP...
SOMEBODY CLAIMS THEY SAW A FIGURE...
...ON TOP OF THE BUILDING THAT NIGHT. SOUNDS MYSTERIOUS, HUH?
THEN THE STEEL FRAMES FELL...

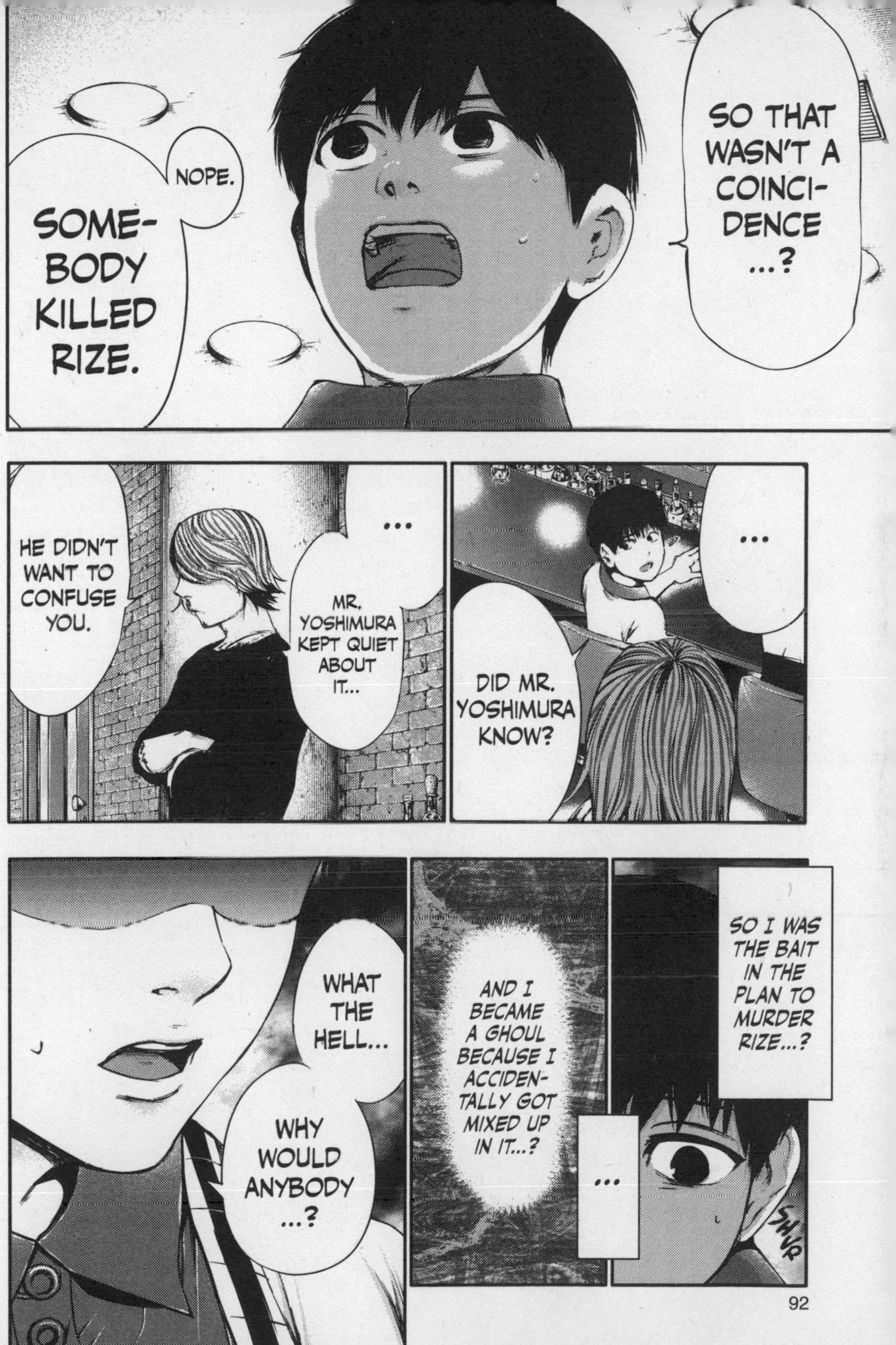
SO THAT WASN'T A COINCIDENCE ...?
NOPE.
SOMEBODY KILLED RIZE.
...
DID MR. YOSHIMURA KNOW?
...
MR. YOSHIMURA KEPT QUIET ABOUT IT...
HE DIDN'T WANT TO CONFUSE YOU.
SO I WAS THE BAIT IN THE PLAN TO MURDER RIZE...?
...
SHUR
AND I BECAME A GHOUL BECAUSE I ACCIDENTALLY GOT MIXED UP IN IT...?
WHAT THE HELL...
WHY WOULD ANYBODY ...?

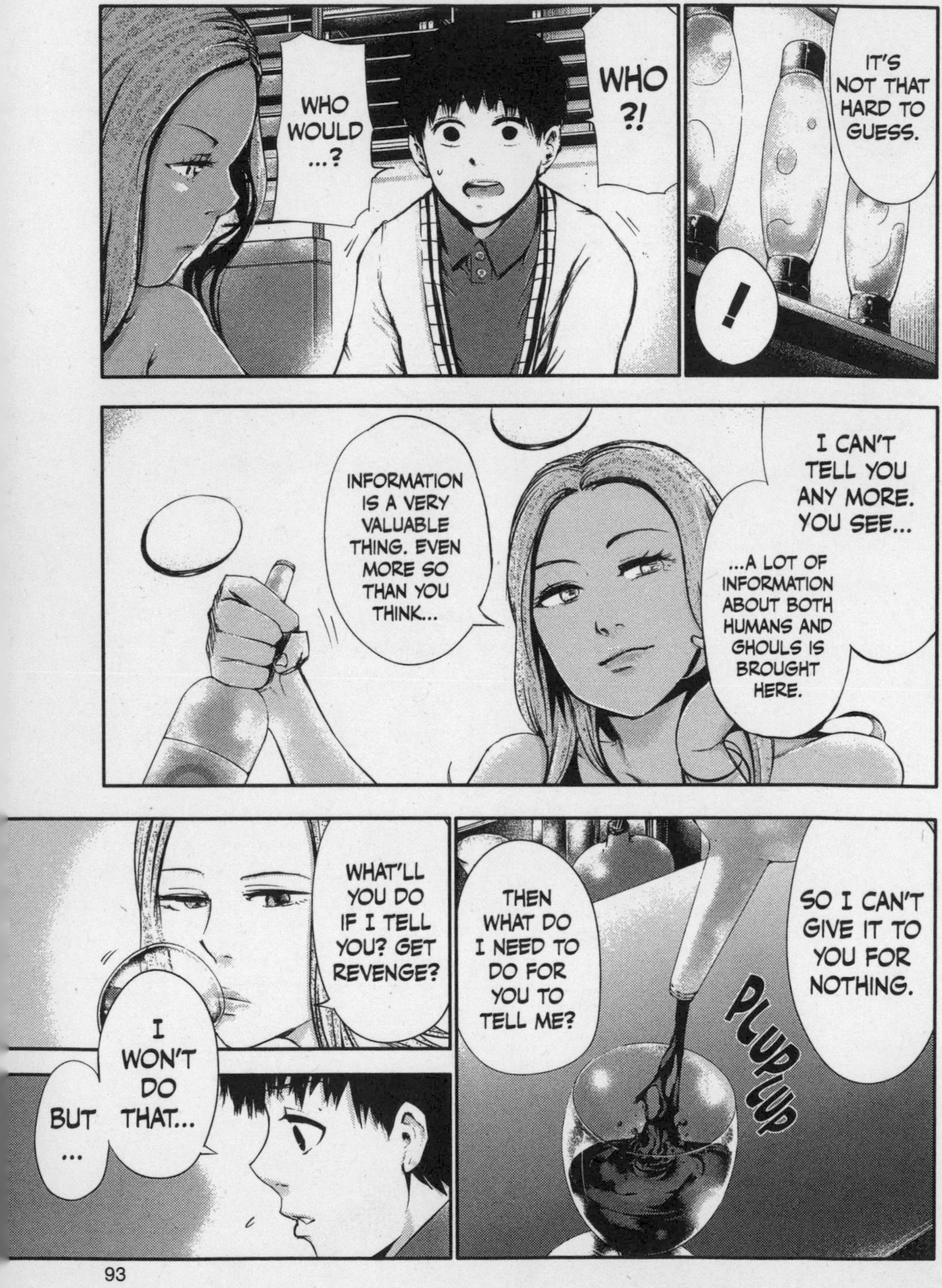
IT'S NOT THAT HARD TO GUESS.
!
WHO ?!
WHO WOULD ...?
I CAN'T TELL YOU ANY MORE. YOU SEE...
...A LOT OF INFORMATION ABOUT BOTH HUMANS AND GHOULS IS BROUGHT HERE.
INFORMATION IS A VERY VALUABLE THING. EVEN MORE SO THAN YOU THINK...
SO I CAN'T GIVE IT TO YOU FOR NOTHING.
PLUP PLUP
THEN WHAT DO I NEED TO DO FOR YOU TO TELL ME?
WHAT'LL YOU DO IF I TELL YOU? GET REVENGE?
I WON'T DO THAT...
BUT ...

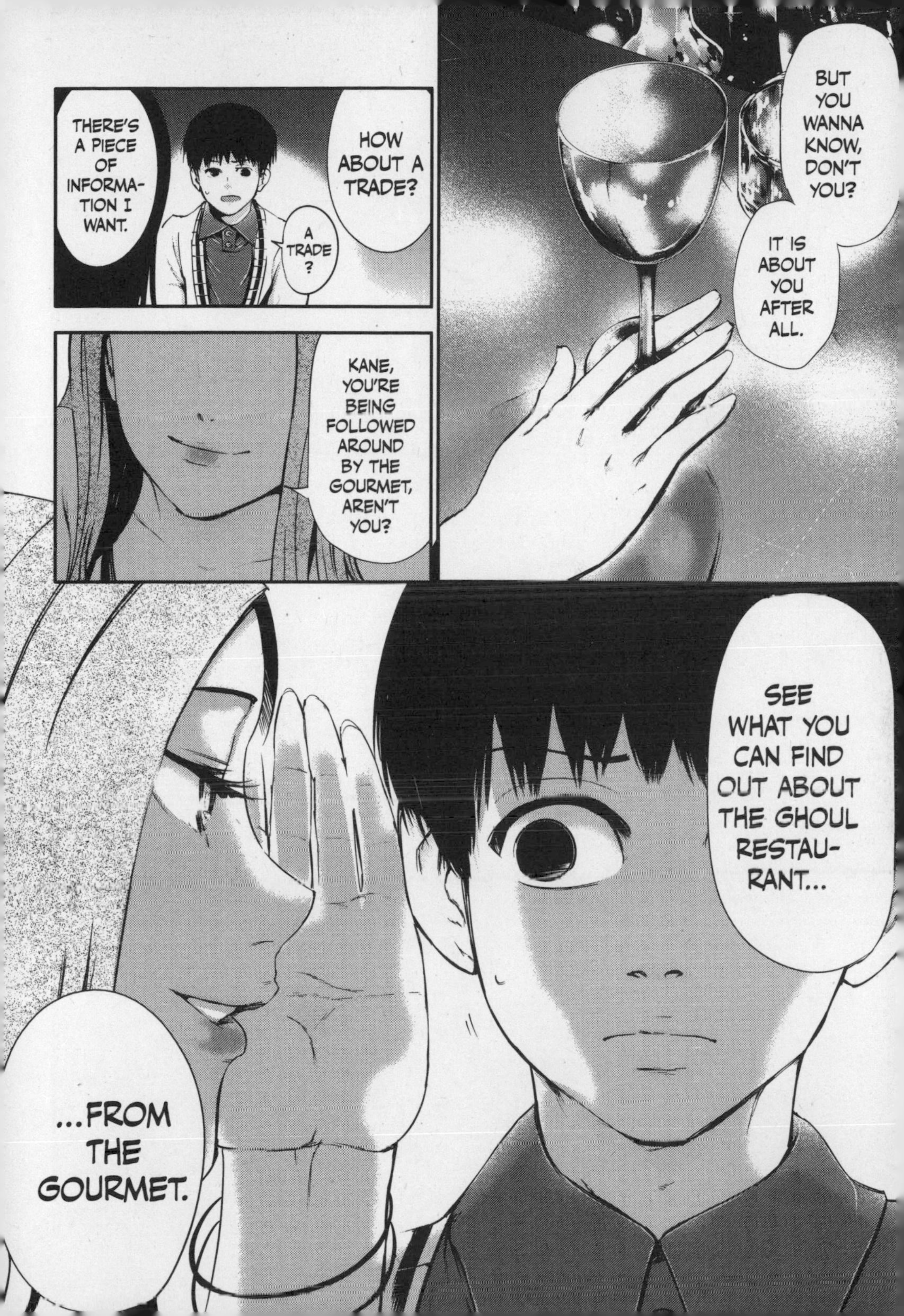
BUT YOU WANNA KNOW, DON'T YOU?
IT IS ABOUT YOU AFTER ALL.
HOW ABOUT A TRADE?
A TRADE?
THERE'S A PIECE OF INFORMATION I WANT.
KANE, YOU'RE BEING FOLLOWED AROUND BY THE GOURMET, AREN'T YOU?
SEE WHAT YOU CAN FIND OUT ABOUT THE GHOUL RESTAURANT...
...FROM THE GOURMET.

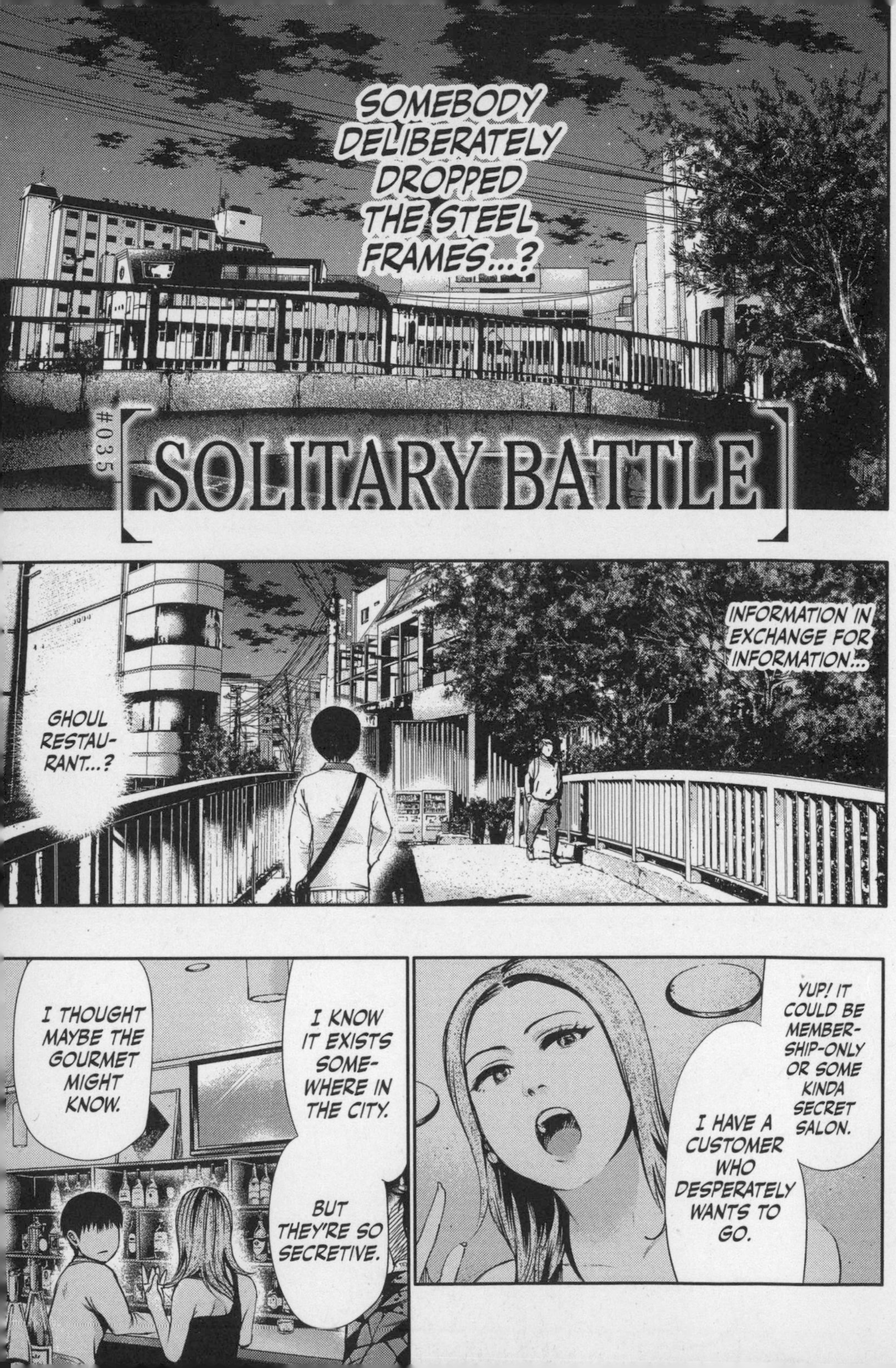
SOMEBODY DELIBERATELY DROPPED THE STEEL FRAMES...?
#035
SOLITARY BATTLE
INFORMATION IN EXCHANGE FOR INFORMATION...
GHOUL RESTAU-RANT...?
YUP! IT COULD BE MEMBER-SHIP-ONLY OR SOME KINDA SECRET SALON.
I HAVE A CUSTOMER WHO DESPERATELY WANTS TO GO.
I KNOW IT EXISTS SOME-WHERE IN THE CITY.
BUT THEY'RE SO SECRETIVE.
I THOUGHT MAYBE THE GOURMET MIGHT KNOW.

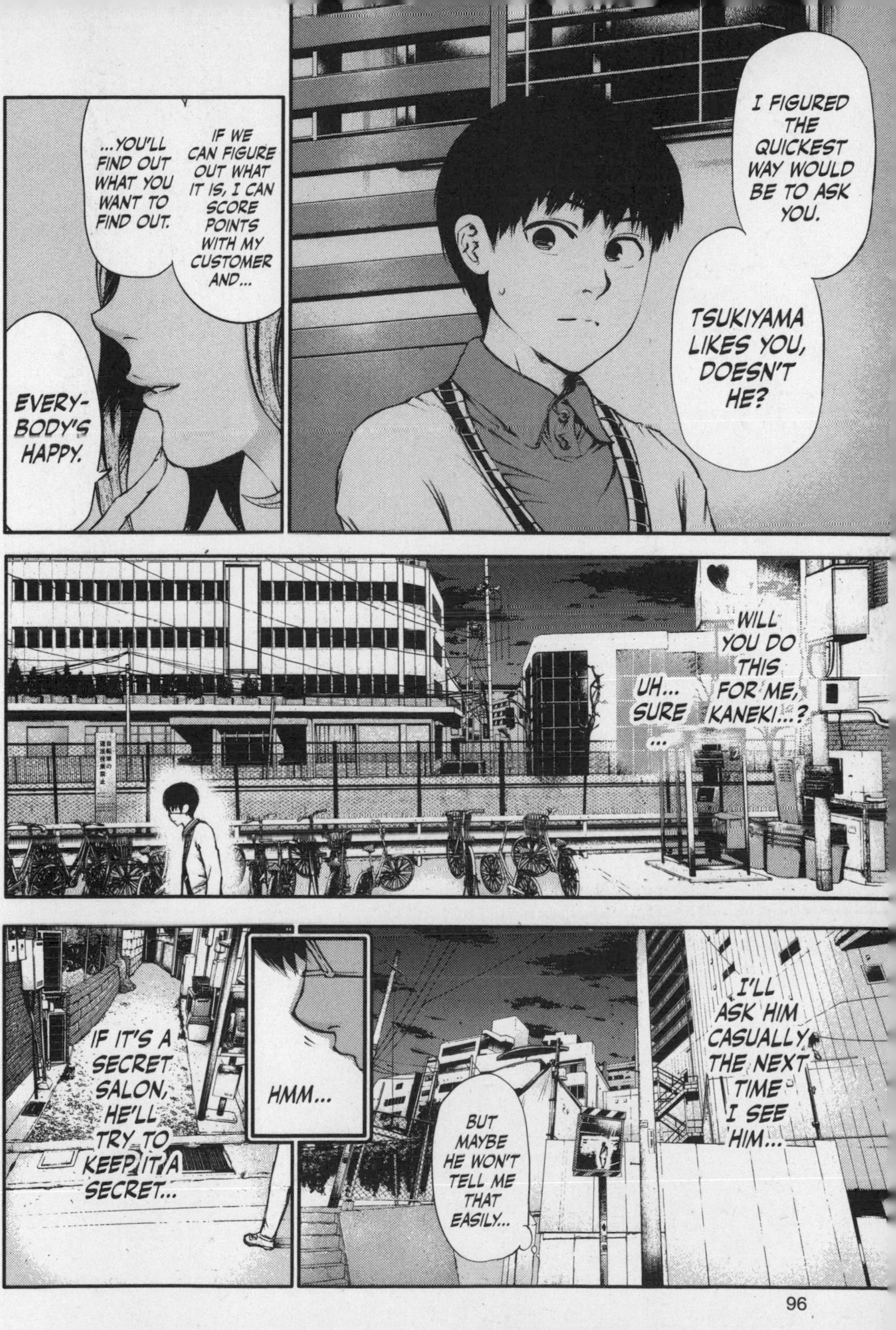
I FIGURED THE QUICKEST WAY WOULD BE TO ASK YOU.
TSUKIYAMA LIKES YOU, DOESN'T HE?
IF WE CAN FIGURE OUT WHAT IT IS, I CAN SCORE POINTS WITH MY CUSTOMER AND...
...YOU'LL FIND OUT WHAT YOU WANT TO FIND OUT.
EVERY-BODY'S HAPPY.
WILL YOU DO THIS FOR ME, KANEKI...?
UH... SURE...
I'LL ASK HIM CASUALLY THE NEXT TIME I SEE HIM...
BUT MAYBE HE WON'T TELL ME THAT EASILY...
HMM...
IF IT'S A SECRET SALON, HE'LL TRY TO KEEP IT A SECRET...

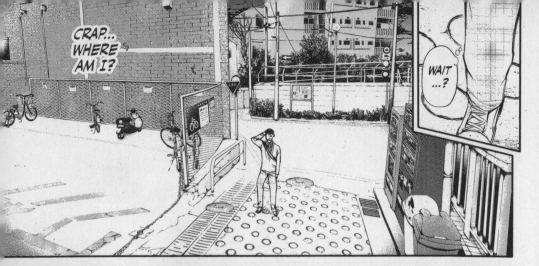

CRAP... WHERE AM I?

WAIT ...?

SHOOT ...

... PREY... ...YOU ...

I WASN'T THINKING ABOUT WHERE I WAS GOING...

A FIGHT ...?

TkAkkS

WHUD

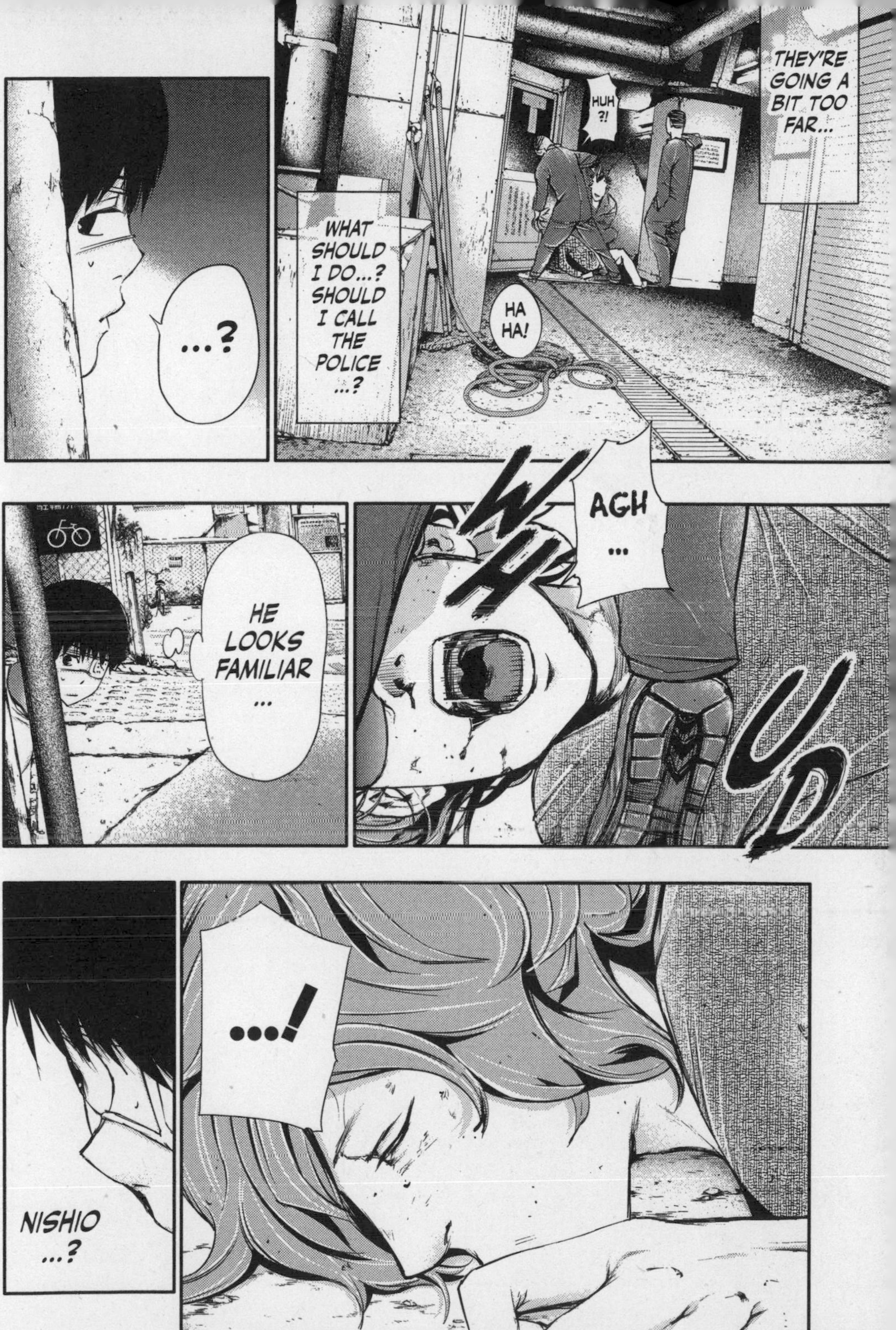
THEY'RE GOING A BIT TOO FAR...
HUH ?!
HA HA!
WHAT SHOULD I DO...? SHOULD I CALL THE POLICE ...?
...?
AGH ...
WHUD
HE LOOKS FAMILIAR ...
...!
NISHIO ...?

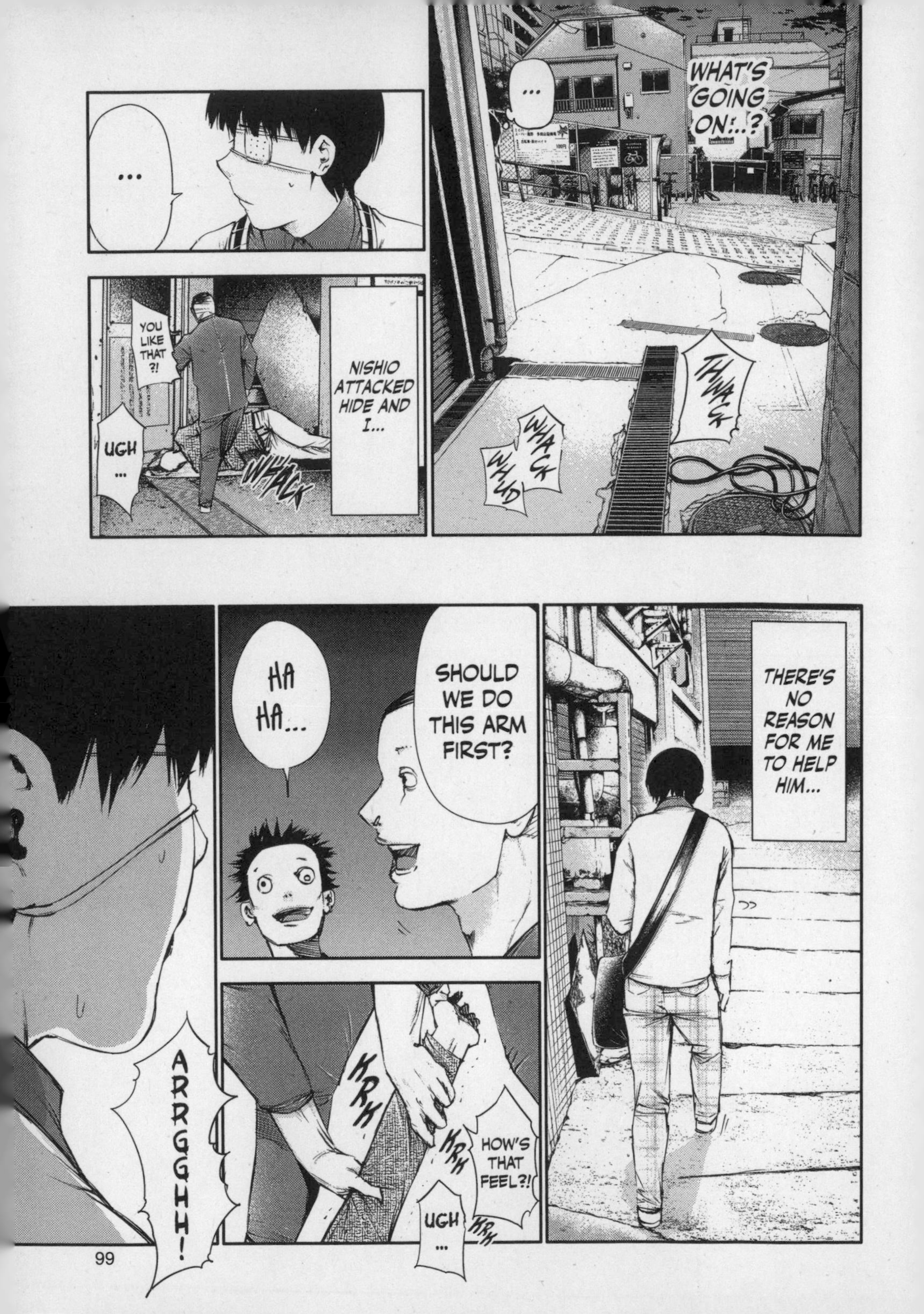
WHAT'S GOING ON...?
...
THWACK
WHACK
WHUD
...
NISHIO ATTACKED HIDE AND I...
YOU LIKE THAT?!
UGH...
WHACK
THERE'S NO REASON FOR ME TO HELP HIM...
SHOULD WE DO THIS ARM FIRST?
HA HA...
KRK
KRK
HOW'S THAT FEEL?!
UGH...
KRK
ARRGGHH!

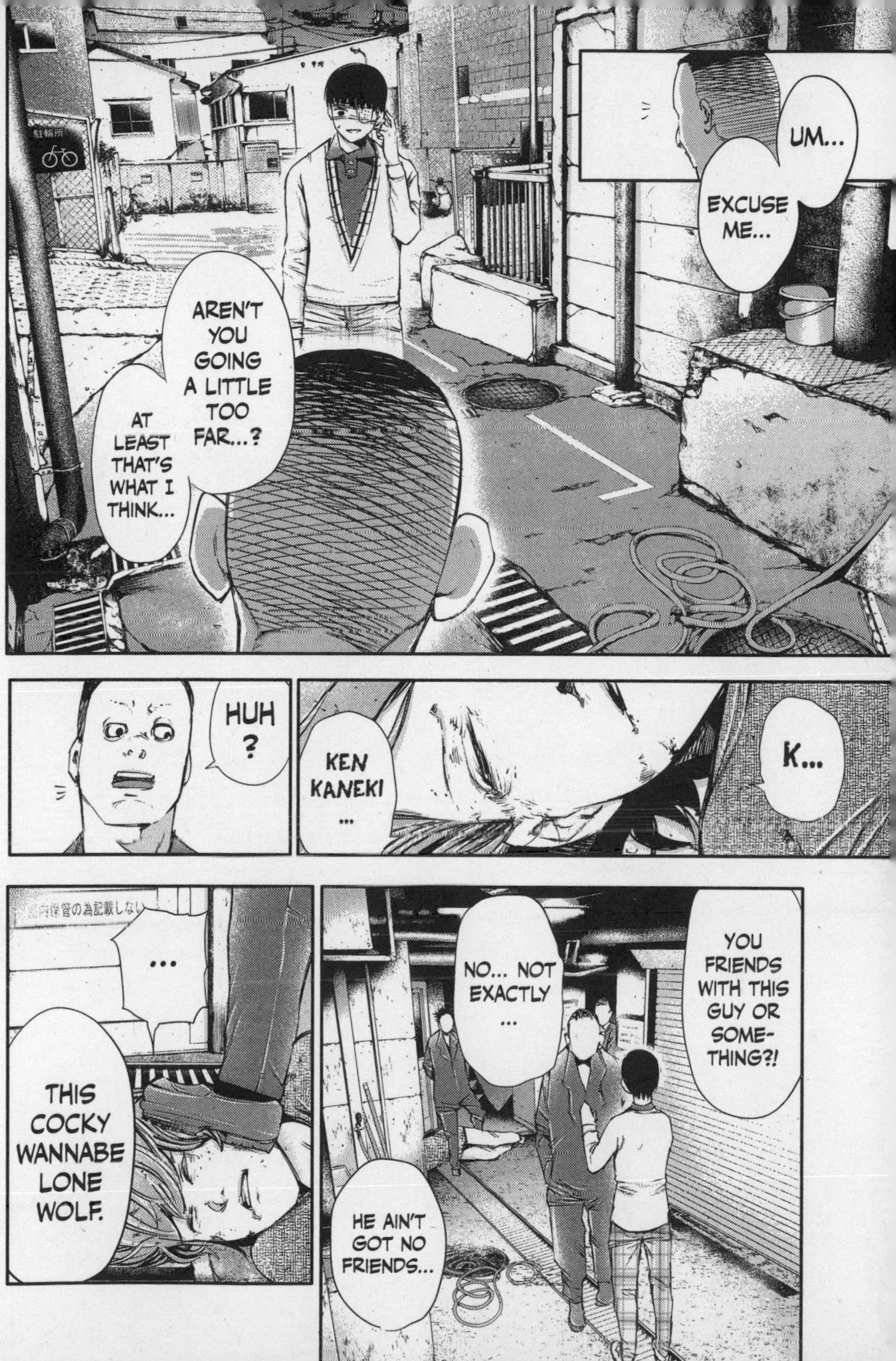
UM...
EXCUSE ME...
AREN'T YOU GOING A LITTLE TOO FAR...?
AT LEAST THAT'S WHAT I THINK...
駐輪所
K...
KEN KANEKI ...
HUH ?
YOU FRIENDS WITH THIS GUY OR SOME-THING?!
NO... NOT EXACTLY ...
HE AIN'T GOT NO FRIENDS...
...
THIS COCKY WANNABE LONE WOLF.

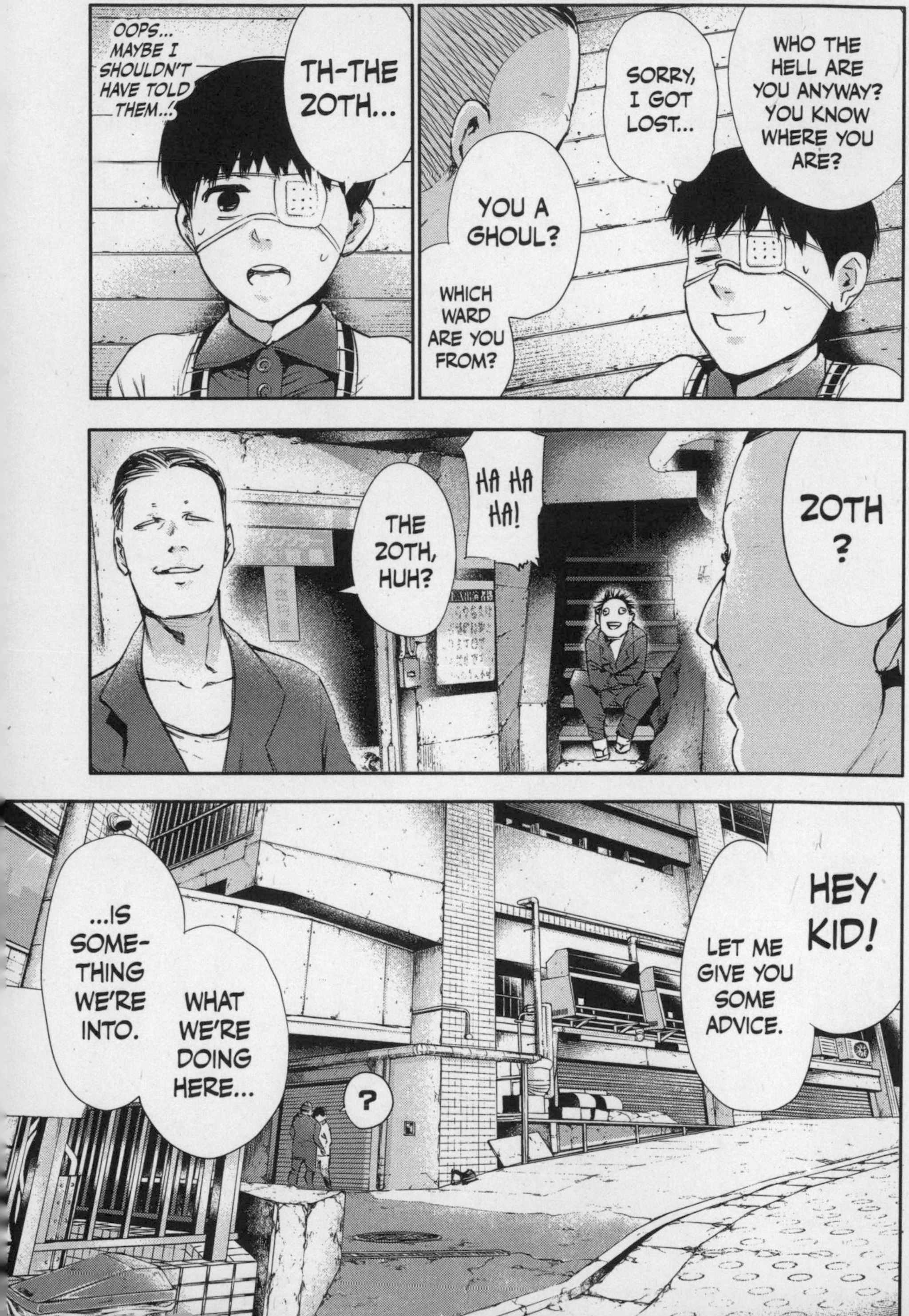
WHO THE HELL ARE YOU ANYWAY? YOU KNOW WHERE YOU ARE?
SORRY, I GOT LOST...
YOU A GHOUL?
WHICH WARD ARE YOU FROM?
TH-THE 20TH...
OOPS... MAYBE I SHOULDN'T HAVE TOLD THEM..!
20TH ?
HA HA HA!
THE 20TH, HUH?
HEY KID!
LET ME GIVE YOU SOME ADVICE.
?
WHAT WE'RE DOING HERE...
...IS SOME-THING WE'RE INTO.

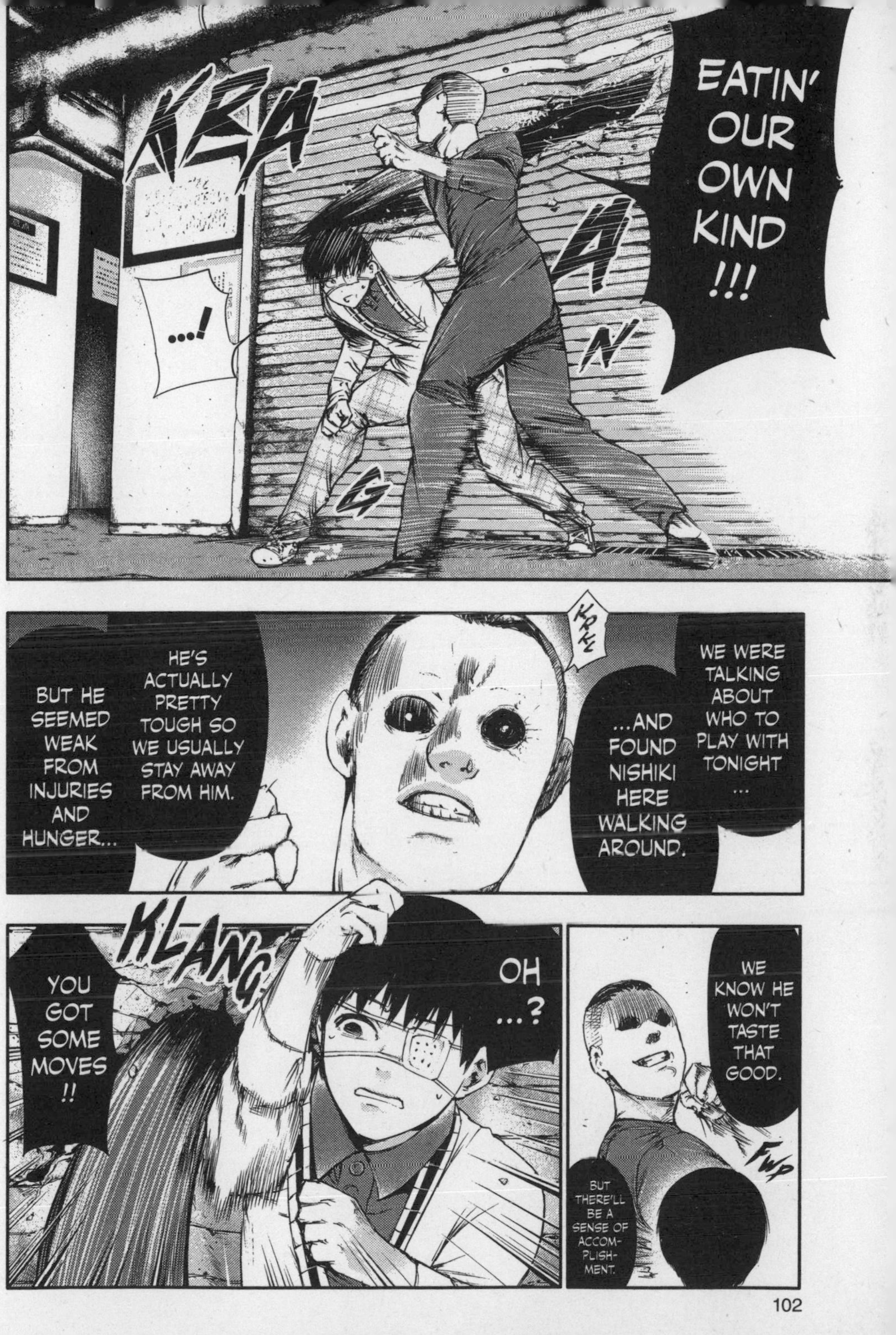
EATIN' OUR OWN KIND !!!
KRAANG
...!
WE WERE TALKING ABOUT WHO TO PLAY WITH TONIGHT ...
...AND FOUND NISHIKI HERE WALKING AROUND.
HE'S ACTUALLY PRETTY TOUGH SO WE USUALLY STAY AWAY FROM HIM.
BUT HE SEEMED WEAK FROM INJURIES AND HUNGER...
WE KNOW HE WON'T TASTE THAT GOOD.
FWP
BUT THERE'LL BE A SENSE OF ACCOMPLISHMENT.
KLANG
OH ...?
YOU GOT SOME MOVES !!

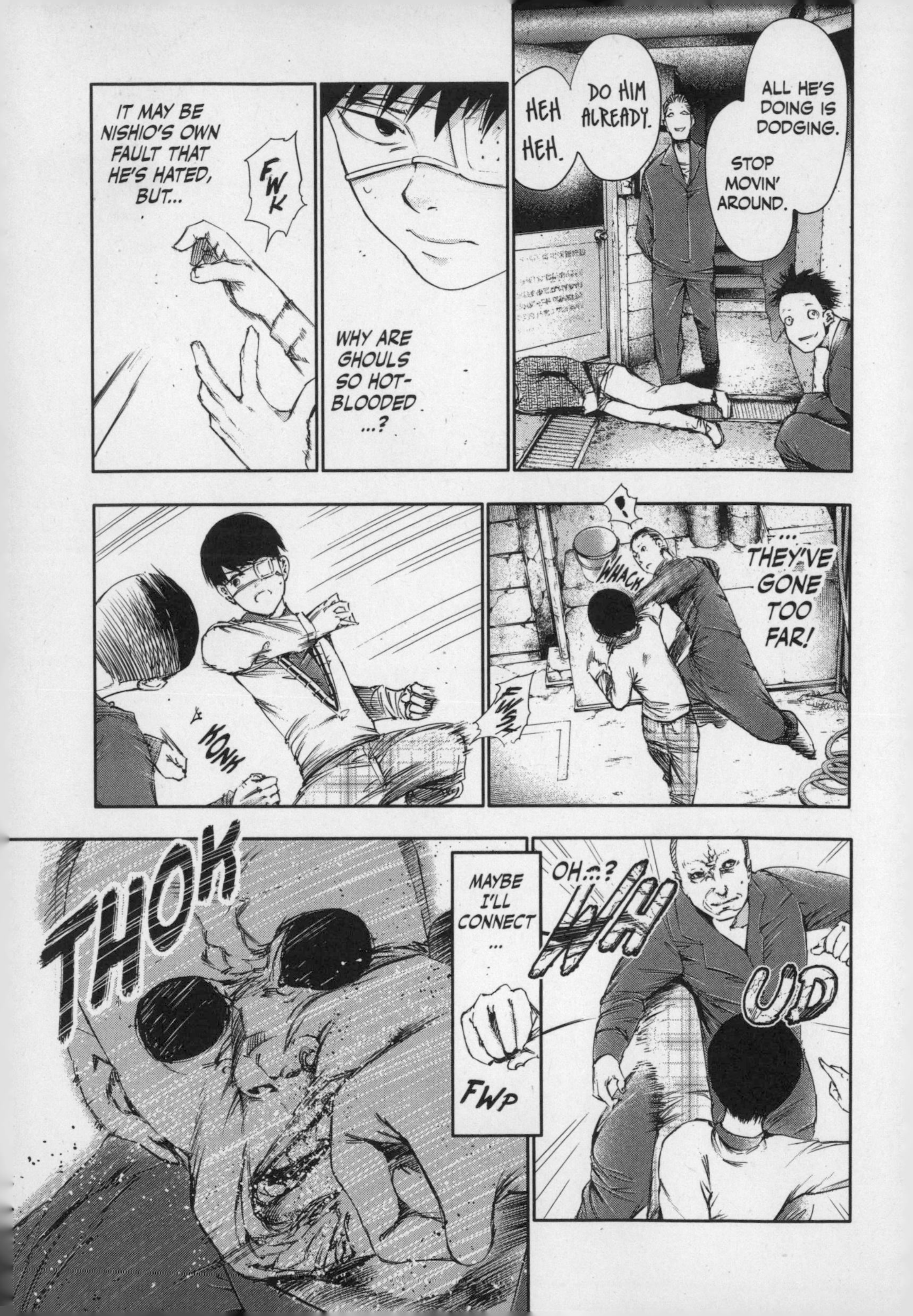
ALL HE'S DOING IS DODGING.
STOP MOVIN' AROUND.
DO HIM ALREADY.
HEH HEH.
WHY ARE GHOULS SO HOT-BLOODED ...?
IT MAY BE NISHIO'S OWN FAULT THAT HE'S HATED, BUT...
FWK
!
...THEY'VE GONE TOO FAR!
WHACK
HONK
OH...?
WH
UD
MAYBE I'LL CONNECT ...
FWP
THOK

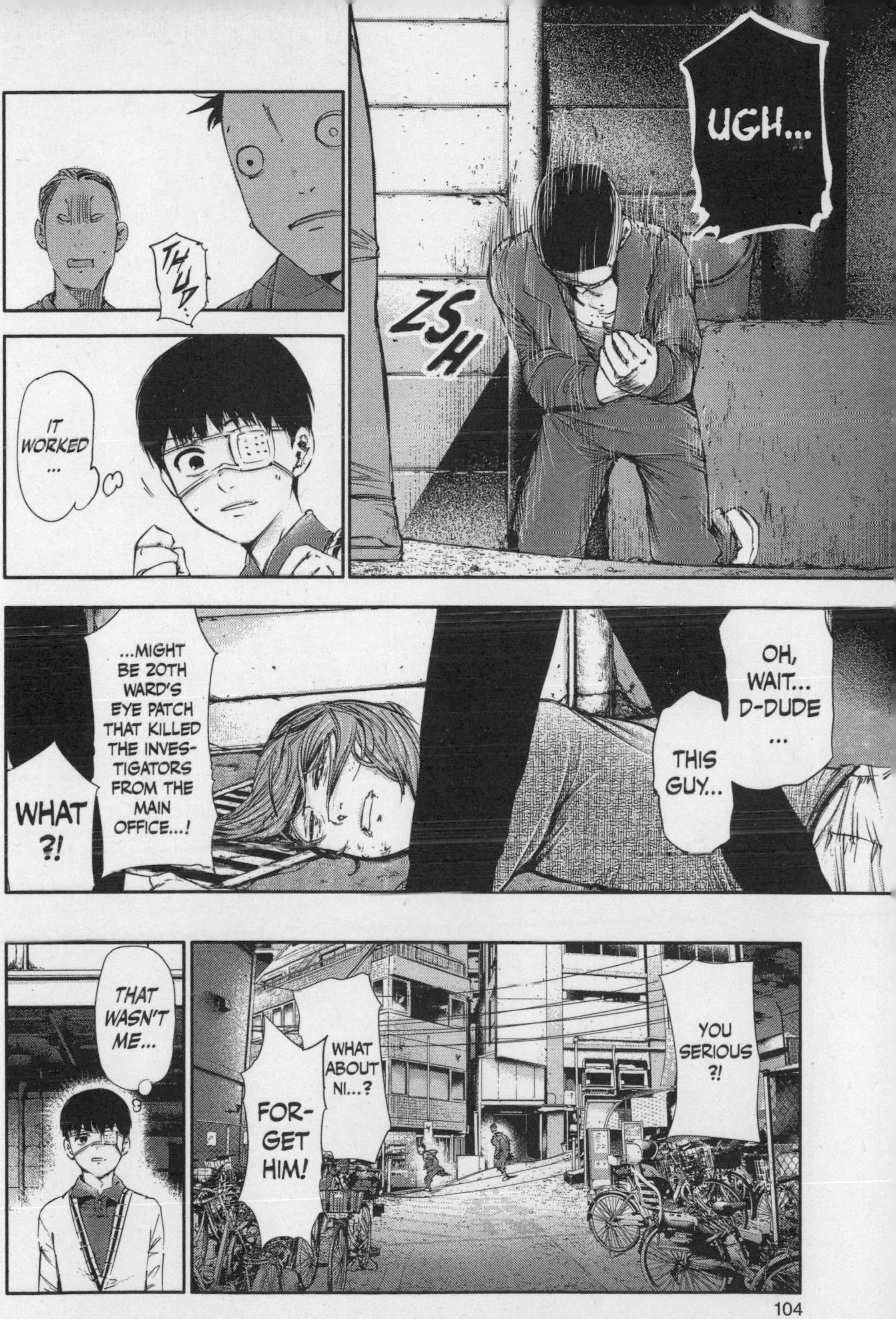
UGH...
ZSH
THUD
IT WORKED...
OH, WAIT... D-DUDE...
THIS GUY...
...MIGHT BE 20TH WARD'S EYE PATCH THAT KILLED THE INVESTIGATORS FROM THE MAIN OFFICE...!
WHAT?!
YOU SERIOUS?!
WHAT ABOUT NI...?
FORGET HIM!
THAT WASN'T ME...

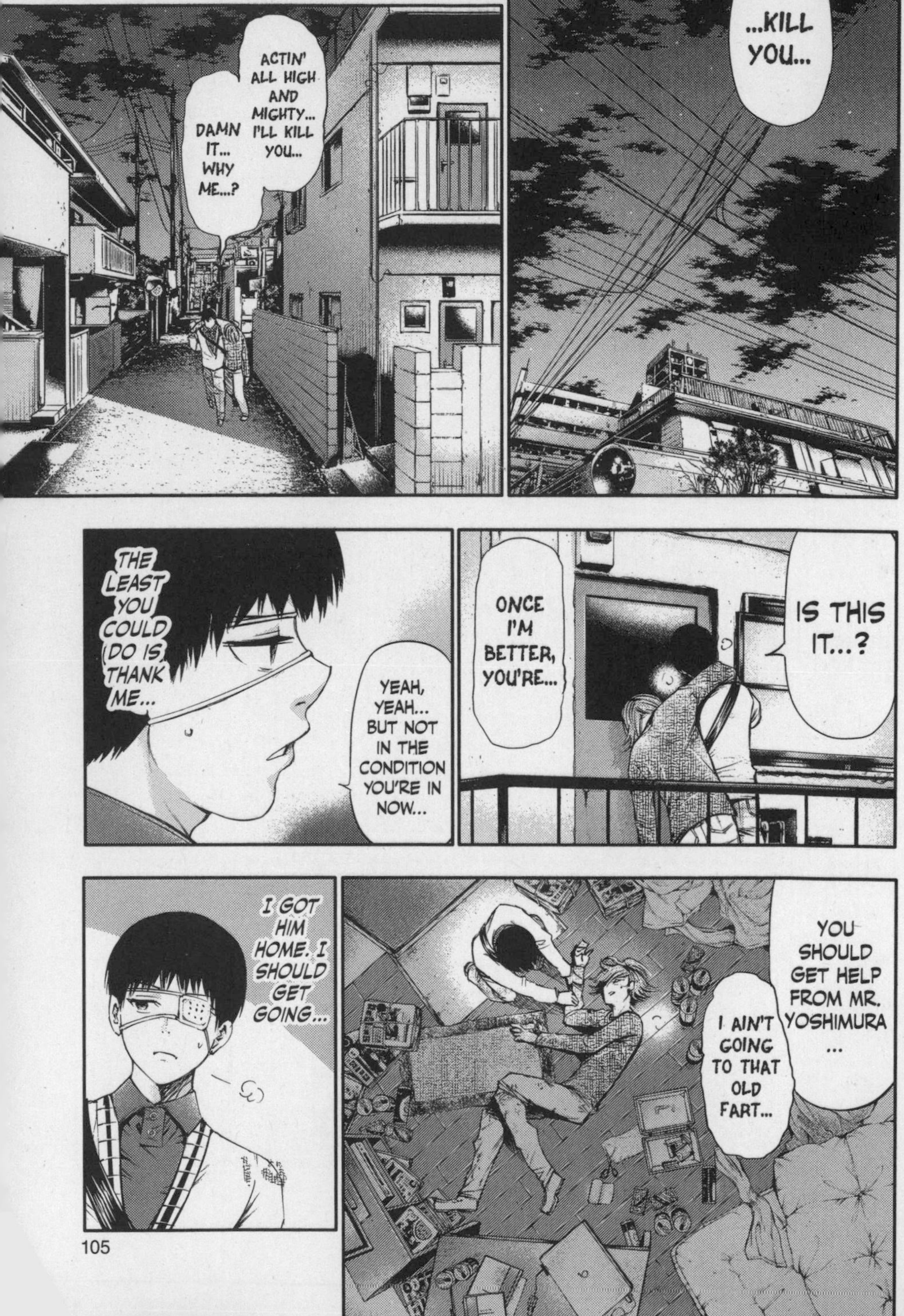
...KILL YOU...
ACTIN' ALL HIGH AND MIGHTY... I'LL KILL YOU...
DAMN IT... WHY ME...?
IS THIS IT...?
ONCE I'M BETTER, YOU'RE...
YEAH, YEAH... BUT NOT IN THE CONDITION YOU'RE IN NOW...
THE LEAST YOU COULD DO IS THANK ME...
YOU SHOULD GET HELP FROM MR. YOSHIMURA...
I AIN'T GOING TO THAT OLD FART...
I GOT HIM HOME. I SHOULD GET GOING...

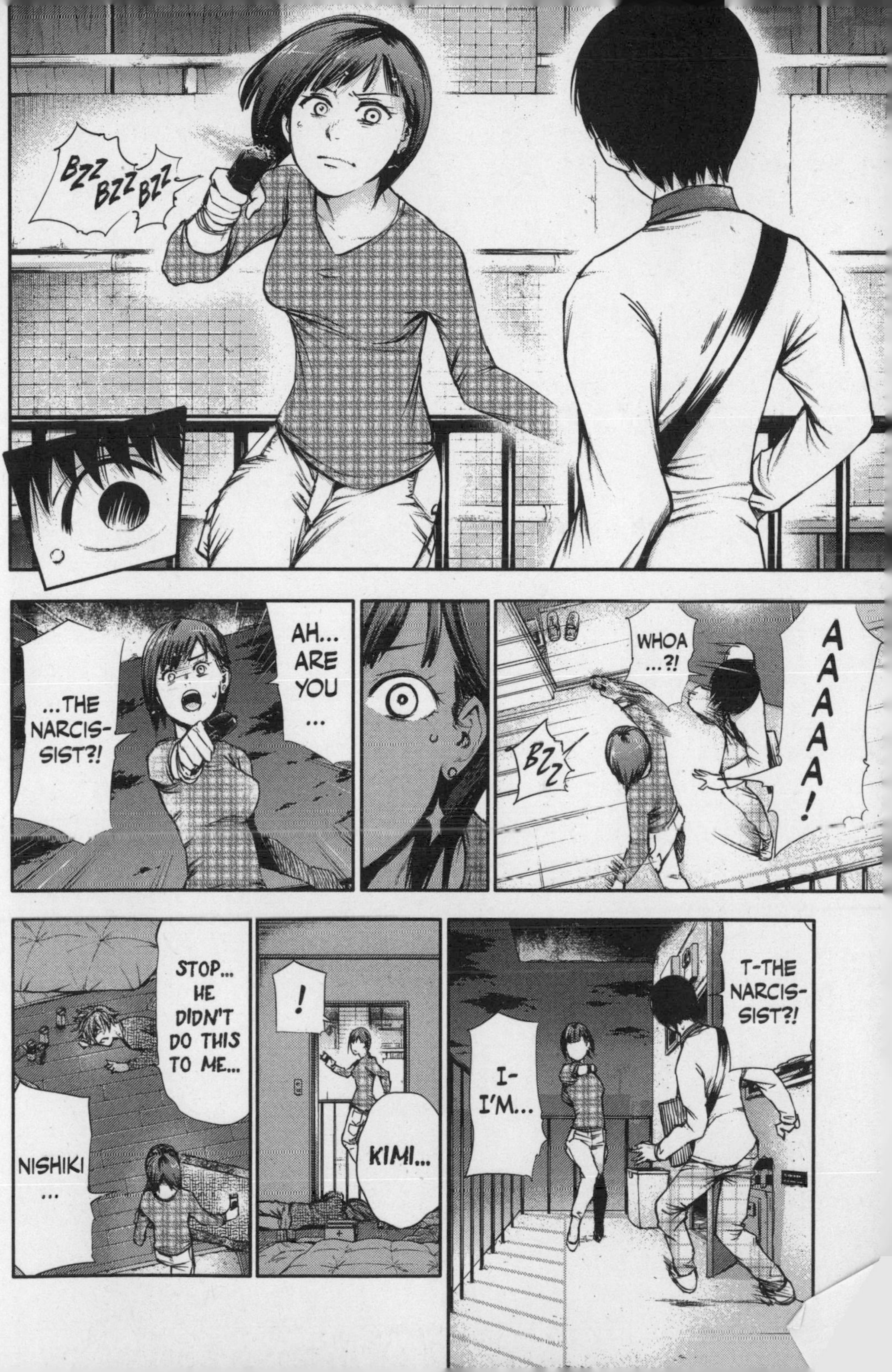
BZZ BZZ BZZ
AAAAAA!
WHOA ...?!
BZZ
AH... ARE YOU ...
...THE NARCIS-SIST?!
T-THE NARCIS-SIST?!
I- I'M...
!
KIMI...
STOP... HE DIDN'T DO THIS TO ME...
NISHIKI ...

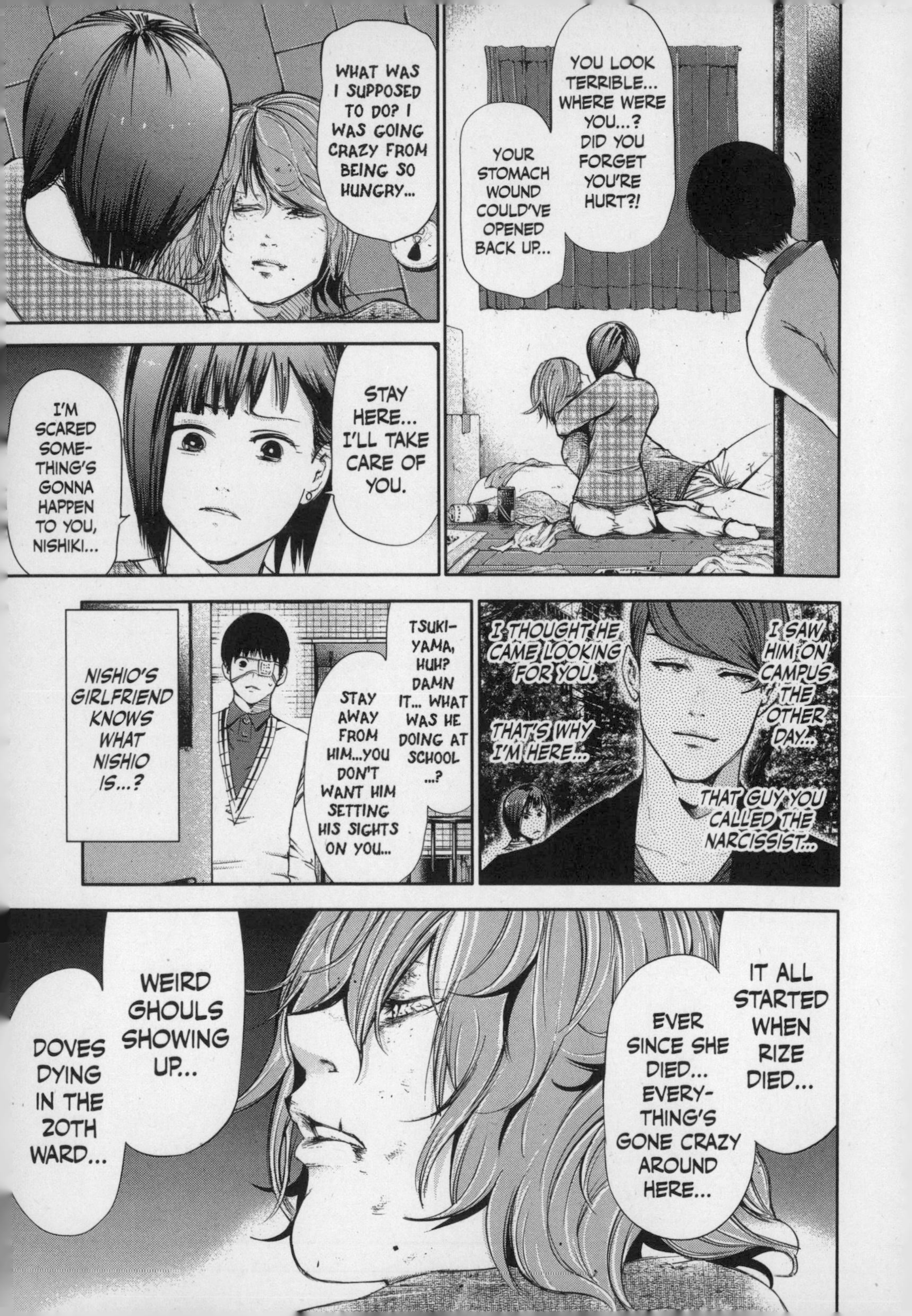
YOU LOOK TERRIBLE... WHERE WERE YOU...? DID YOU FORGET YOU'RE HURT?!
YOUR STOMACH WOUND COULD'VE OPENED BACK UP...
WHAT WAS I SUPPOSED TO DO? I WAS GOING CRAZY FROM BEING SO HUNGRY...
STAY HERE... I'LL TAKE CARE OF YOU.
I'M SCARED SOME-THING'S GONNA HAPPEN TO YOU, NISHIKI...
I SAW HIM ON CAMPUS THE OTHER DAY...
THAT GUY YOU CALLED THE NARCISSIST...
I THOUGHT HE CAME LOOKING FOR YOU.
THAT'S WHY I'M HERE...
TSUKI-YAMA, HUH? DAMN IT... WHAT WAS HE DOING AT SCHOOL ...?
STAY AWAY FROM HIM...YOU DON'T WANT HIM SETTING HIS SIGHTS ON YOU...
NISHIO'S GIRLFRIEND KNOWS WHAT NISHIO IS...?
IT ALL STARTED WHEN RIZE DIED...
EVER SINCE SHE DIED... EVERY-THING'S GONE CRAZY AROUND HERE...
WEIRD GHOULS SHOWING UP...
DOVES DYING IN THE 20TH WARD...

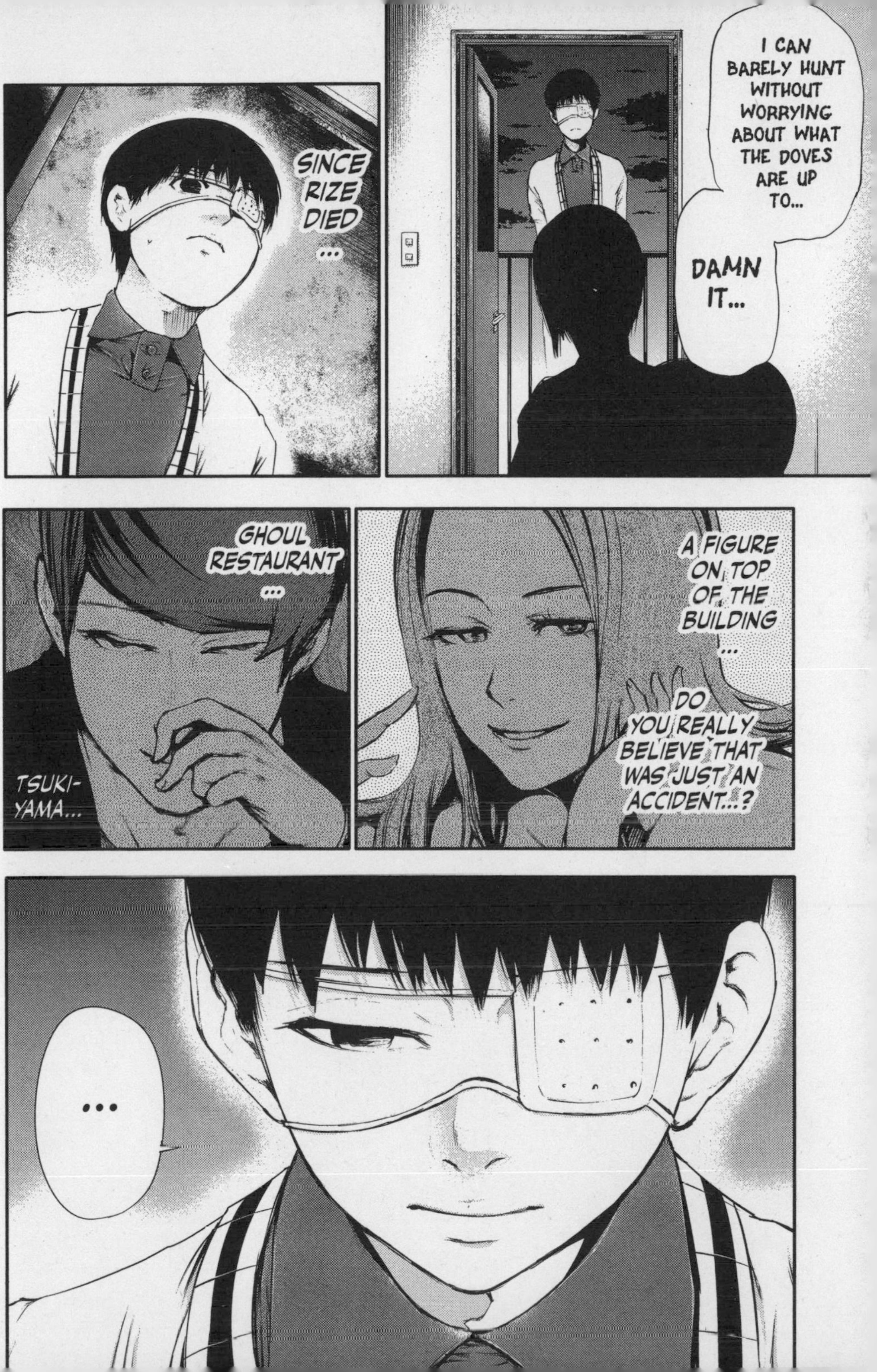
I CAN BARELY HUNT WITHOUT WORRYING ABOUT WHAT THE DOVES ARE UP TO...
DAMN IT...
SINCE RIZE DIED ...
A FIGURE ON TOP OF THE BUILDING ...
DO YOU REALLY BELIEVE THAT WAS JUST AN ACCIDENT...?
GHOUL RESTAURANT ...
TSUKI-YAMA...
...

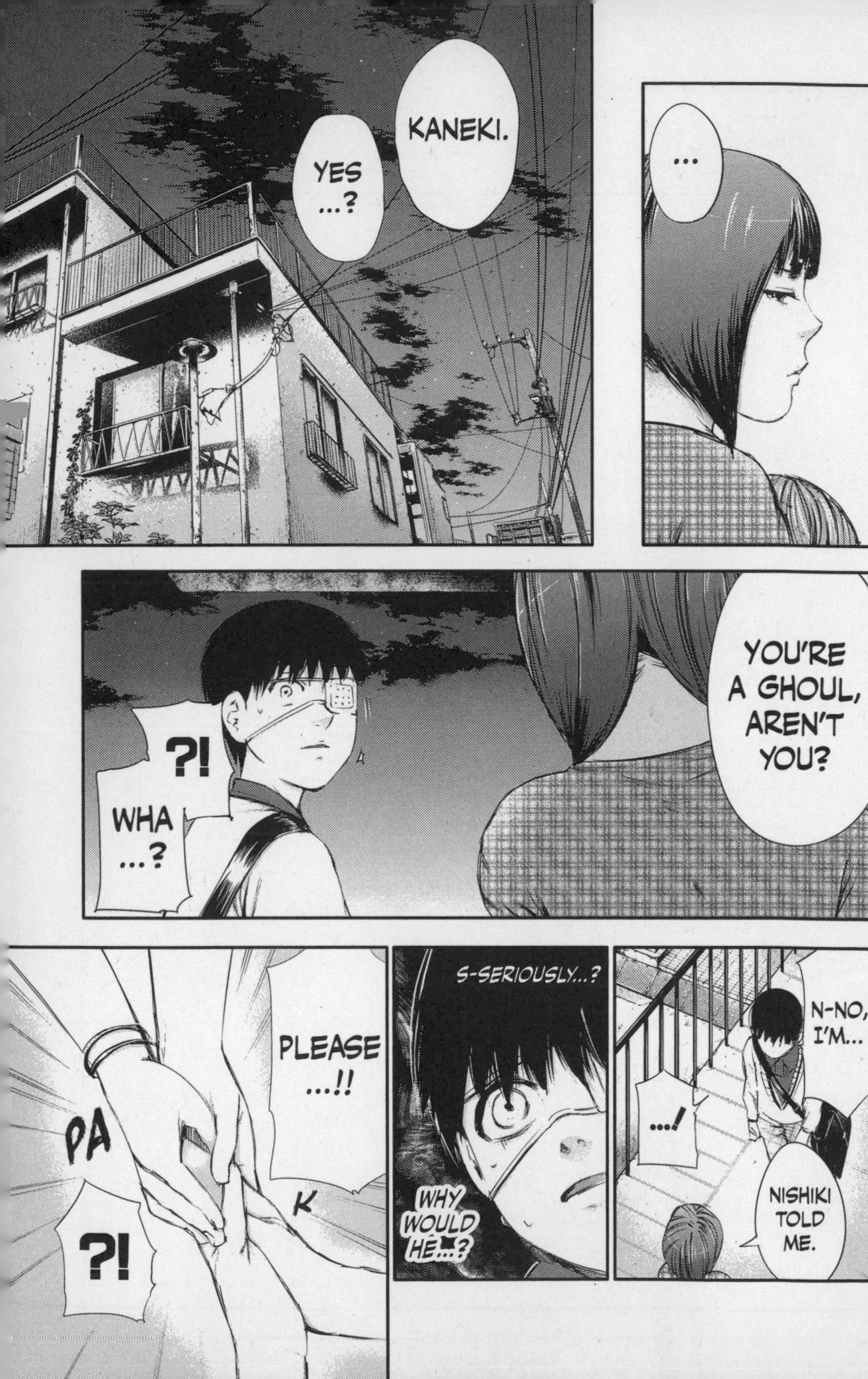
...
KANEKI.
YES ...?
YOU'RE A GHOUL, AREN'T YOU?
?!
WHA ...?
N-NO, I'M...
...!
NISHIKI TOLD ME.
S-SERIOUSLY...?
WHY WOULD HE...?
PLEASE ...!!
PA
K
?!

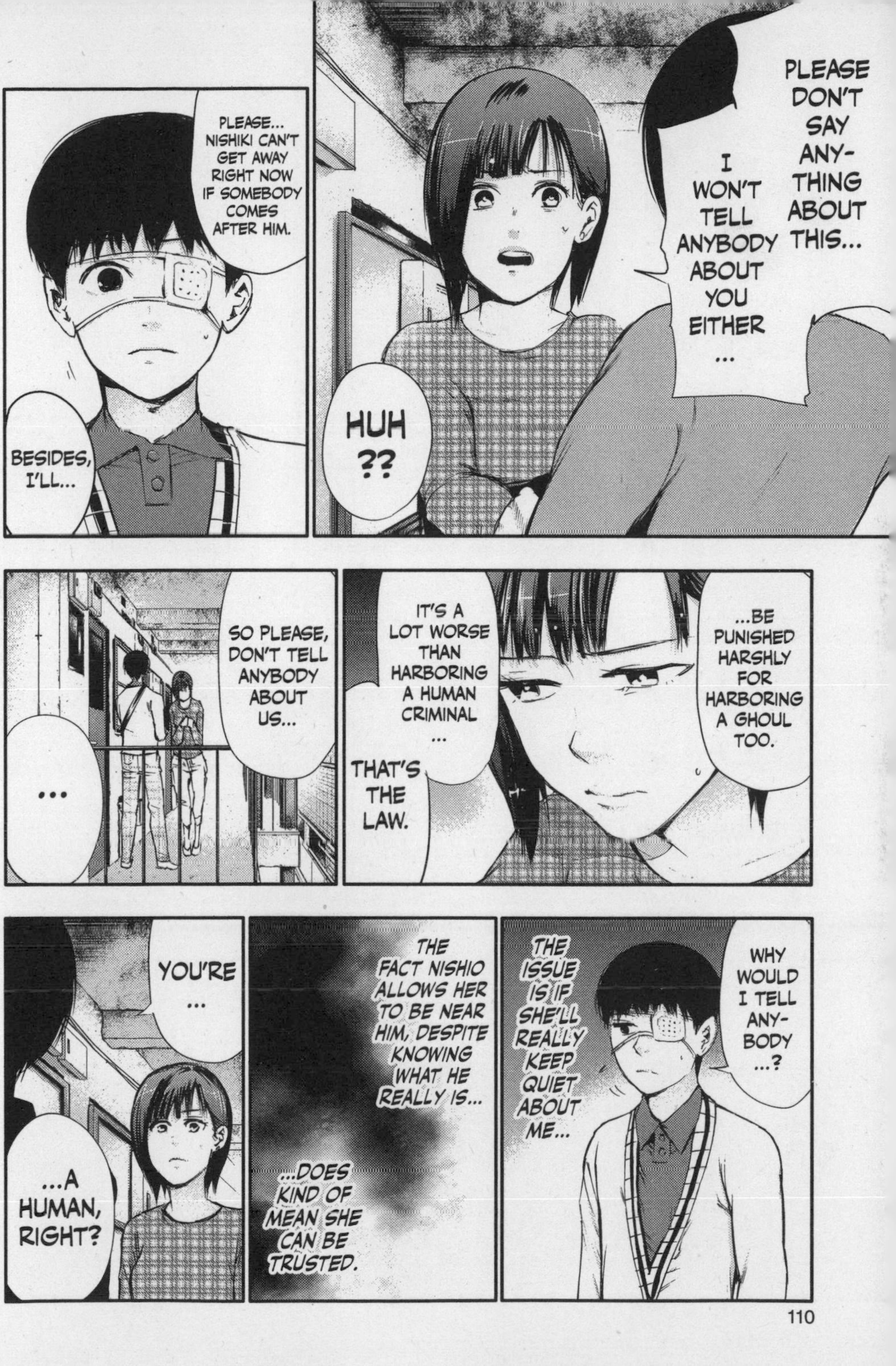
PLEASE DON'T SAY ANYTHING ABOUT THIS...
I WON'T TELL ANYBODY ABOUT YOU EITHER ...
HUH ??
PLEASE... NISHIKI CAN'T GET AWAY RIGHT NOW IF SOMEBODY COMES AFTER HIM.
BESIDES, I'LL...
...BE PUNISHED HARSHLY FOR HARBORING A GHOUL TOO.
IT'S A LOT WORSE THAN HARBORING A HUMAN CRIMINAL ...
THAT'S THE LAW.
SO PLEASE, DON'T TELL ANYBODY ABOUT US...
...
WHY WOULD I TELL ANYBODY ...?
THE ISSUE IS IF SHE'LL REALLY KEEP QUIET ABOUT ME...
THE FACT NISHIO ALLOWS HER TO BE NEAR HIM, DESPITE KNOWING WHAT HE REALLY IS...
...DOES KIND OF MEAN SHE CAN BE TRUSTED.
YOU'RE ...
...A HUMAN, RIGHT?

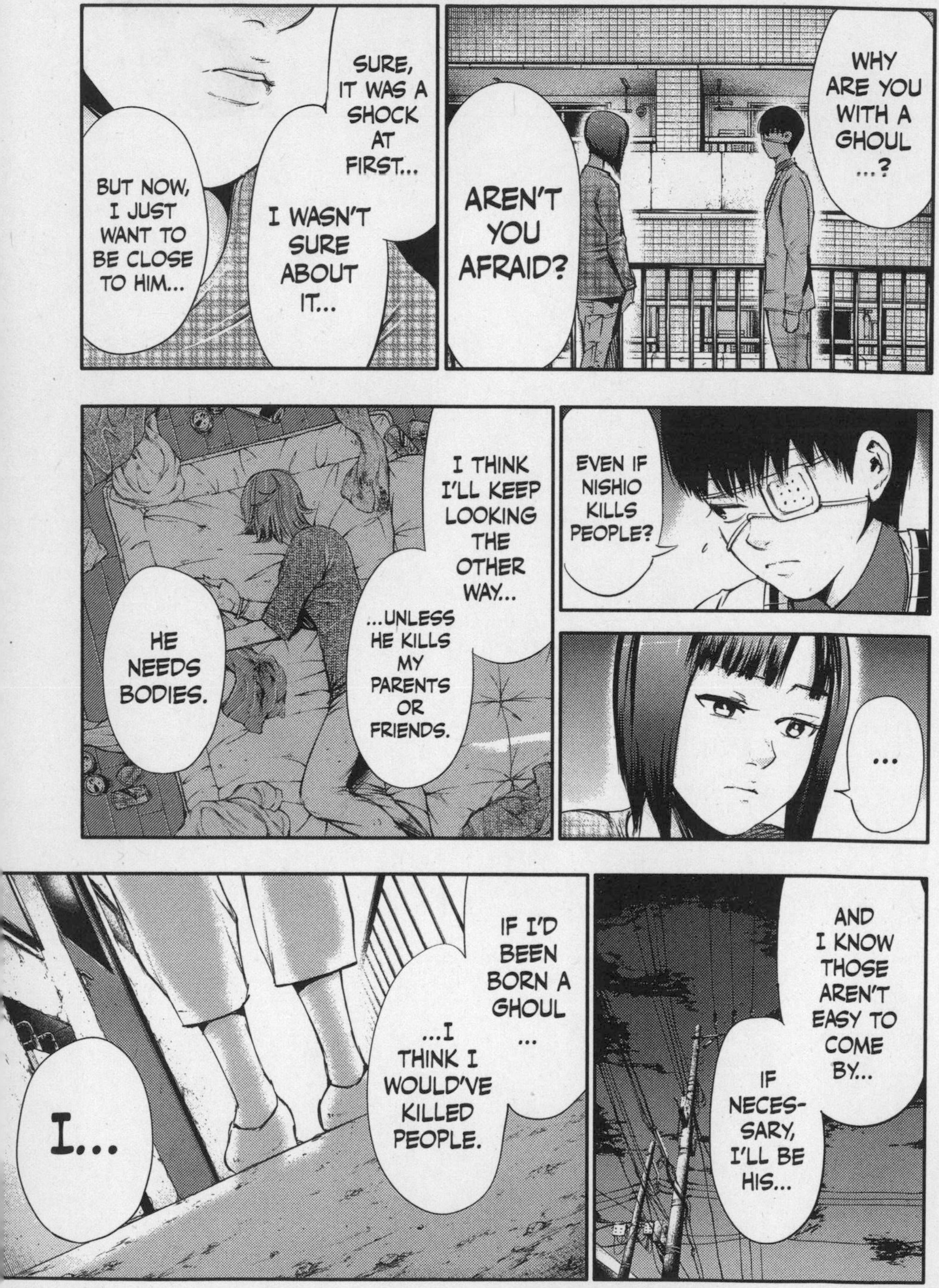
WHY ARE YOU WITH A GHOUL ...?
AREN'T YOU AFRAID?
SURE, IT WAS A SHOCK AT FIRST...
I WASN'T SURE ABOUT IT...
BUT NOW, I JUST WANT TO BE CLOSE TO HIM...
EVEN IF NISHIO KILLS PEOPLE?
...
I THINK I'LL KEEP LOOKING THE OTHER WAY...
...UNLESS HE KILLS MY PARENTS OR FRIENDS.
HE NEEDS BODIES.
AND I KNOW THOSE AREN'T EASY TO COME BY...
IF NECES-SARY, I'LL BE HIS...
IF I'D BEEN BORN A GHOUL ...
...I THINK I WOULD'VE KILLED PEOPLE.
I...

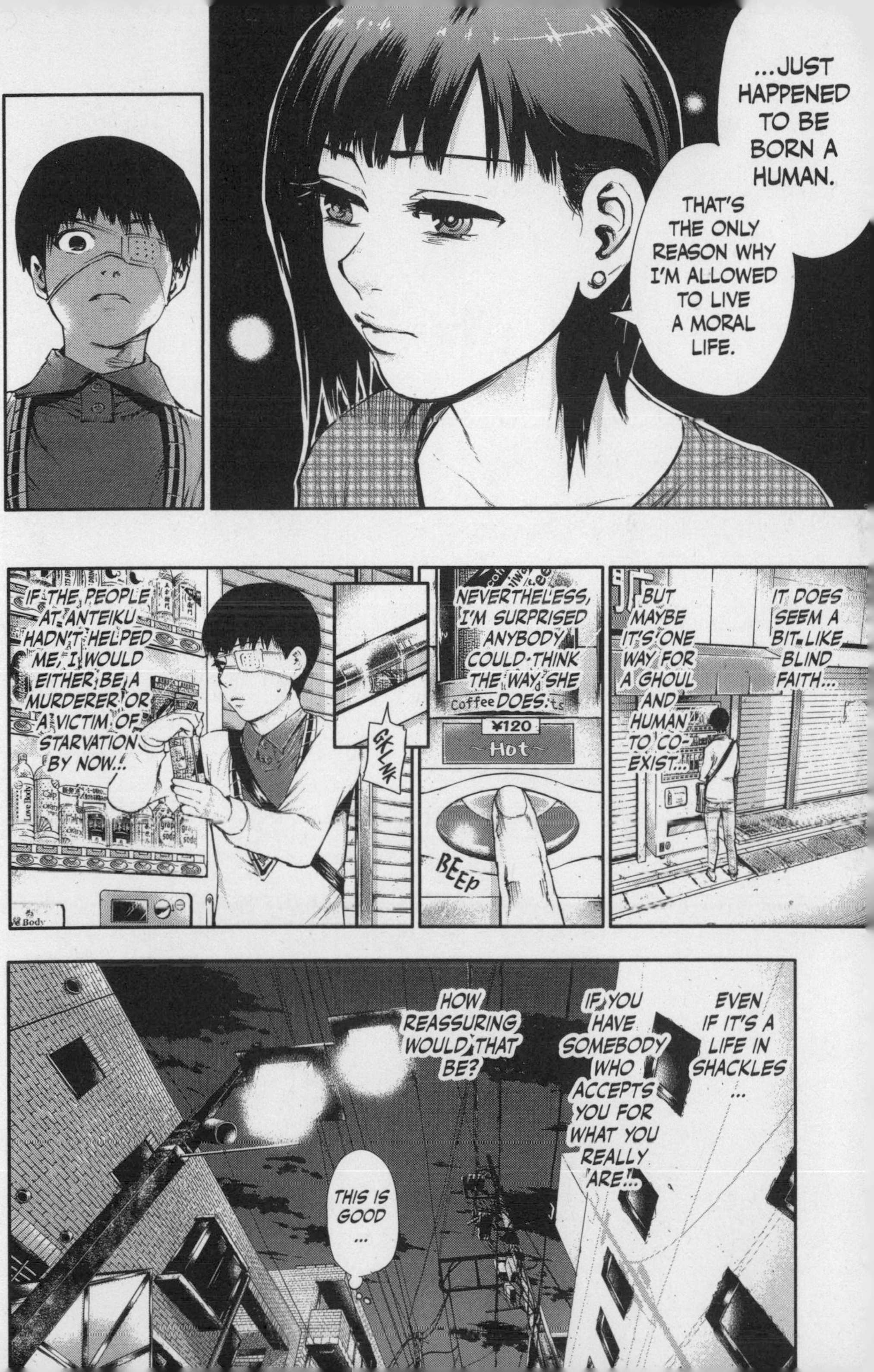
...JUST HAPPENED TO BE BORN A HUMAN.
THAT'S THE ONLY REASON WHY I'M ALLOWED TO LIVE A MORAL LIFE.
IT DOES SEEM A BIT LIKE BLIND FAITH...
BUT MAYBE IT'S ONE WAY FOR A GHOUL AND HUMAN TO CO-EXIST...
NEVERTHELESS, I'M SURPRISED ANYBODY COULD THINK THE WAY SHE DOES.
Coffee
¥120
Hot
BEEp
GKLNK
IF THE PEOPLE AT ANTEIKU HADN'T HELPED ME, I WOULD EITHER BE A MURDERER OR A VICTIM OF STARVATION BY NOW...
EVEN IF IT'S A LIFE IN SHACKLES...
IF YOU HAVE SOMEBODY WHO ACCEPTS YOU FOR WHAT YOU REALLY ARE...
HOW REASSURING WOULD THAT BE?
THIS IS GOOD...

#036
TOKYO GHOUL

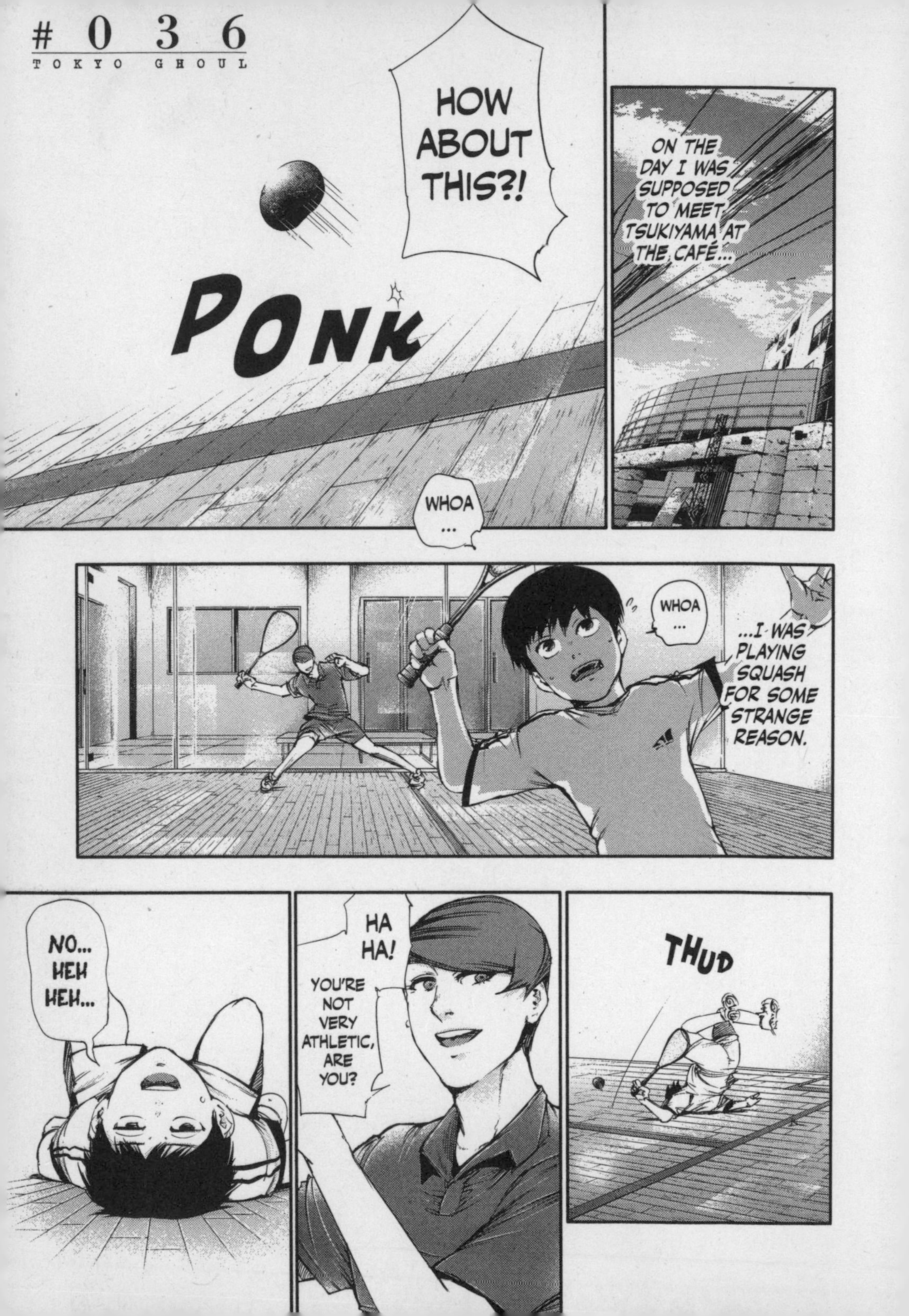

ON THE DAY I WAS SUPPOSED TO MEET TSUKIYAMA AT THE CAFÉ...
HOW ABOUT THIS?!
PONK
WHOA ...
WHOA ...
...I WAS PLAYING SQUASH FOR SOME STRANGE REASON.
THUD
HA HA!
YOU'RE NOT VERY ATHLETIC, ARE YOU?
NO... HEH HEH...

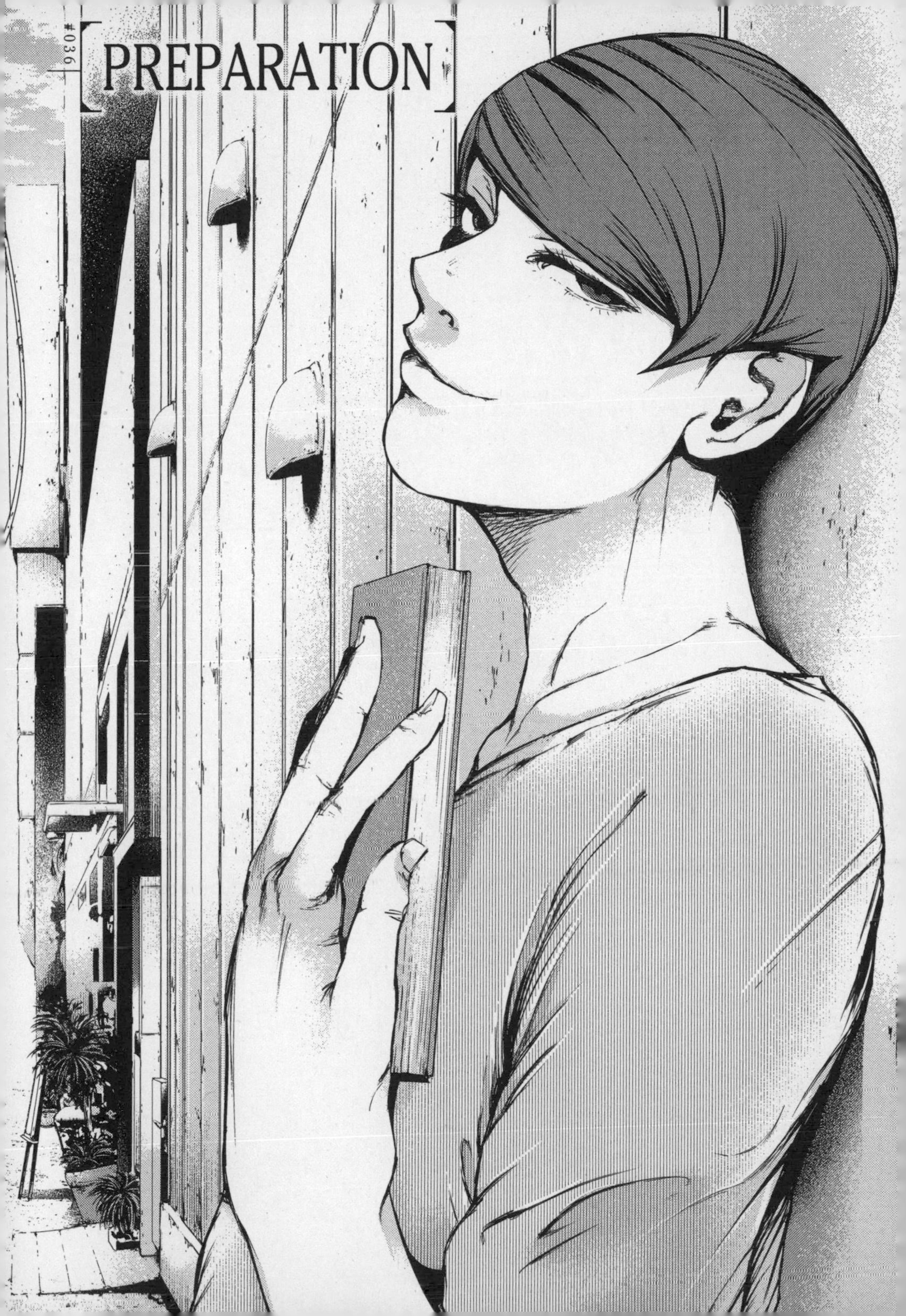
#036
PREPARATION

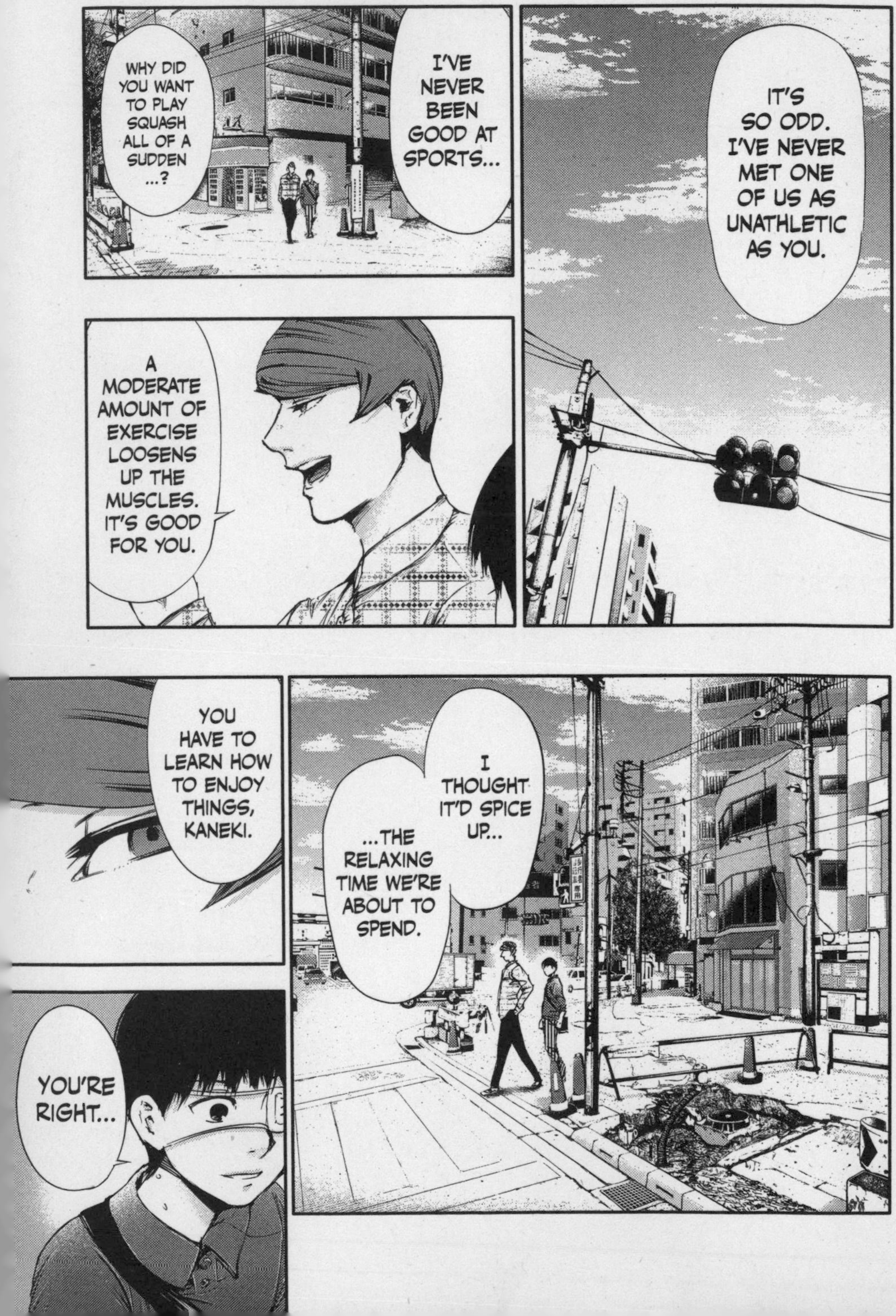
IT'S SO ODD. I'VE NEVER MET ONE OF US AS UNATHLETIC AS YOU.
I'VE NEVER BEEN GOOD AT SPORTS...
WHY DID YOU WANT TO PLAY SQUASH ALL OF A SUDDEN ...?
A MODERATE AMOUNT OF EXERCISE LOOSENS UP THE MUSCLES. IT'S GOOD FOR YOU.
I THOUGHT IT'D SPICE UP...
...THE RELAXING TIME WE'RE ABOUT TO SPEND.
YOU HAVE TO LEARN HOW TO ENJOY THINGS, KANEKI.
YOU'RE RIGHT...

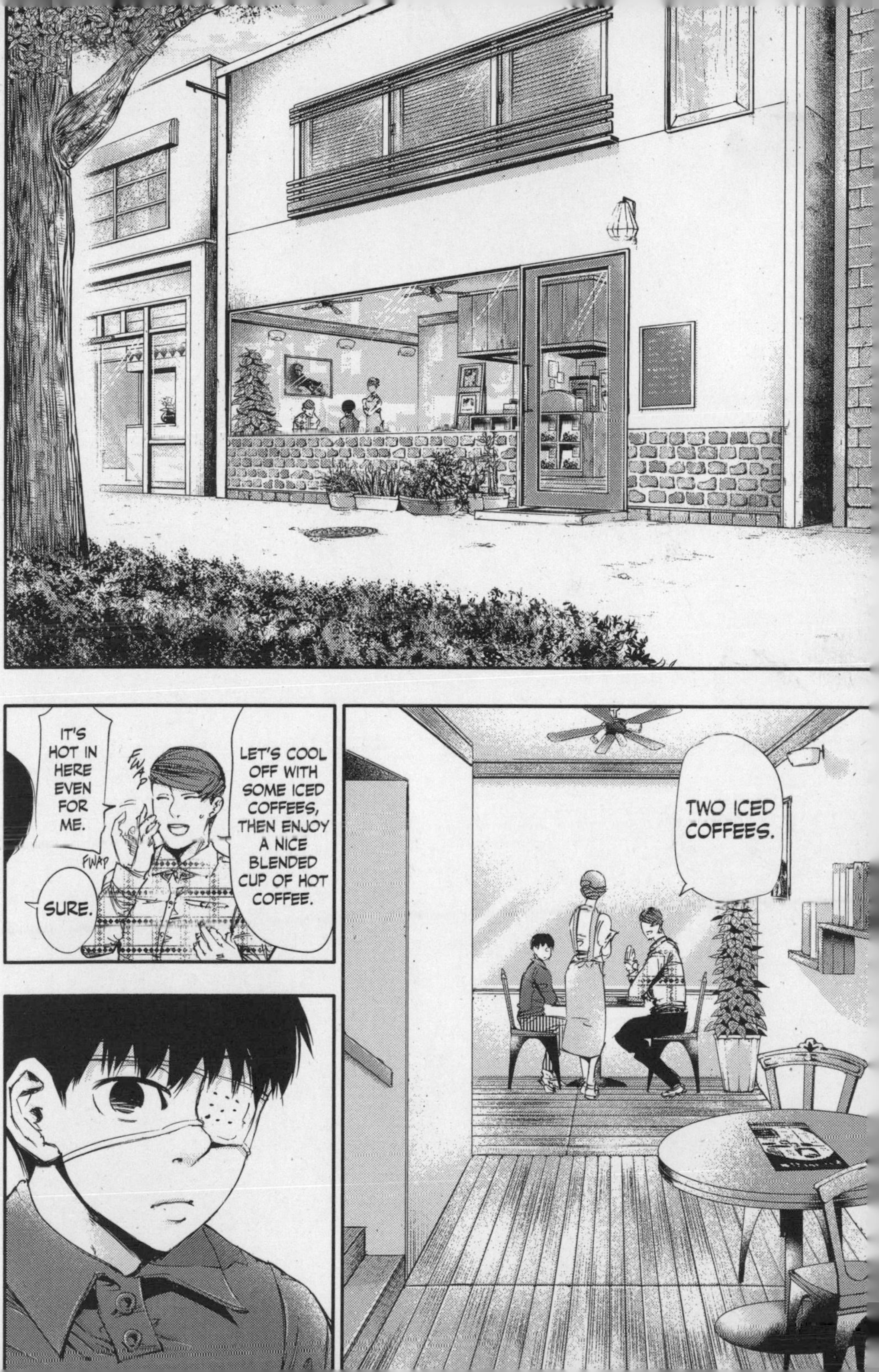
TWO ICED COFFEES.
IT'S HOT IN HERE EVEN FOR ME.
FWAP
LET'S COOL OFF WITH SOME ICED COFFEES, THEN ENJOY A NICE BLENDED CUP OF HOT COFFEE.
FWAP
SURE.

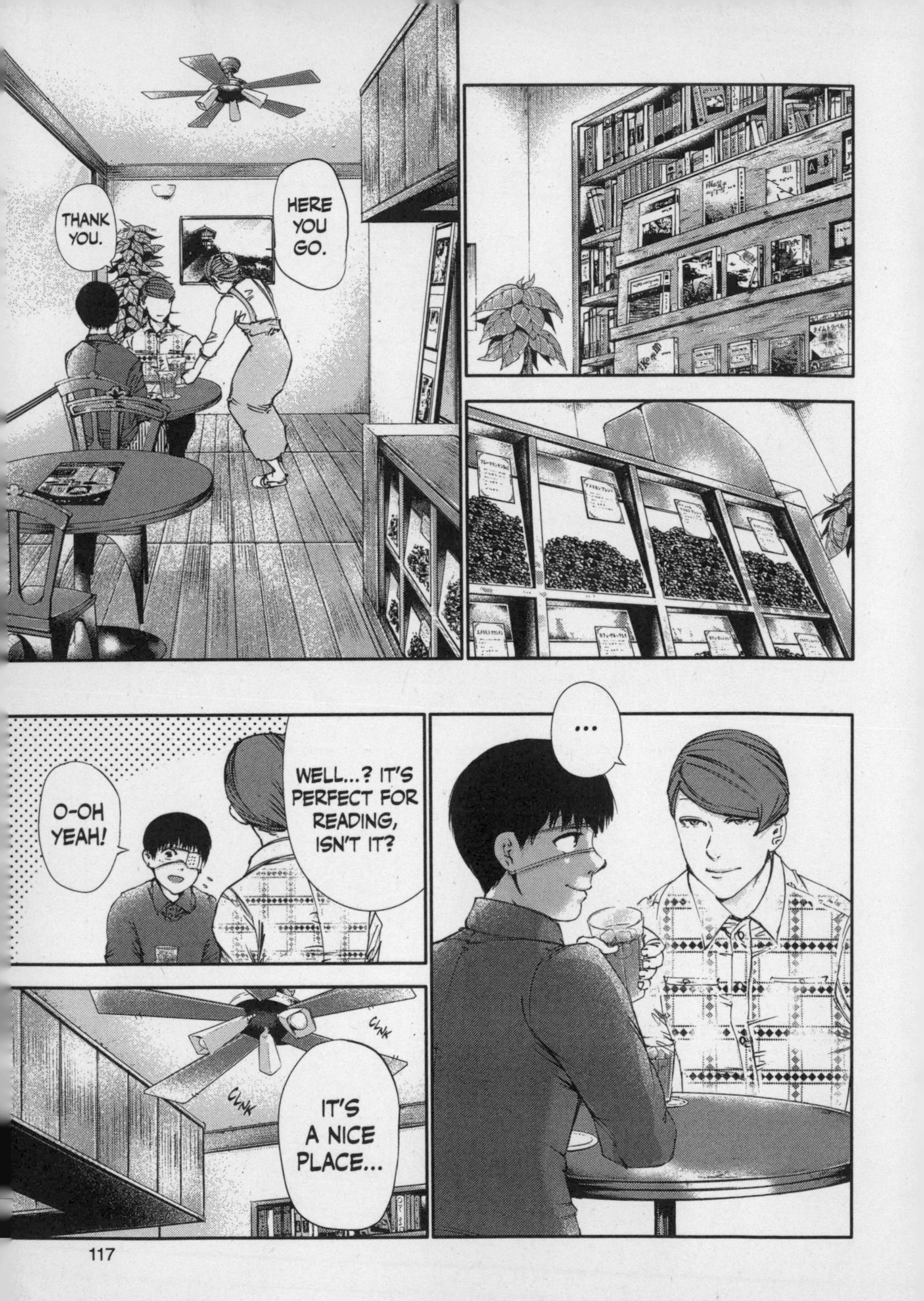
HERE YOU GO.
THANK YOU.
...
WELL...? IT'S PERFECT FOR READING, ISN'T IT?
O-OH YEAH!
CLNK
CLNK
IT'S A NICE PLACE...

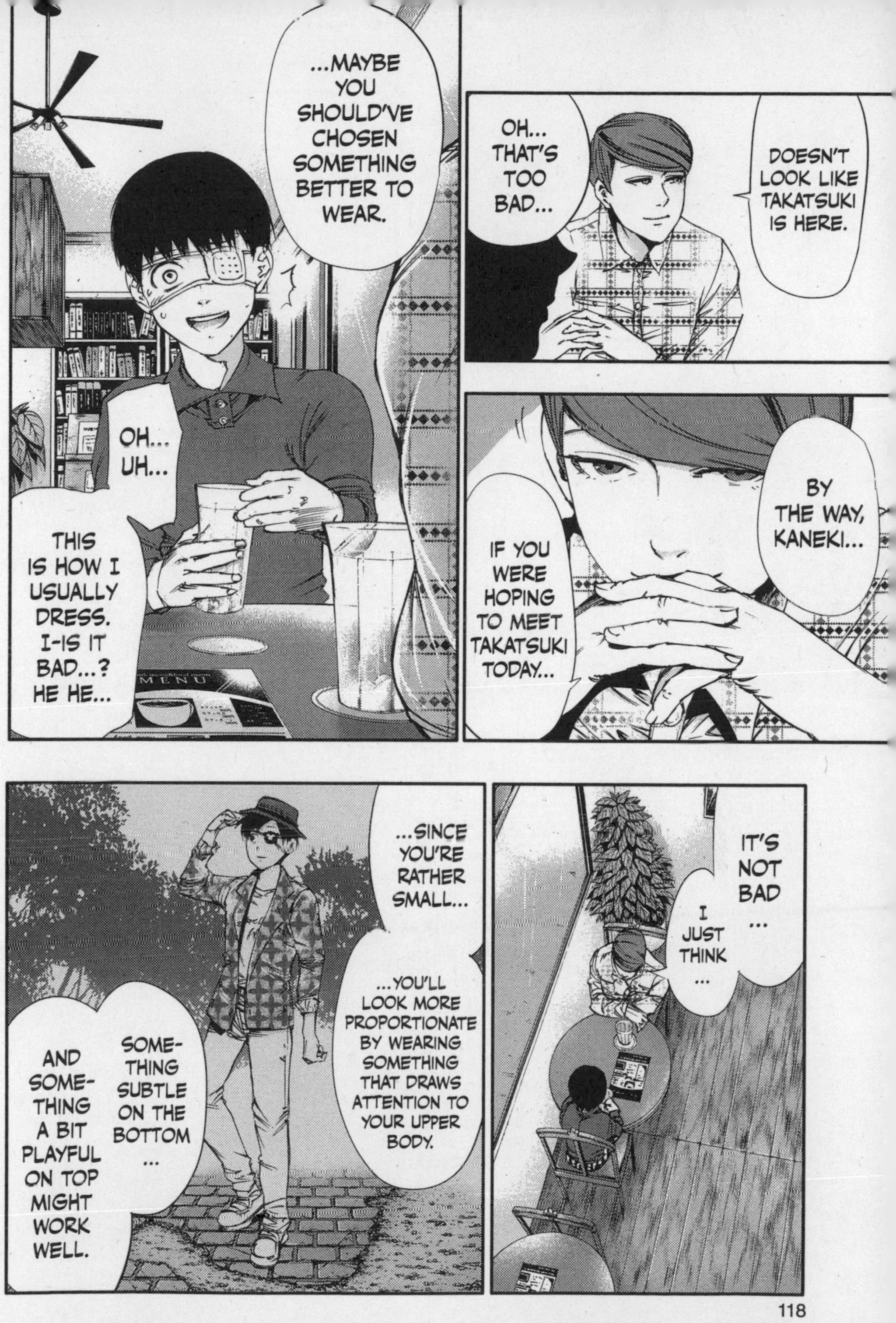
DOESN'T LOOK LIKE TAKATSUKI IS HERE.
OH... THAT'S TOO BAD...
BY THE WAY, KANEKI...
IF YOU WERE HOPING TO MEET TAKATSUKI TODAY...
...MAYBE YOU SHOULD'VE CHOSEN SOMETHING BETTER TO WEAR.
OH... UH...
THIS IS HOW I USUALLY DRESS. I-IS IT BAD...? HE HE...
IT'S NOT BAD...
I JUST THINK...
...SINCE YOU'RE RATHER SMALL...
...YOU'LL LOOK MORE PROPORTIONATE BY WEARING SOMETHING THAT DRAWS ATTENTION TO YOUR UPPER BODY.
SOMETHING SUBTLE ON THE BOTTOM...
AND SOMETHING A BIT PLAYFUL ON TOP MIGHT WORK WELL.

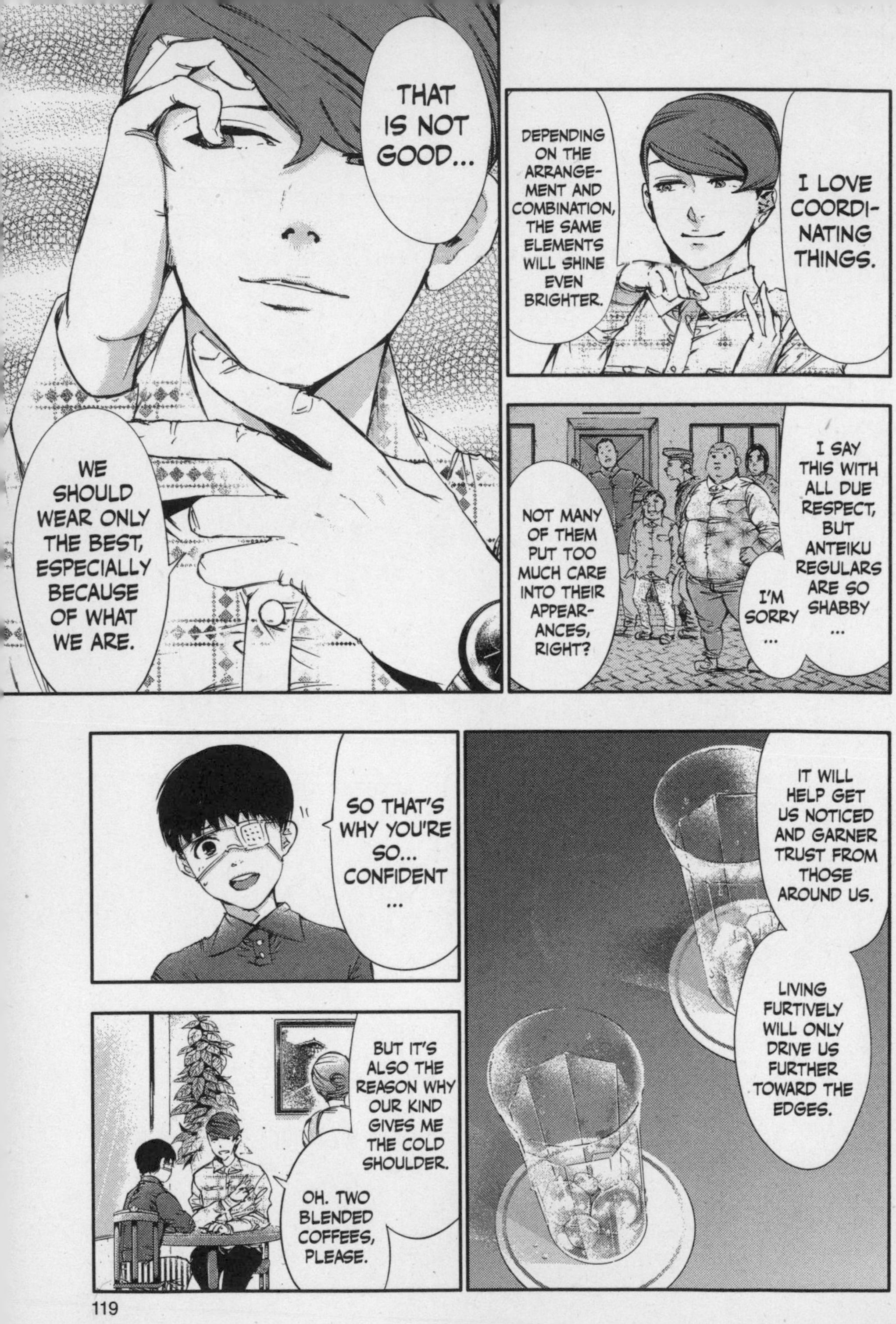
I LOVE COORDINATING THINGS.
DEPENDING ON THE ARRANGEMENT AND COMBINATION, THE SAME ELEMENTS WILL SHINE EVEN BRIGHTER.
I SAY THIS WITH ALL DUE RESPECT, BUT ANTEIKU REGULARS ARE SO SHABBY...
I'M SORRY...
NOT MANY OF THEM PUT TOO MUCH CARE INTO THEIR APPEARANCES, RIGHT?
THAT IS NOT GOOD...
WE SHOULD WEAR ONLY THE BEST, ESPECIALLY BECAUSE OF WHAT WE ARE.
IT WILL HELP GET US NOTICED AND GARNER TRUST FROM THOSE AROUND US.
LIVING FURTIVELY WILL ONLY DRIVE US FURTHER TOWARD THE EDGES.
SO THAT'S WHY YOU'RE SO... CONFIDENT...
BUT IT'S ALSO THE REASON WHY OUR KIND GIVES ME THE COLD SHOULDER.
OH. TWO BLENDED COFFEES, PLEASE.

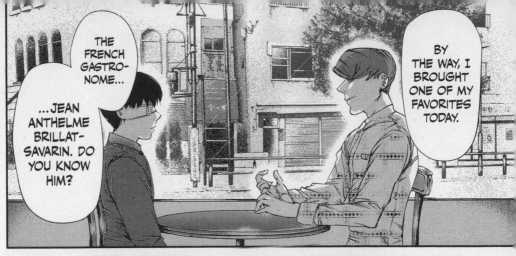

BY THE WAY, I BROUGHT ONE OF MY FAVORITES TODAY.
THE FRENCH GASTRONOME...
...JEAN ANTHELME BRILLAT-SAVARIN. DO YOU KNOW HIM?
THE PHYSIOLOGY OF TASTE?
SO YOU'VE READ IT...
THE WORKS OF FOOD CONNOISSEURS ARE OF GREAT INTEREST TO ME...
THE FLAVORS I COULD NEVER TASTE. THE EMOTIONS I COULD NEVER FEEL.
IT'S ALL SO NEW AND UNIMAGINABLE.
J'aime beaucoup le fromage...
HIS ADAGE "A DESSERT WITHOUT CHEESE IS LIKE A BEAUTIFUL WOMAN WITH ONLY ONE EYE."
THAT TOO IS FASCINATING.

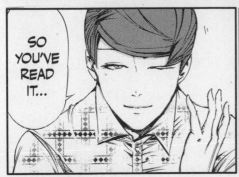

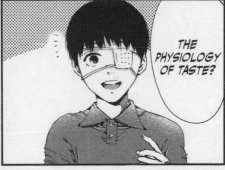

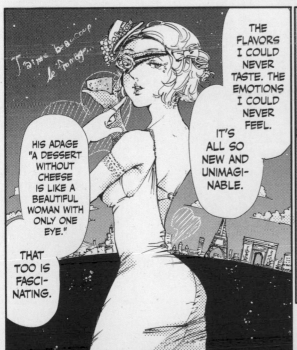

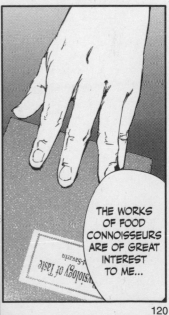

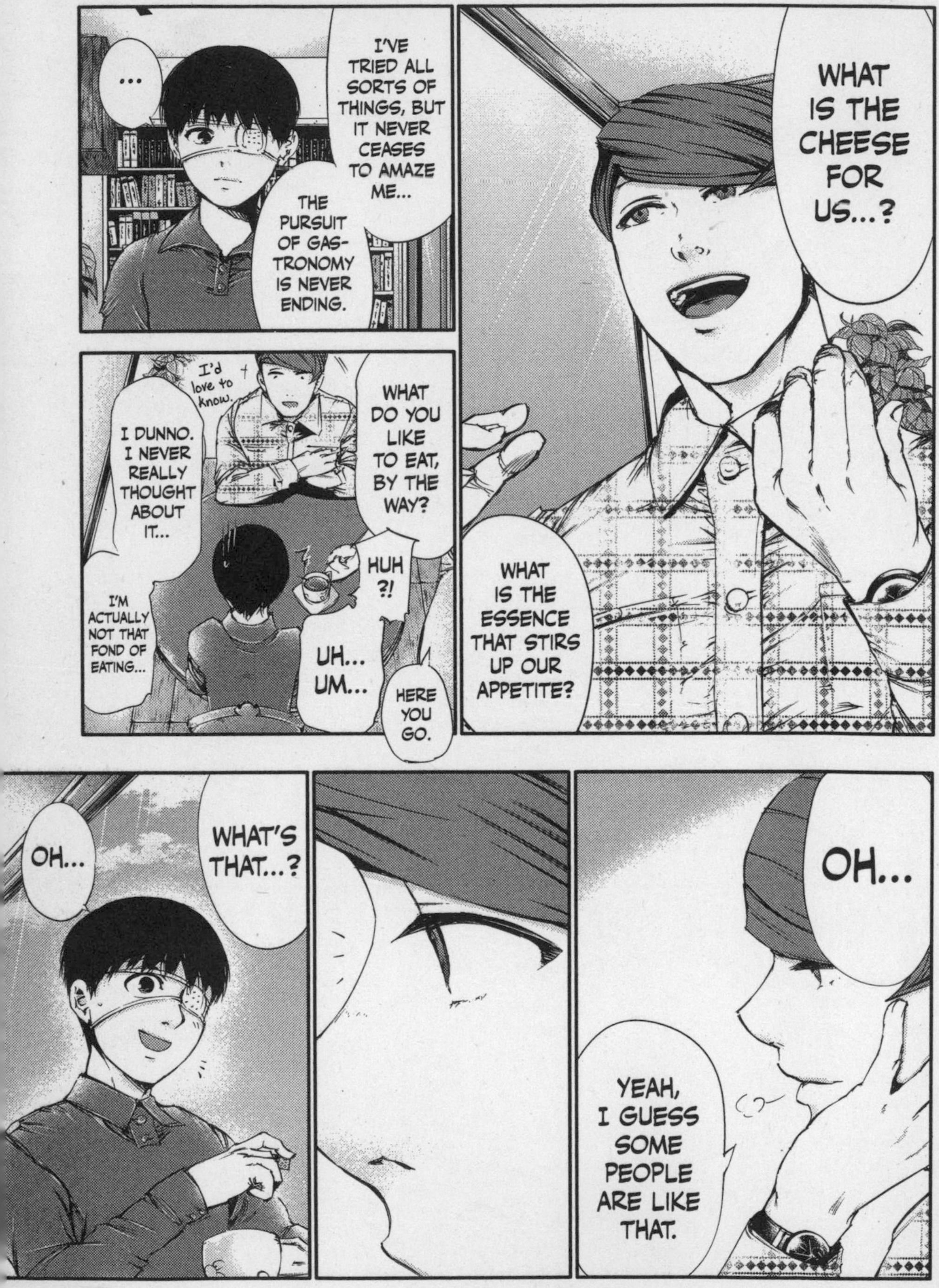
WHAT IS THE CHEESE FOR US...?
WHAT IS THE ESSENCE THAT STIRS UP OUR APPETITE?
I'VE TRIED ALL SORTS OF THINGS, BUT IT NEVER CEASES TO AMAZE ME...
THE PURSUIT OF GAS-TRONOMY IS NEVER ENDING.
...
WHAT DO YOU LIKE TO EAT, BY THE WAY?
I'd love to know.
HUH?!
UH... UM...
HERE YOU GO.
I DUNNO. I NEVER REALLY THOUGHT ABOUT IT...
I'M ACTUALLY NOT THAT FOND OF EATING...
OH...
YEAH, I GUESS SOME PEOPLE ARE LIKE THAT.
WHAT'S THAT...?
OH...

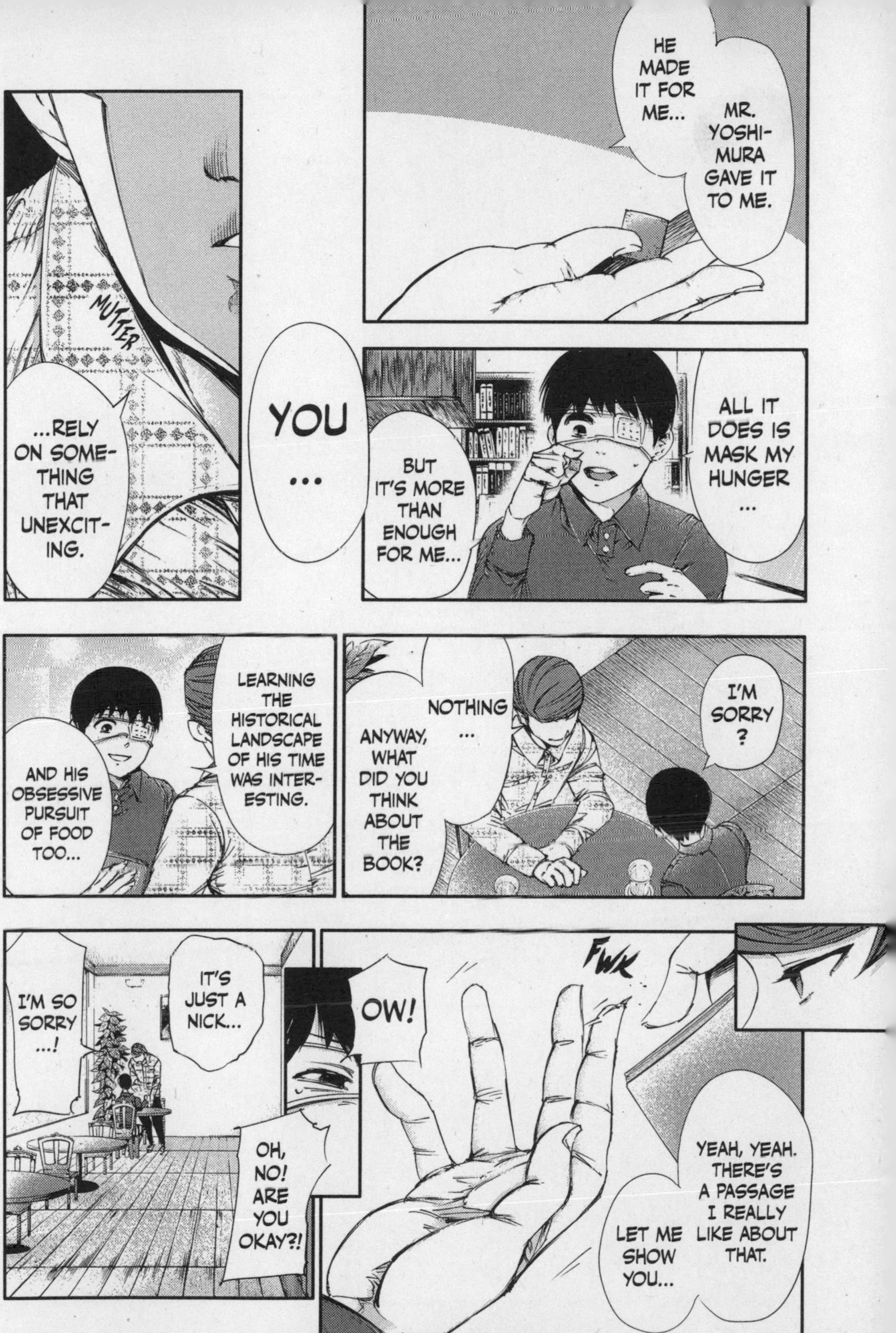
MR. YOSHIMURA GAVE IT TO ME.
HE MADE IT FOR ME...
ALL IT DOES IS MASK MY HUNGER...
BUT IT'S MORE THAN ENOUGH FOR ME...
YOU...
MUTTER
...RELY ON SOMETHING THAT UNEXCITING.
I'M SORRY?
NOTHING...
ANYWAY, WHAT DID YOU THINK ABOUT THE BOOK?
LEARNING THE HISTORICAL LANDSCAPE OF HIS TIME WAS INTERESTING.
AND HIS OBSESSIVE PURSUIT OF FOOD TOO...
YEAH, YEAH. THERE'S A PASSAGE I REALLY LIKE ABOUT THAT.
LET ME SHOW YOU...
FWK
OW!
OH, NO! ARE YOU OKAY?!
IT'S JUST A NICK...
I'M SO SORRY...!

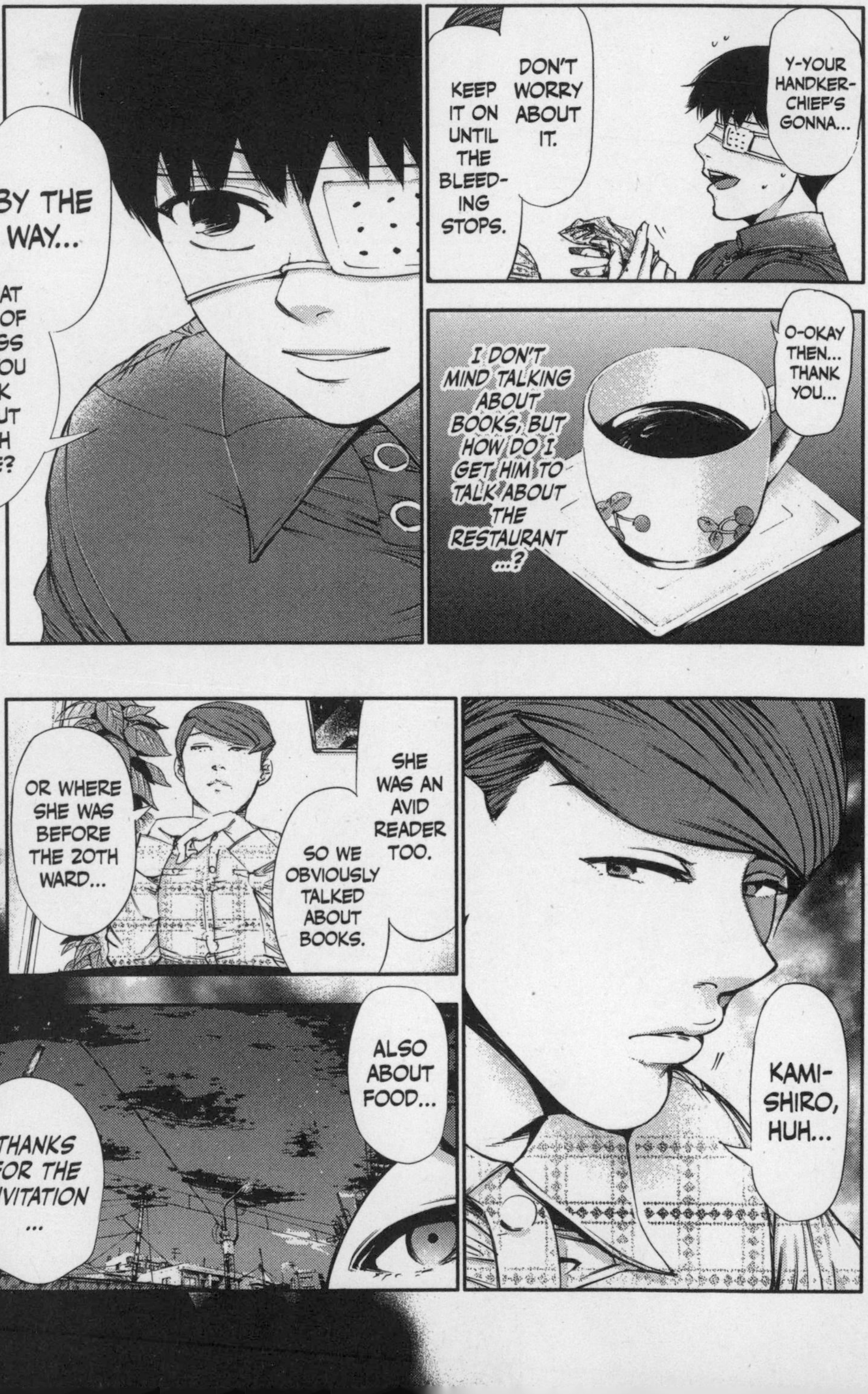
Y-YOUR HANDKER-CHIEF'S GONNA...
DON'T WORRY ABOUT IT.
KEEP IT ON UNTIL THE BLEED-ING STOPS.
O-OKAY THEN... THANK YOU...
I DON'T MIND TALKING ABOUT BOOKS, BUT HOW DO I GET HIM TO TALK ABOUT THE RESTAURANT ...?
BY THE WAY...
...WHAT KIND OF THINGS DID YOU TALK ABOUT WITH RIZE?
KAMI-SHIRO, HUH...
SHE WAS AN AVID READER TOO.
SO WE OBVIOUSLY TALKED ABOUT BOOKS.
OR WHERE SHE WAS BEFORE THE 20TH WARD...
ALSO ABOUT FOOD...
THANKS FOR THE INVITATION ...

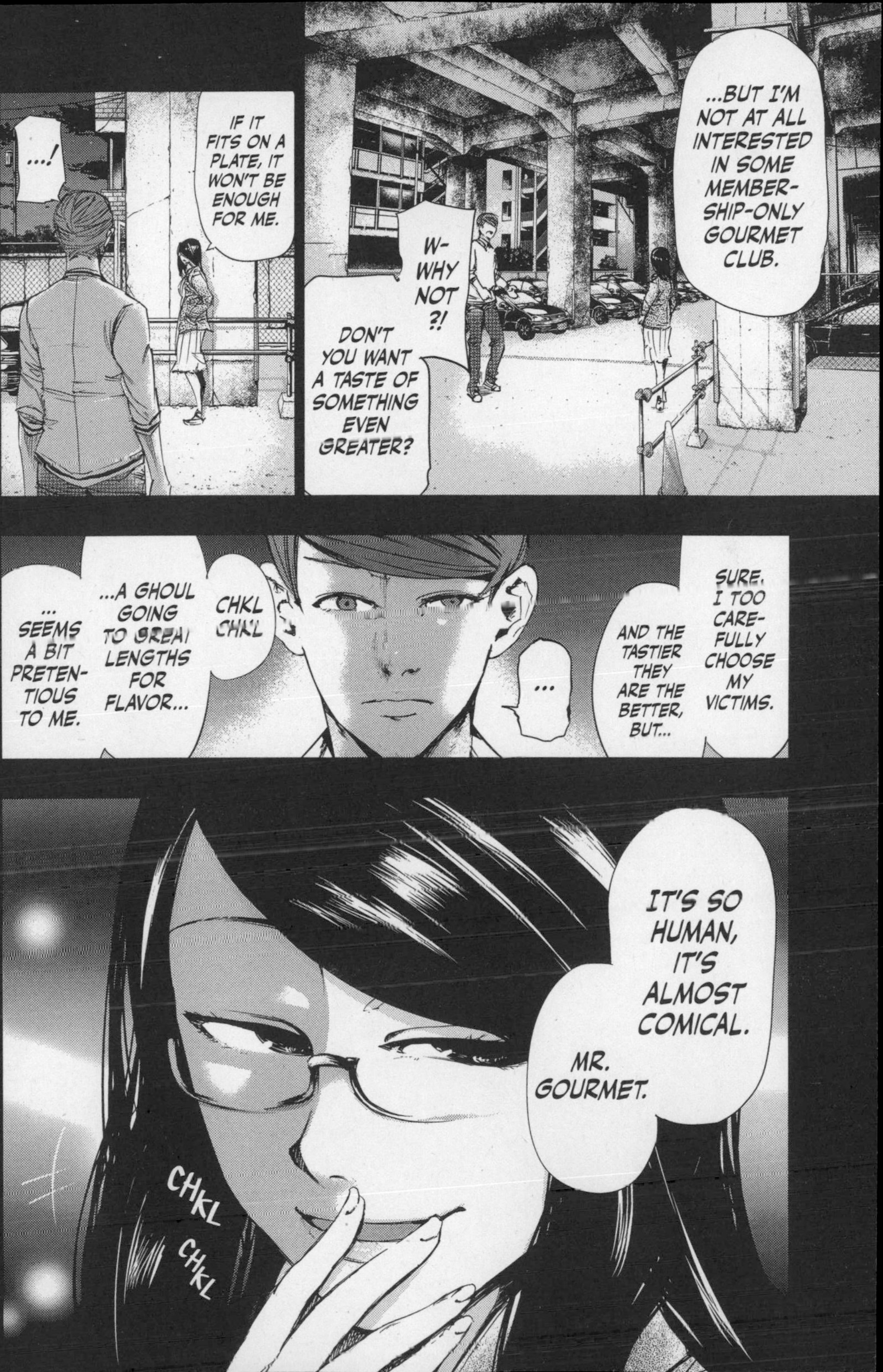
...BUT I'M NOT AT ALL INTERESTED IN SOME MEMBERSHIP-ONLY GOURMET CLUB.
W-WHY NOT?!
DON'T YOU WANT A TASTE OF SOMETHING EVEN GREATER?
IF IT FITS ON A PLATE, IT WON'T BE ENOUGH FOR ME.
...!
SURE. I TOO CAREFULLY CHOOSE MY VICTIMS.
AND THE TASTIER THEY ARE THE BETTER, BUT...
...
CHKL CHKL
...A GHOUL GOING TO GREAT LENGTHS FOR FLAVOR...
...SEEMS A BIT PRETENTIOUS TO ME.
IT'S SO HUMAN, IT'S ALMOST COMICAL.
MR. GOURMET.
CHKL CHKL

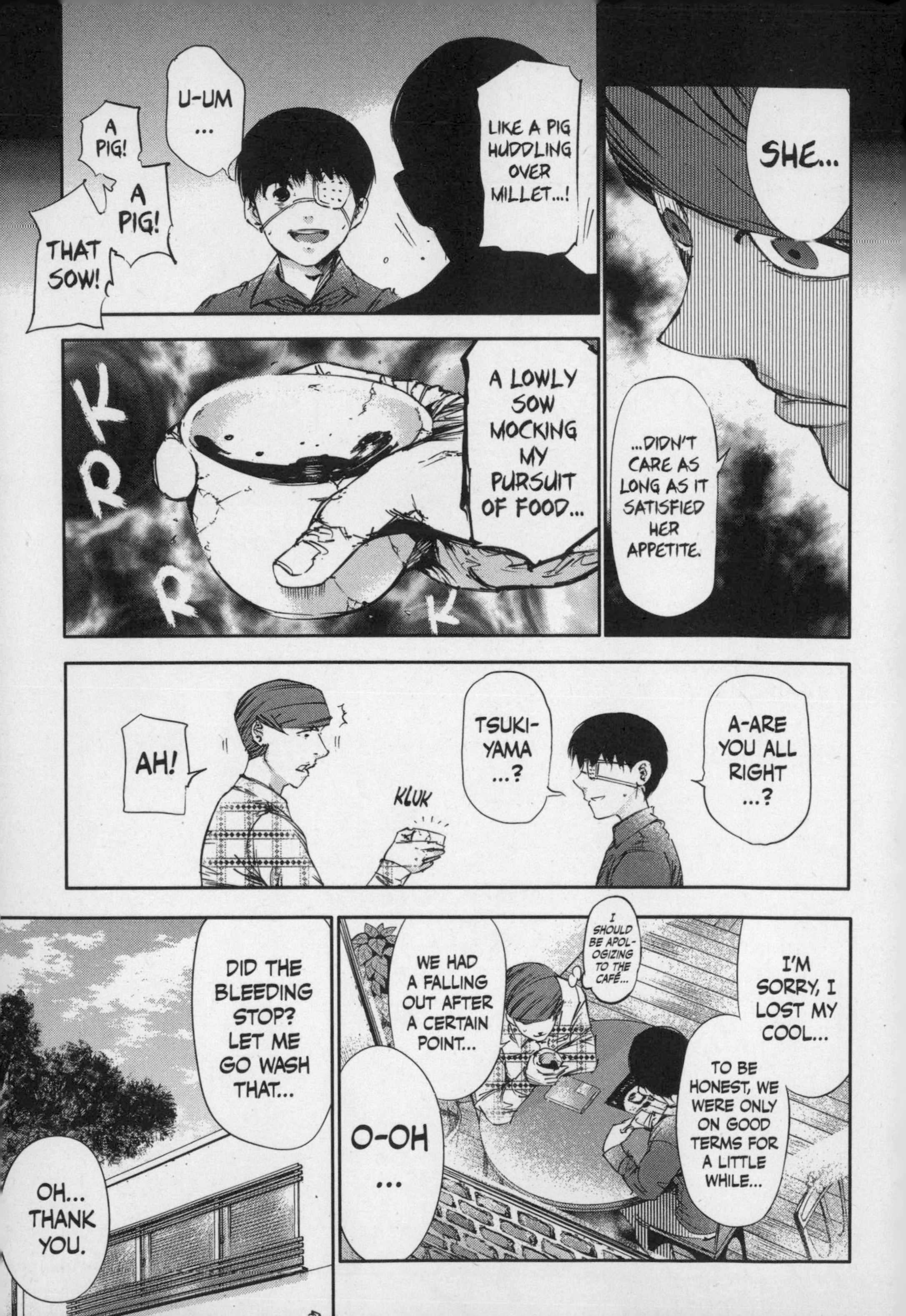
SHE...
...DIDN'T CARE AS LONG AS IT SATISFIED HER APPETITE.
LIKE A PIG HUDDLING OVER MILLET...!
U-UM ...
A PIG!
A PIG!
THAT SOW!
A LOWLY SOW MOCKING MY PURSUIT OF FOOD...
KRRK
A-ARE YOU ALL RIGHT ...?
TSUKI-YAMA ...?
KLUK
AH!
I'M SORRY, I LOST MY COOL...
I SHOULD BE APOLOGIZING TO THE CAFÉ...
TO BE HONEST, WE WERE ONLY ON GOOD TERMS FOR A LITTLE WHILE...
WE HAD A FALLING OUT AFTER A CERTAIN POINT...
O-OH ...
DID THE BLEEDING STOP? LET ME GO WASH THAT...
OH... THANK YOU.

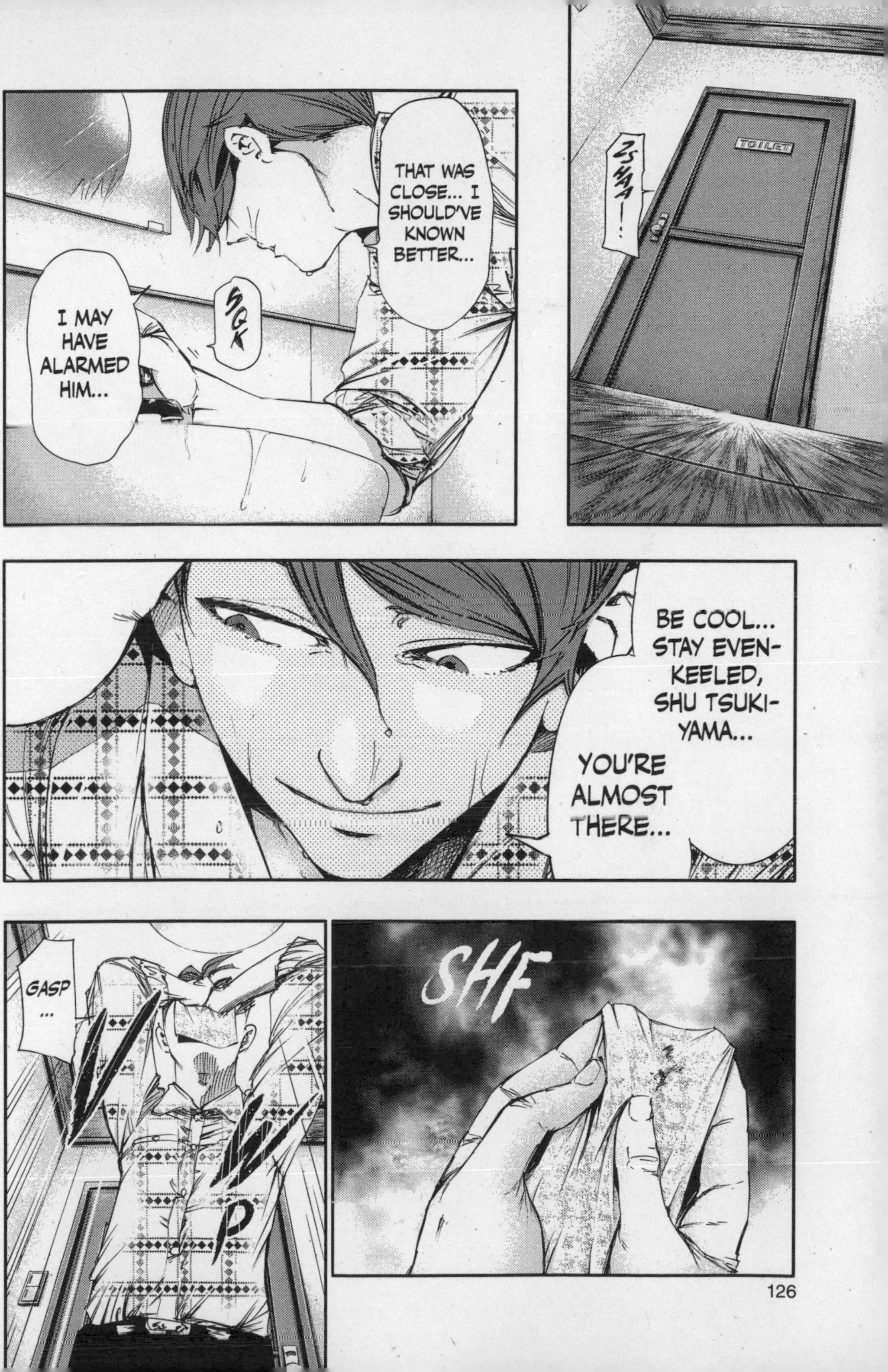
ZSHAA!!
THAT WAS CLOSE... I SHOULD'VE KNOWN BETTER...
SQK
I MAY HAVE ALARMED HIM...
BE COOL... STAY EVEN-KEELED, SHU TSUKI-YAMA...
YOU'RE ALMOST THERE...
SHF
GASP ...

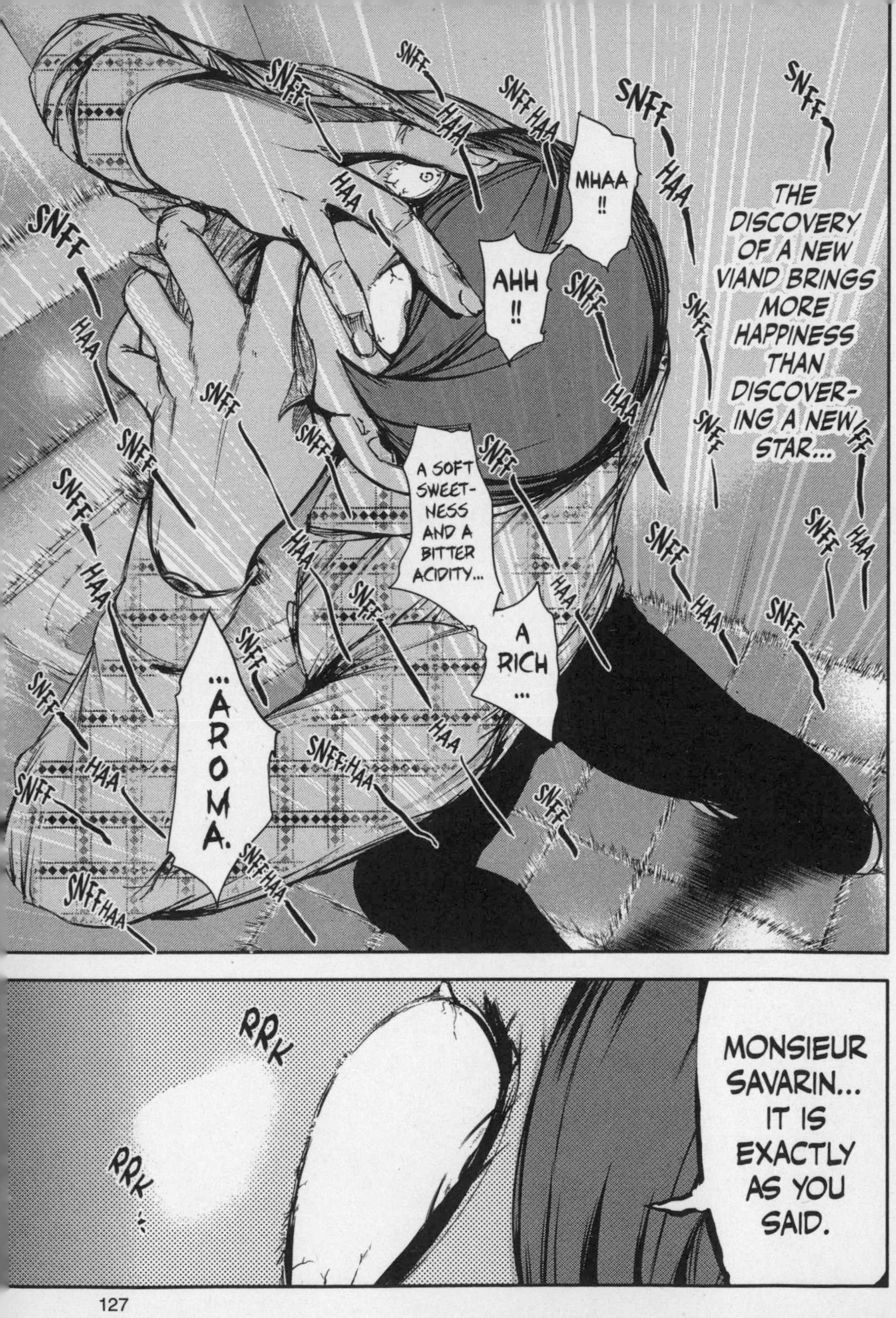
SNFF HAA
THE DISCOVERY OF A NEW VIAND BRINGS MORE HAPPINESS THAN DISCOVERING A NEW STAR...
SNFF HAA
SNFF
SNFF HAA
SNFF HAA
MHAA!!
SNFF HAA
AHH!!
SNFF HAA
SNFF HAA
A SOFT SWEETNESS AND A BITTER ACIDITY...
SNFF HAA
A RICH...
SNFF HAA
SNFF HAA
SNFF HAA
...AROMA.
SNFF HAA
SNFF HAA
SNFF HAA
SNFF HAA
SNFFHAA
SNFFHAA
MONSIEUR SAVARIN... IT IS EXACTLY AS YOU SAID.
RRK
RRK

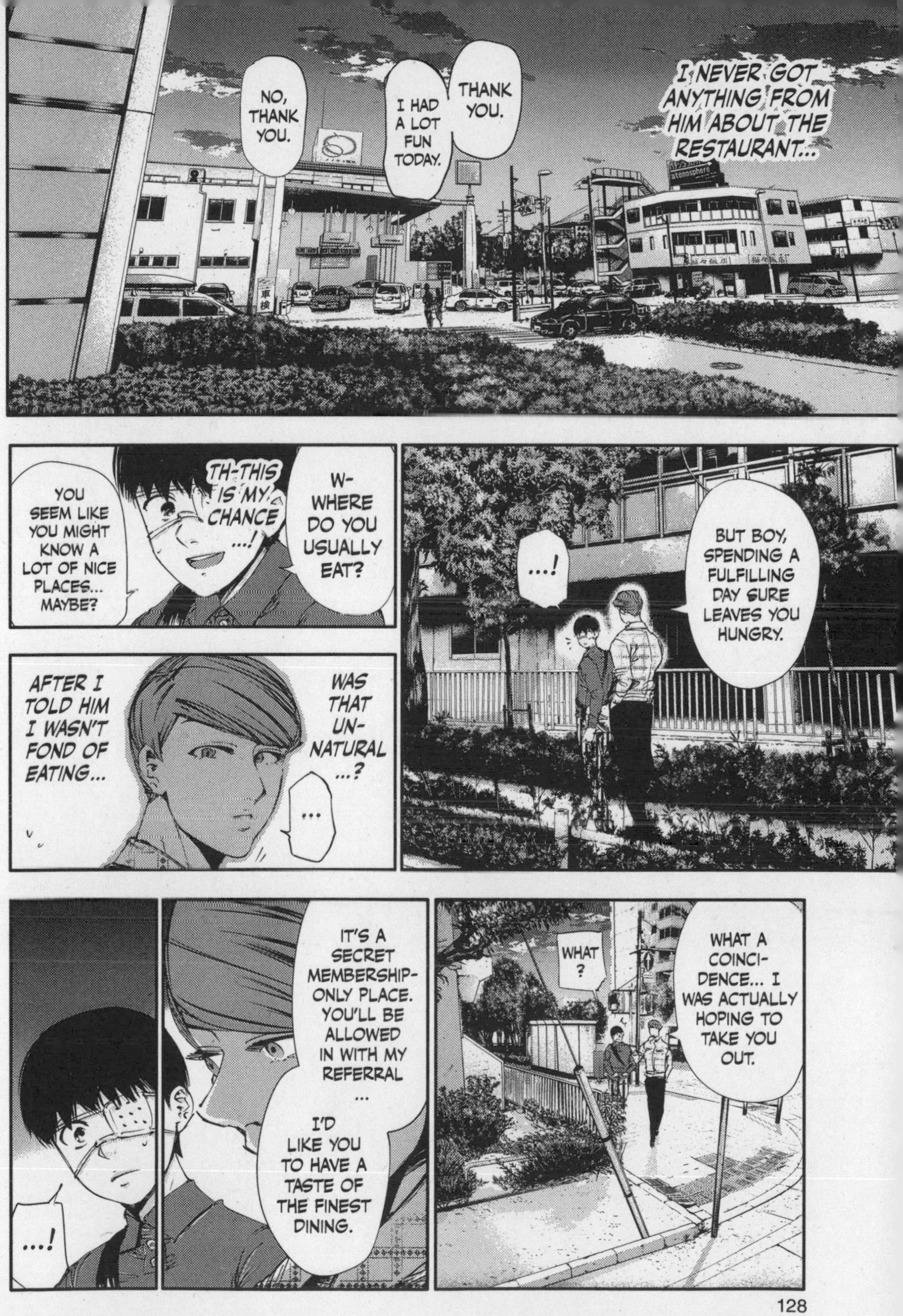
I NEVER GOT ANYTHING FROM HIM ABOUT THE RESTAURANT...
THANK YOU.
I HAD A LOT FUN TODAY.
NO, THANK YOU.
BUT BOY, SPENDING A FULFILLING DAY SURE LEAVES YOU HUNGRY.
...!
W-WHERE DO YOU USUALLY EAT?
TH-THIS IS MY CHANCE...!
YOU SEEM LIKE YOU MIGHT KNOW A LOT OF NICE PLACES... MAYBE?
WAS THAT UN-NATURAL...?
AFTER I TOLD HIM I WASN'T FOND OF EATING...
...
WHAT A COINCI-DENCE... I WAS ACTUALLY HOPING TO TAKE YOU OUT.
WHAT?
IT'S A SECRET MEMBERSHIP-ONLY PLACE. YOU'LL BE ALLOWED IN WITH MY REFERRAL ...
I'D LIKE YOU TO HAVE A TASTE OF THE FINEST DINING.
...!

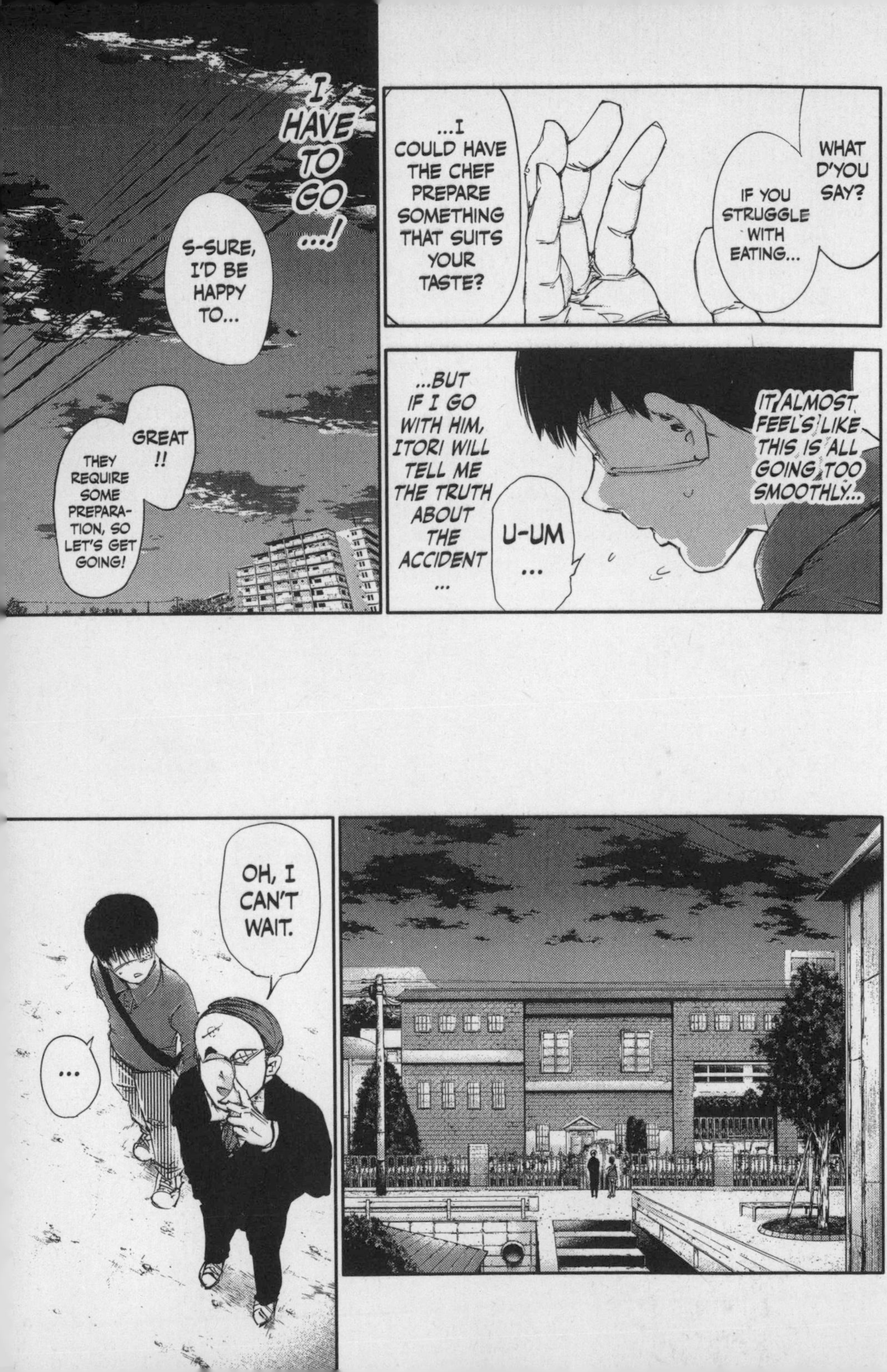
WHAT D'YOU SAY?
IF YOU STRUGGLE WITH EATING...
...I COULD HAVE THE CHEF PREPARE SOMETHING THAT SUITS YOUR TASTE?
IT ALMOST FEELS LIKE THIS IS ALL GOING TOO SMOOTHLY...
...BUT IF I GO WITH HIM, ITORI WILL TELL ME THE TRUTH ABOUT THE ACCIDENT...
U-UM...
I HAVE TO GO...!
S-SURE, I'D BE HAPPY TO...
GREAT!!
THEY REQUIRE SOME PREPARATION, SO LET'S GET GOING!
OH, I CAN'T WAIT.
...

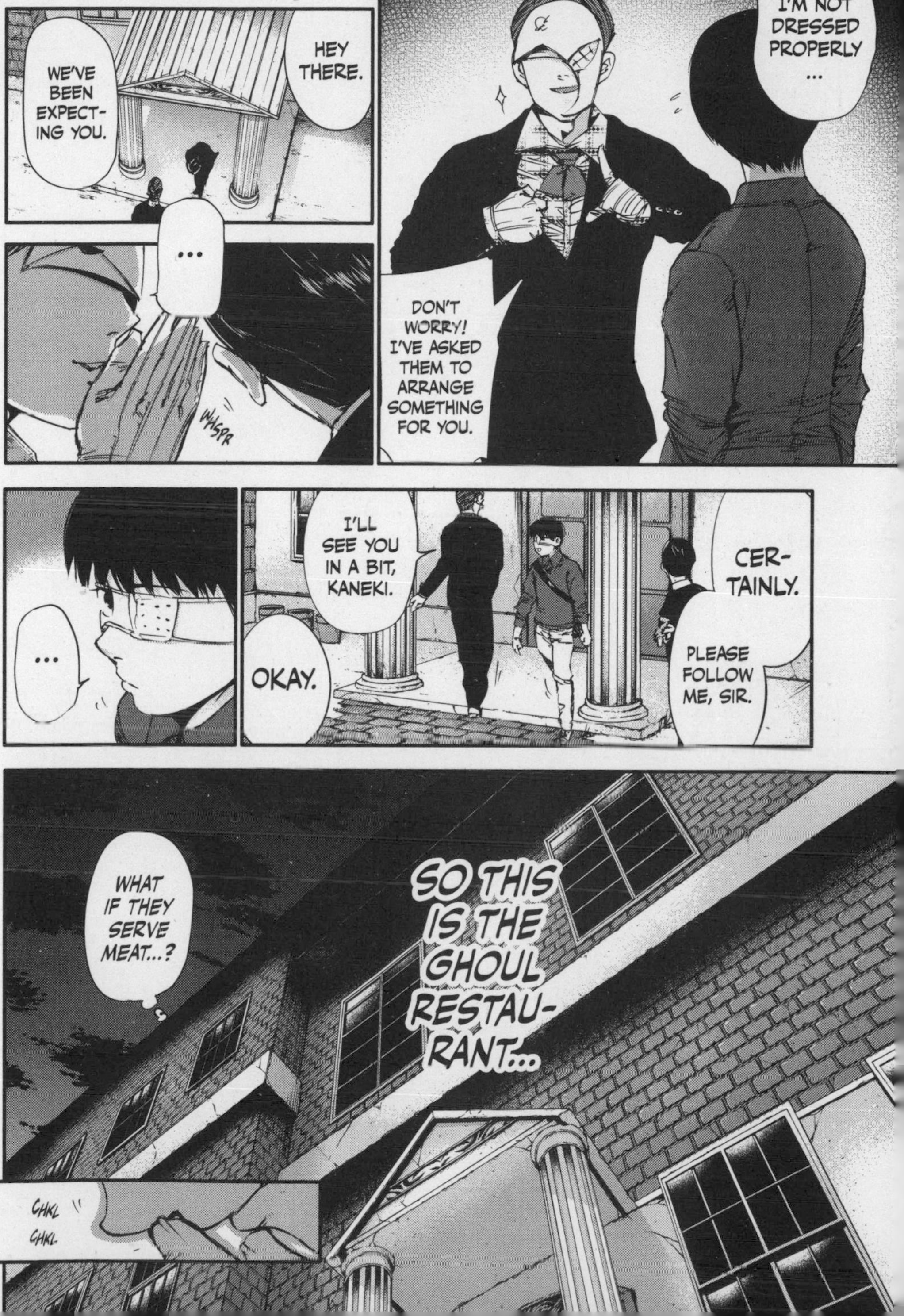
UM... I'M NOT DRESSED PROPERLY ...
DON'T WORRY! I'VE ASKED THEM TO ARRANGE SOMETHING FOR YOU.
HEY THERE.
WE'VE BEEN EXPECTING YOU.
...
WHSPR
CER-TAINLY.
I'LL SEE YOU IN A BIT, KANEKI.
PLEASE FOLLOW ME, SIR.
OKAY.
...
SO THIS IS THE GHOUL RESTAU-RANT...
WHAT IF THEY SERVE MEAT...?
CHKL
CHKL

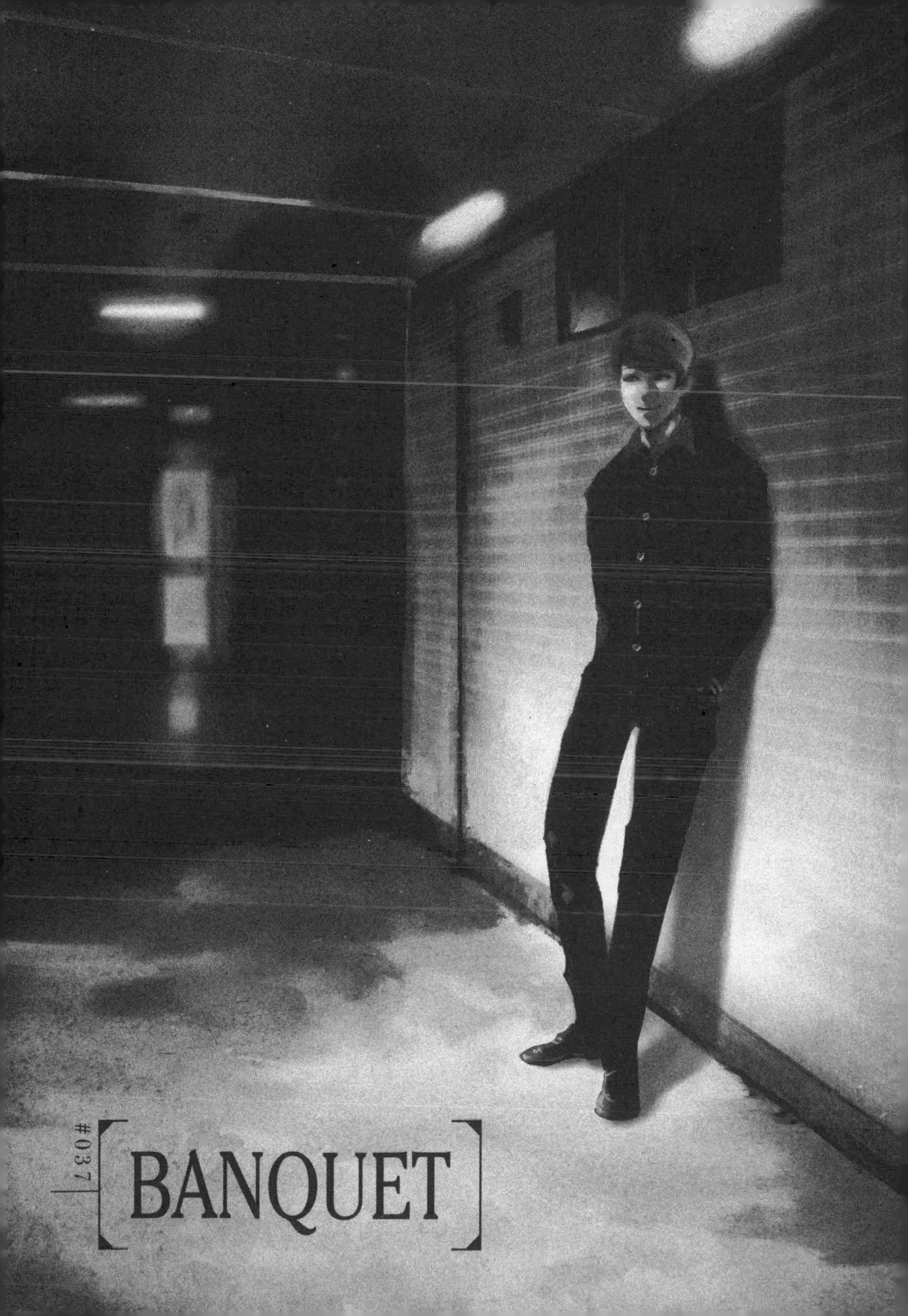
#037
BANQUET

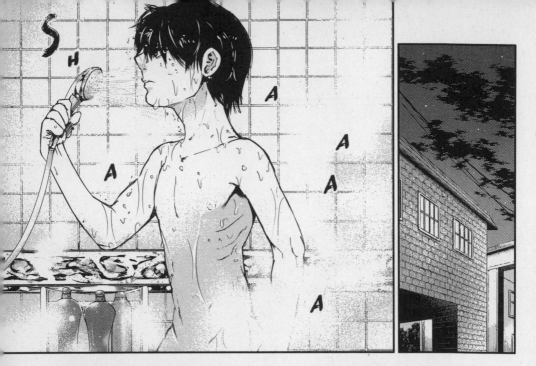

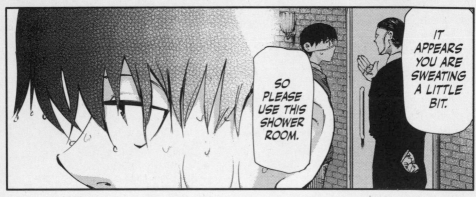

SHAAAAAA
IT APPEARS YOU ARE SWEATING A LITTLE BIT.
SO PLEASE USE THIS SHOWER ROOM.
DID I SMELL OF SWEAT FROM PLAYING SQUASH ...?
IN ANY CASE, I'VE NEVER TAKEN A SHOWER AT A RESTAURANT BEFORE...
SHAAA

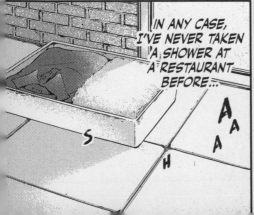

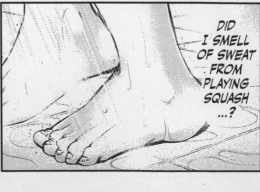

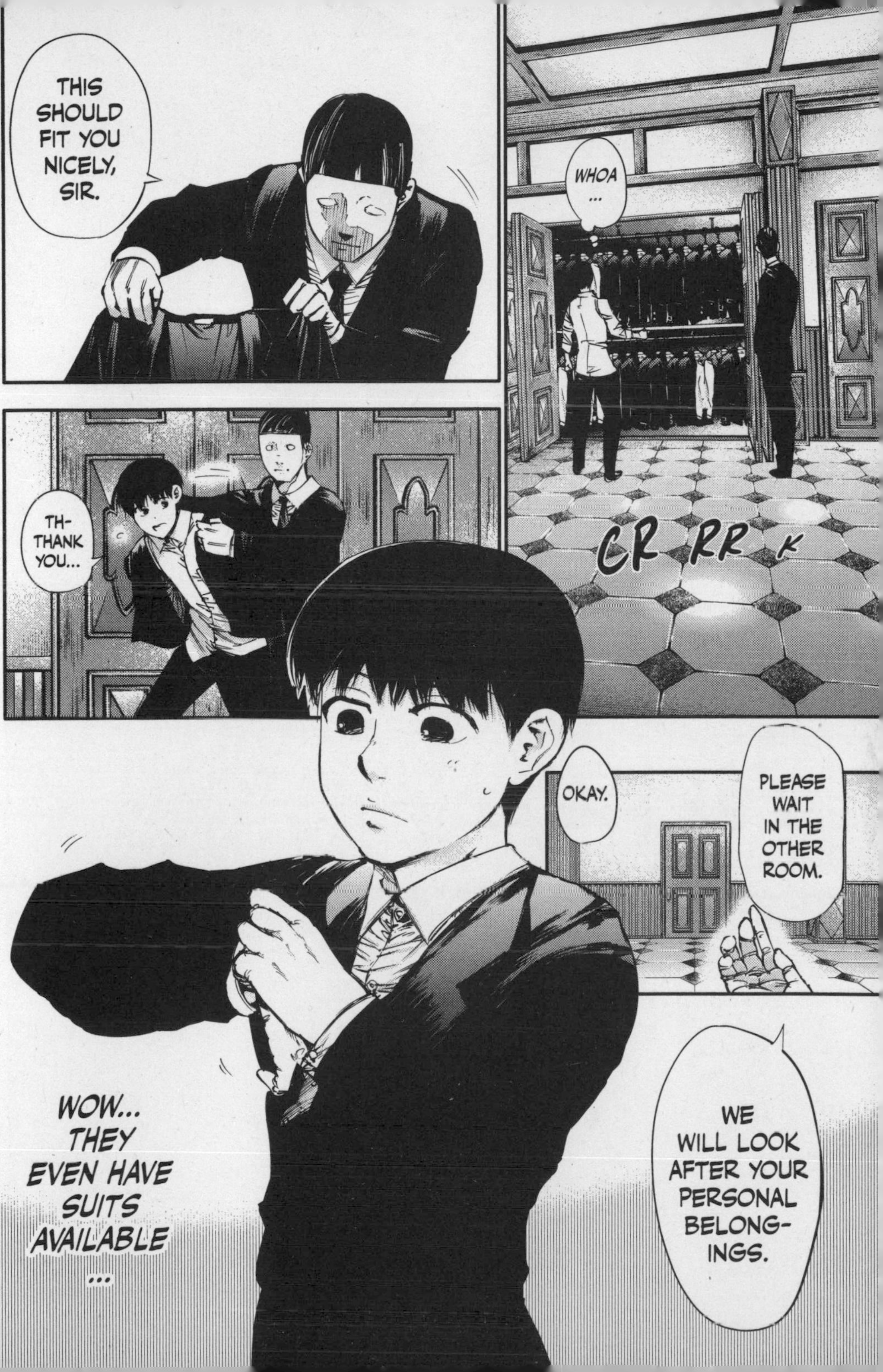
WHOA ...
CR RR K
THIS SHOULD FIT YOU NICELY, SIR.
TH-THANK YOU...
PLEASE WAIT IN THE OTHER ROOM.
OKAY.
WE WILL LOOK AFTER YOUR PERSONAL BELONG-INGS.
WOW... THEY EVEN HAVE SUITS AVAILABLE ...

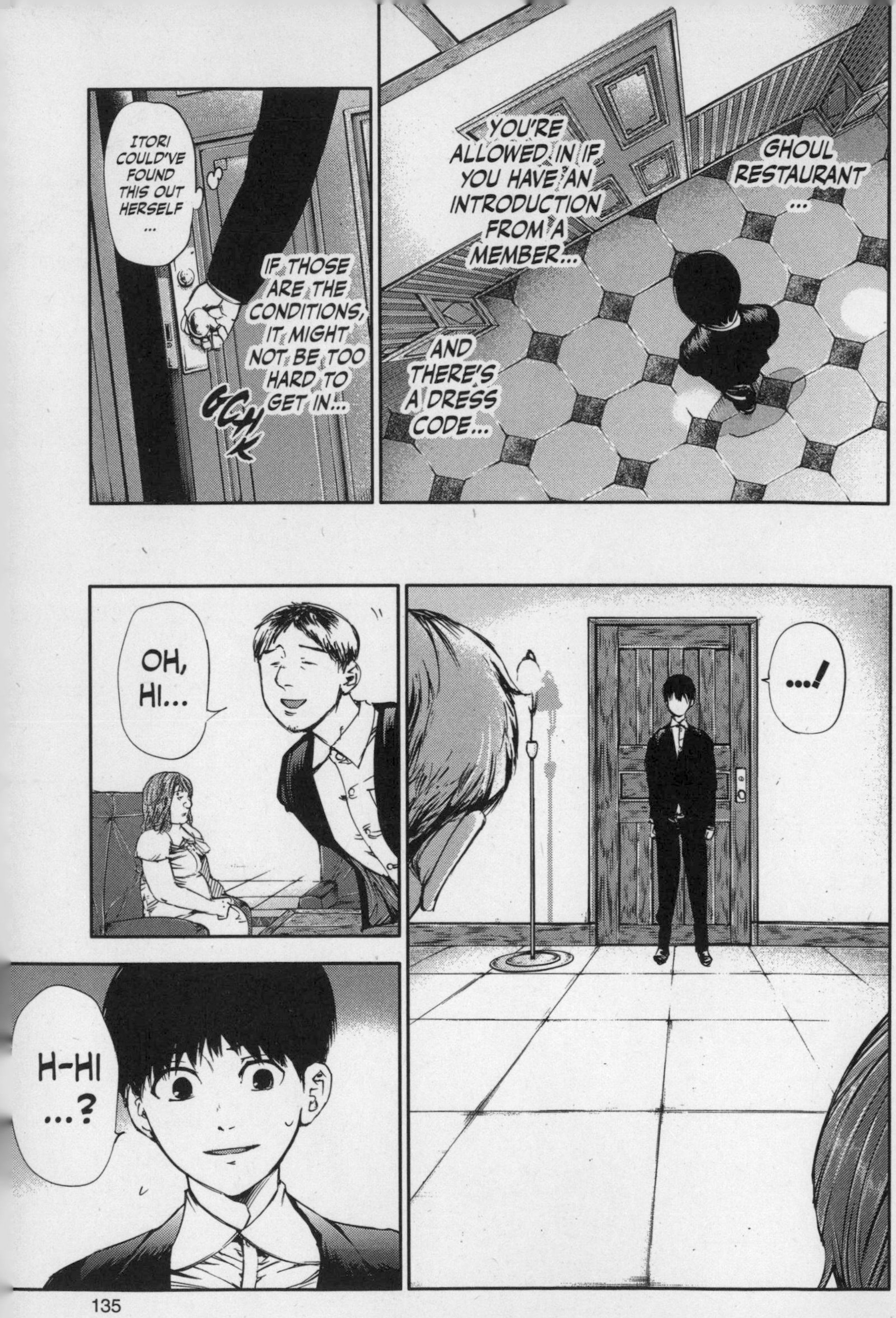
GHOUL RESTAURANT ...
YOU'RE ALLOWED IN IF YOU HAVE AN INTRODUCTION FROM A MEMBER...
AND THERE'S A DRESS CODE...
ITORI COULD'VE FOUND THIS OUT HERSELF ...
IF THOSE ARE THE CONDITIONS, IT MIGHT NOT BE TOO HARD TO GET IN...
GCHK
...!
OH, HI...
H-HI ...?

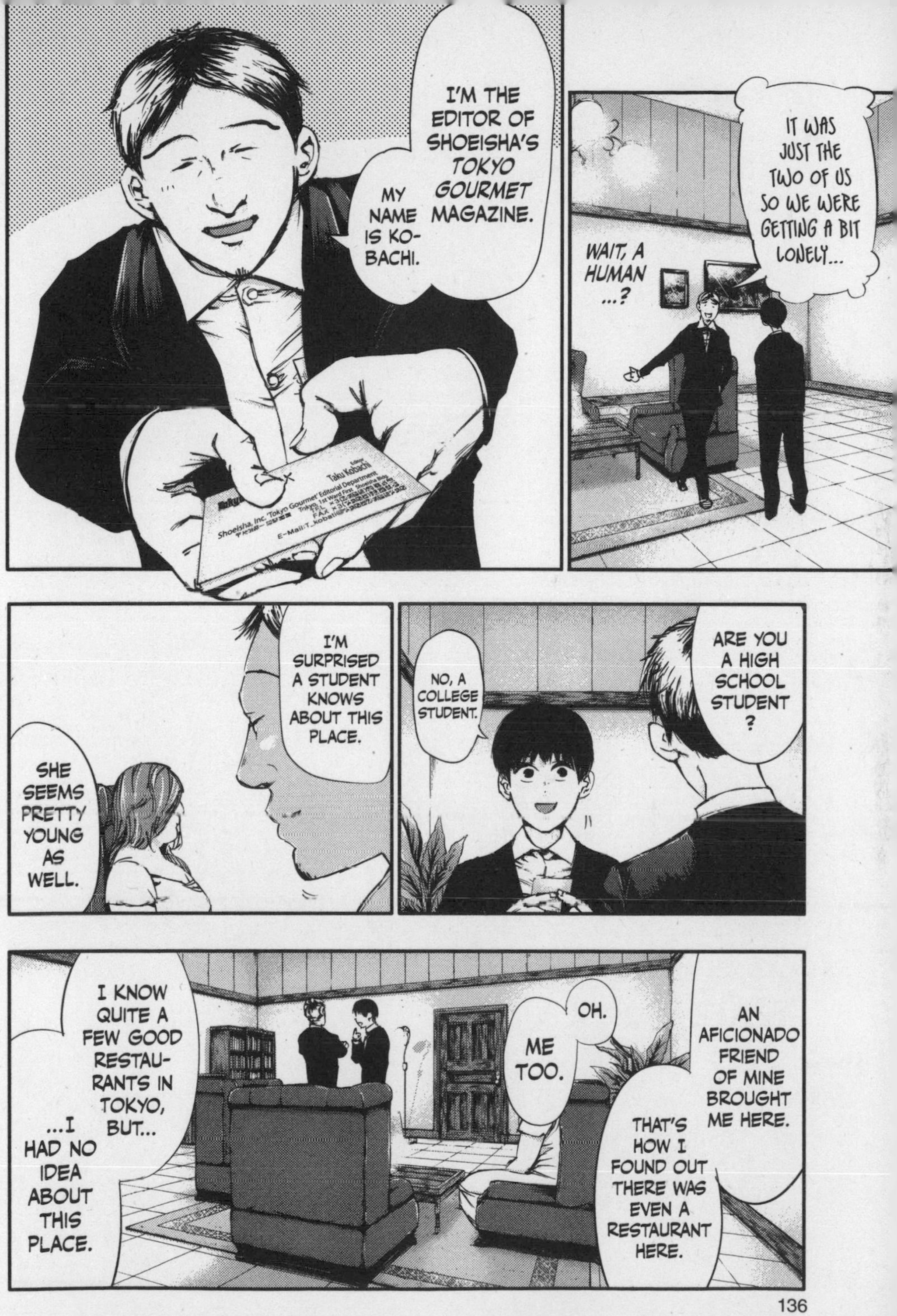
IT WAS JUST THE TWO OF US SO WE WERE GETTING A BIT LONELY...
WAIT, A HUMAN ...?
I'M THE EDITOR OF SHOEISHA'S *TOKYO GOURMET* MAGAZINE.
MY NAME IS KO-BACHI.
Taku Kobachi
Shoeisha, Inc. 'Tokyo Gourmet' Editorial Department
ARE YOU A HIGH SCHOOL STUDENT ?
NO, A COLLEGE STUDENT.
I'M SURPRISED A STUDENT KNOWS ABOUT THIS PLACE.
SHE SEEMS PRETTY YOUNG AS WELL.
AN AFICIONADO FRIEND OF MINE BROUGHT ME HERE.
THAT'S HOW I FOUND OUT THERE WAS EVEN A RESTAURANT HERE.
OH.
ME TOO.
I KNOW QUITE A FEW GOOD RESTAU-RANTS IN TOKYO, BUT...
...I HAD NO IDEA ABOUT THIS PLACE.

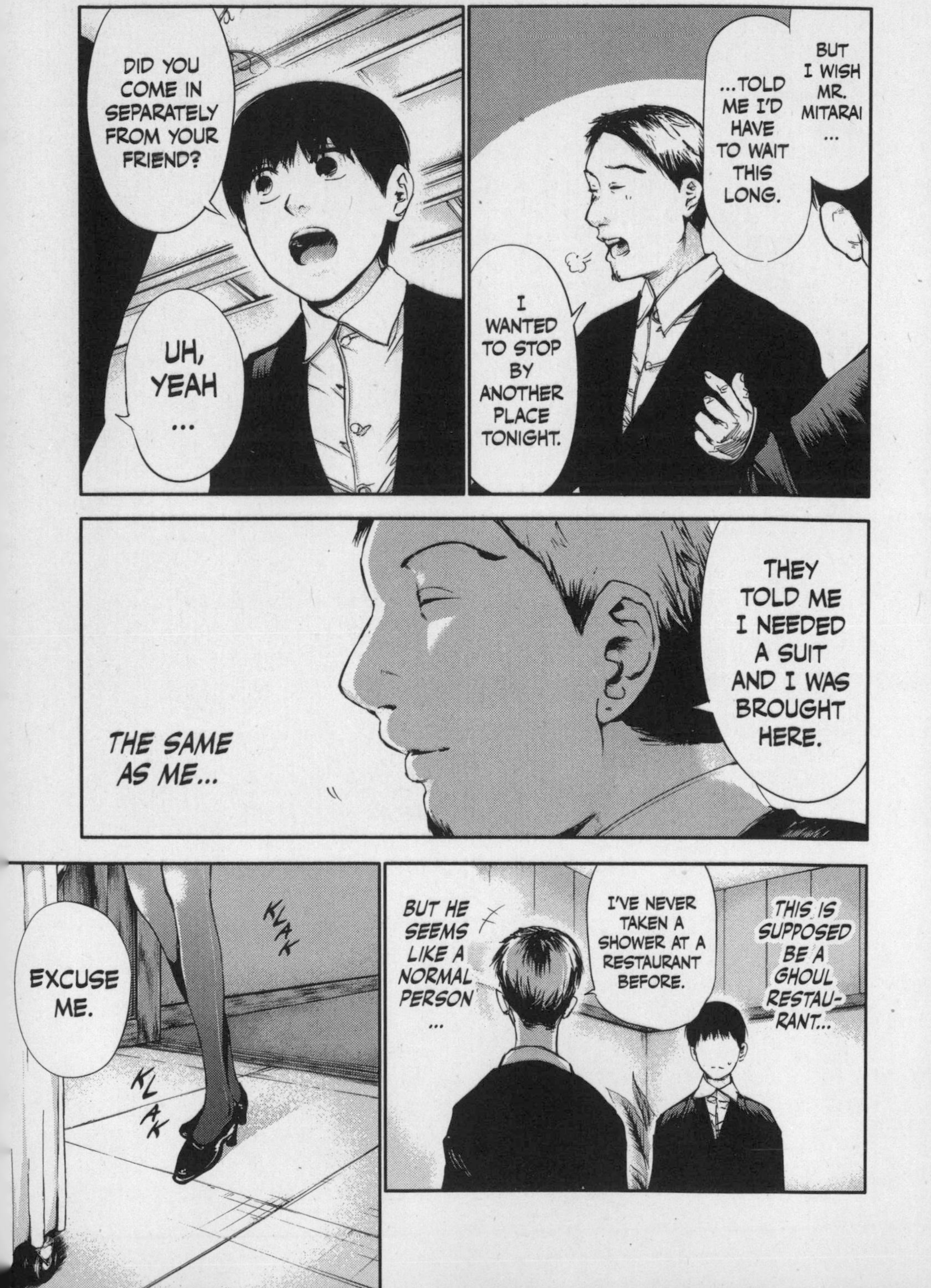
BUT I WISH MR. MITARAI ...
...TOLD ME I'D HAVE TO WAIT THIS LONG.
I WANTED TO STOP BY ANOTHER PLACE TONIGHT.
DID YOU COME IN SEPARATELY FROM YOUR FRIEND?
UH, YEAH ...
THEY TOLD ME I NEEDED A SUIT AND I WAS BROUGHT HERE.
THE SAME AS ME...
THIS IS SUPPOSED BE A GHOUL RESTAU-RANT...
I'VE NEVER TAKEN A SHOWER AT A RESTAURANT BEFORE.
BUT HE SEEMS LIKE A NORMAL PERSON ...
KLAK
EXCUSE ME.
KLAK

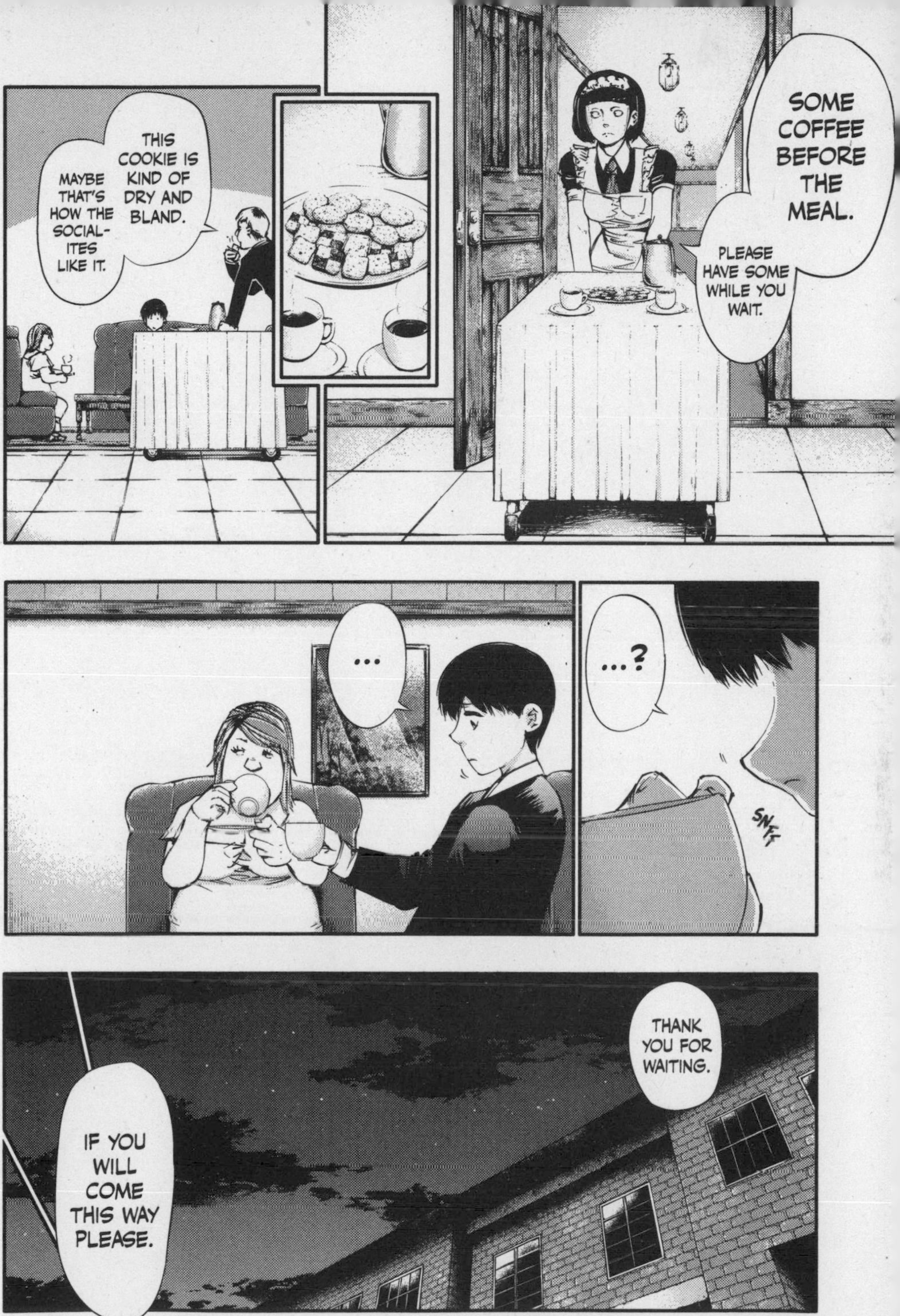
SOME COFFEE BEFORE THE MEAL.
PLEASE HAVE SOME WHILE YOU WAIT.
THIS COOKIE IS KIND OF DRY AND BLAND.
MAYBE THAT'S HOW THE SOCIAL-ITES LIKE IT.
...?
SNFF
...
THANK YOU FOR WAITING.
IF YOU WILL COME THIS WAY PLEASE.

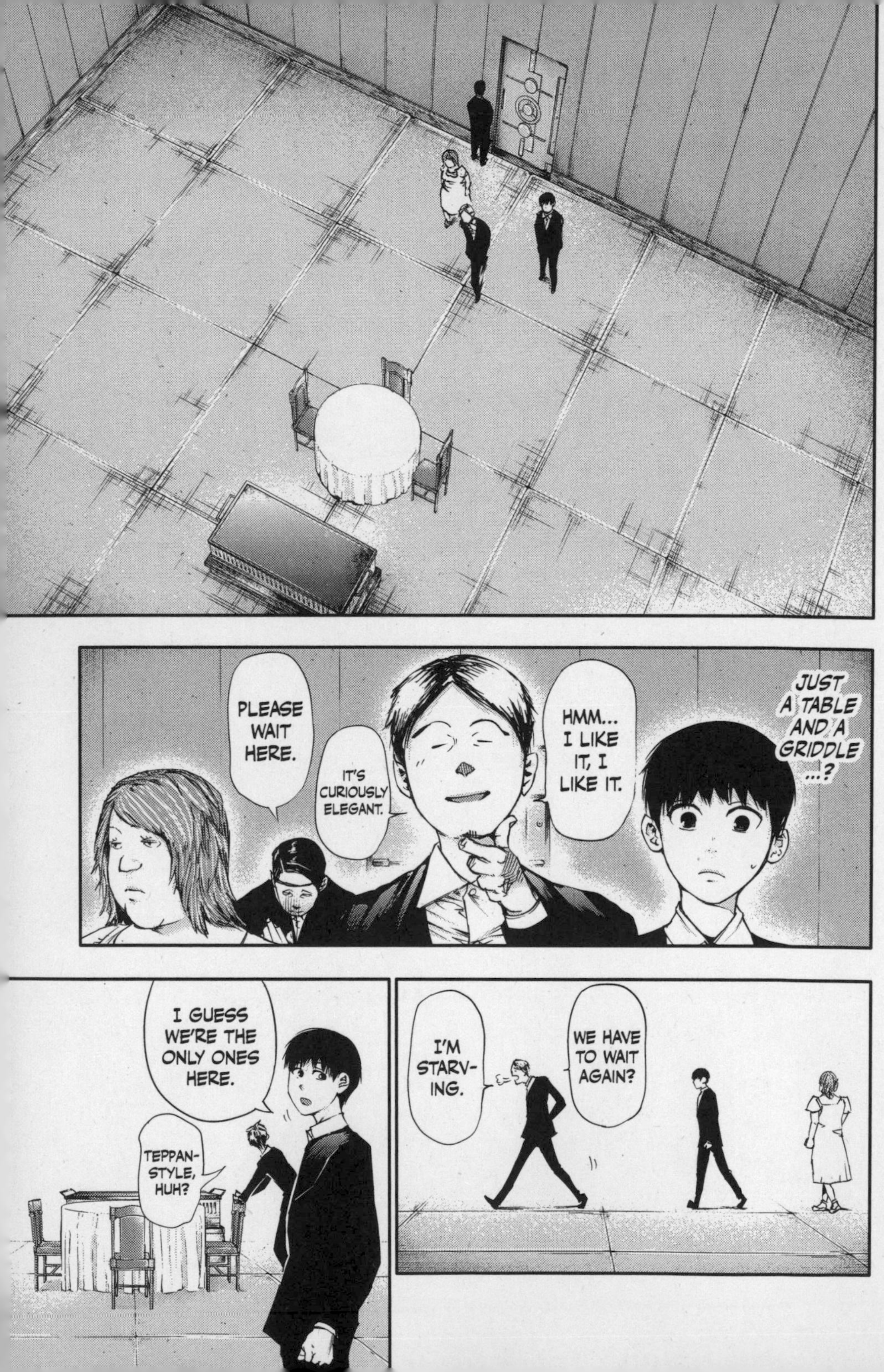
JUST A TABLE AND A GRIDDLE ...?
HMM... I LIKE IT, I LIKE IT.
PLEASE WAIT HERE.
IT'S CURIOUSLY ELEGANT.
WE HAVE TO WAIT AGAIN?
I'M STARV-ING.
I GUESS WE'RE THE ONLY ONES HERE.
TEPPAN-STYLE, HUH?

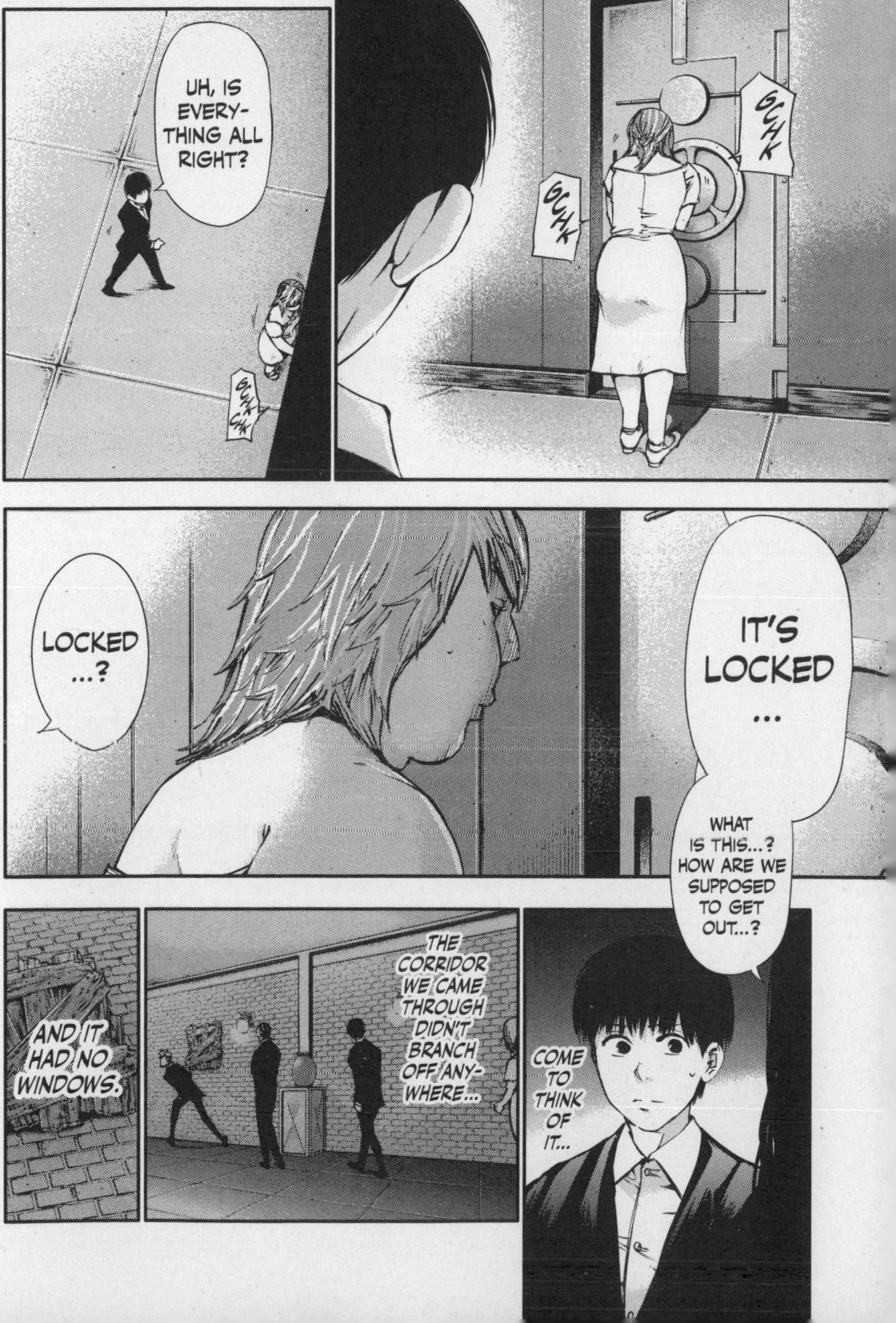
GCHK
GCHK
UH, IS EVERYTHING ALL RIGHT?
GCHK CHK
IT'S LOCKED ...
LOCKED ...?
WHAT IS THIS...? HOW ARE WE SUPPOSED TO GET OUT...?
COME TO THINK OF IT...
THE CORRIDOR WE CAME THROUGH DIDN'T BRANCH OFF ANYWHERE...
AND IT HAD NO WINDOWS.

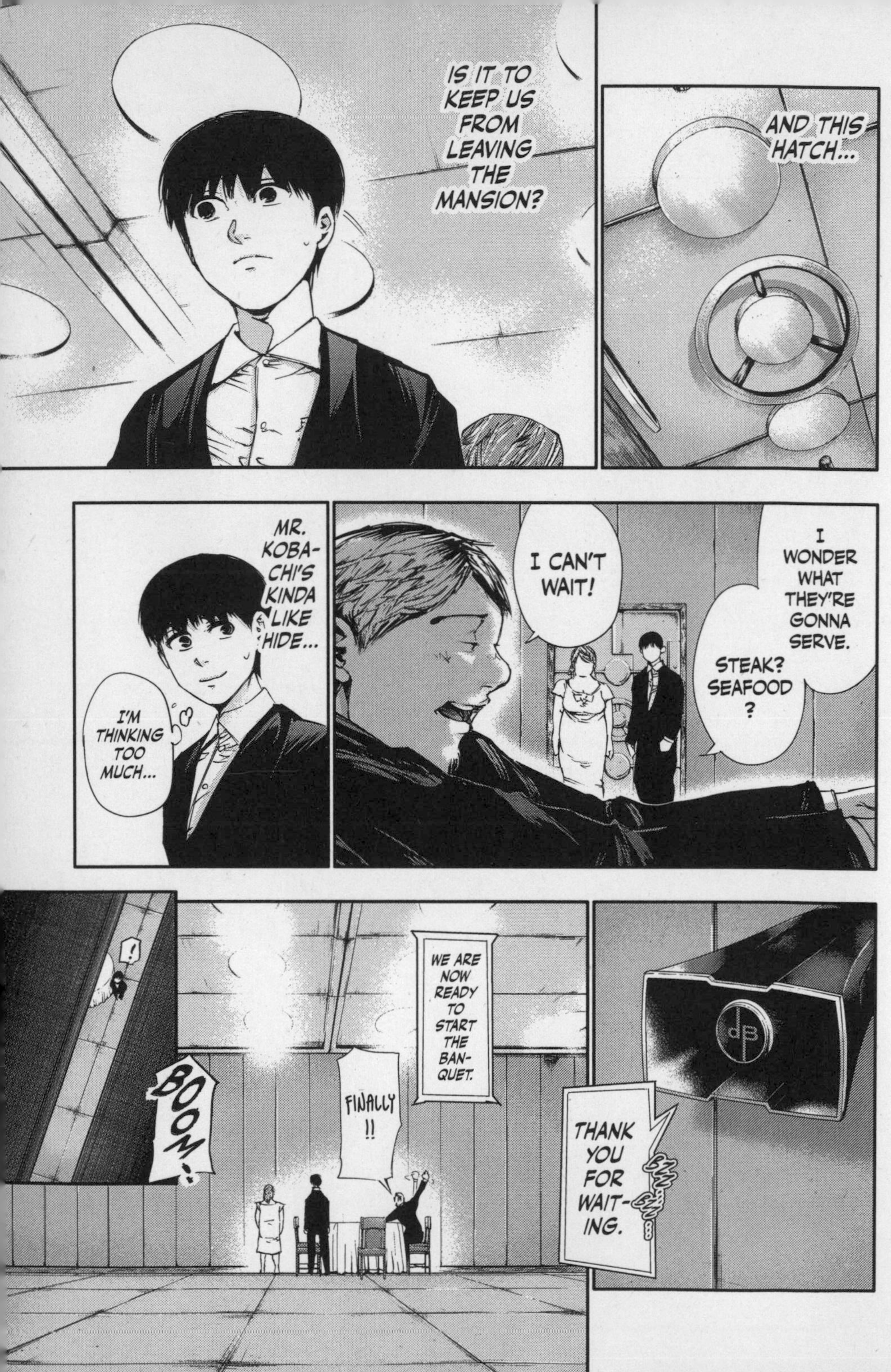
AND THIS HATCH...
IS IT TO KEEP US FROM LEAVING THE MANSION?
I WONDER WHAT THEY'RE GONNA SERVE.
I CAN'T WAIT!
STEAK? SEAFOOD?
MR. KOBACHI'S KINDA LIKE HIDE...
I'M THINKING TOO MUCH...
THANK YOU FOR WAITING.
WE ARE NOW READY TO START THE BANQUET.
FINALLY!!
BOOM!
!

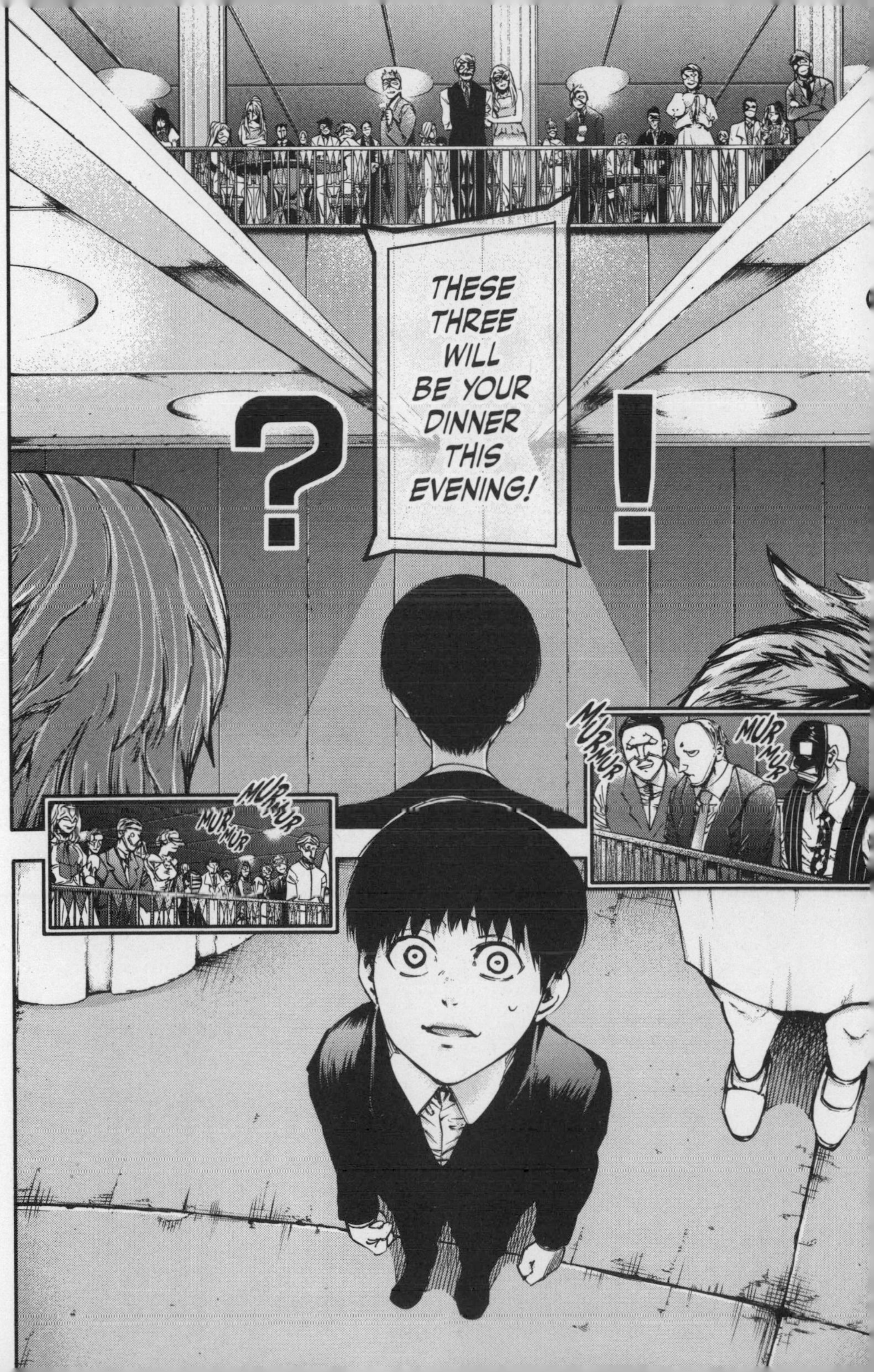
!
THESE THREE WILL BE YOUR DINNER THIS EVENING!
?
MURMUR
MUR MUR
MURMUR
MUR MUR

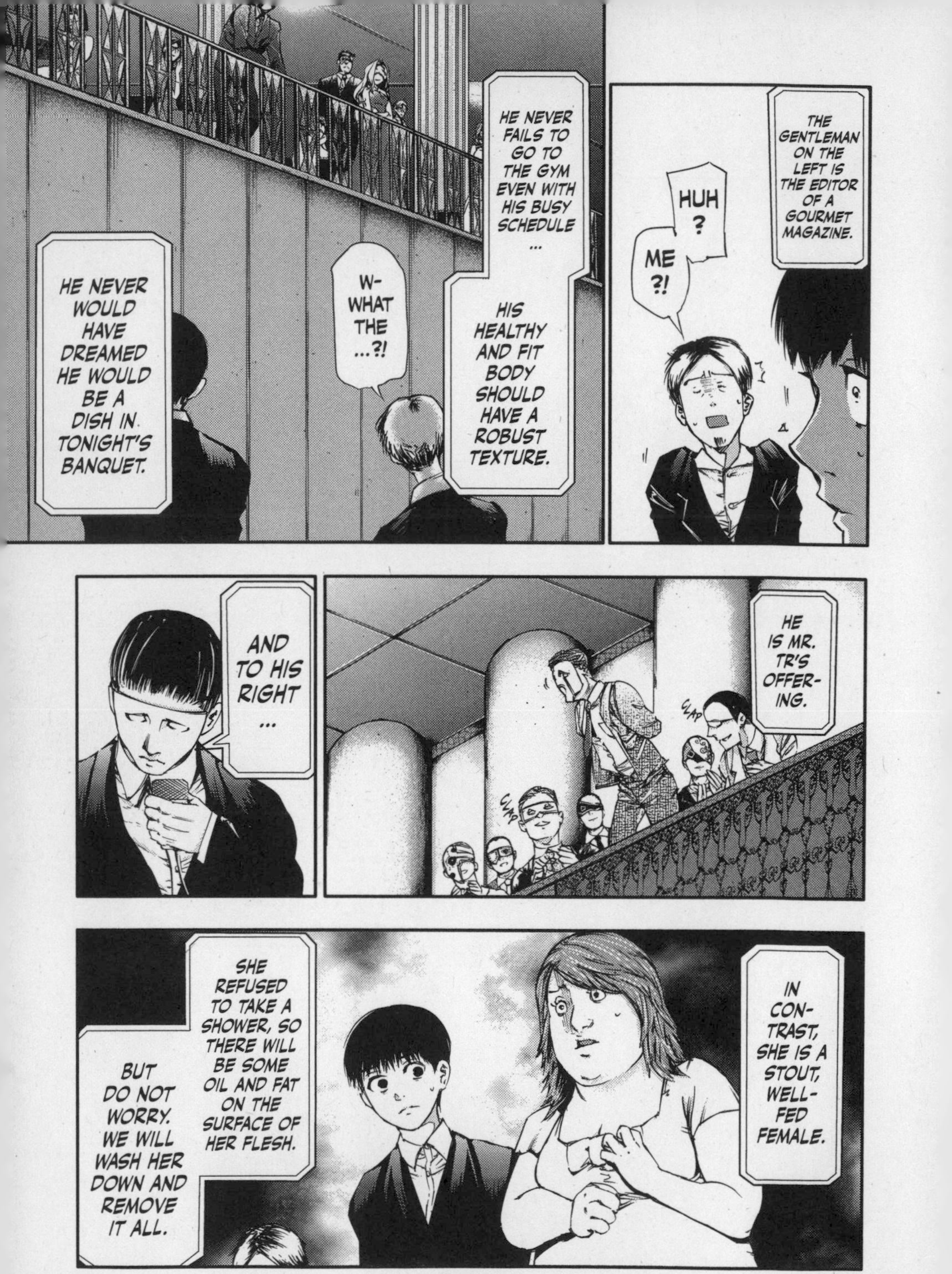
THE GENTLEMAN ON THE LEFT IS THE EDITOR OF A GOURMET MAGAZINE.
HUH?
ME?!
HE NEVER FAILS TO GO TO THE GYM EVEN WITH HIS BUSY SCHEDULE ...
HIS HEALTHY AND FIT BODY SHOULD HAVE A ROBUST TEXTURE.
W- WHAT THE ...?!
HE NEVER WOULD HAVE DREAMED HE WOULD BE A DISH IN TONIGHT'S BANQUET.
HE IS MR. TR'S OFFERING.
CLAP
CLAP
AND TO HIS RIGHT ...
IN CONTRAST, SHE IS A STOUT, WELL-FED FEMALE.
SHE REFUSED TO TAKE A SHOWER, SO THERE WILL BE SOME OIL AND FAT ON THE SURFACE OF HER FLESH.
BUT DO NOT WORRY. WE WILL WASH HER DOWN AND REMOVE IT ALL.

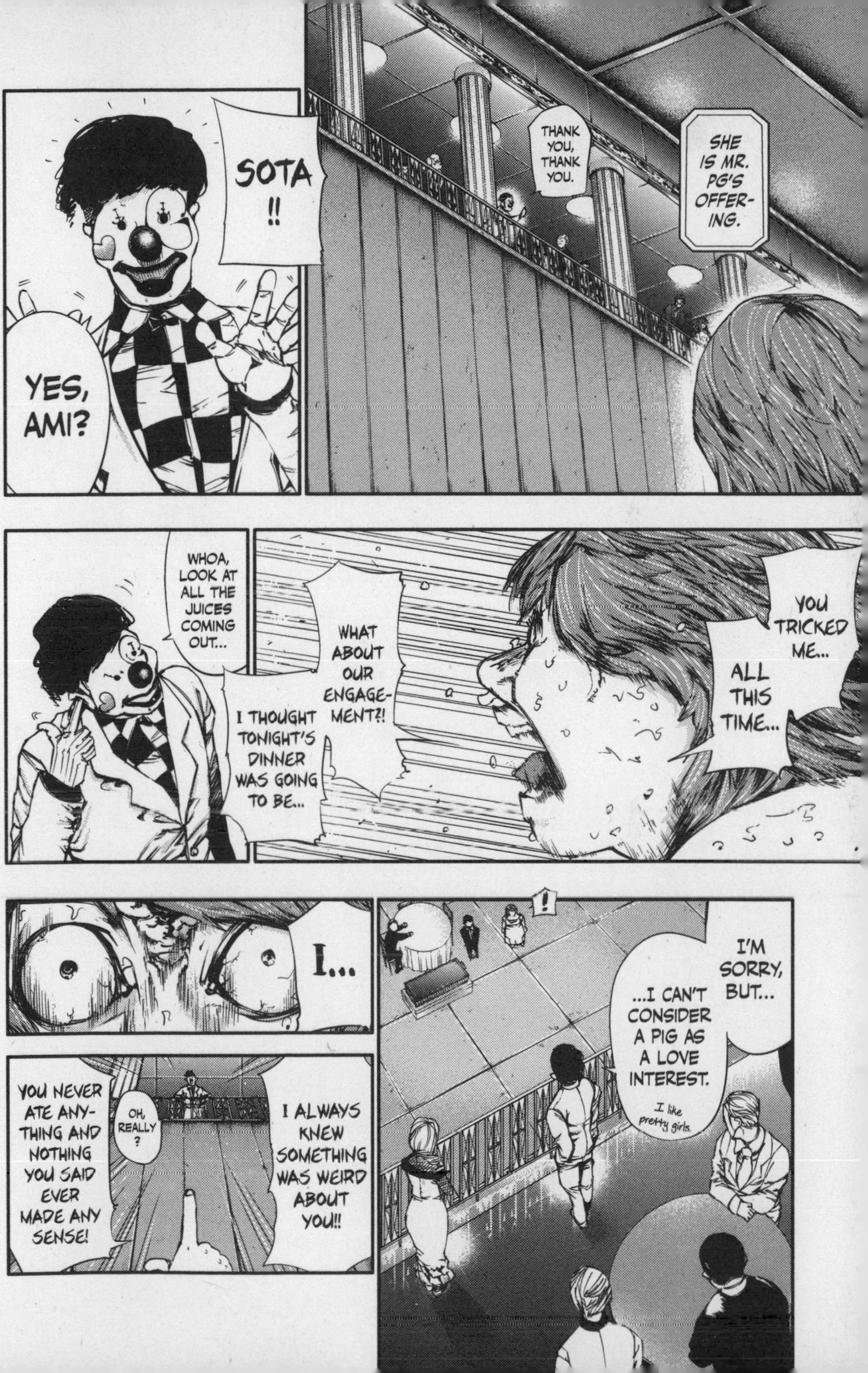
SHE IS MR. PG'S OFFER-ING.
THANK YOU, THANK YOU.
SOTA!!
YES, AMI?
YOU TRICKED ME...
ALL THIS TIME...
WHAT ABOUT OUR ENGAGE-MENT?!
I THOUGHT TONIGHT'S DINNER WAS GOING TO BE...
WHOA, LOOK AT ALL THE JUICES COMING OUT...
!
I'M SORRY, BUT...
...I CAN'T CONSIDER A PIG AS A LOVE INTEREST.
I like pretty girls.
I...
I ALWAYS KNEW SOMETHING WAS WEIRD ABOUT YOU!!
OH, REALLY?
YOU NEVER ATE ANY-THING AND NOTHING YOU SAID EVER MADE ANY SENSE!

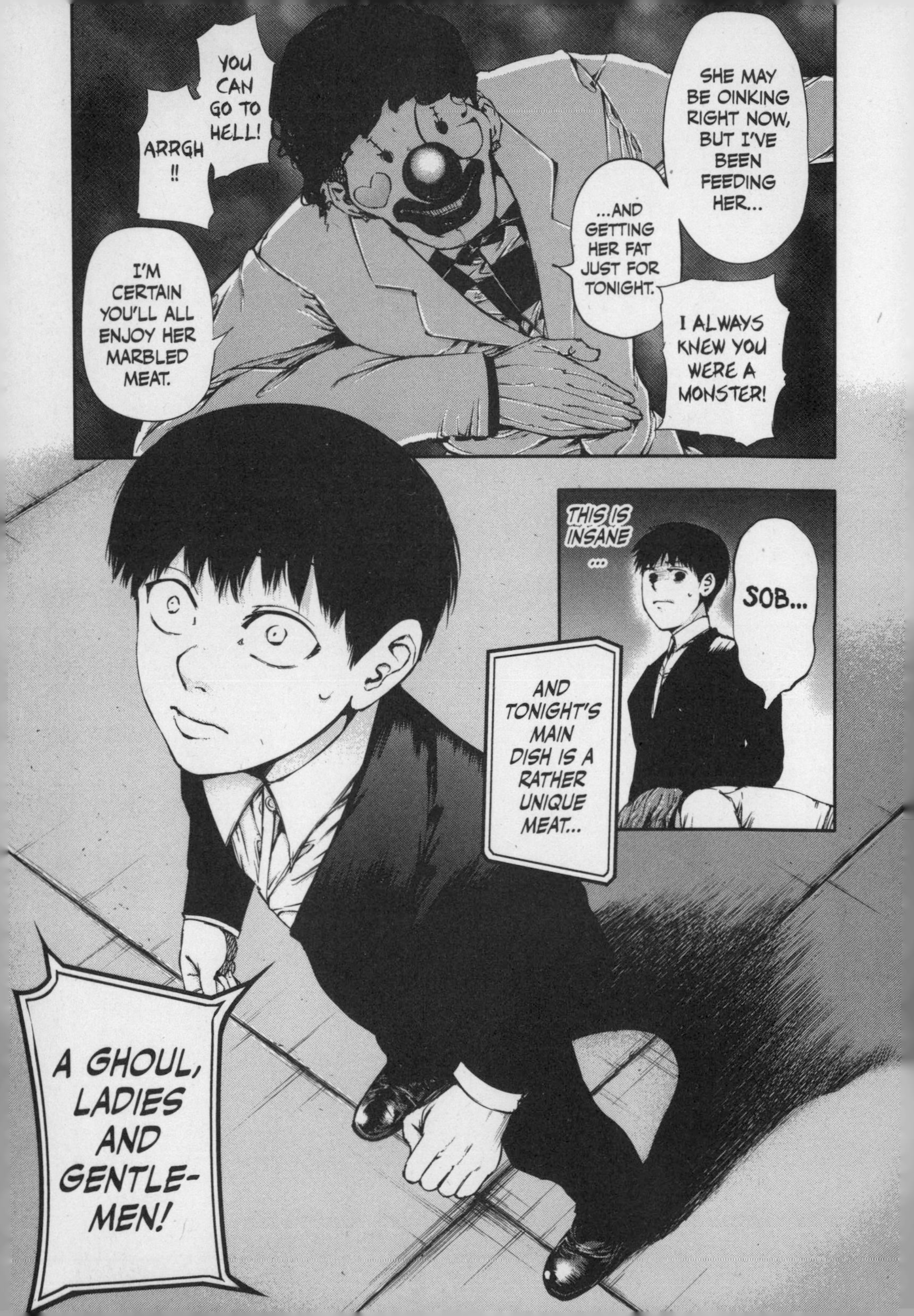
SHE MAY BE OINKING RIGHT NOW, BUT I'VE BEEN FEEDING HER...
...AND GETTING HER FAT JUST FOR TONIGHT.
YOU CAN GO TO HELL!
ARRGH!!
I ALWAYS KNEW YOU WERE A MONSTER!
I'M CERTAIN YOU'LL ALL ENJOY HER MARBLED MEAT.
SOB...
THIS IS INSANE...
AND TONIGHT'S MAIN DISH IS A RATHER UNIQUE MEAT...
A GHOUL, LADIES AND GENTLE-MEN!

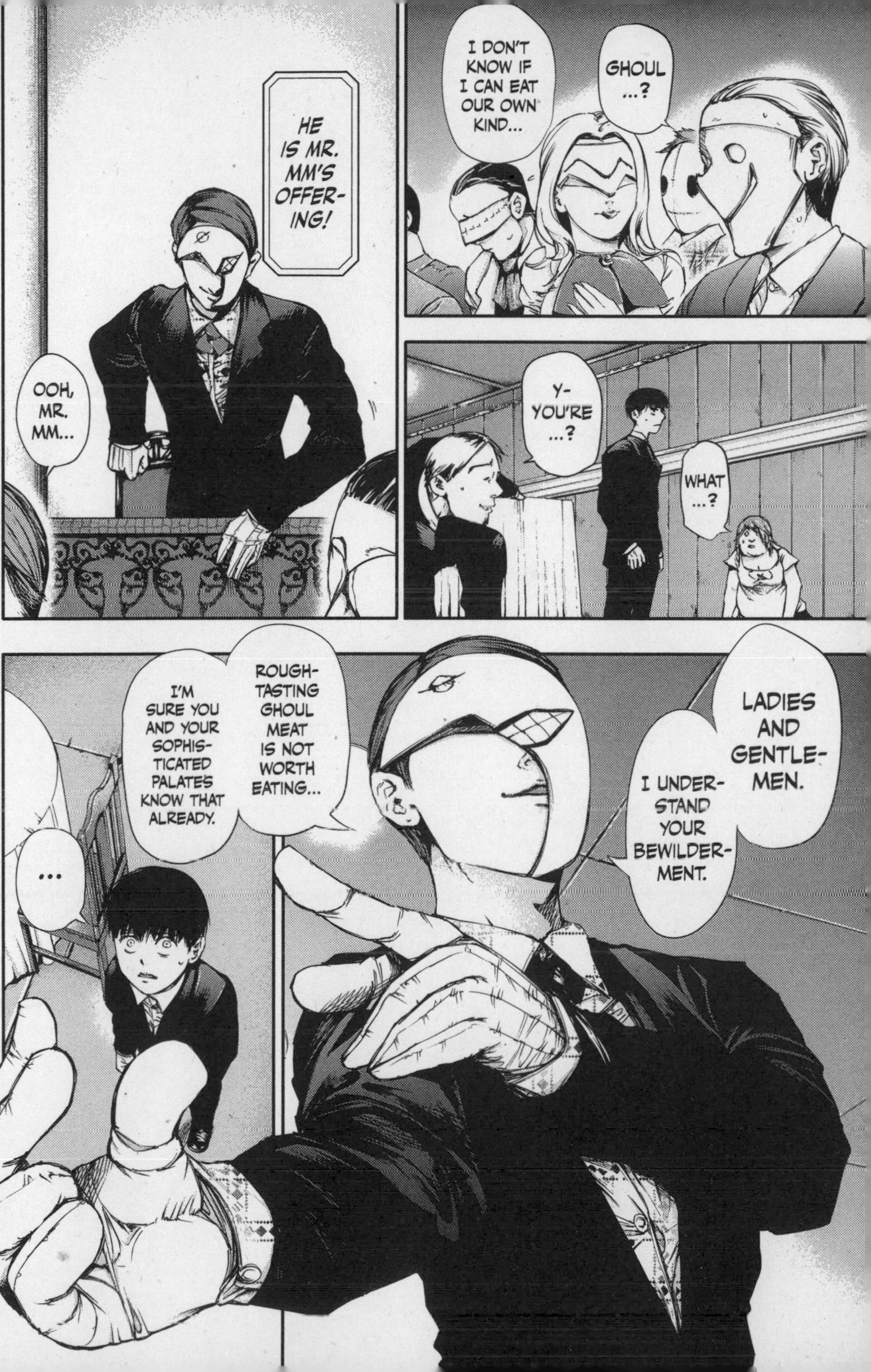
GHOUL ...?
I DON'T KNOW IF I CAN EAT OUR OWN KIND...
Y- YOU'RE ...?
WHAT ...?
HE IS MR. MM'S OFFERING!
OOH, MR. MM...
LADIES AND GENTLEMEN.
I UNDERSTAND YOUR BEWILDERMENT.
ROUGH-TASTING GHOUL MEAT IS NOT WORTH EATING...
I'M SURE YOU AND YOUR SOPHISTICATED PALATES KNOW THAT ALREADY.
...

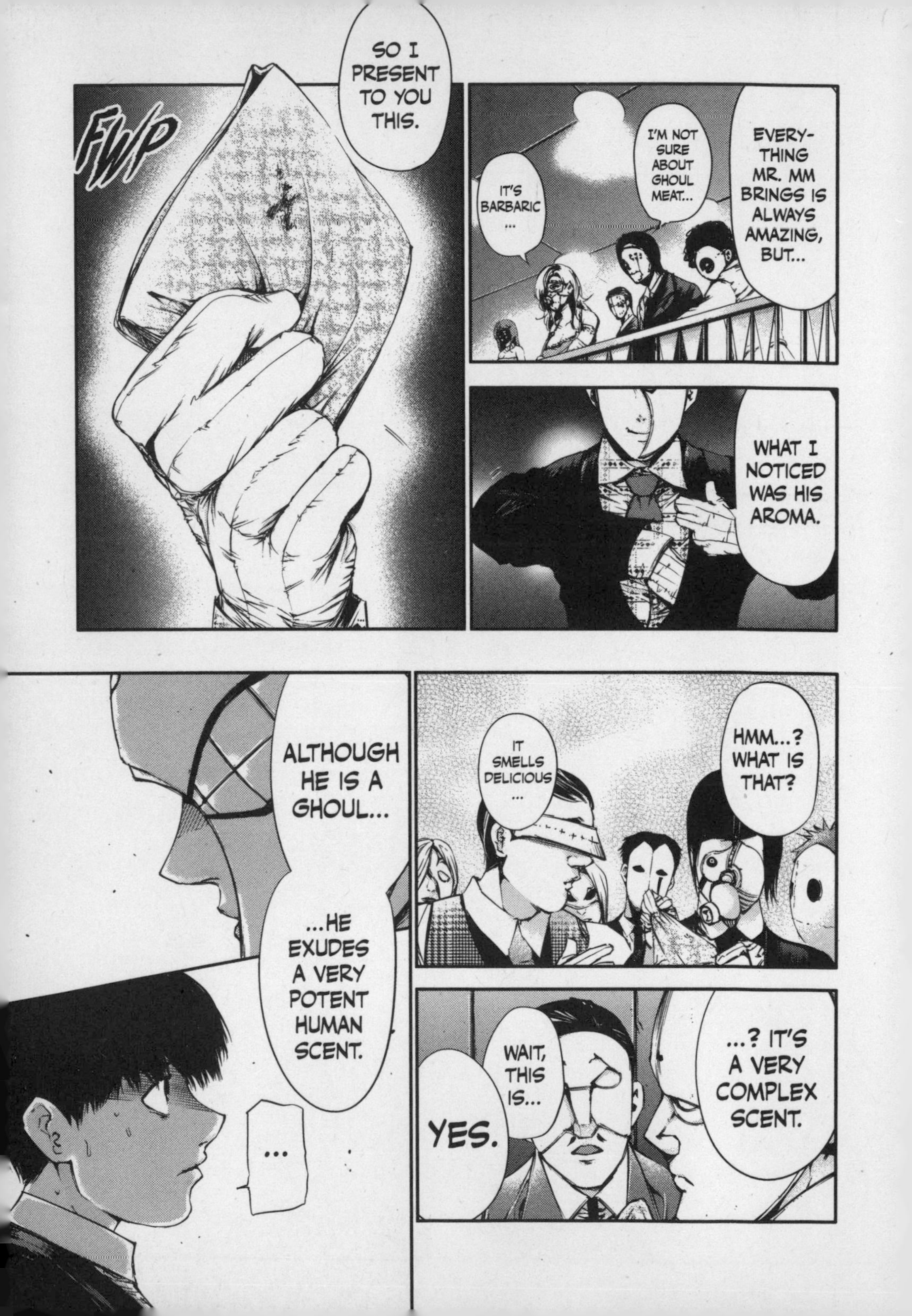
EVERY-THING MR. MM BRINGS IS ALWAYS AMAZING, BUT...
I'M NOT SURE ABOUT GHOUL MEAT...
IT'S BARBARIC...
WHAT I NOTICED WAS HIS AROMA.
SO I PRESENT TO YOU THIS.
FWP
HMM...? WHAT IS THAT?
IT SMELLS DELICIOUS...
...? IT'S A VERY COMPLEX SCENT.
WAIT, THIS IS...
YES.
ALTHOUGH HE IS A GHOUL...
...HE EXUDES A VERY POTENT HUMAN SCENT.
...

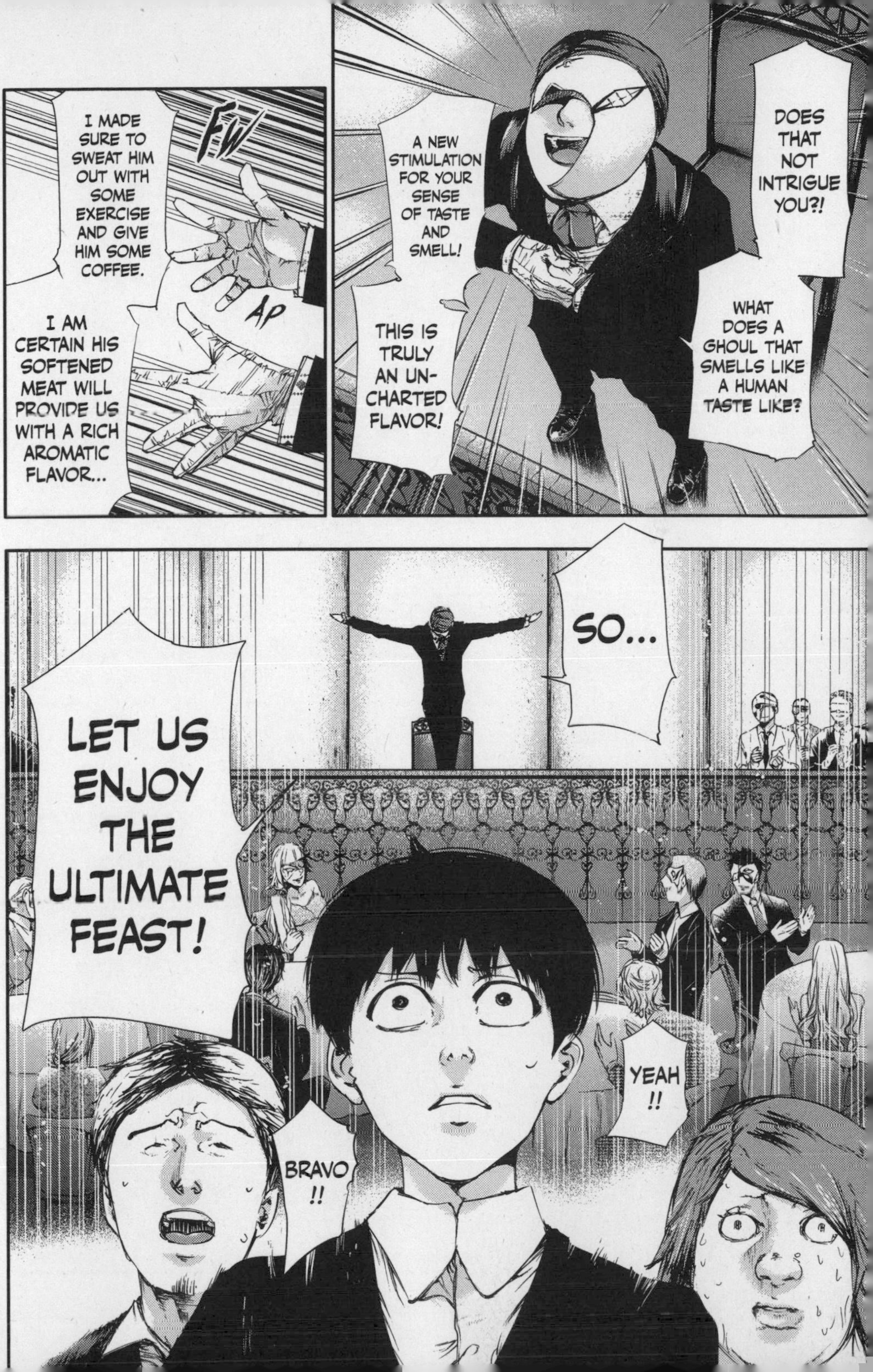
DOES THAT NOT INTRIGUE YOU?!
A NEW STIMULATION FOR YOUR SENSE OF TASTE AND SMELL!
WHAT DOES A GHOUL THAT SMELLS LIKE A HUMAN TASTE LIKE?
THIS IS TRULY AN UN-CHARTED FLAVOR!
FW
I MADE SURE TO SWEAT HIM OUT WITH SOME EXERCISE AND GIVE HIM SOME COFFEE.
AP
I AM CERTAIN HIS SOFTENED MEAT WILL PROVIDE US WITH A RICH AROMATIC FLAVOR...
SO...
LET US ENJOY THE ULTIMATE FEAST!
YEAH !!
BRAVO !!

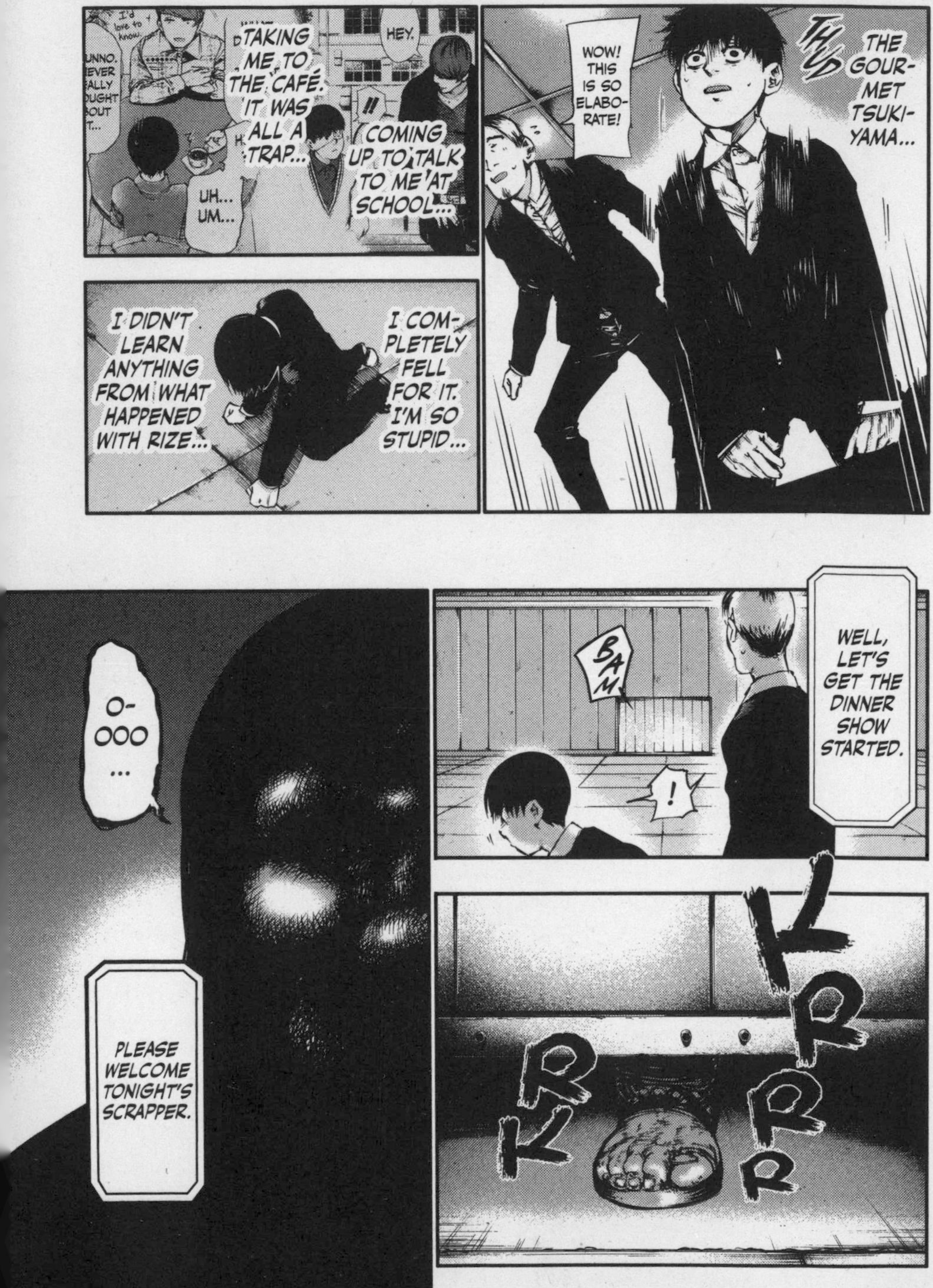
THUD
THE GOURMET TSUKIYAMA...
WOW! THIS IS SO ELABORATE!
HEY.
!!
COMING UP TO TALK TO ME AT SCHOOL...
TAKING ME TO THE CAFÉ. IT WAS ALL A TRAP...
I'd love to know.
UH... UM...
I COMPLETELY FELL FOR IT. I'M SO STUPID...
I DIDN'T LEARN ANYTHING FROM WHAT HAPPENED WITH RIZE...
WELL, LET'S GET THE DINNER SHOW STARTED.
BAM
!
KRRR
KRRR
O-OOO...
PLEASE WELCOME TONIGHT'S SCRAPPER.

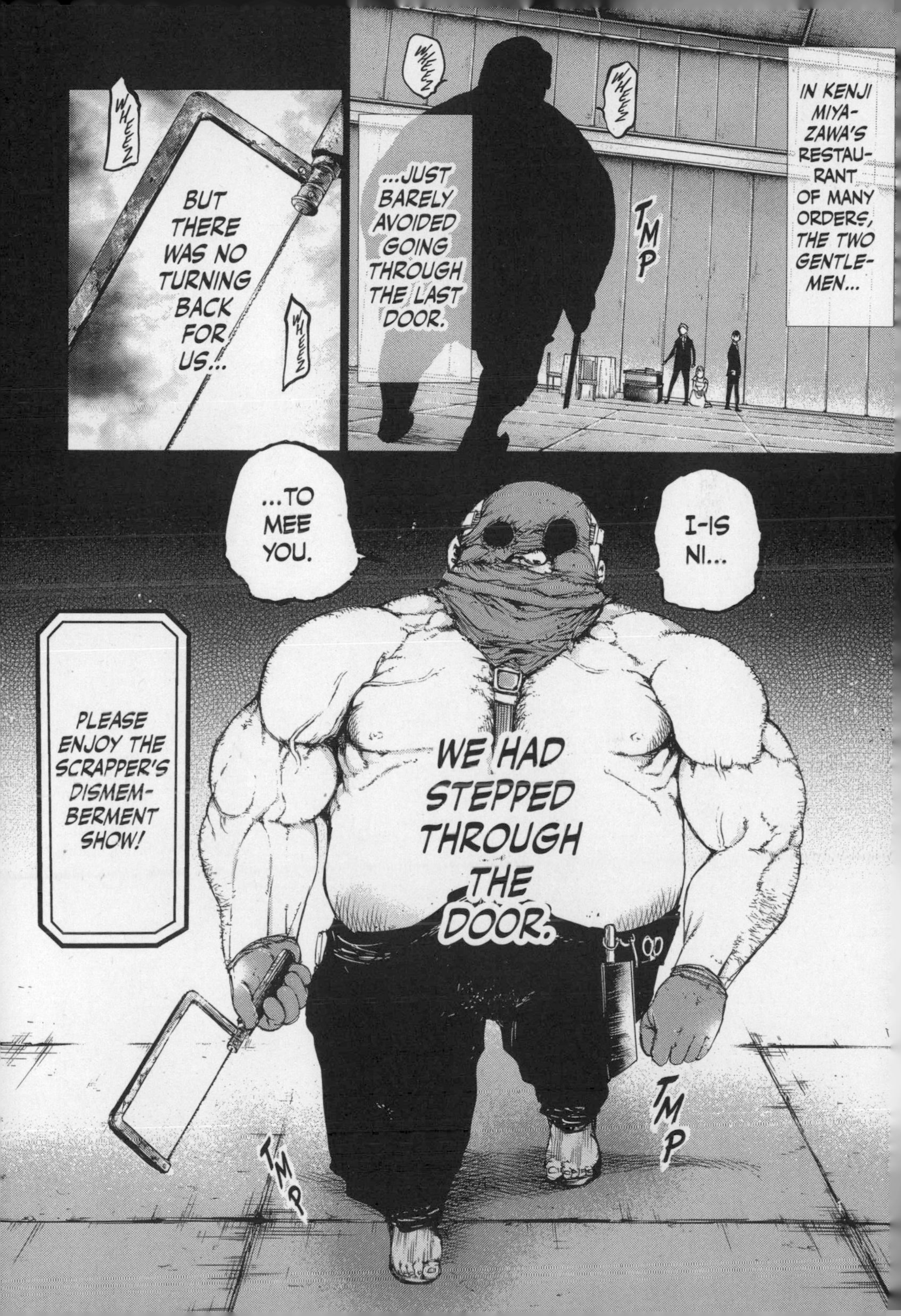
IN KENJI MIYAZAWA'S RESTAURANT OF MANY ORDERS, THE TWO GENTLEMEN...
WHEEZ
WHEEZ
TMP
...JUST BARELY AVOIDED GOING THROUGH THE LAST DOOR.
WHEEZ
BUT THERE WAS NO TURNING BACK FOR US...
WHEEZ
I-IS NI...
...TO MEE YOU.
WE HAD STEPPED THROUGH THE DOOR.
PLEASE ENJOY THE SCRAPPER'S DISMEMBERMENT SHOW!
TMP
TMP

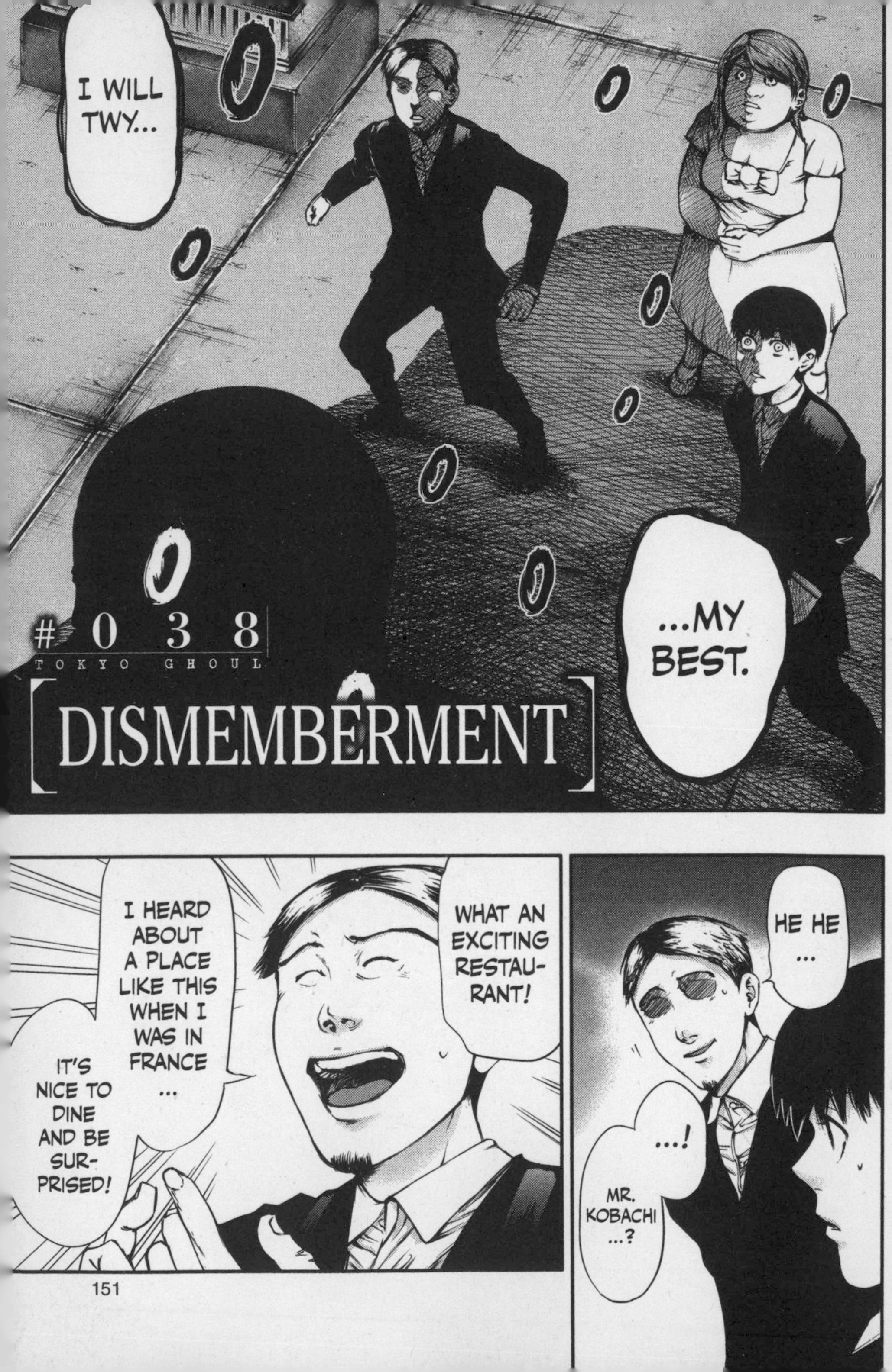
I WILL TWY...
...MY BEST.
#038
TOKYO GHOUL
DISMEMBERMENT
HE HE ...
...!
MR. KOBACHI ...?
WHAT AN EXCITING RESTAU-RANT!
I HEARD ABOUT A PLACE LIKE THIS WHEN I WAS IN FRANCE ...
IT'S NICE TO DINE AND BE SUR-PRISED!

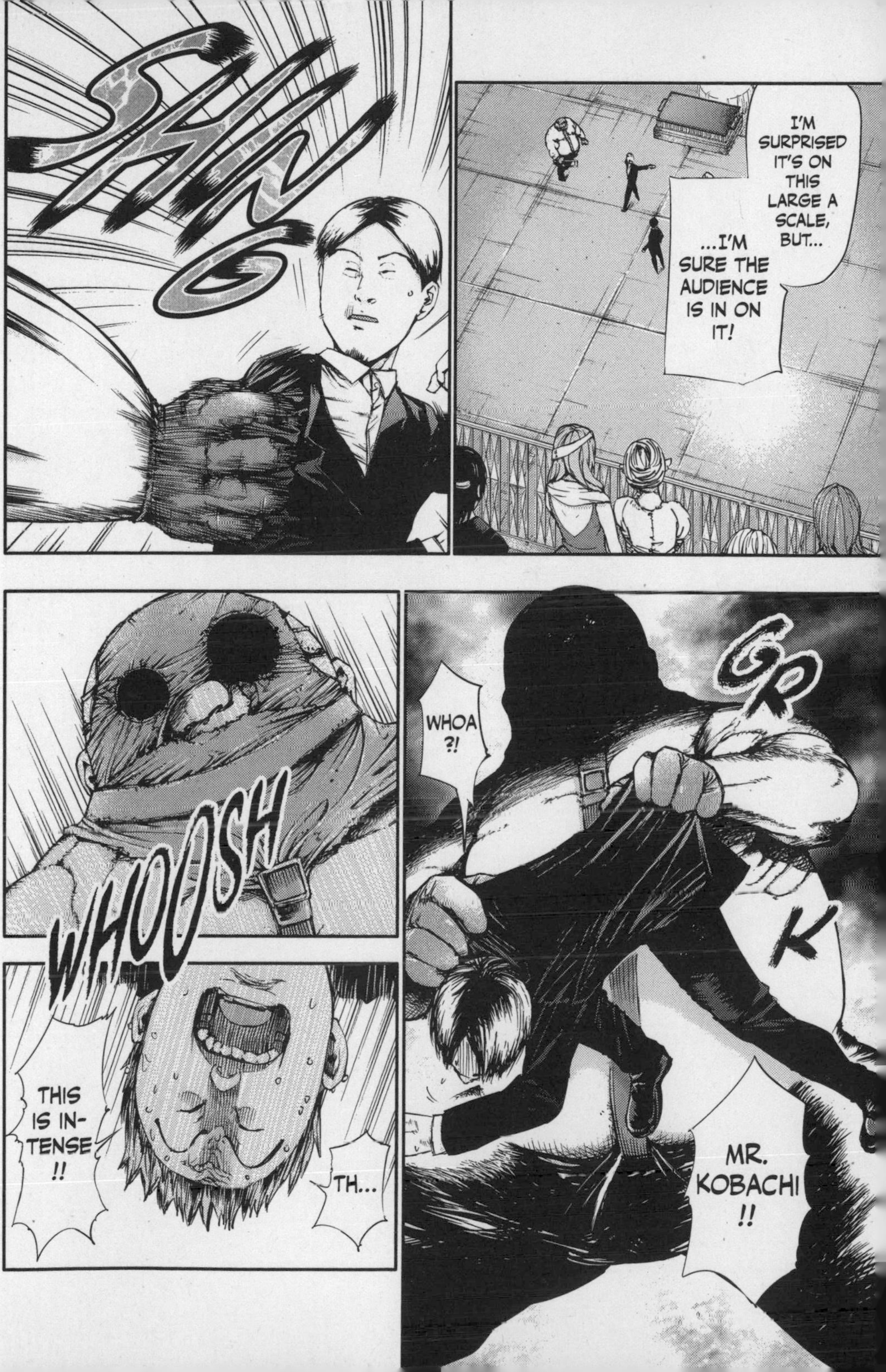
I'M SURPRISED IT'S ON THIS LARGE A SCALE, BUT...
...I'M SURE THE AUDIENCE IS IN ON IT!
SHING
GRK
WHOA?!
MR. KOBACHI!!
WHOOSH
TH...
THIS IS IN-TENSE!!

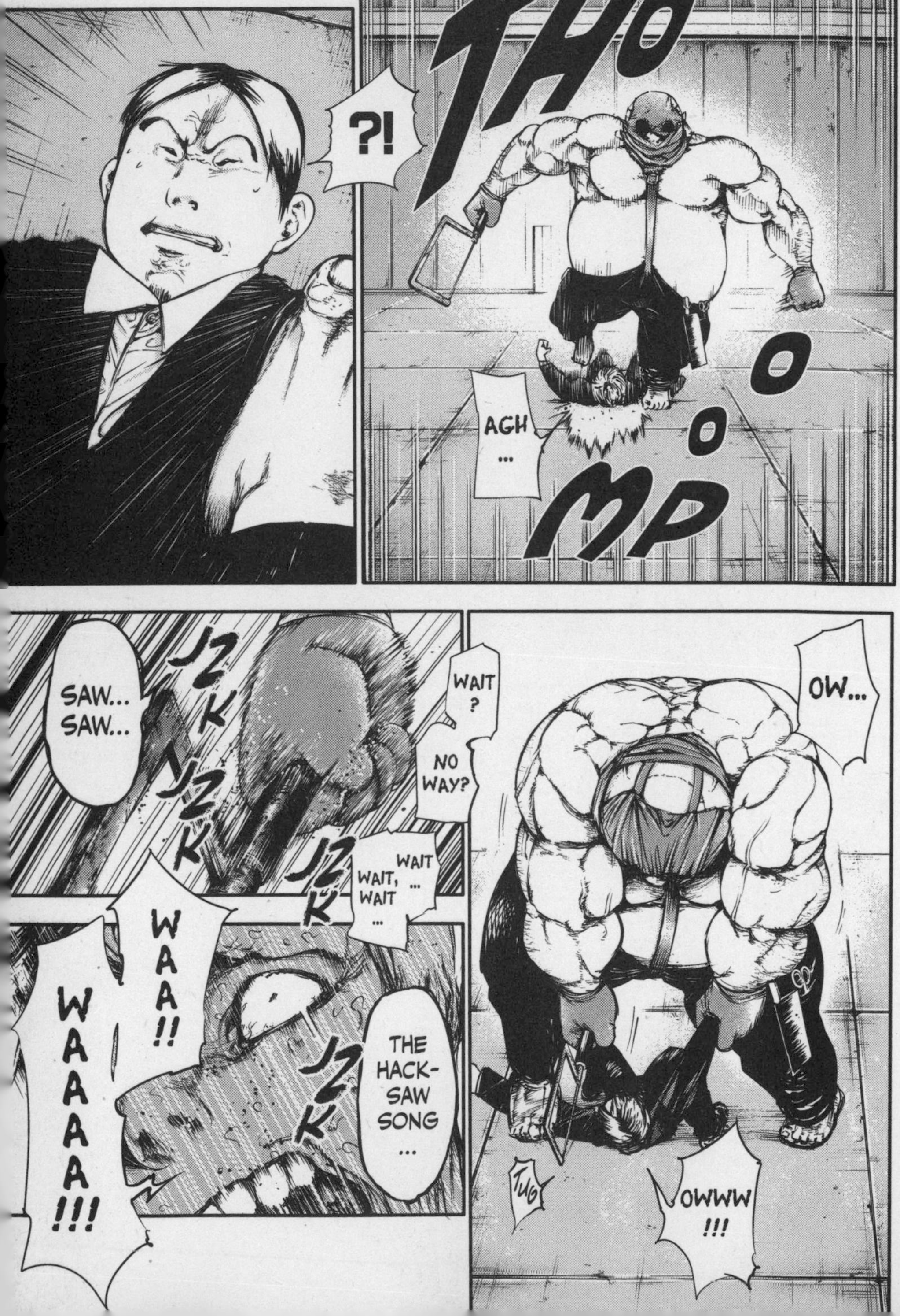
THOOOOMP
AGH ...
?!
OW...
TUG
OWWW !!!
WAIT ?
NO WAY?
SAW... SAW...
JZK
JZK
JZK
WAIT, WAIT ... WAIT ...
THE HACK-SAW SONG ...
JZK
WAAA!!
WAAAAAA!!!

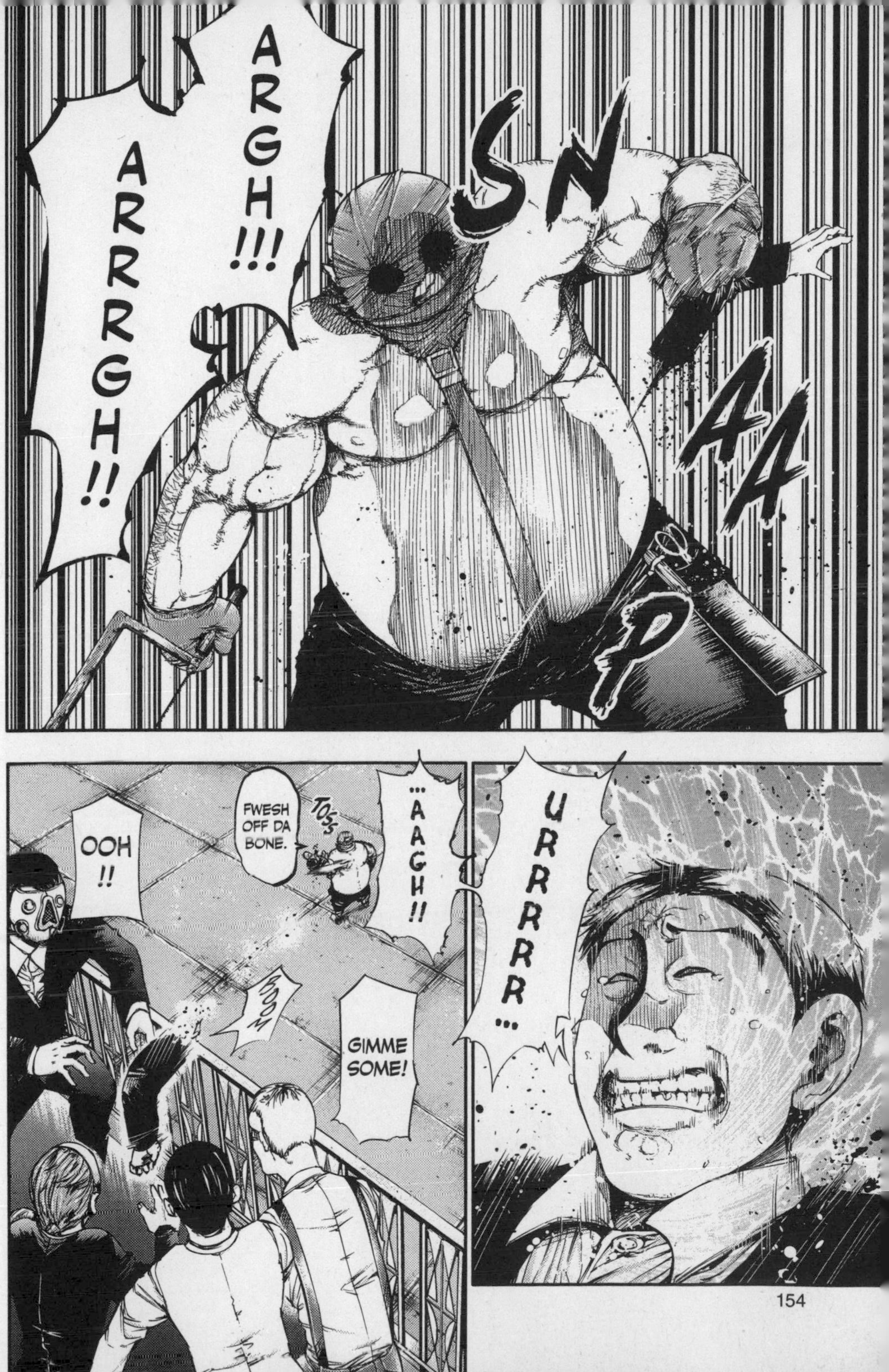
ARGH!!!
ARRRGH!!
SNAP
URRRRR...
...AAGH!!
FWESH OFF DA BONE.
TOSS
OOH!!
GIMME SOME!

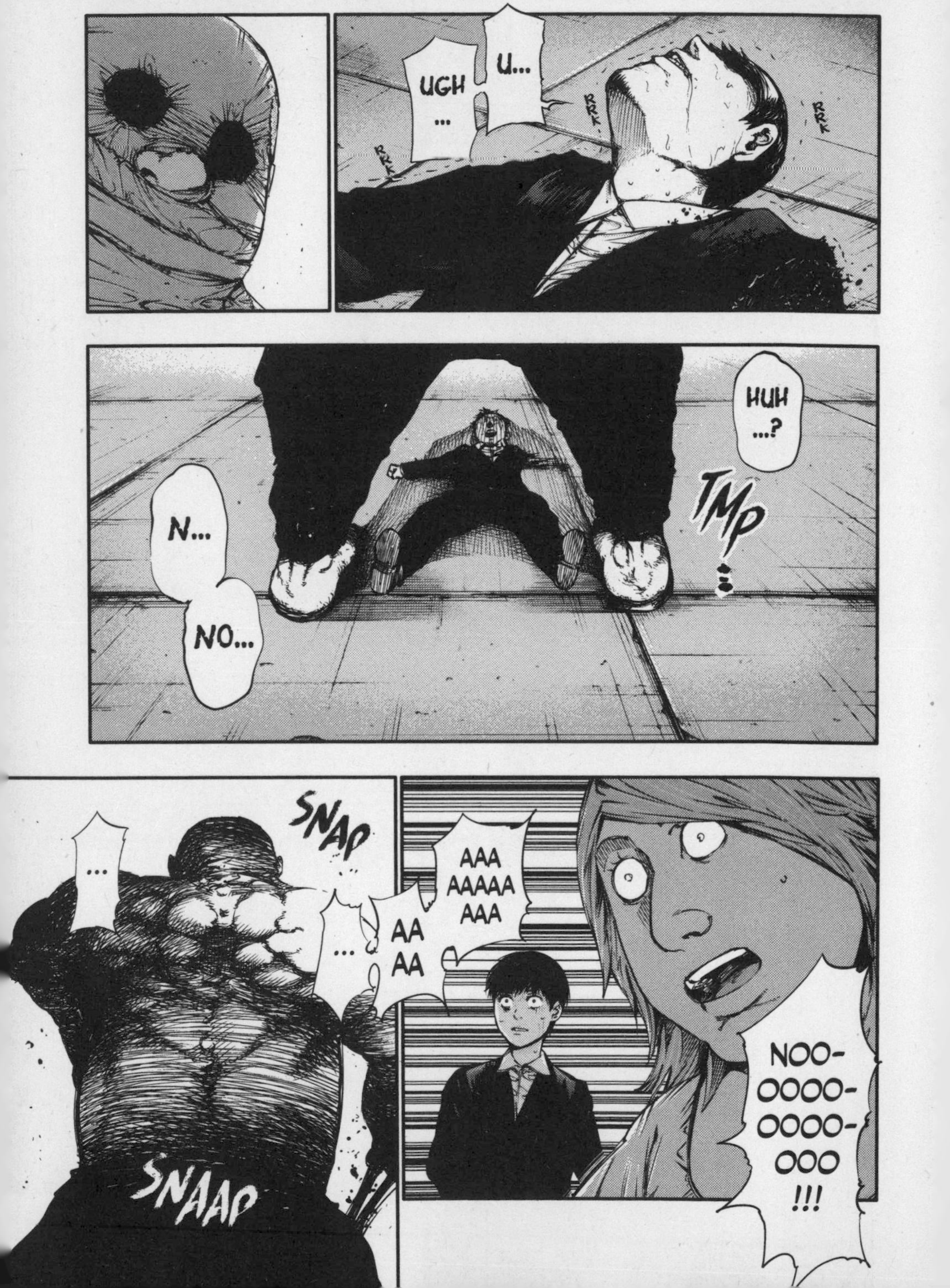
RRK
U...
UGH ...
RRK
RRK
HUH ...?
TMP
N...
NO...
AAA AAAAA AAA
NOO-OOOO-OOOO-OOO !!!
SNAP
...
AA AA
...
SNAAP

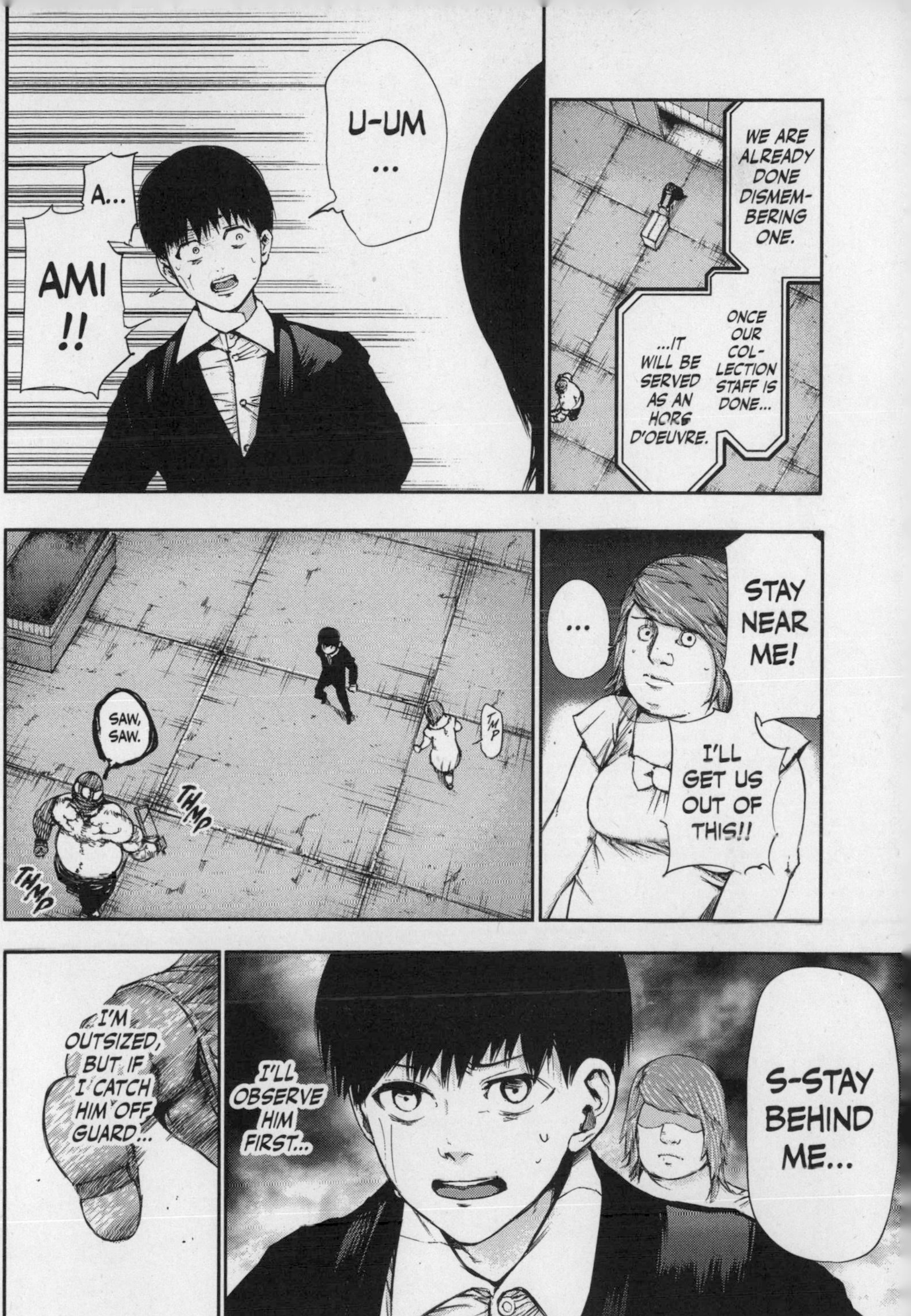
WE ARE ALREADY DONE DISMEMBERING ONE.
ONCE OUR COLLECTION STAFF IS DONE...
...IT WILL BE SERVED AS AN HORS D'OEUVRE.
U-UM ...
A...
AMI !!
STAY NEAR ME!
...
I'LL GET US OUT OF THIS!!
TMP
SAW, SAW.
THMP
THMP
S-STAY BEHIND ME...
I'LL OBSERVE HIM FIRST...
I'M OUTSIZED, BUT IF I CATCH HIM OFF GUARD...

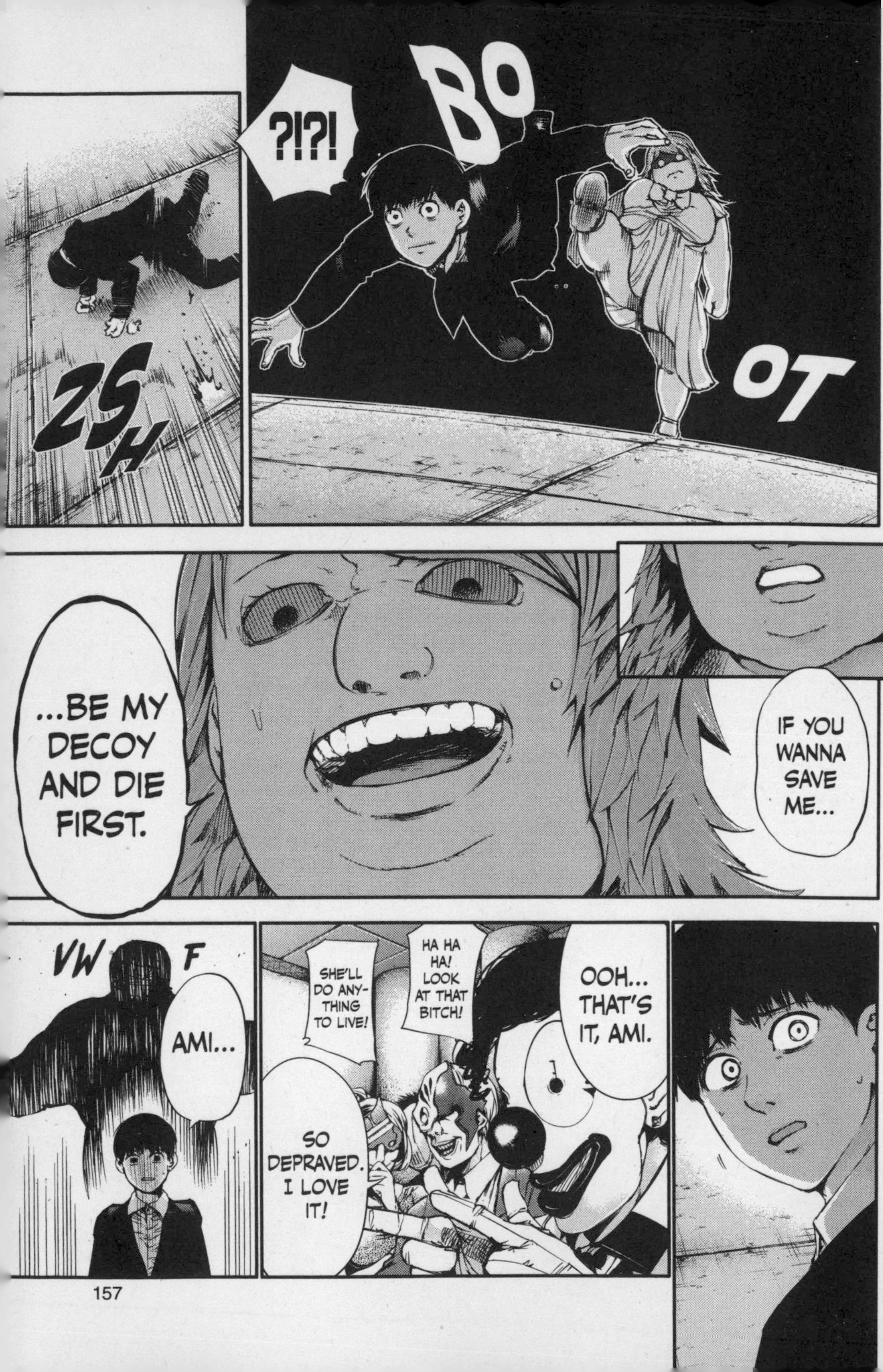

?!?!
BO
OT
ZSH
IF YOU WANNA SAVE ME...
...BE MY DECOY AND DIE FIRST.
OOH... THAT'S IT, AMI.
HA HA HA! LOOK AT THAT BITCH!
SHE'LL DO ANYTHING TO LIVE!
SO DEPRAVED. I LOVE IT!
VW F
AMI...

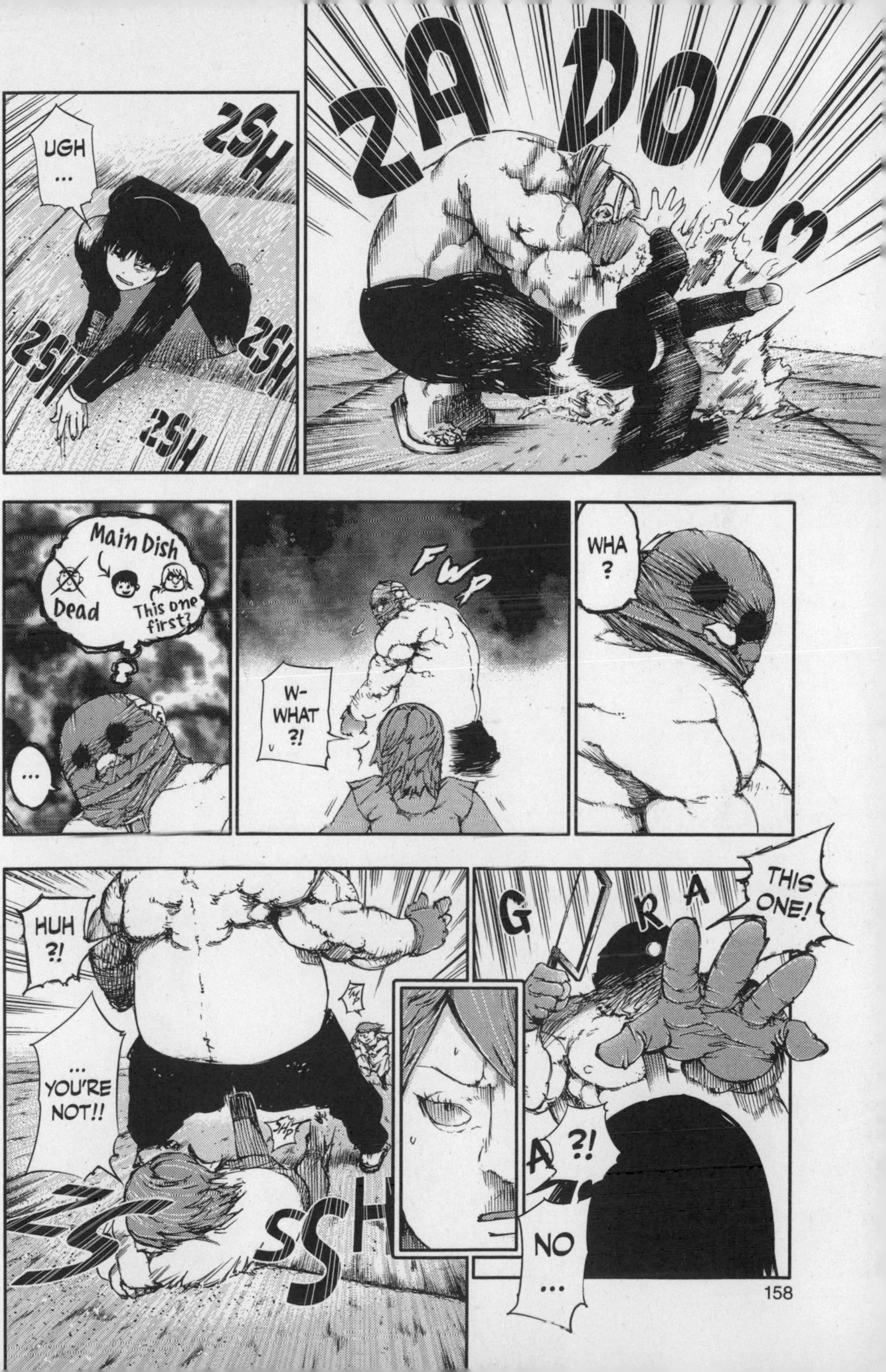
ZA DOOM
UGH ...
ZSH
ZSH
ZSH
ZSH
WHA ?
FWP
W- WHAT ?!
Main Dish
Dead
This one first?
...
GRA
THIS ONE!
A ?!
NO ...
HUH ?!
... YOU'RE NOT!!
SSH

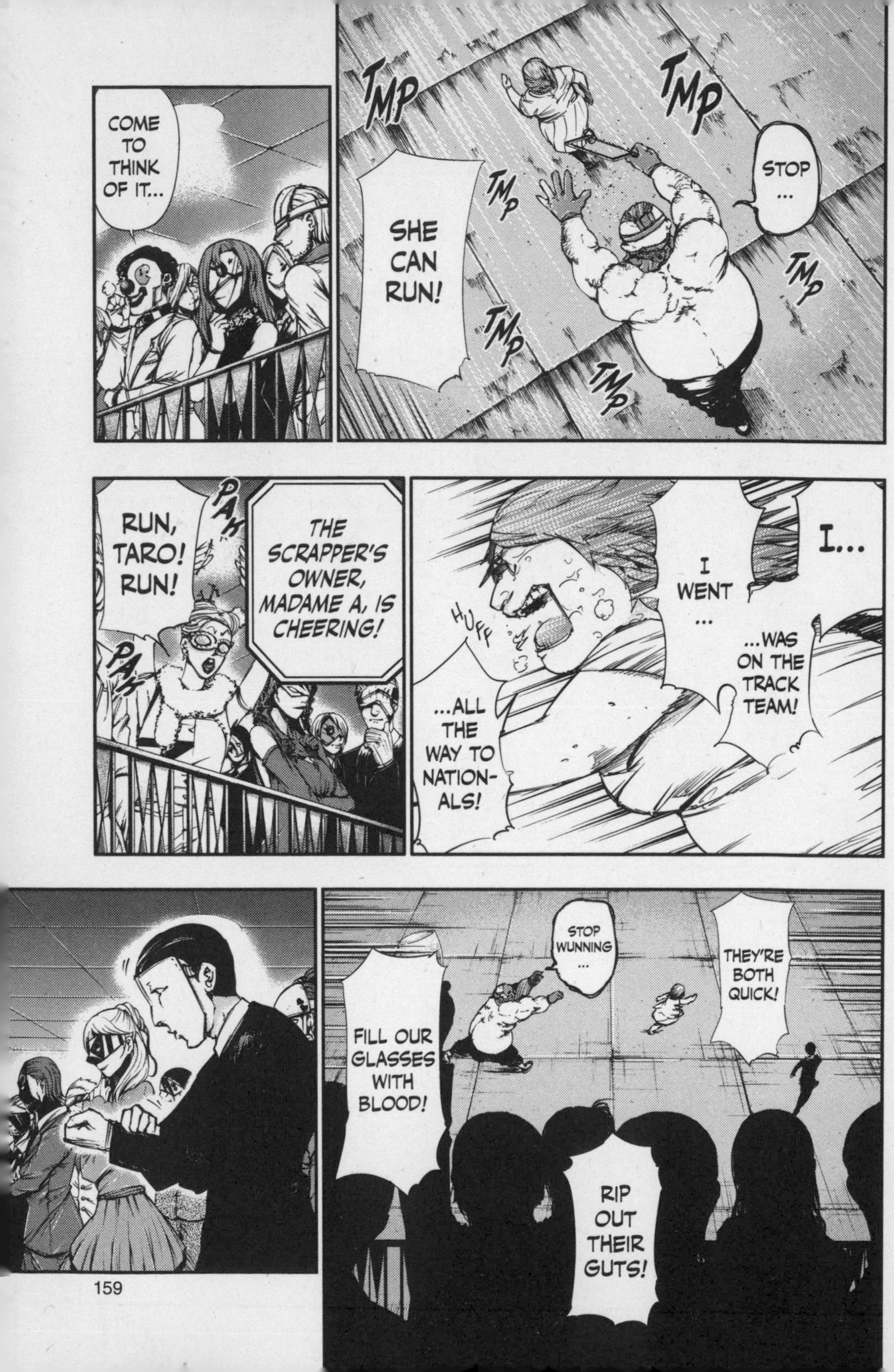
TMP
TMP
STOP ...
SHE CAN RUN!
TMP
TMP
TMP
TMP
COME TO THINK OF IT...
I...
I WENT ...
...WAS ON THE TRACK TEAM!
HUFF
...ALL THE WAY TO NATION-ALS!
THE SCRAPPER'S OWNER, MADAME A, IS CHEERING!
PAK
RUN, TARO! RUN!
PAK
THEY'RE BOTH QUICK!
STOP WUNNING ...
FILL OUR GLASSES WITH BLOOD!
RIP OUT THEIR GUTS!

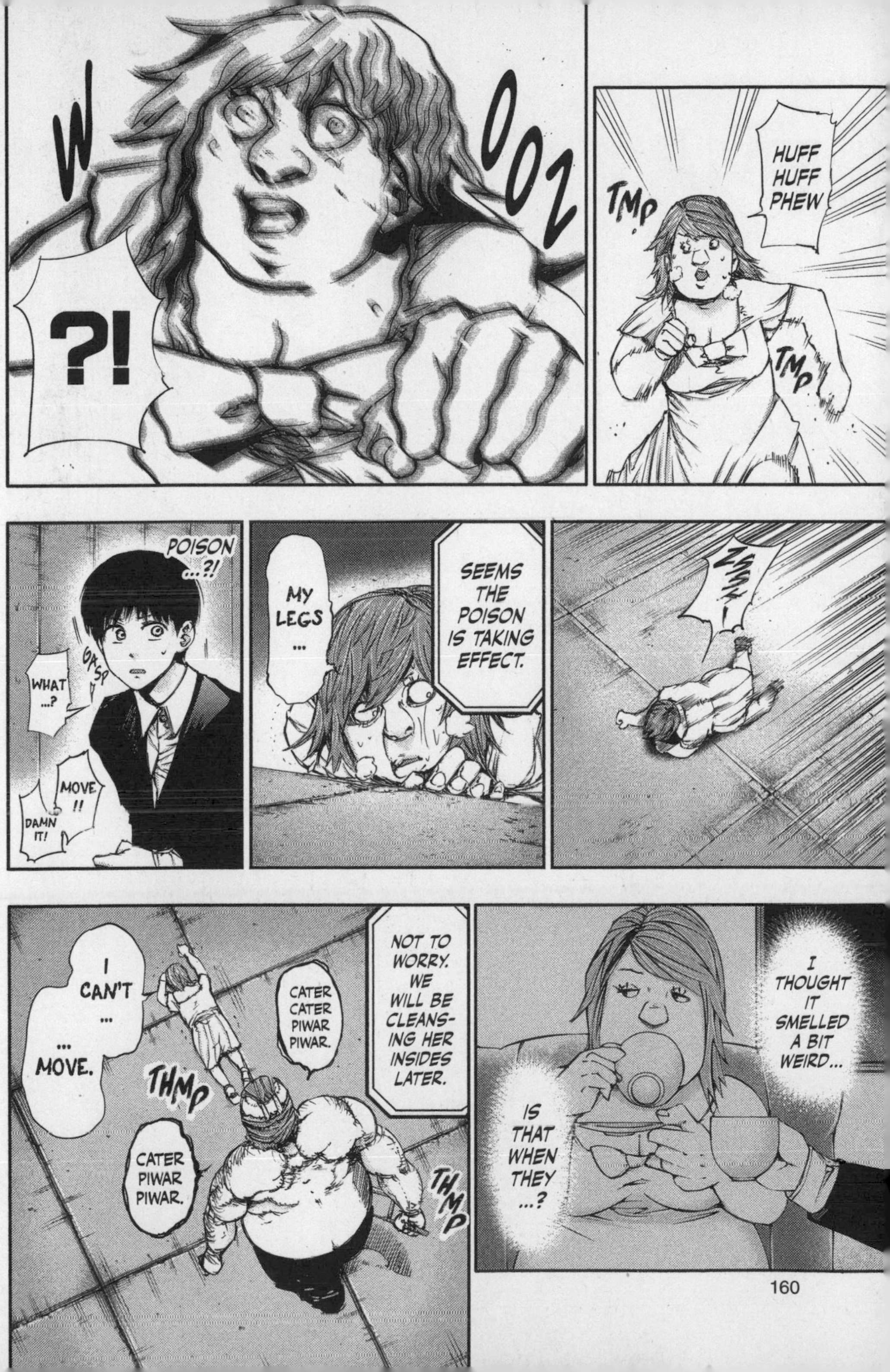
HUFF HUFF PHEW
TMP
TMP
WOOZ
?!
SEEMS THE POISON IS TAKING EFFECT.
MY LEGS ...
POISON ...?!
GASP
WHAT ...?
MOVE !!
DAMN IT!
I THOUGHT IT SMELLED A BIT WEIRD...
IS THAT WHEN THEY ...?
NOT TO WORRY. WE WILL BE CLEANS-ING HER INSIDES LATER.
CATER CATER PIWAR PIWAR.
I CAN'T ... ... MOVE.
THMP
CATER PIWAR PIWAR.
THMP

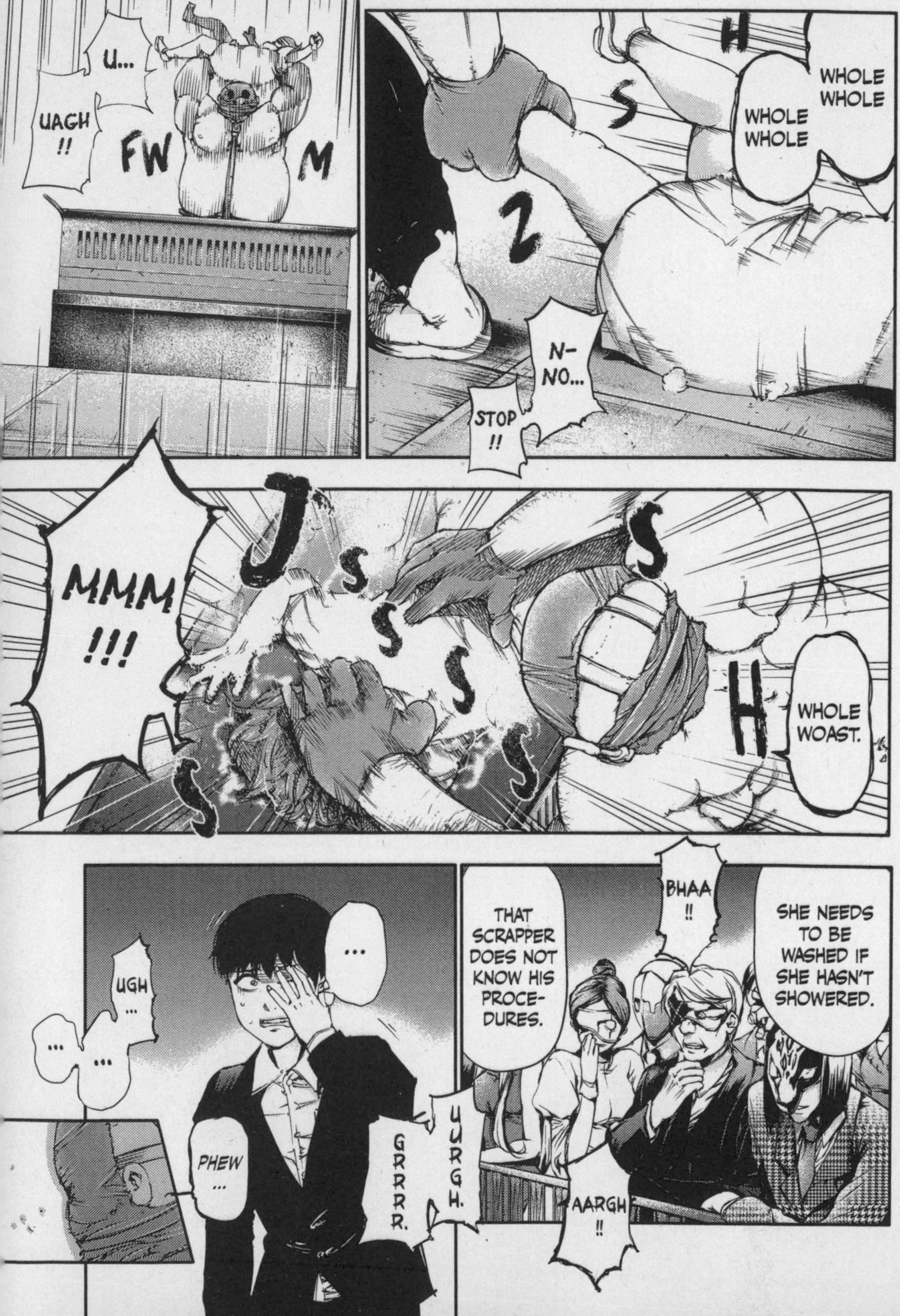

WHOLE WHOLE
WHOLE WHOLE
H
S
Z
N- NO...
STOP !!
U...
UAGH !!
FW
M
WHOLE WOAST.
H
S
S
S
S
S
J
MMM !!!
S
SHE NEEDS TO BE WASHED IF SHE HASN'T SHOWERED.
BHAA !!
THAT SCRAPPER DOES NOT KNOW HIS PROCE- DURES.
AARGH !!
...
UGH ...
... ...
YURGH.
GRRRR.
PHEW ...

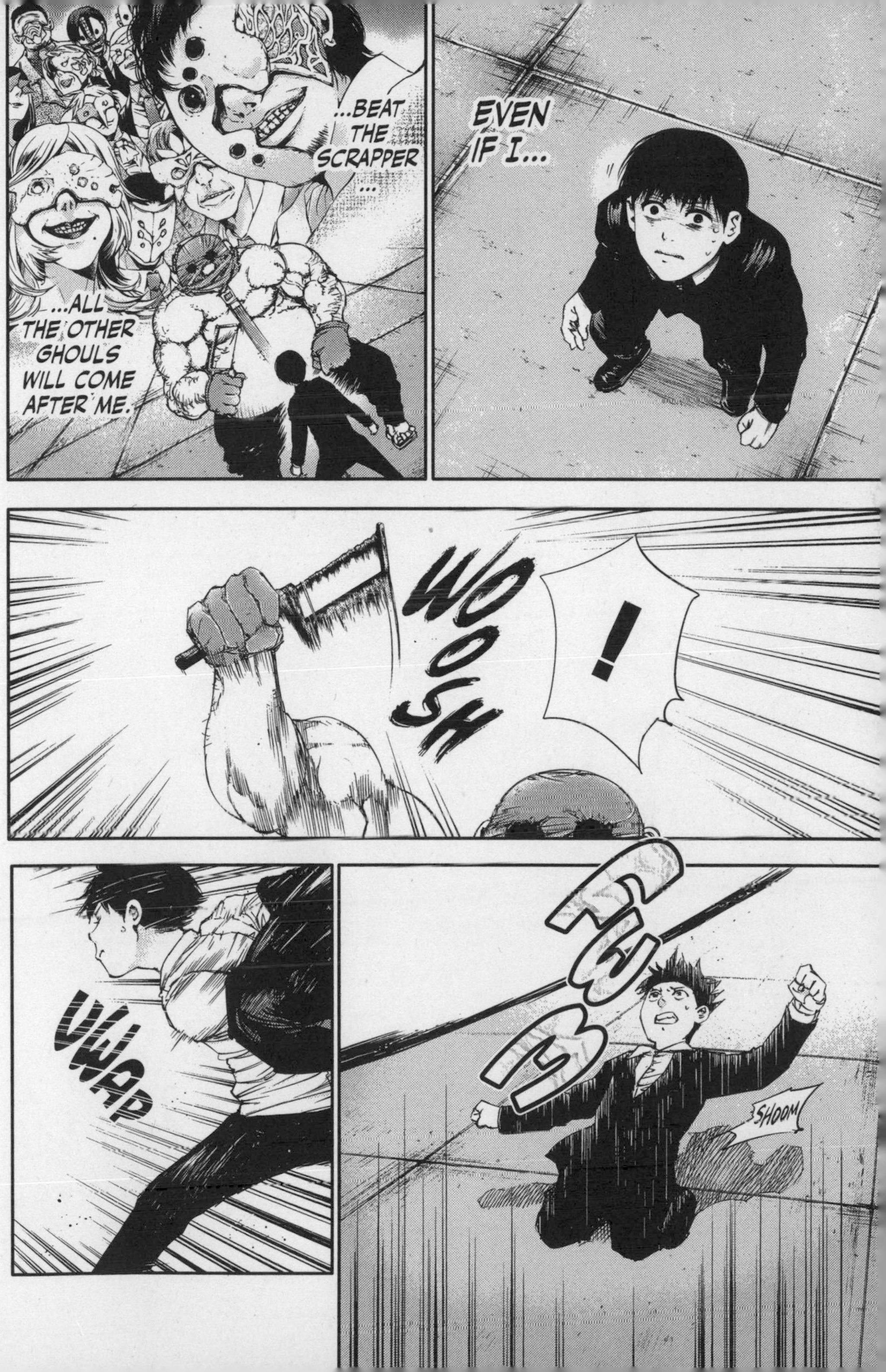
EVEN IF I...
...BEAT THE SCRAPPER ...
...ALL THE OTHER GHOULS WILL COME AFTER ME.
!
WOOSH
FWUM
SHOOM
VWAP

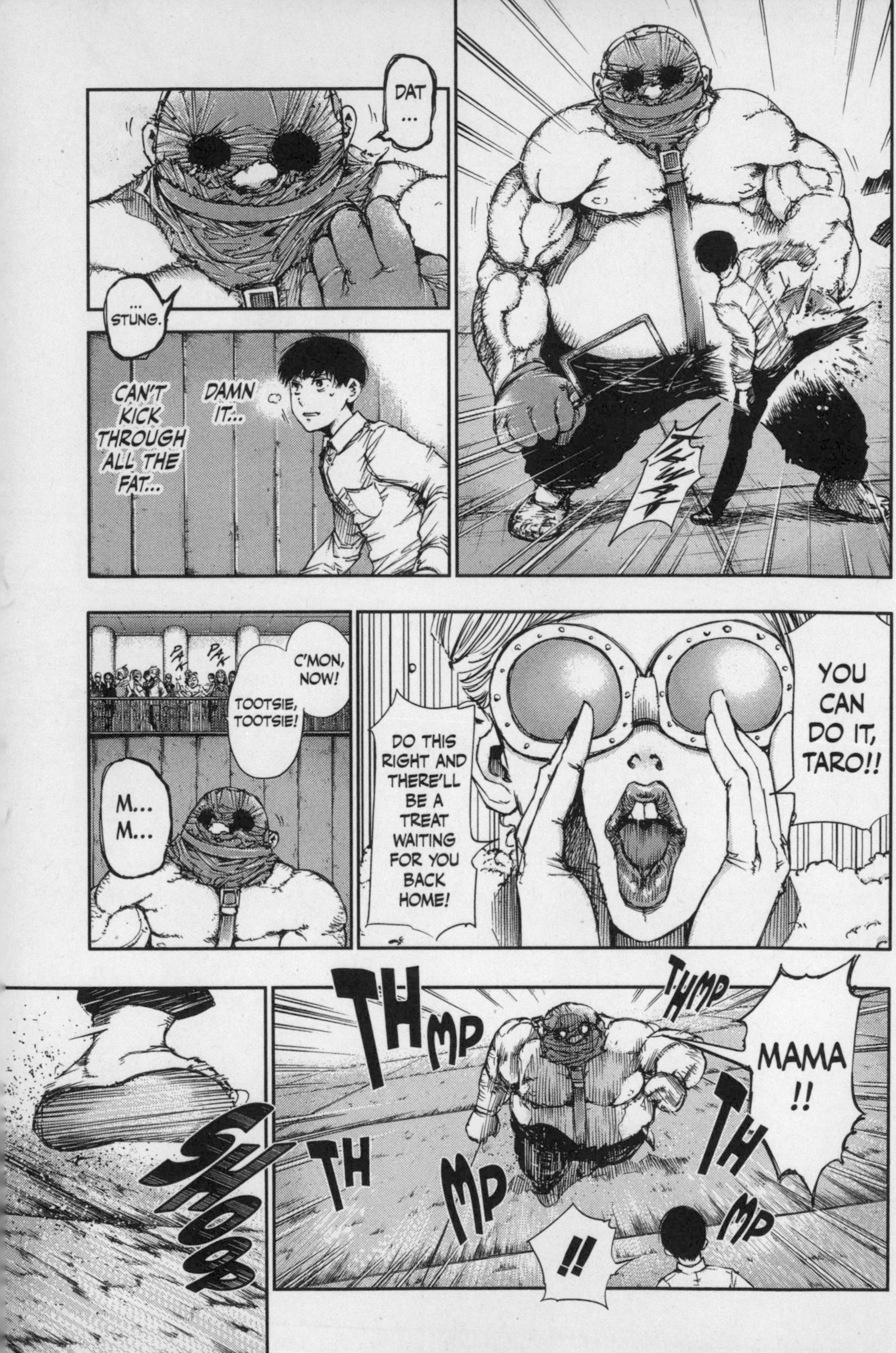
THWAK
DAT ...
... STUNG.
DAMN IT...
CAN'T KICK THROUGH ALL THE FAT...
YOU CAN DO IT, TARO!!
DO THIS RIGHT AND THERE'LL BE A TREAT WAITING FOR YOU BACK HOME!
PAK PAK
C'MON, NOW!
TOOTSIE, TOOTSIE!
M... M...
MAMA!!
THMP
THMP
TH MP
TH MP
TH MP
!!
SHOOP

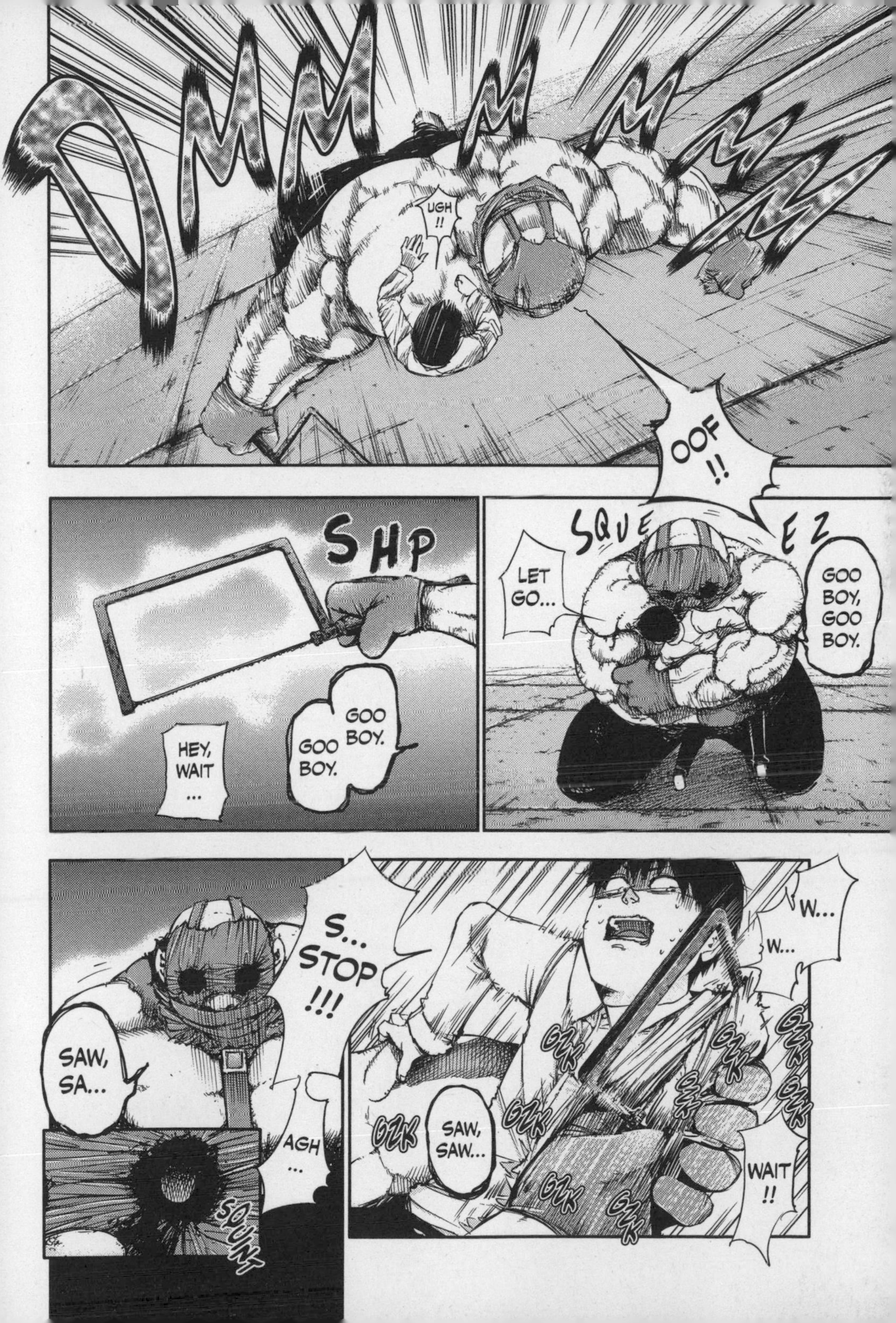
DMMMMMMM
UGH !!
OOF !!
SQUEEZ
LET GO...
GOO BOY, GOO BOY.
SHP
GOO BOY.
GOO BOY.
HEY, WAIT ...
W...
W...
GZK GZK GZK GZK GZK GZK GZK GZK GZK GZK
SAW, SAW...
WAIT !!
S... STOP !!!
SAW, SA...
AGH ...
SQUNT

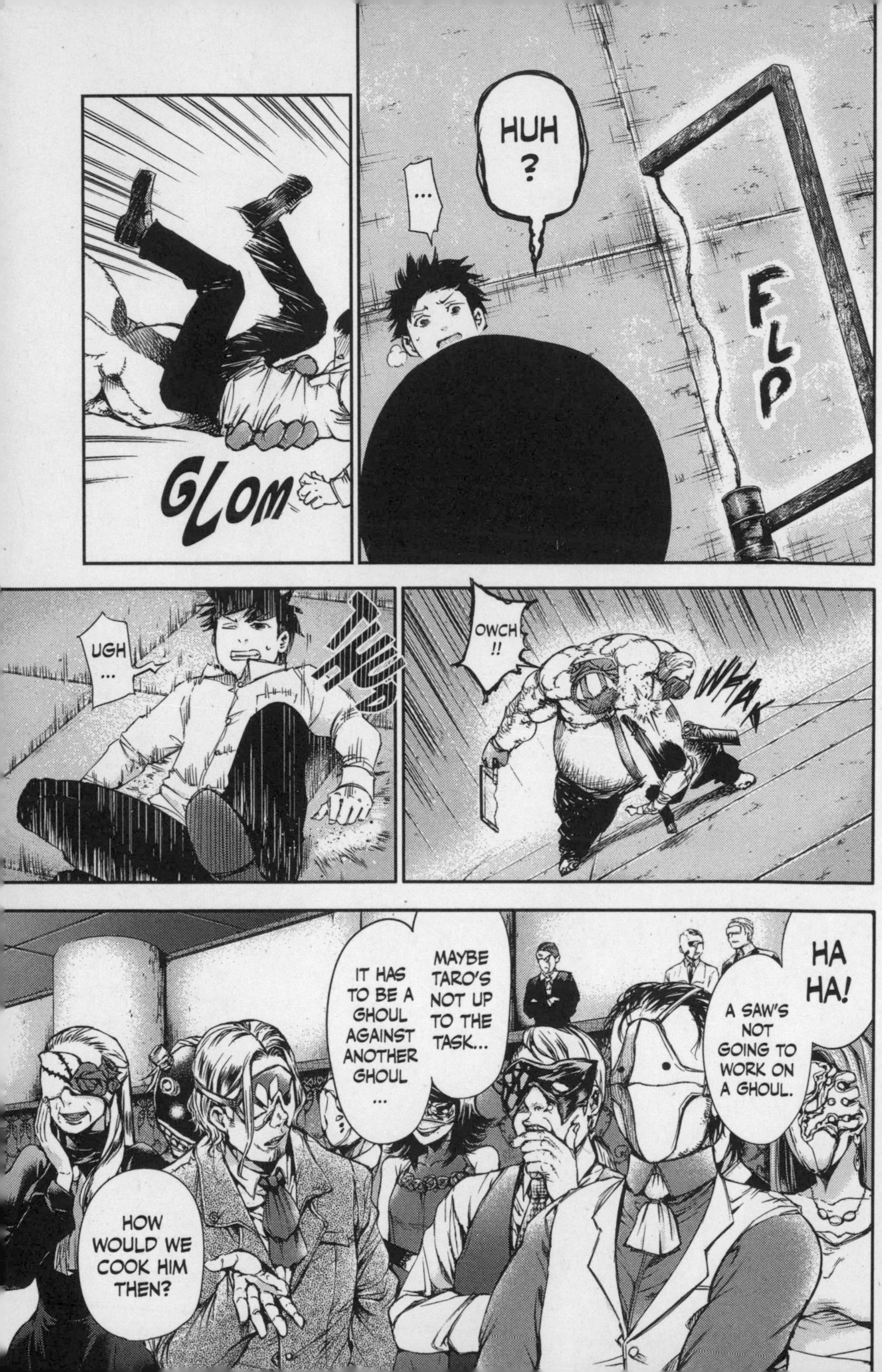
HUH ?
...
FLP
GLOM
OWCH !!
WHAK
UGH ...
THUD
HA HA!
A SAW'S NOT GOING TO WORK ON A GHOUL.
MAYBE TARO'S NOT UP TO THE TASK...
IT HAS TO BE A GHOUL AGAINST ANOTHER GHOUL ...
HOW WOULD WE COOK HIM THEN?

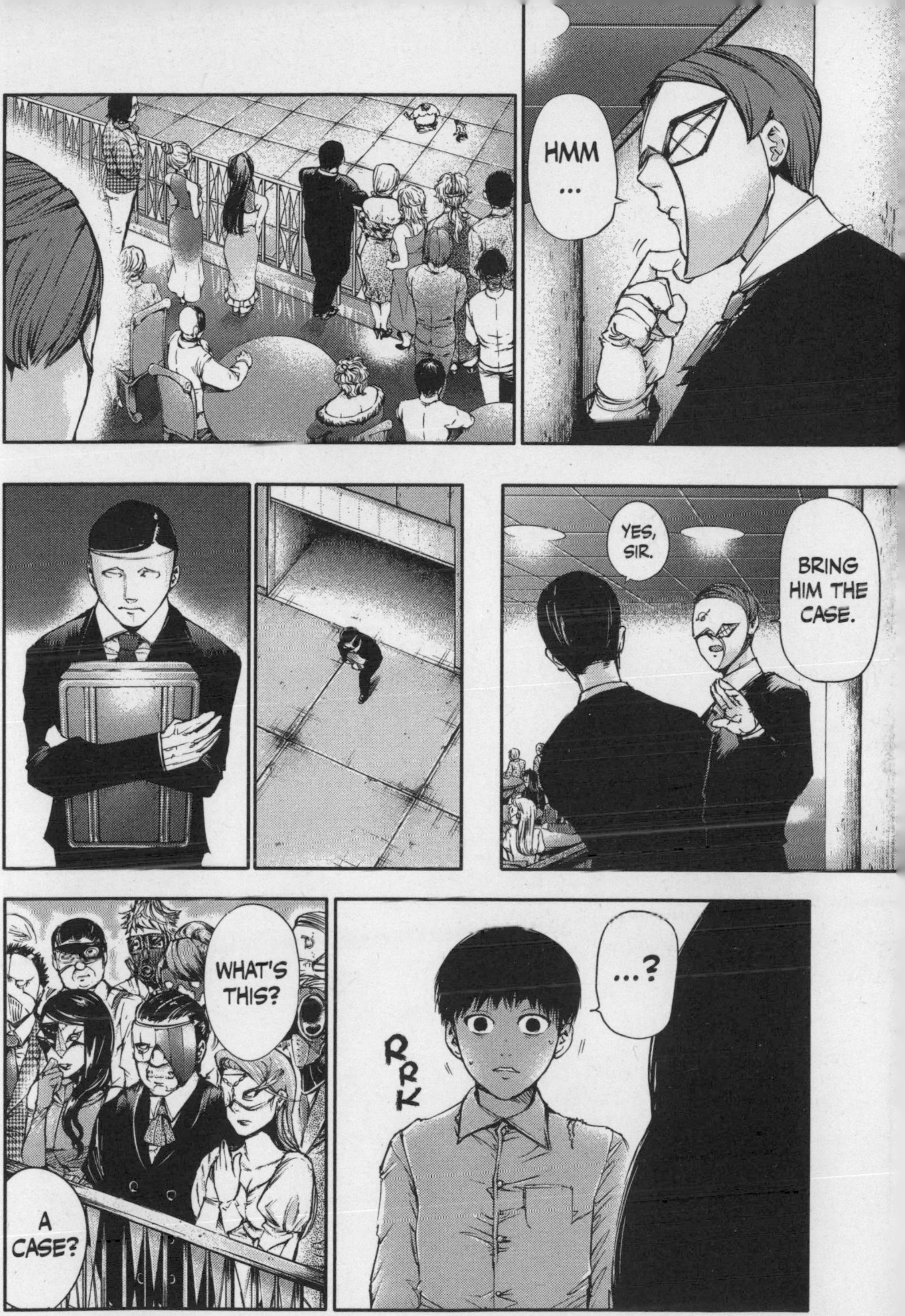
HMM ...
BRING HIM THE CASE.
YES, SIR.
...?
RRK
WHAT'S THIS?
A CASE?

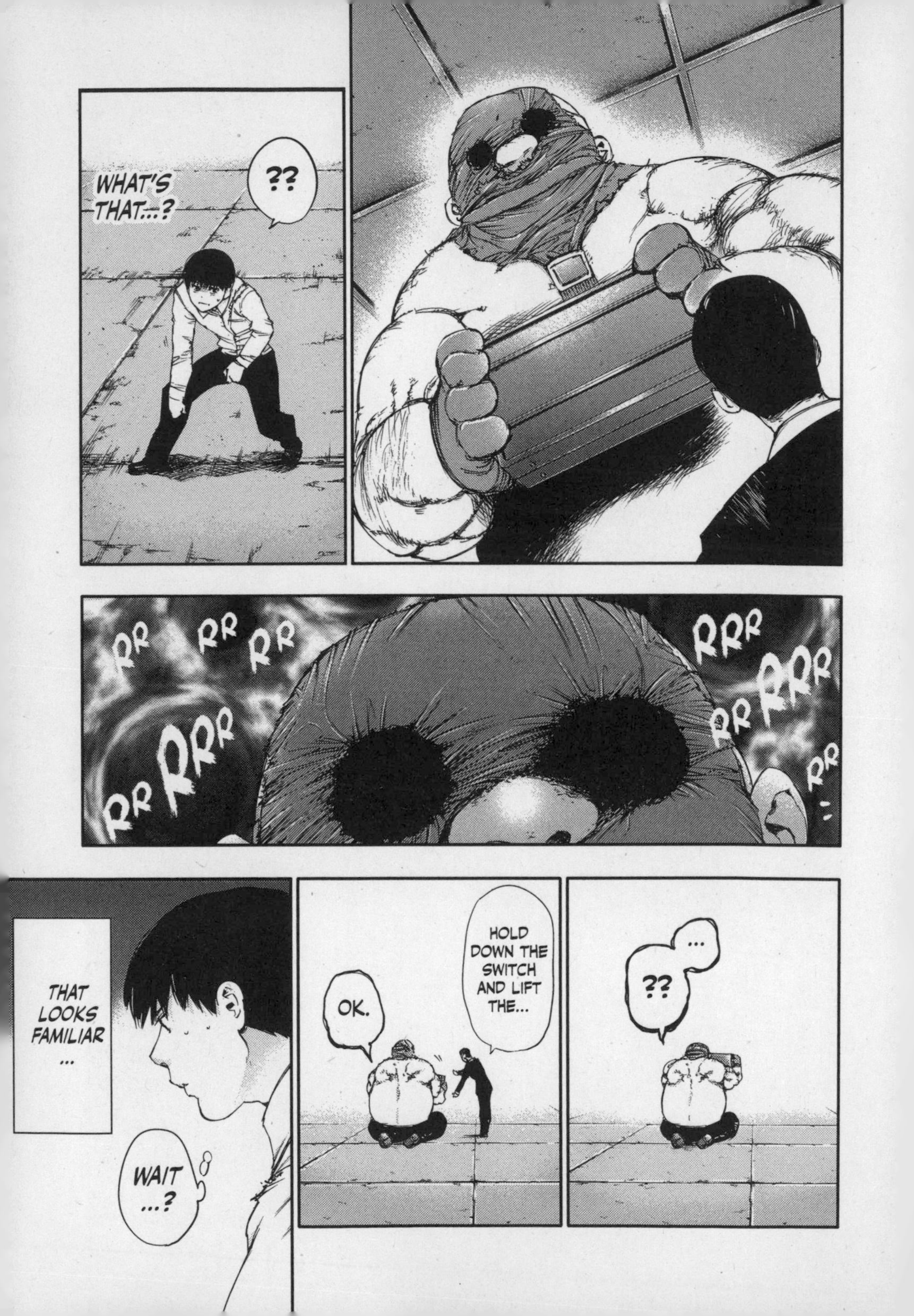
WHAT'S THAT...?
??
RR RR RR
RRR
RR RRRR
RR
RR RRR
RR
...
??
HOLD DOWN THE SWITCH AND LIFT THE...
OK.
THAT LOOKS FAMILIAR ...
WAIT ...?

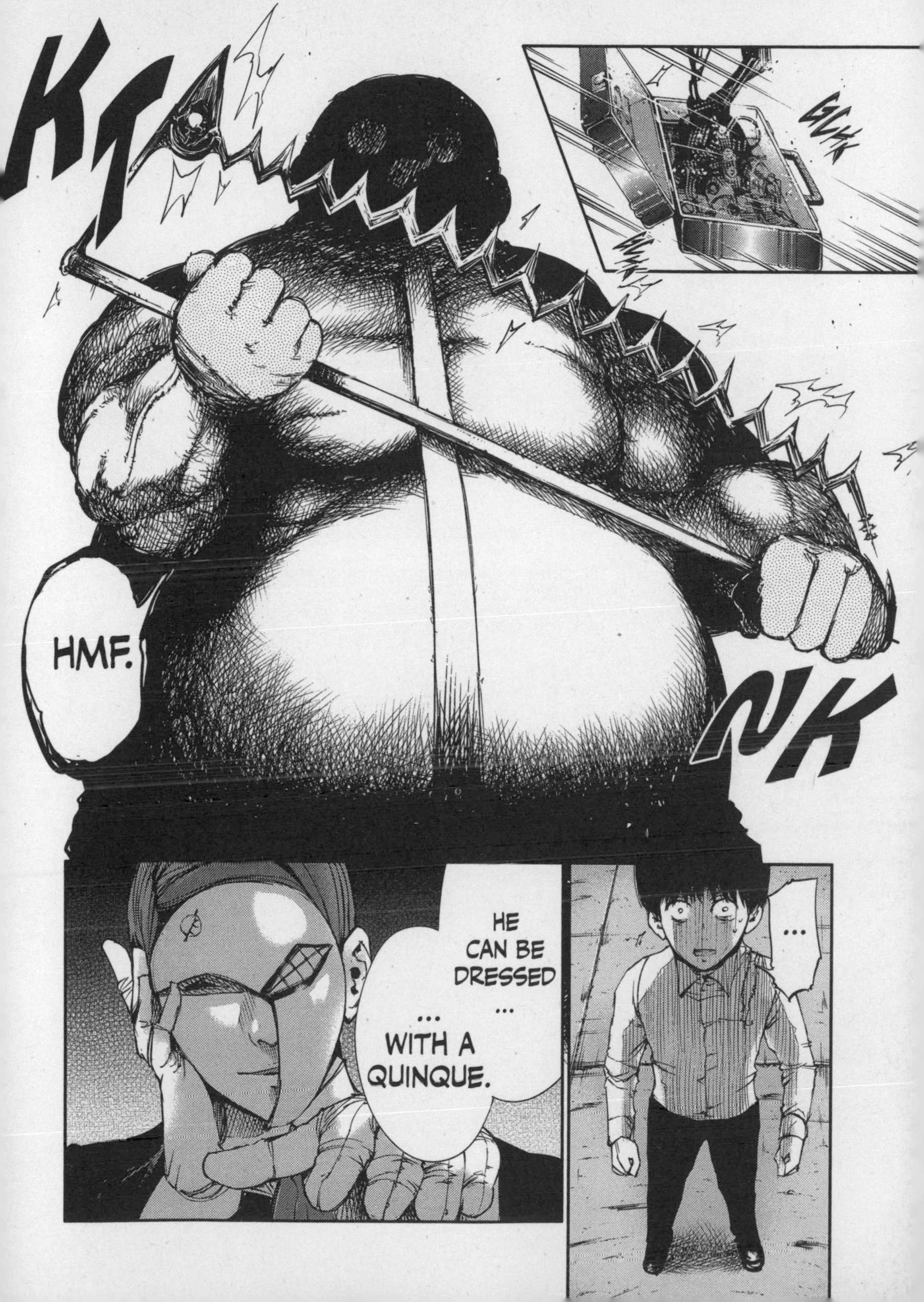
GCKK
KTA
HMF.
NK
...
HE CAN BE DRESSED ...
... WITH A QUINQUE.

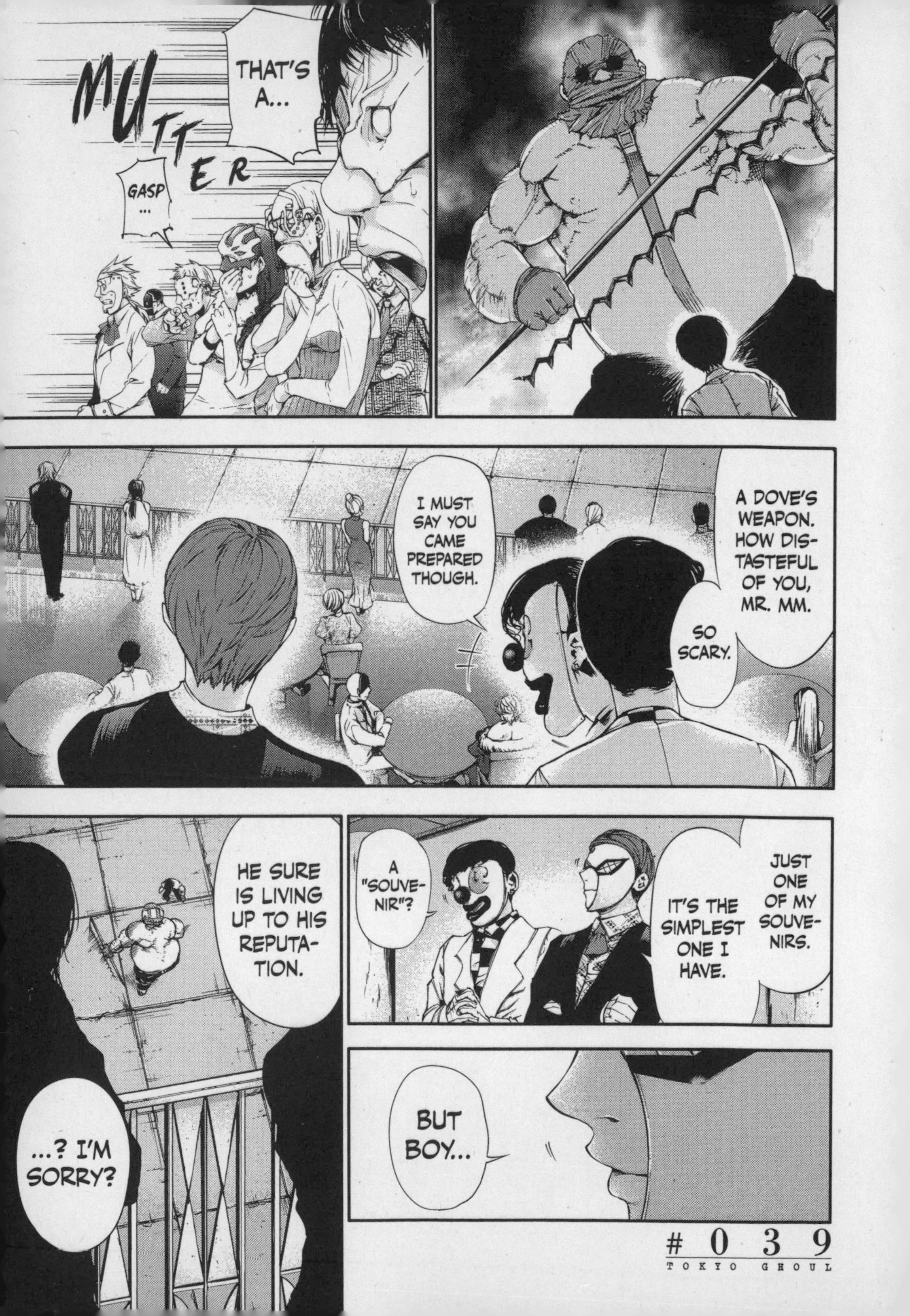
MUTTER
THAT'S A...
GASP...
A DOVE'S WEAPON. HOW DISTASTEFUL OF YOU, MR. MM.
SO SCARY.
I MUST SAY YOU CAME PREPARED THOUGH.
JUST ONE OF MY SOUVENIRS.
IT'S THE SIMPLEST ONE I HAVE.
A "SOUVENIR"?
BUT BOY...
HE SURE IS LIVING UP TO HIS REPUTATION.
...? I'M SORRY?

0 3 9
TOKYO GHOUL

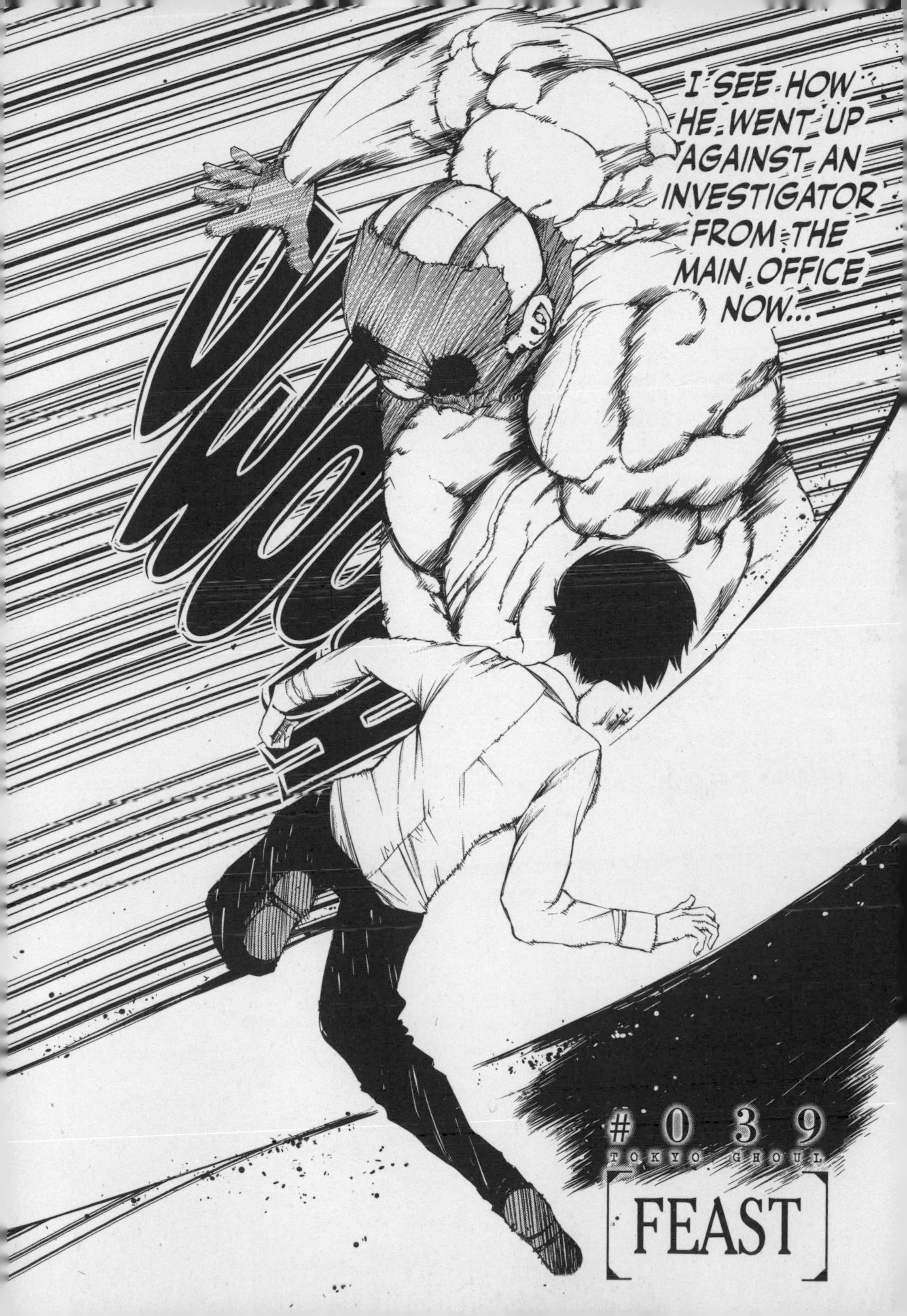
I SEE HOW HE WENT UP AGAINST AN INVESTIGATOR FROM THE MAIN OFFICE NOW...
#039
TOKYO GHOUL
FEAST

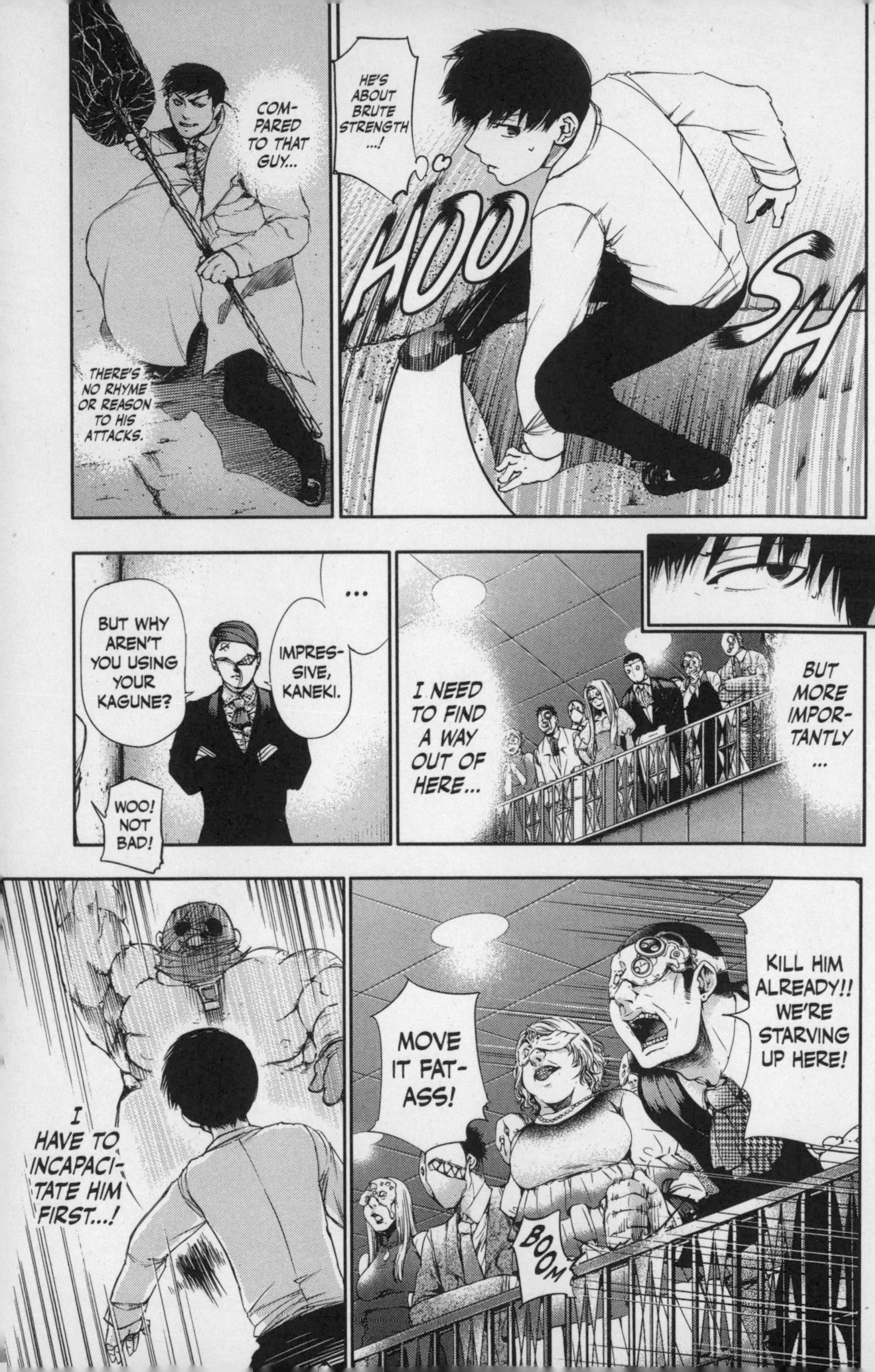
HE'S ABOUT BRUTE STRENGTH ...!
HOOSH
COMPARED TO THAT GUY...
THERE'S NO RHYME OR REASON TO HIS ATTACKS.
BUT MORE IMPORTANTLY ...
I NEED TO FIND A WAY OUT OF HERE...
...
IMPRESSIVE, KANEKI.
BUT WHY AREN'T YOU USING YOUR KAGUNE?
WOO! NOT BAD!
KILL HIM ALREADY!! WE'RE STARVING UP HERE!
MOVE IT FAT-ASS!
BOOM
I HAVE TO INCAPACITATE HIM FIRST...!

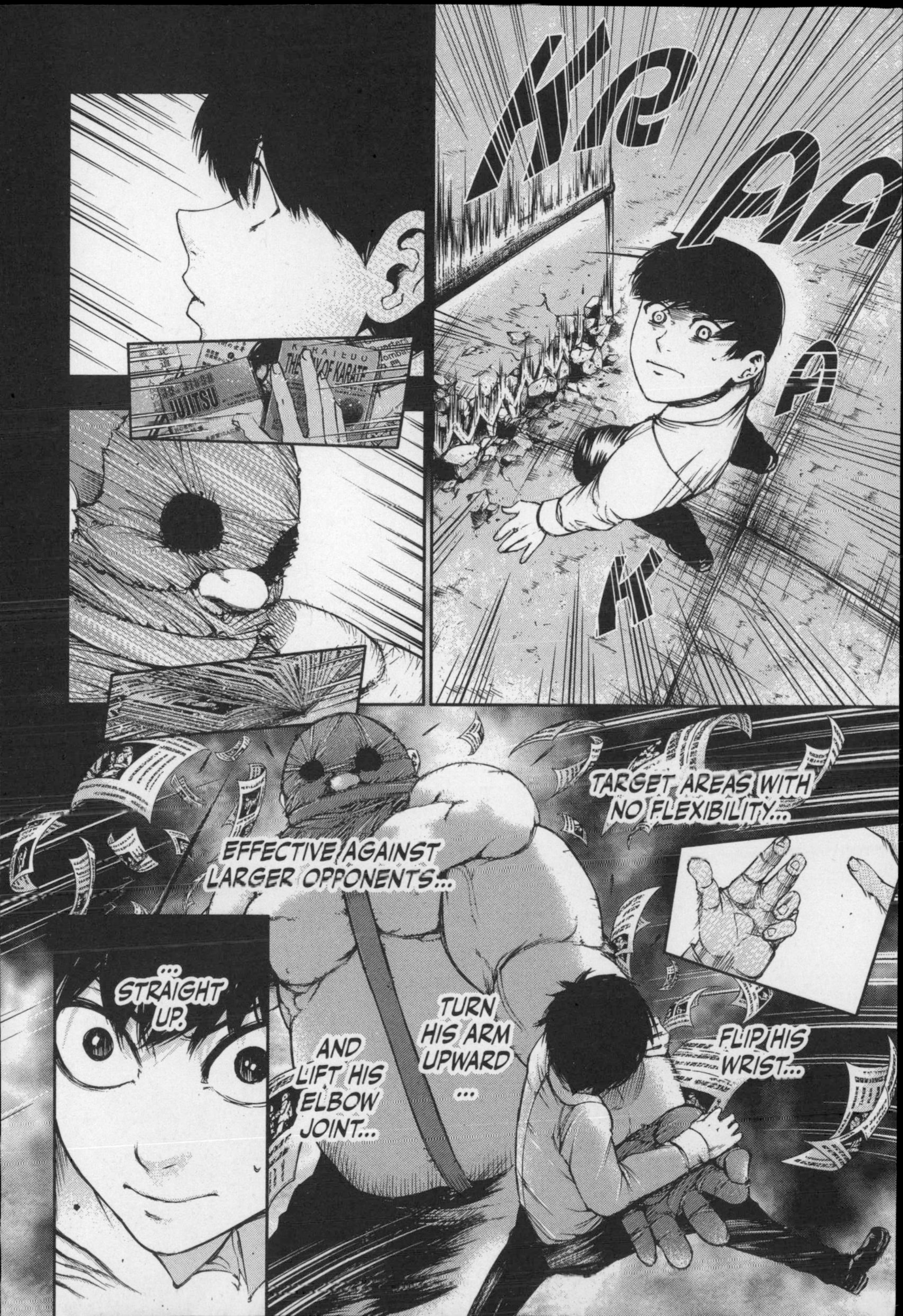

JUJITSU
TARGET AREAS WITH NO FLEXIBILITY...
EFFECTIVE AGAINST LARGER OPPONENTS...
FLIP HIS WRIST...
TURN HIS ARM UPWARD ...
AND LIFT HIS ELBOW JOINT...
...STRAIGHT UP.

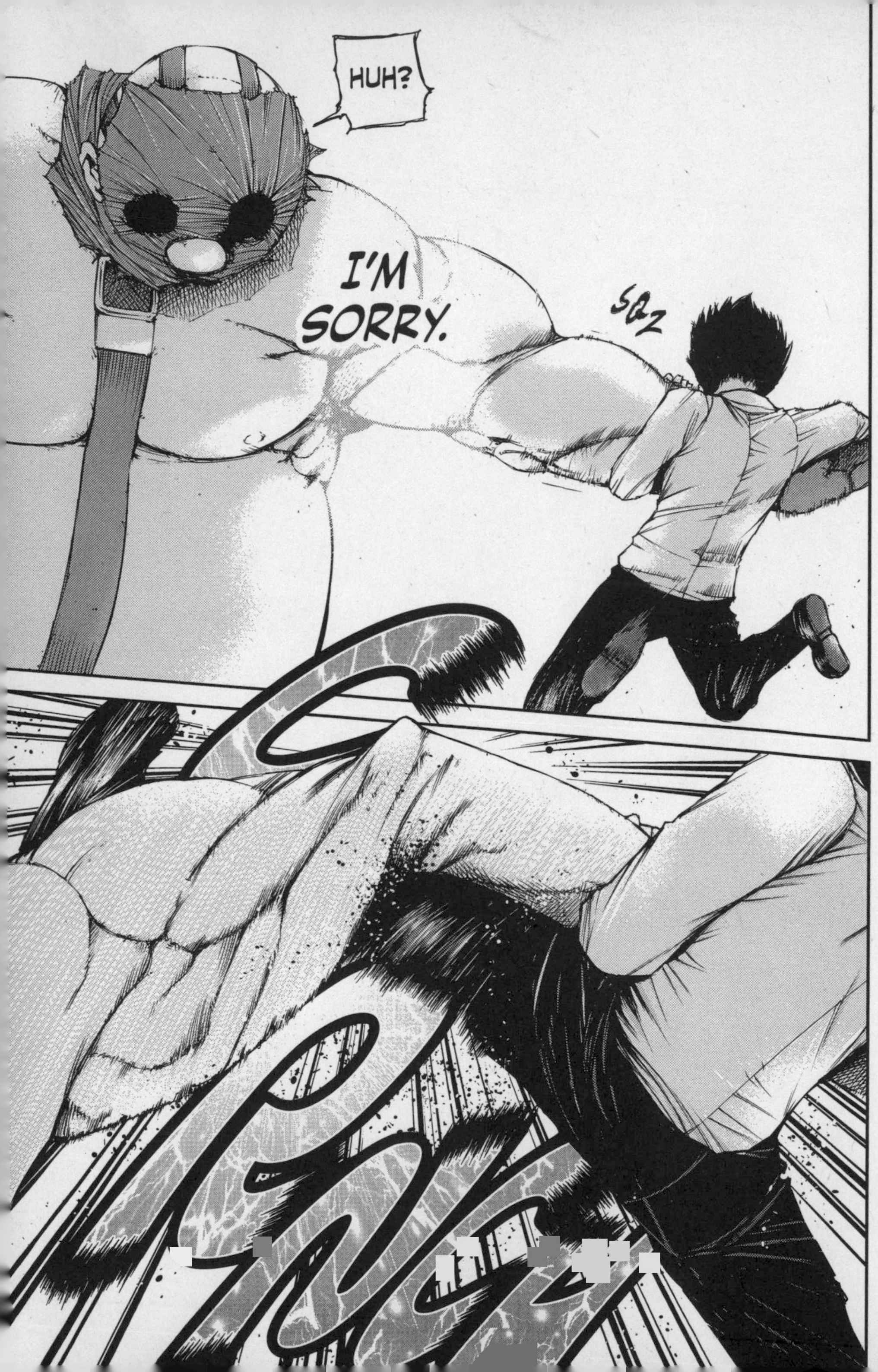
HUH?
I'M SORRY.
SQZ

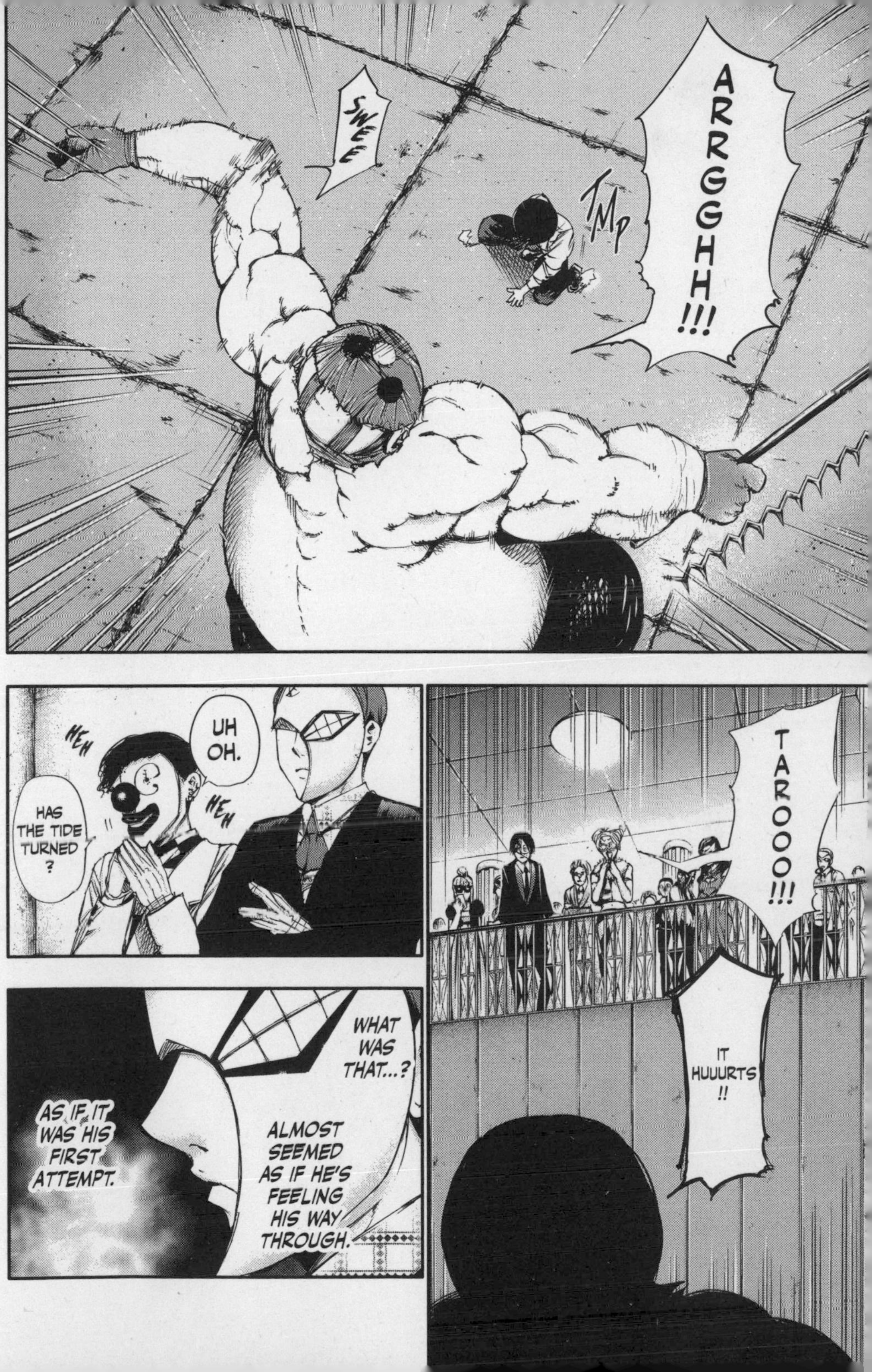
ARRRGGHH!!!
TMP
SWEEE
TAROOOO!!!
IT HUUURTS!!
UH OH.
HEH
HEH
HAS THE TIDE TURNED?
WHAT WAS THAT...?
ALMOST SEEMED AS IF HE'S FEELING HIS WAY THROUGH.
AS IF IT WAS HIS FIRST ATTEMPT.

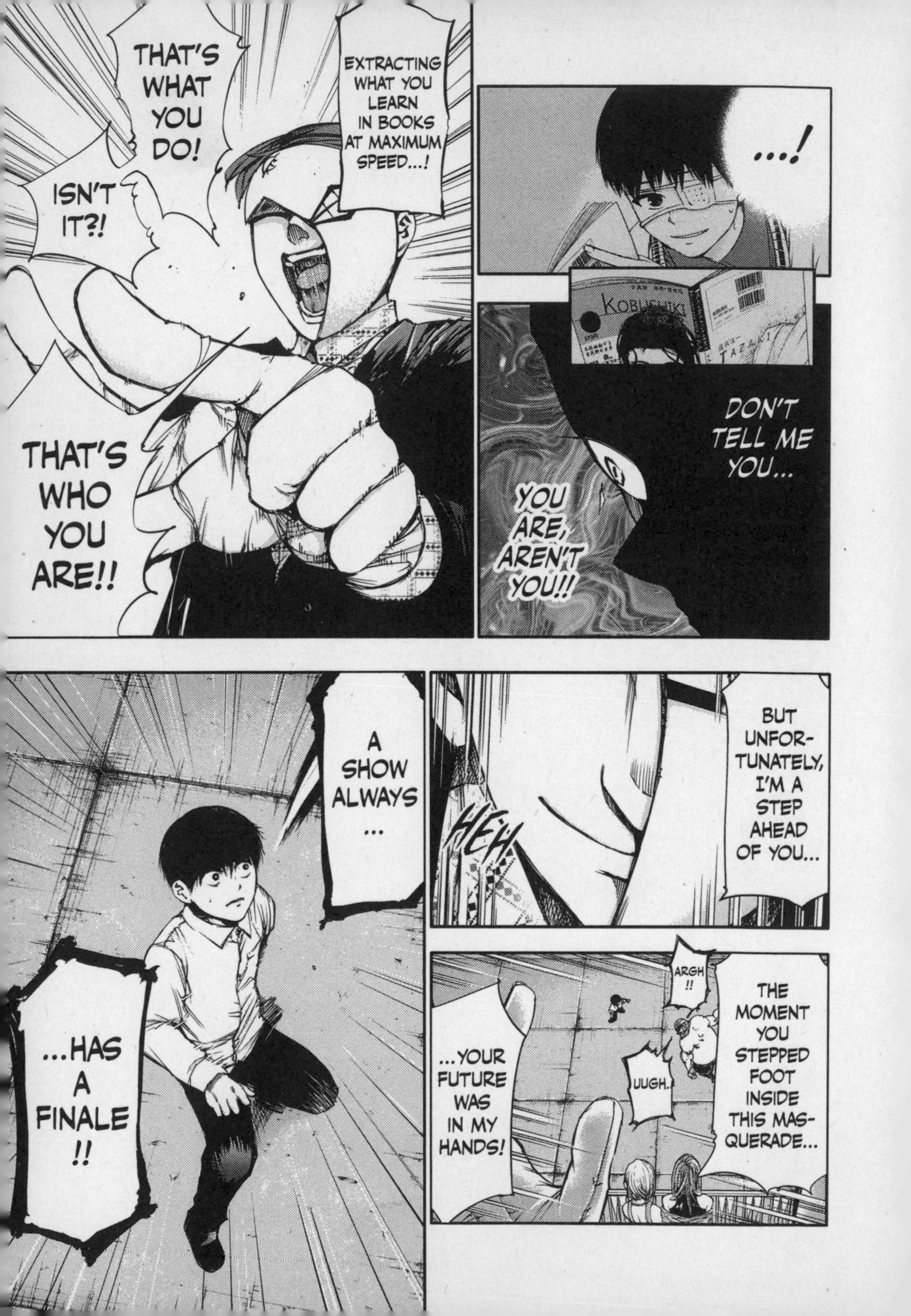
...!
KOBUSHIKI
TAZAKI
DON'T TELL ME YOU...
YOU ARE, AREN'T YOU!!
EXTRACTING WHAT YOU LEARN IN BOOKS AT MAXIMUM SPEED...!
THAT'S WHAT YOU DO!
ISN'T IT?!
THAT'S WHO YOU ARE!!
BUT UNFOR-TUNATELY, I'M A STEP AHEAD OF YOU...
HEH
THE MOMENT YOU STEPPED FOOT INSIDE THIS MAS-QUERADE...
ARGH!!
UUGH.
...YOUR FUTURE WAS IN MY HANDS!
A SHOW ALWAYS...
...HAS A FINALE!!

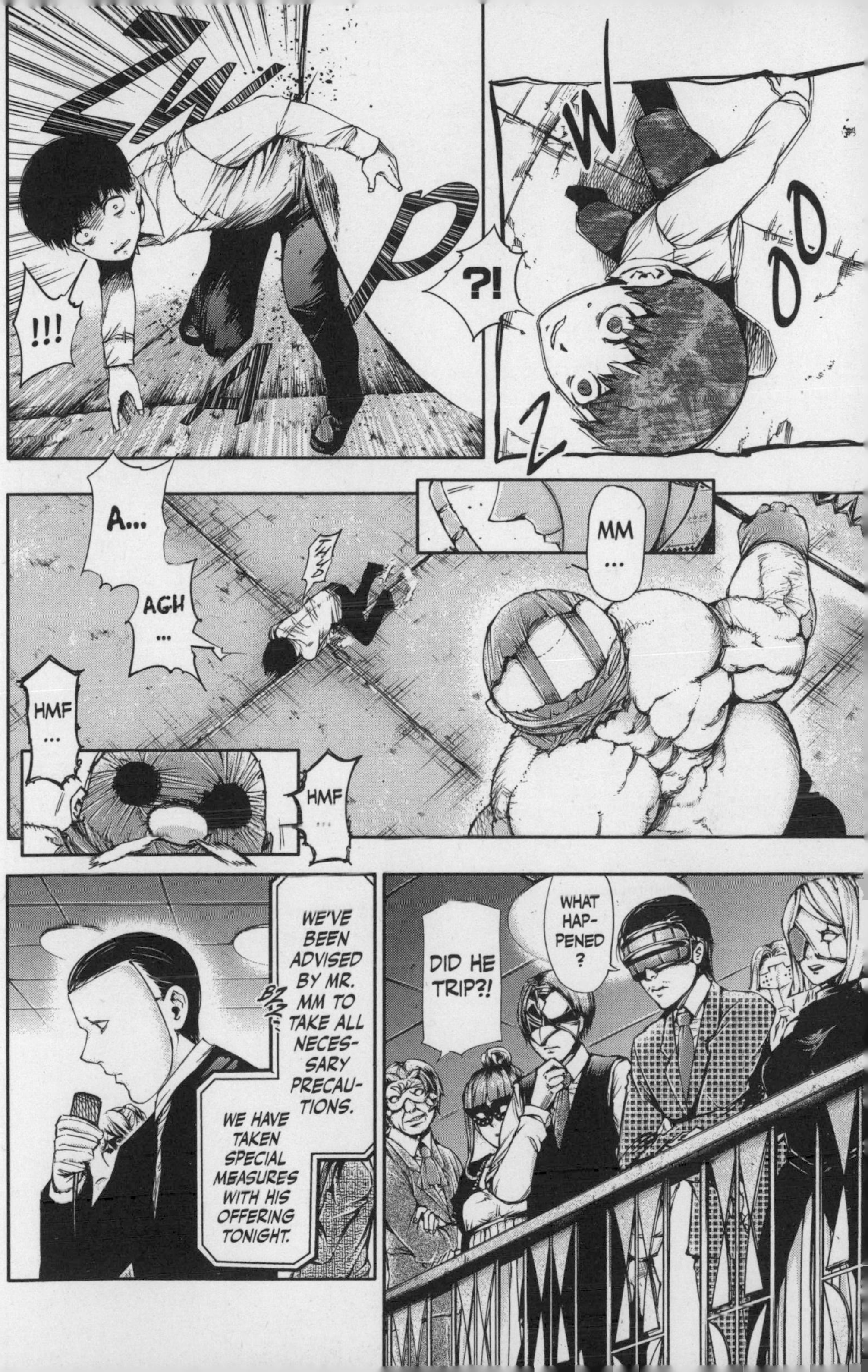
?!
!!!
MM ...
A...
AGH ...
THUD
HMF ...
HMF ...
WHAT HAP-PENED ?
DID HE TRIP?!
WE'VE BEEN ADVISED BY MR. MM TO TAKE ALL NECES-SARY PRECAU-TIONS.
BZZ
WE HAVE TAKEN SPECIAL MEASURES WITH HIS OFFERING TONIGHT.

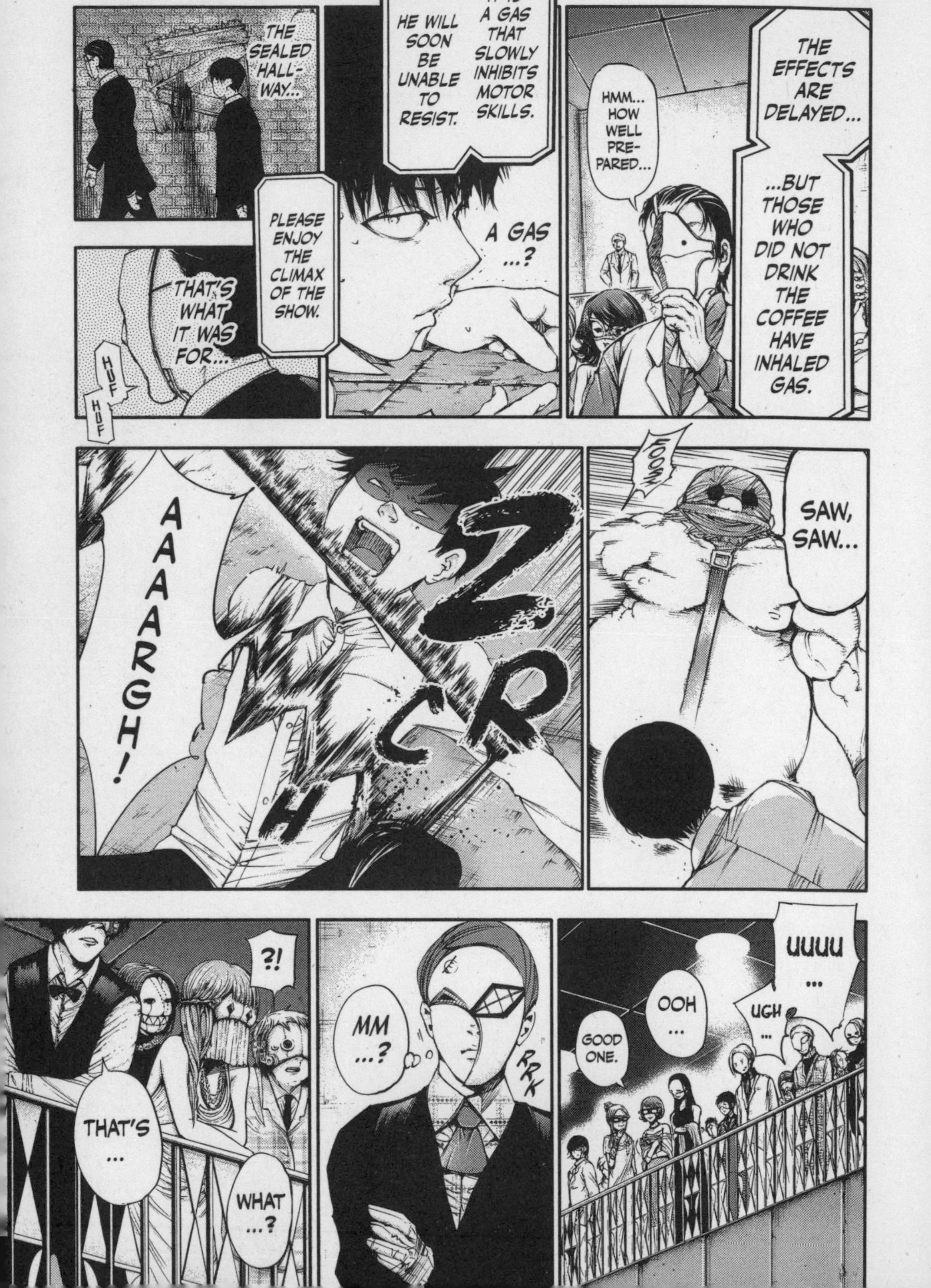
THE EFFECTS ARE DELAYED...
...BUT THOSE WHO DID NOT DRINK THE COFFEE HAVE INHALED GAS.
HMM... HOW WELL PRE-PARED...
IT IS A GAS THAT SLOWLY INHIBITS MOTOR SKILLS.
HE WILL SOON BE UNABLE TO RESIST.
PLEASE ENJOY THE CLIMAX OF THE SHOW.
A GAS ...?
THE SEALED HALL-WAY...
THAT'S WHAT IT WAS FOR...
HUF
HUF
FOOM
SAW, SAW...
AAAAARGH!
UUUU ...
UGH ...
OOH ...
GOOD ONE.
RRK
MM ...?
?!
THAT'S ...
WHAT ...?

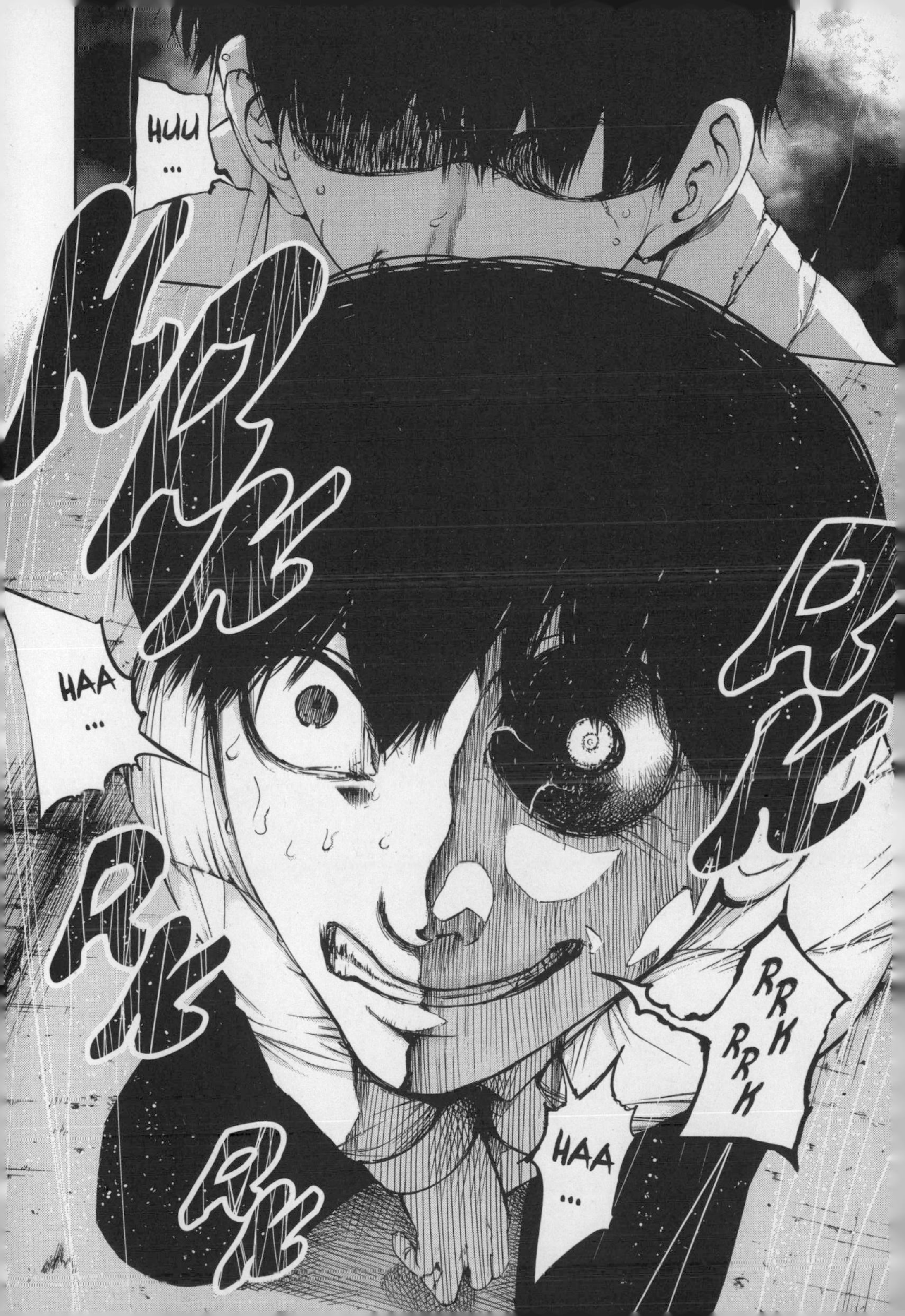
HUU ...
HAA ...
RRK RRK
HAA ...

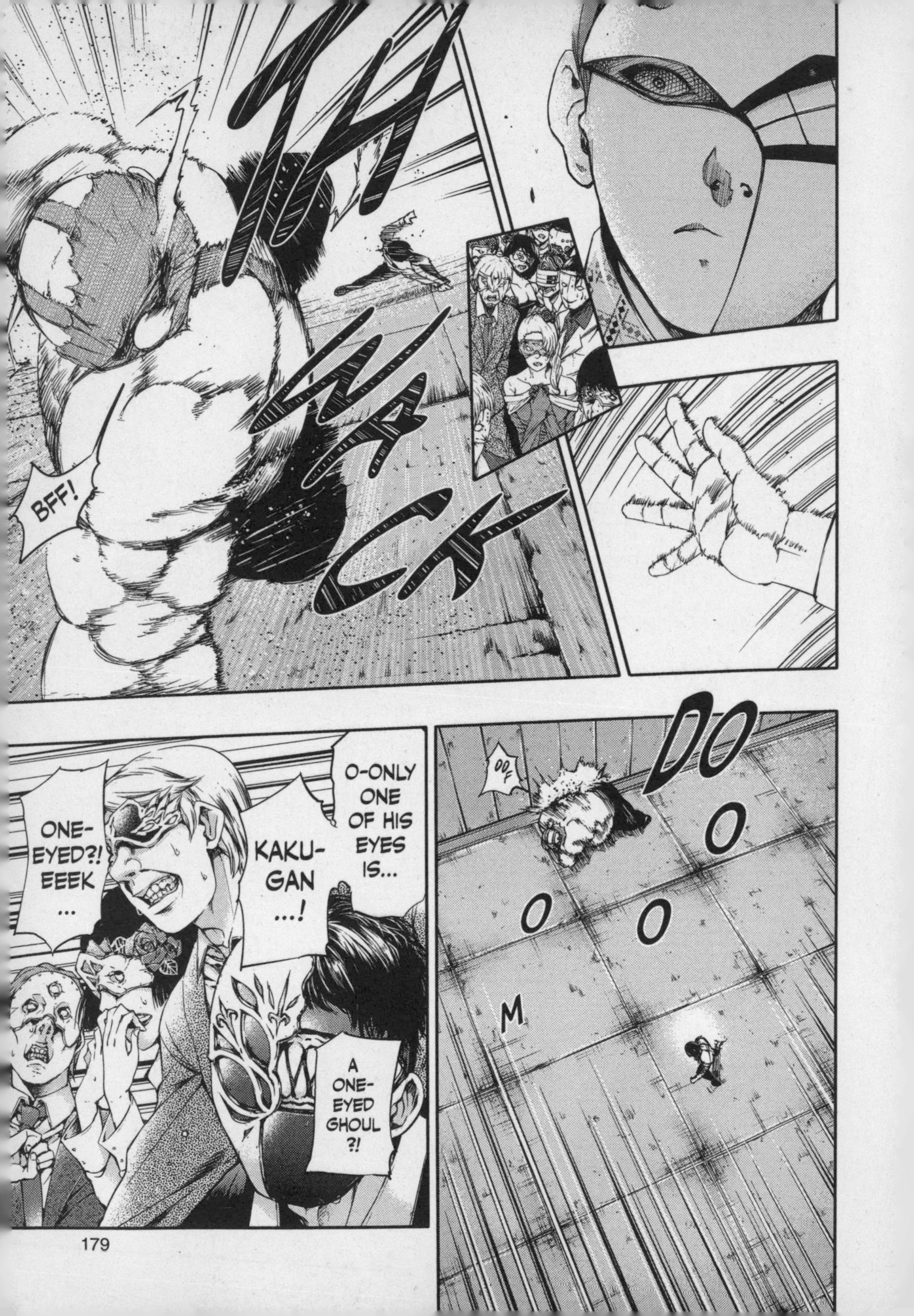
WHACK
BFF!
DOOOOM
OOF
O-ONLY ONE OF HIS EYES IS...
KAKU-GAN ...!
ONE-EYED?! EEEK ...
A ONE-EYED GHOUL ?!

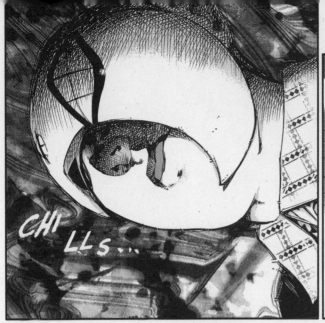

CHILLS...

A ONE-EYED... YOU SERIOUS?

I DIDN'T THINK THEY ACTUALLY EXISTED...

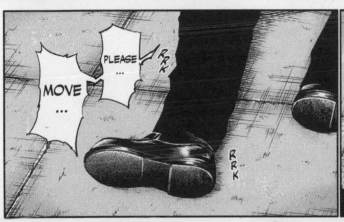

MOVE...

PLEASE...

RRK

RRK

GASP...

I'M GOING NUMB...

THUD

OWCH...

G...

GO TARO!!

KILL HIM!

NOW'S YOUR CHANCE!!

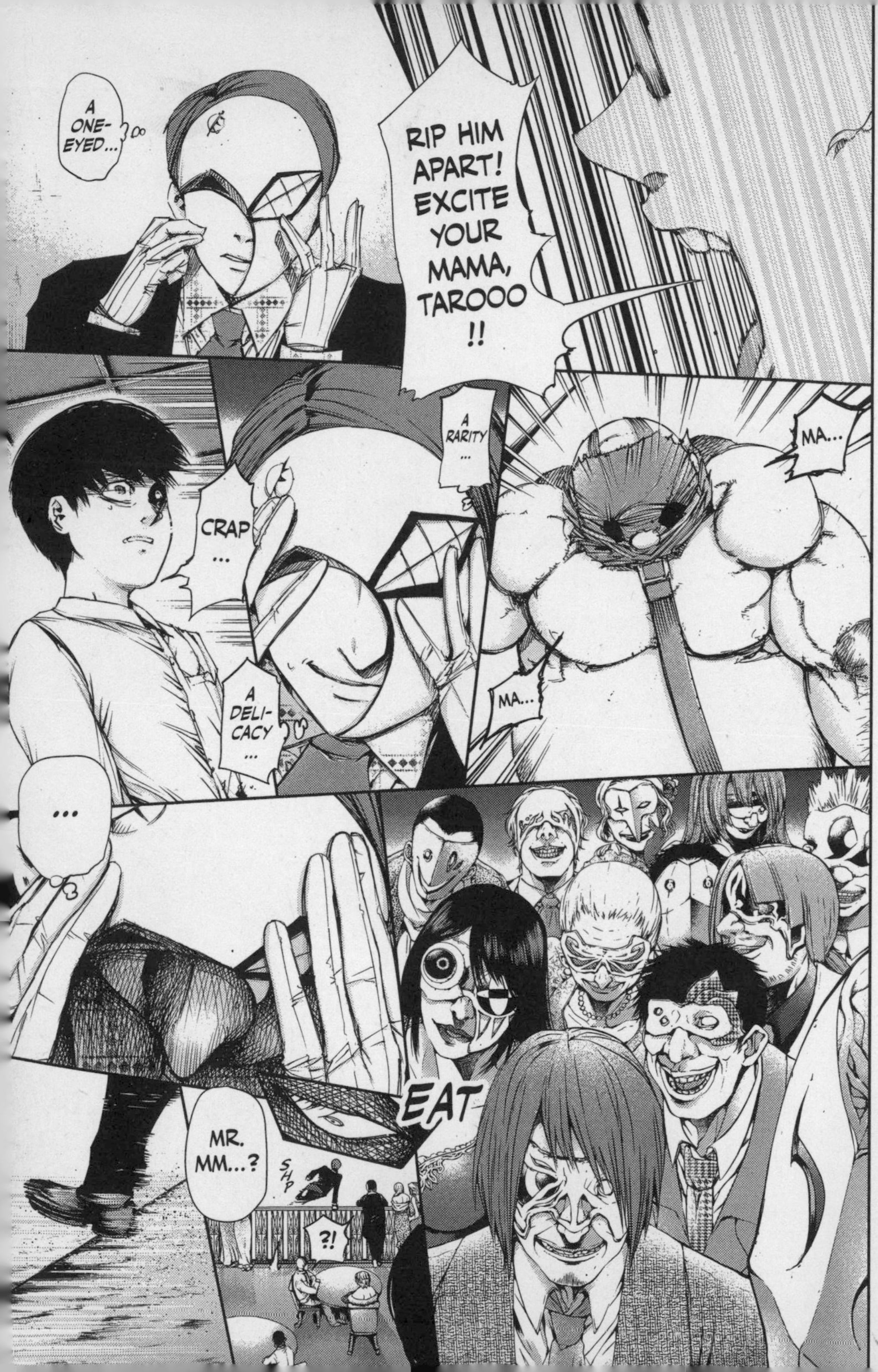
RIP HIM APART! EXCITE YOUR MAMA, TAROOO !!
A ONE-EYED...
MA...
MA...
A RARITY ...
A DELI-CACY ...
CRAP ...
EAT
...
MR. MM...?
SHP
?!

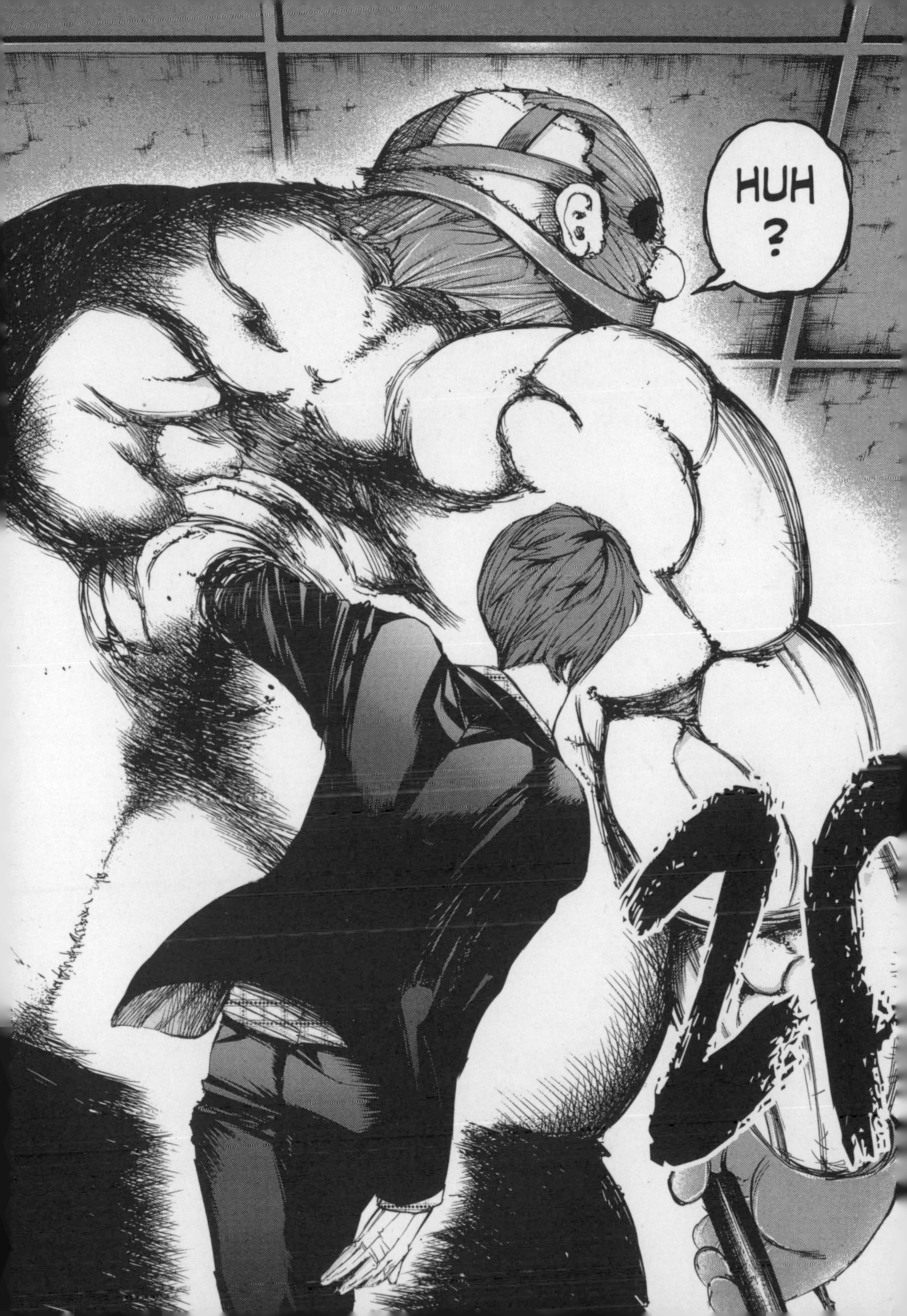
HUH ?

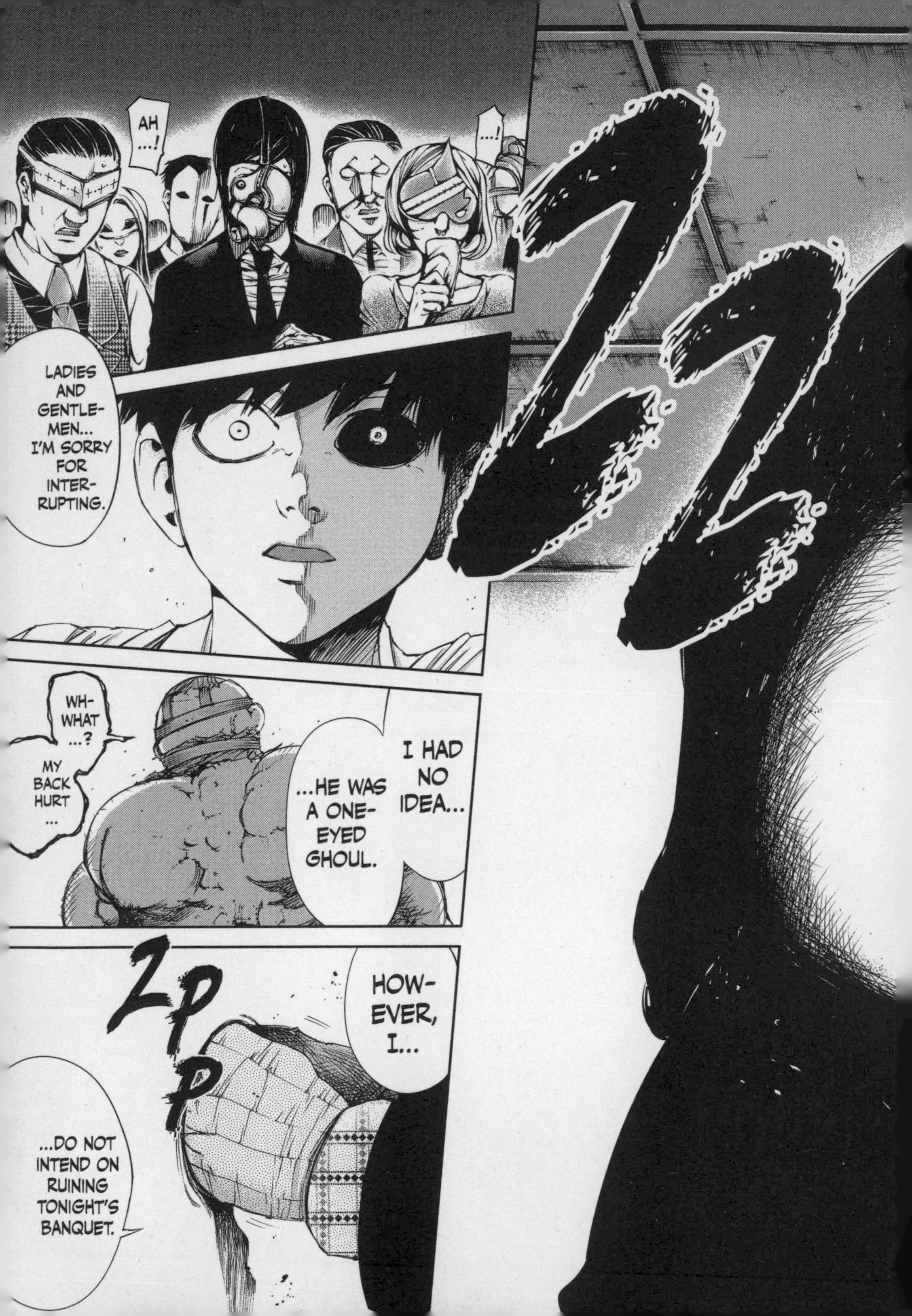
ZZ
...!
AH ...!
LADIES AND GENTLEMEN... I'M SORRY FOR INTERRUPTING.
I HAD NO IDEA...
...HE WAS A ONE-EYED GHOUL.
WH-WHAT ...?
MY BACK HURT ...
HOWEVER, I...
ZP P
...DO NOT INTEND ON RUINING TONIGHT'S BANQUET.

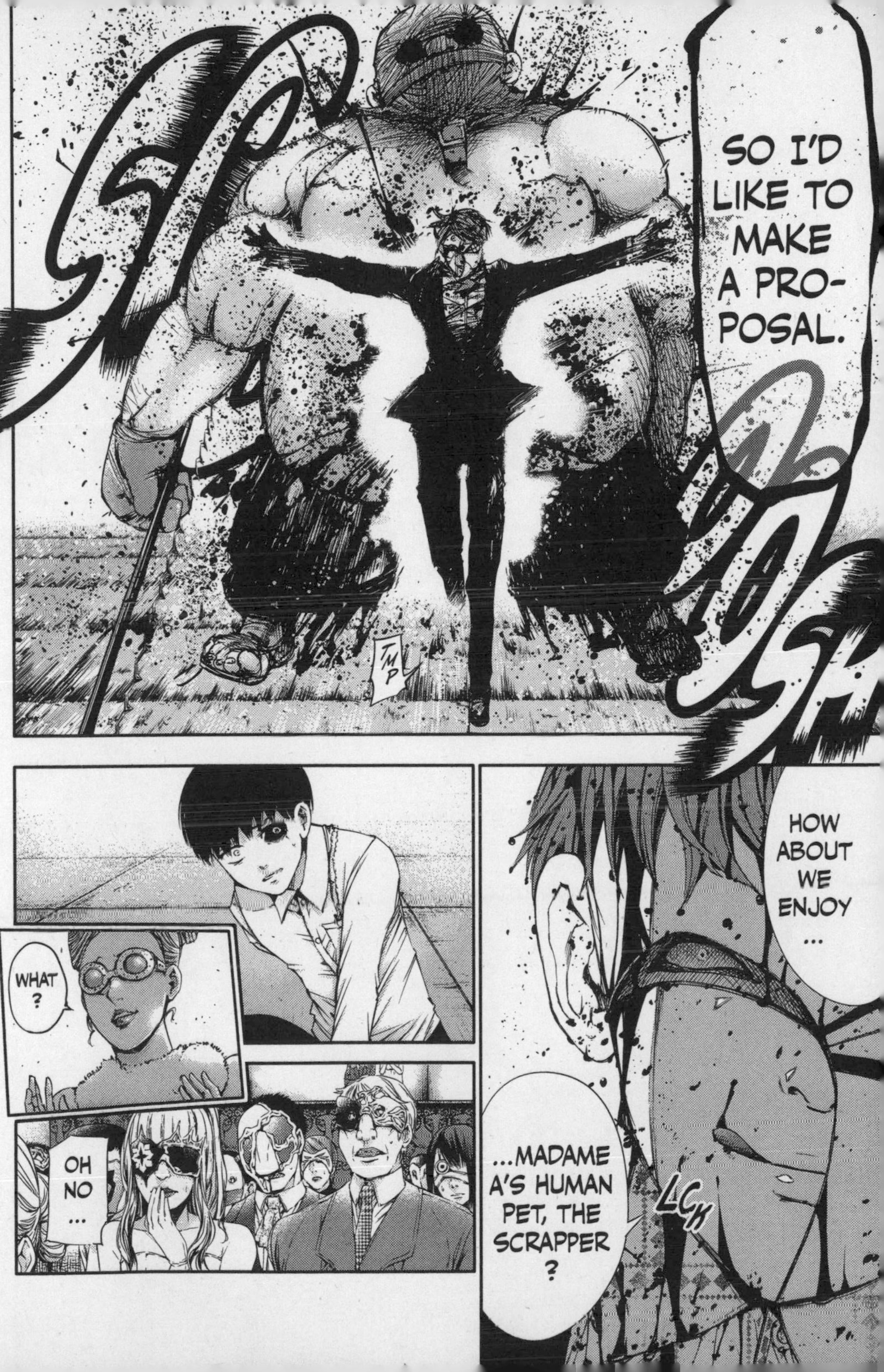
SO I'D LIKE TO MAKE A PRO-POSAL.
TMP
HOW ABOUT WE ENJOY ...
...MADAME A'S HUMAN PET, THE SCRAPPER ?
LCK
WHAT ?
OH NO ...

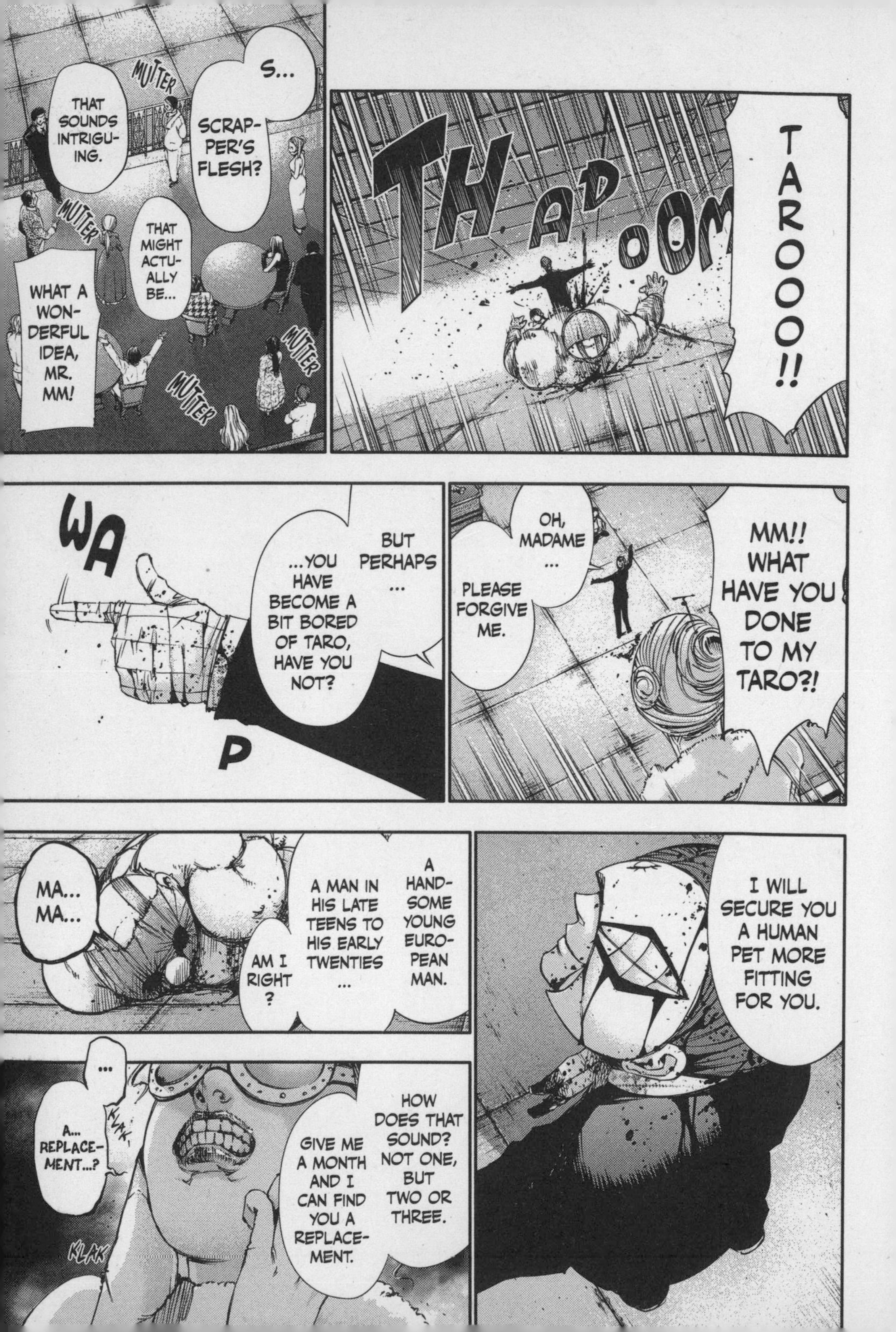
TAROOO!!
THADOOM
S...
SCRAPPER'S FLESH?
THAT SOUNDS INTRIGUING.
MUTTER
THAT MIGHT ACTUALLY BE...
WHAT A WONDERFUL IDEA, MR. MM!
MUTTER
MUTTER
MUTTER
MM!! WHAT HAVE YOU DONE TO MY TARO?!
OH, MADAME...
PLEASE FORGIVE ME.
BUT PERHAPS...
...YOU HAVE BECOME A BIT BORED OF TARO, HAVE YOU NOT?
WAP
I WILL SECURE YOU A HUMAN PET MORE FITTING FOR YOU.
A HANDSOME YOUNG EUROPEAN MAN.
A MAN IN HIS LATE TEENS TO HIS EARLY TWENTIES...
AM I RIGHT?
MA... MA...
HOW DOES THAT SOUND? NOT ONE, BUT TWO OR THREE.
GIVE ME A MONTH AND I CAN FIND YOU A REPLACEMENT.
...
A... REPLACEMENT...?
KLAK
KLAK

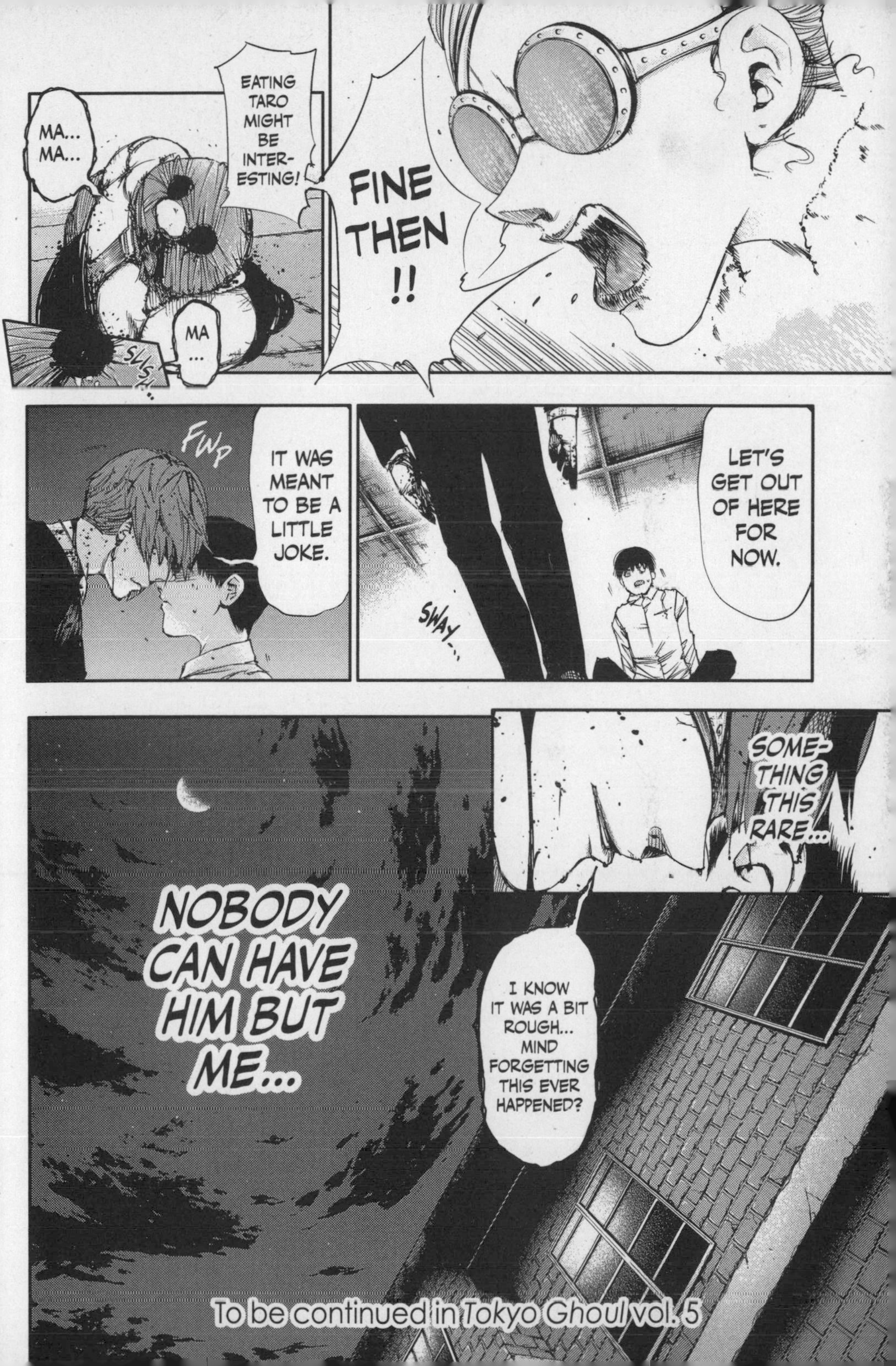
FINE THEN !!
EATING TARO MIGHT BE INTER-ESTING!
MA... MA...
MA ...
SLISH
LET'S GET OUT OF HERE FOR NOW.
SWAY...
FWP
IT WAS MEANT TO BE A LITTLE JOKE.
SOME-THING THIS RARE...
I KNOW IT WAS A BIT ROUGH... MIND FORGETTING THIS EVER HAPPENED?
NOBODY CAN HAVE HIM BUT ME...
To be continued in *Tokyo Ghoul* vol. 5

Tokyo Ghoul

SUI ISHIDA

assistant   Eda
Ryuji Miyamoto
Mizuki Ide
Matsuzaki

design
Hideaki Shimada
(L.S.D.)
cover
Miyuki Takaoka
(POCKET)

editor
Jumpei Matsuo

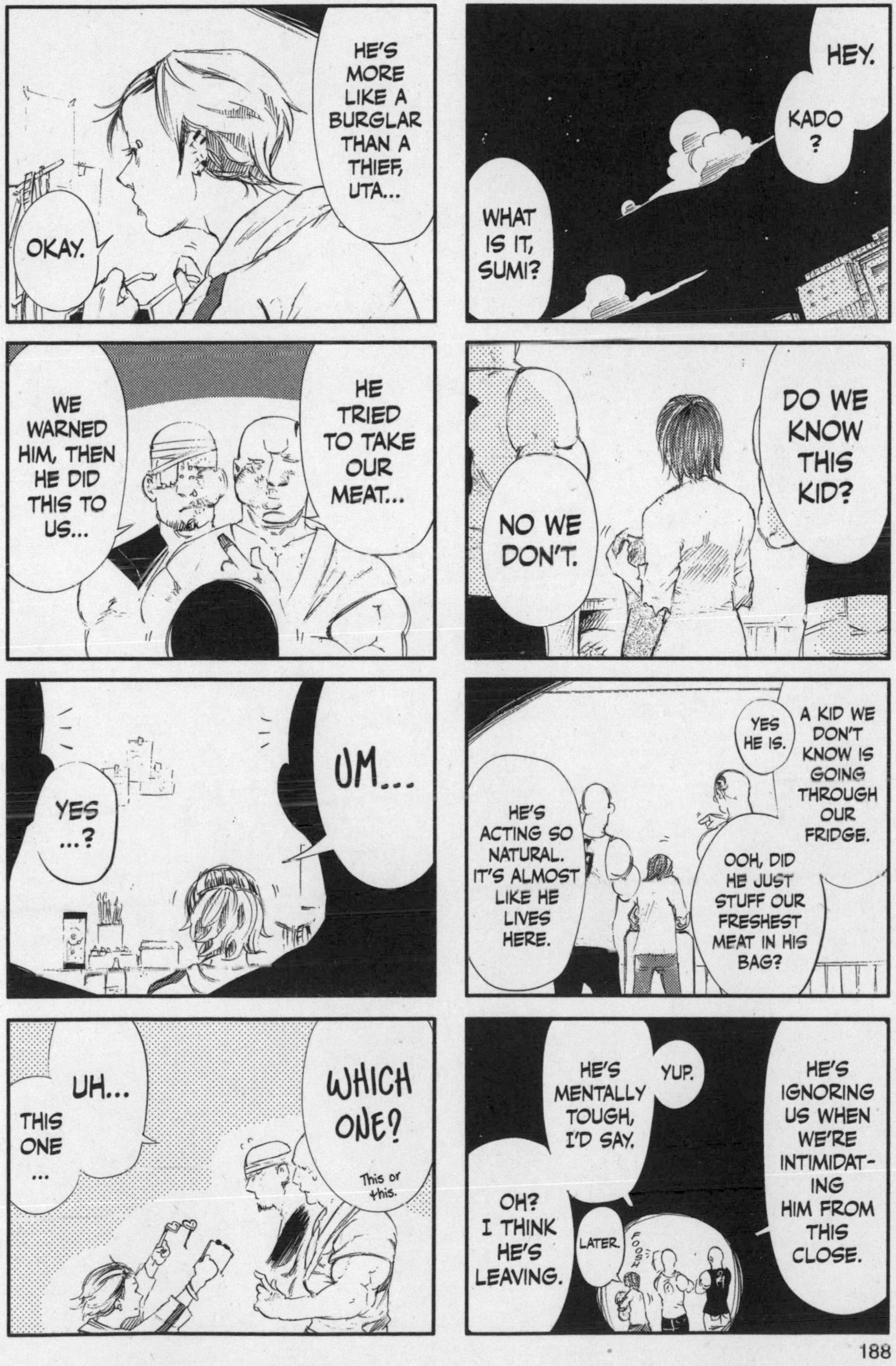
HEY.
KADO ?
WHAT IS IT, SUMI?
HE'S MORE LIKE A BURGLAR THAN A THIEF, UTA...
OKAY.
DO WE KNOW THIS KID?
NO WE DON'T.
HE TRIED TO TAKE OUR MEAT...
WE WARNED HIM, THEN HE DID THIS TO US...
A KID WE DON'T KNOW IS GOING THROUGH OUR FRIDGE.
YES HE IS.
OOH, DID HE JUST STUFF OUR FRESHEST MEAT IN HIS BAG?
HE'S ACTING SO NATURAL. IT'S ALMOST LIKE HE LIVES HERE.
UM...
YES ...?
HE'S IGNORING US WHEN WE'RE INTIMIDAT-ING HIM FROM THIS CLOSE.
YUP.
HE'S MENTALLY TOUGH, I'D SAY.
OH? I THINK HE'S LEAVING.
LATER.
FOOSH
WHICH ONE?
This or this.
UH...
THIS ONE ...

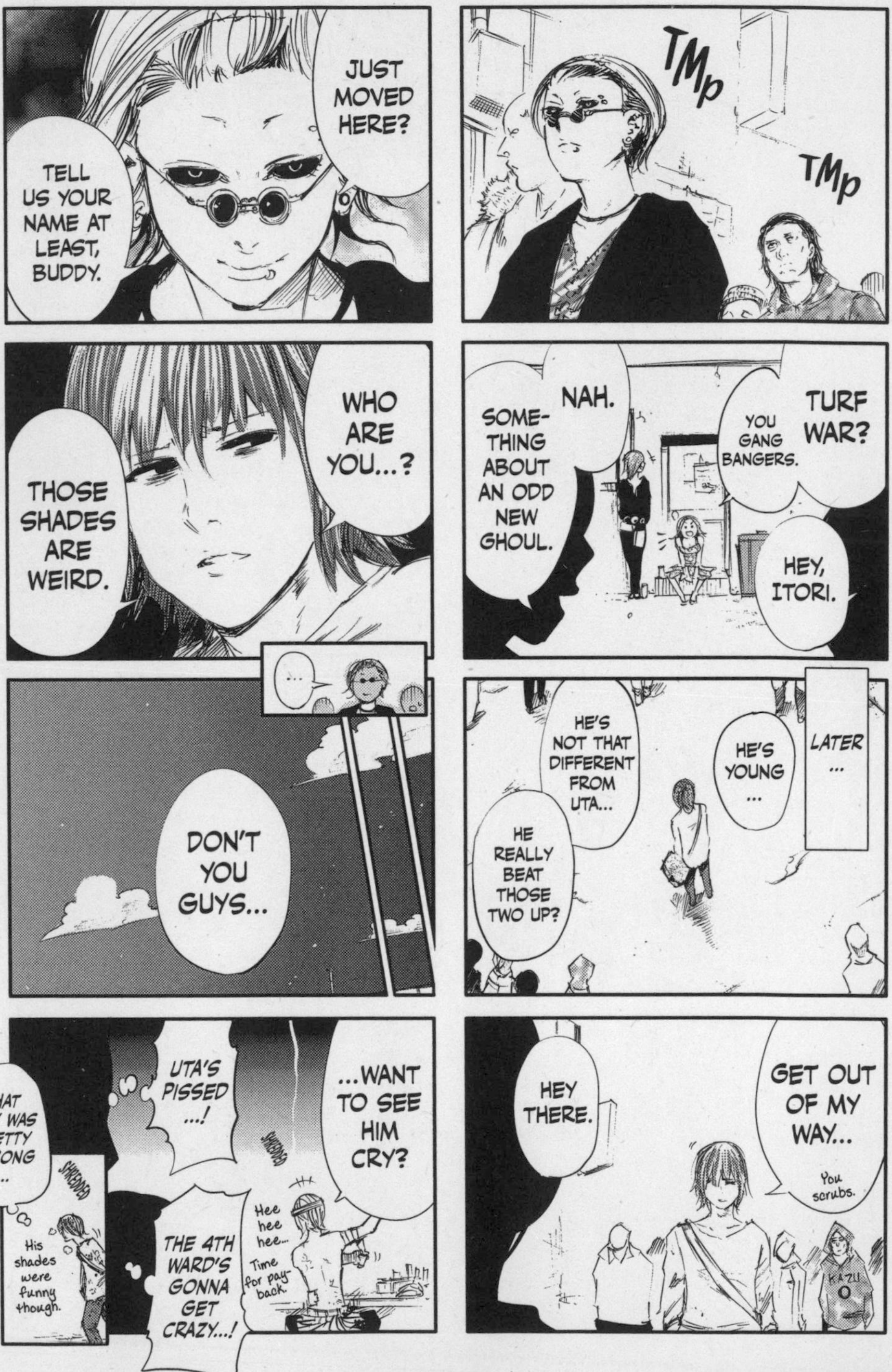
TMp
TMp
JUST MOVED HERE?
TELL US YOUR NAME AT LEAST, BUDDY.
TURF WAR?
YOU GANG BANGERS.
NAH.
SOME-THING ABOUT AN ODD NEW GHOUL.
HEY, ITORI.
WHO ARE YOU...?
THOSE SHADES ARE WEIRD.
LATER...
HE'S YOUNG...
HE'S NOT THAT DIFFERENT FROM UTA...
HE REALLY BEAT THOSE TWO UP?
...
DON'T YOU GUYS...
GET OUT OF MY WAY...
You scrubs.
KAZU
HEY THERE.
...WANT TO SEE HIM CRY?
UTA'S PISSED...!
Hee hee hee... Time for payback.
THE 4TH WARD'S GONNA GET CRAZY...!
THAT GUY WAS PRETTY STRONG...
His shades were funny though.

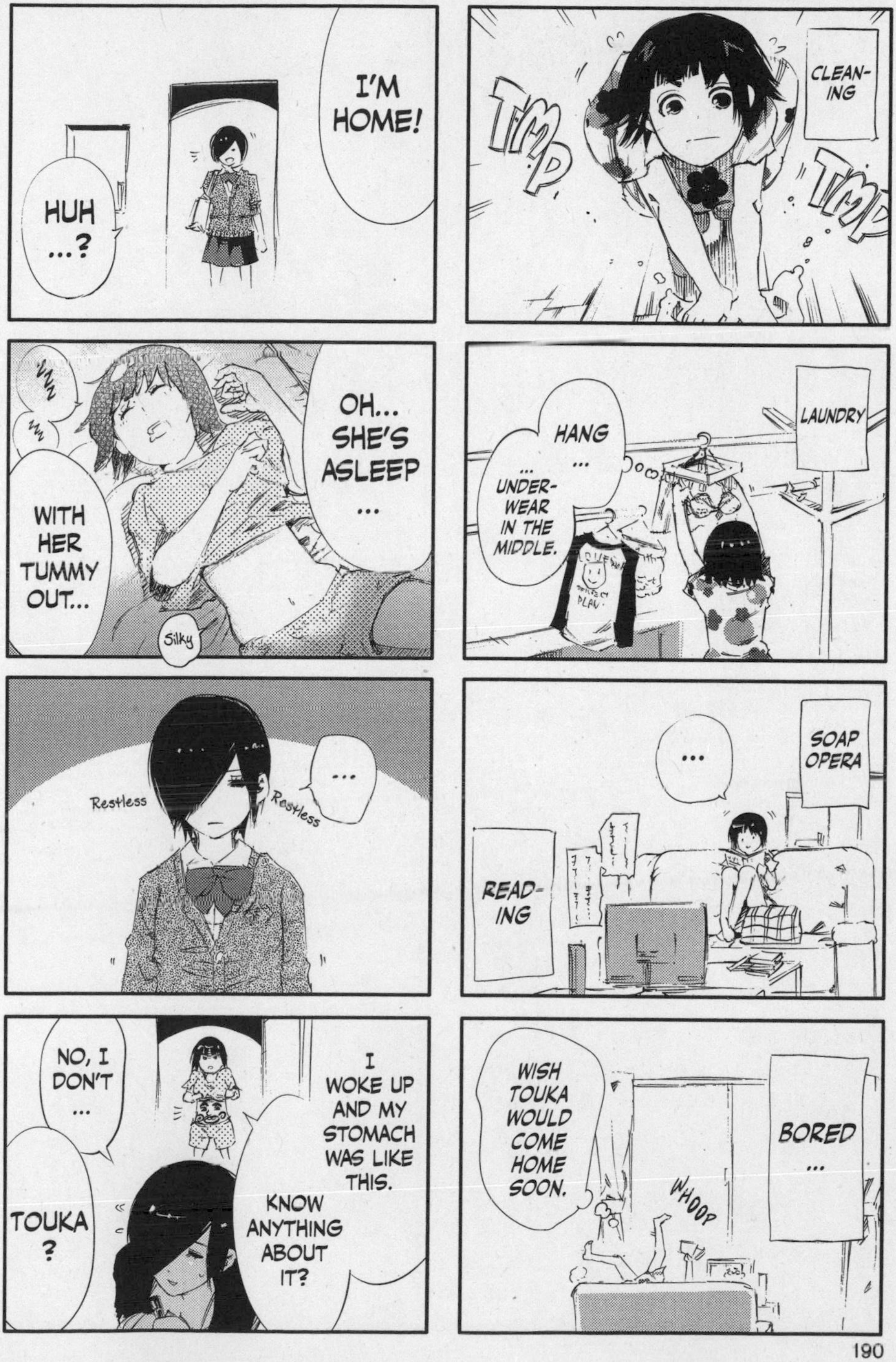
CLEAN-ING
TMP
TMP
LAUNDRY
HANG...
...UNDER-WEAR IN THE MIDDLE.
SOAP OPERA
...
READ-ING
BORED...
WISH TOUKA WOULD COME HOME SOON.
WHOOP
I'M HOME!
HUH...?
OH... SHE'S ASLEEP...
WITH HER TUMMY OUT...
Silky
...
Restless
Restless
I WOKE UP AND MY STOMACH WAS LIKE THIS.
KNOW ANYTHING ABOUT IT?
TOUKA?
NO, I DON'T...

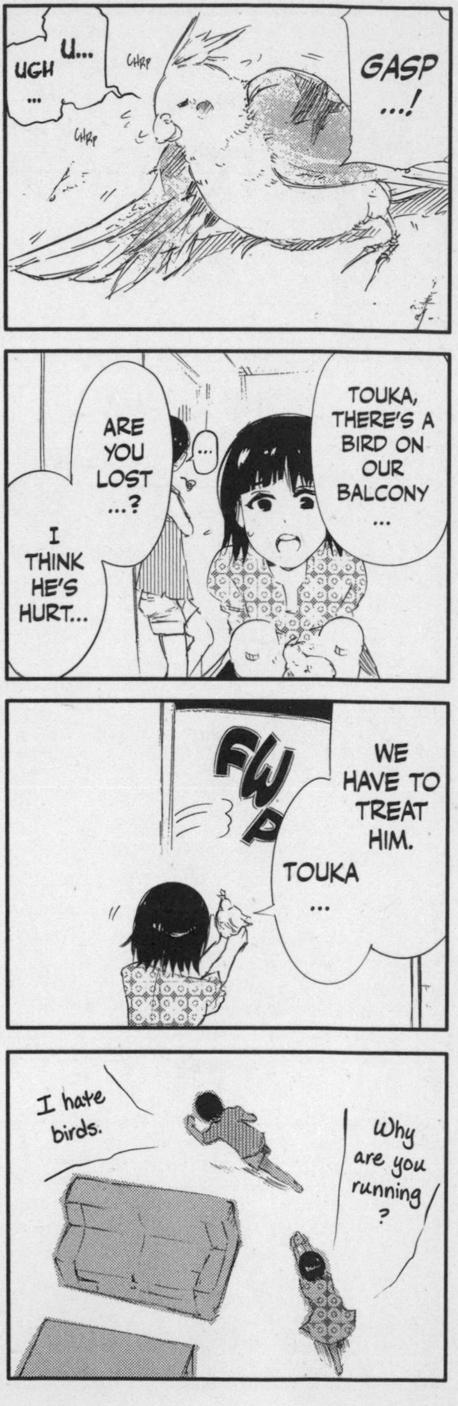
GASP ...!
CHRP
U...
UGH ...
CHRP
TOUKA, THERE'S A BIRD ON OUR BALCONY ...
...
ARE YOU LOST ...?
I THINK HE'S HURT...
WE HAVE TO TREAT HIM.
FWP
TOUKA ...
Why are you running ?
I hate birds.

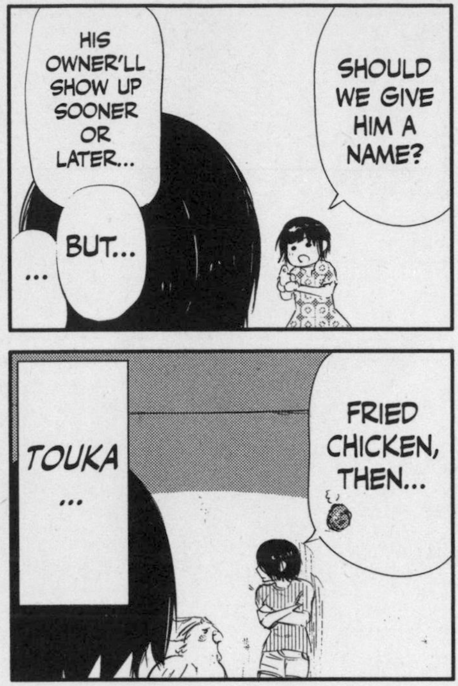
SHOULD WE GIVE HIM A NAME?
HIS OWNER'LL SHOW UP SOONER OR LATER...
BUT...
...
FRIED CHICKEN, THEN...
TOUKA ...

Thank you for reading volume 4.

A year's gone by already.

My first series, first time drawing all digitally. It seems so long ago that I crazily claimed I would do it all by myself with no assistants.

The period when I was working on volume 1 with just one assistant was a period of pure anguish. Thank you Mr. Eda for helping me out.

I'm still inexperienced, but I would be grateful if you would continue sticking by me.

Thank you.

Sui Ishida

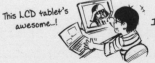

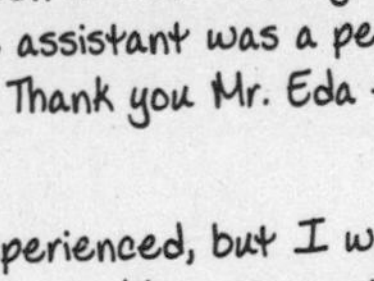
This LCD tablet's awesome...!
It's so easy to draw!

TOKYO GHOUL

THIS IS THE LAST PAGE

TOKYO GHOUL READS RIGHT TO LEFT

TOKYO GHOUL
東京喰種

VOLUME 4
VIZ Signature Edition

Story and art by
SUI ISHIDA

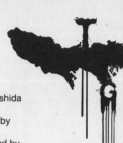

First published in Japan in 2011 by SHUEISHA Inc., Tokyo.
English translation rights arranged by SHUEISHA Inc.

TRANSLATION. Joe Yamazaki
TOUCH-UP ART AND LETTERING. Vanessa Satone
DESIGN. Fawn Lau
EDITOR. Joel Enos

Printed in the U.S.A.

Published by VIZ Media, LLC
P.O. Box 77010
San Francisco, CA 94107

10 9 8 7 6 5
First printing, December 2015
Fifth printing, March 2019

VIZ MEDIA
viz.com
VIZ SIGNATURE
vizsignature.com

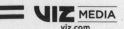

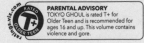